Workshop on Simple and Efficient Natural Language Processing (SustaiNLP 2021)

Online
10 November 2021

ISBN: 978-1-7138-9181-9

Printed from e-media with permission by:

Curran Associates, Inc.
57 Morehouse Lane
Red Hook, NY 12571

proceedings.com

Some format issues inherent in the e-media version may also appear in this print version.

Printed with permission by Curran Associates, Inc. (2024)

Association for Computational Linguistics
209 N. Eighth Street
Stroudsburg, Pennsylvania 18360

Phone: 1-570-476-8006
Fax: 1-570-476-0860

acl@aclweb.org

Additional copies of this publication are available from:

Curran Associates, Inc.
57 Morehouse Lane
Red Hook, NY 12571 USA
Phone: 845-758-0400
Fax: 845-758-2633
Email: curran@proceedings.com
Web: www.proceedings.com

SustaiNLP 2021

2nd Workshop on Simple and Efficient Natural Language Processing (SustaiNLP)

Proceedings of SustaiNLP

November 10, 2021
Online workshop

Introduction

It is our great pleasure to welcome you to the second edition of SustaiNLP: Workshop on Simple and Efficient Natural Language Processing.

The Natural Language Processing community has, in recent years, demonstrated a notable focus on improving higher scores on standard benchmarks and taking the lead on community-wide leaderboards (e.g., GLUE, SentEval). While this aspiration has led to improvements in benchmark performance of (predominantly neural) models, it has also came at a cost, i.e., increased model complexity and the evergrowing amount of computational resources required for training and using the current state-of-the-art models. Moreover, the recent research efforts have, for the most part, failed to identify sources of empirical gains in models, often failing to empirically justify the model complexity beyond benchmark performance.

Because of these easily observable trends, we organized the SustaiNLP workshop with the goal of promoting more sustainable NLP research and practices, with two main objectives: (1) encouraging development of more efficient NLP models; and (2) providing simpler architectures and empirical justification of model complexity. For both aspects, we encouraged submissions from all topical areas of NLP.

Besides the original research papers (short and long), we encouraged cross-submissions of work that has been published at other events as well as extended abstracts of work in progress that fit the scope and aims of the workshop (only the original research papers, however, are included in these workshop proceedings).

We received 51 submissions, proposing a multitude of viable resource-efficient NLP methods and spanning a wide range of NLP applications. We have selected 21 submissions for presentation at the workshop, yielding an acceptance rate of $\sim$41%.

Many thanks to our program committee for their thorough and thoughtful reviews. We would also like to thank to our panelists and invited speakers whose discussions and talks we strongly believe will make the workshop exciting and memorable.

We are looking forward to the second edition of the SustaiNLP workshop!

SustaiNLP Organizers
September 2021

Organizers:
Nafise Sadat Moosavi, TU Darmstadt
Iryna Gurevych, TU Darmstadt
Angela Fan, INRIA Nancy and Facebook AI Research
Thomas Wolf, Huggingface Inc.
Yufang Hou, IBM Research
Ana Marasović, Allen Institute for AI and University of Washington
Zornitsa Kozareva, Facebook AI Research
Sujith Ravi, SliceX AI

Program Committee:
Dennis Aumiller, Emily M. Bender, Rajarshi Bhowmik, Samuel Cahyawijaya, Han Cai, Qingqing Cao, Rotem Dror, gerard DUPONT, Marzieh Fadaee, Benjamin Heinzerling, Ari Holtzman, Zhiqi Huang, Peter Izsak, Ehsan Kamalloo, Abhinav Ramesh Kashyap, Young Jin Kim, Gyuwan Kim, Tuan Lai, Anne Lauscher, Phong Le, Ji-Ung Lee, Zhaojiang Lin, Zeyu Liu, Alexandra Luccioni, Sandya Mannarswamy, Mohsen Mesgar, Seyed Abolghasem Mirroshandel, Marius Mosbach, Tapas Nayak, Myle Ott, Nikolaos Pappas, Daraksha Parveen, Mohammad Taher Pilehvar, Barbara Plank, Roi Reichart, Victor Sanh, Roy Schwartz, Sheng Shen, Edwin Simpson, Sameer Singh, Urmish Thakker, Rakesh Verma, Ivan Vulić, Moshe Wasserblat, Genta Indra Winata, Mengzhou Xia, Patrick Xia, Canwen Xu, Peng Xu, Yan Xu, Makoto Yamada, Yichun Yin, Naoki Yoshinaga, Tiezheng Yu, Zhuosheng Zhang

Invited Speakers:
Jacob Andreas, MIT
Colin Raffel, University of North Carolina, Chapel Hill
Nazneen Rajani, Salesforce Research
Dan Roth, University of Pennsylvania
Roy Schwartz, Hebrew University of Jerusalem
Yulia Tsvetkov, University of Washington

Panelists:
Emily M. Bender, University of Washington
Goran Glavaš, Universität Mannheim
Perez Ogayo, Carnegie Mellon University
Colin Raffel, University of North Carolina, Chapel Hill
Roy Schwartz, Hebrew University of Jerusalem
Moshe Wasserblat, Intel

Table of Contents

Conference Program

November 10, 2021

Low Resource Quadratic Forms for Knowledge Graph Embeddings
Zachary Zhou, Jeffery Kline, Devin Conathan and Glenn Fung

Evaluating the carbon footprint of NLP methods: a survey and analysis of existing tools
Nesrine bannour, Sahar Ghannay, Aurélie Névéol and Anne-Laure Ligozat

Limitations of Knowledge Distillation for Zero-shot Transfer Learning
Saleh Soltan, Haidar Khan and Wael Hamza

Countering the Influence of Essay Length in Neural Essay Scoring
Sungho Jeon and Michael Strube

Memory-efficient Transformers via Top-k Attention
Ankit Gupta, Guy Dar, Shaya Goodman, David Ciprut and Jonathan Berant

BioCopy: A Plug-And-Play Span Copy Mechanism in Seq2Seq Models
Yi Liu, Guoan Zhang, Puning Yu, Jianlin Su and Shengfeng Pan

Combining Lexical and Dense Retrieval for Computationally Efficient Multi-hop Question Answering
Georgios Sidiropoulos, Nikos Voskarides, Svitlana Vakulenko and Evangelos Kanoulas

Learning to Rank in the Age of Muppets: Effectiveness–Efficiency Tradeoffs in Multi-Stage Ranking
Yue Zhang, ChengCheng Hu, Yuqi Liu, Hui Fang and Jimmy Lin

Improving Synonym Recommendation Using Sentence Context
Maria Glenski, William I. Sealy, Kate Miller and Dustin Arendt

Semantic Categorization of Social Knowledge for Commonsense Question Answering
Gengyu Wang, Xiaochen Hou, Diyi Yang, Kathleen McKeown and Jing Huang

Speeding Up Transformer Training By Using Dataset Subsampling - An Exploratory Analysis
Lovre Torbarina, Velimir Mihelčić, Bruno Šarlija, Lukasz Roguski and Željko Kraljević

November 10, 2021 (continued)

Low Resource Quadratic Forms for Knowledge Graph Embeddings

Zachary Zhou
University of Wisconsin – Madison
Industrial & Systems Engineering
1415 Engineering Drive
Madison, WI 53706
zzhou246@wisc.edu

Jeffery Kline
Devin Conathan
Glenn Fung
American Family Insurance
6000 American Parkway
Madison, WI 53783
{jklin1,dconatha,gfung}@amfam.com

Abstract

We address the problem of *link prediction* between entities and relations of knowledge graphs. State of the art techniques that address this problem, while increasingly accurate, are computationally intensive. In this paper we cast link prediction as a sparse convex program whose solution defines a quadratic form that is used as a ranking function. The structure of our convex program is such that standard support vector machine software packages, which are numerically robust and efficient, can solve it. We show that on benchmark data sets, our model's performance is competitive with state of the art models, but training times can be reduced by a factor of 40 using only CPU-based (and not GPU-accelerated) computing resources. This approach may be suitable for applications where balancing the demands of graph completion performance against computational efficiency is a desirable trade-off.

1 Introduction

Digital representations of knowledge are essential to many machine learning domains including social networks, citation networks, question-answering, information retrieval, recommender systems, and natural language processing (Zhang et al., 2016; Xiong et al., 2017; Hao et al., 2017; Yang and Mitchell, 2017). Multirelational data, when represented as a directed graph whose nodes (entities) are connected to each other by one or more edges (relations) are *knowledge graphs*.

Knowledge graphs are often both large and incomplete. As a result, the task of *link prediction* is a basic challenge. Much recent work on knowledge graph representation has focused on constructing embeddings of the relations and entities of a graph to facilitate good performance on the link prediction problem. But training modern models on large graphs often consumes many hours of GPU time.

In this paper, we formulate the link prediction problem as a sparse convex program that can be efficiently solved by off-the-shelf support vector machine (SVM) software packages. We demonstrate performance that is competitive with state of the art methods, but our programs are solved in substantially shorter times and without requiring specialized GPU hardware. Our approach takes advantage of existing SVM technology: large-scale convex problems are routinely solved using an arsenal of first and second order methods, as well as decades of empirically-derived heuristics. Solutions to convex problems are global, often unique, and in some cases (e.g. linear programs), solutions come with theoretical guarantees about program complexity. While we do not pursue this idea in the present work, it is possible to naturally incorporate external knowledge about relationships into convex programs (Fung et al., 2002). An unusual feature of our program is that the solution is not used as a binary classifier, but instead, the solution is used to define a symmetric quadratic form that ranks facts in the knowledge graph.

The main contributions of this work include 1) a novel convex formulation of the link prediction problem 2) a scalable approach to link prediction that that can be efficiently solved using standard SVM solvers and 3) a link prediction model that exhibits competitive performance.

We now describe the remaining sections of this paper. In the next section we present notation and background information on SVMs and the TransE model that we base our method on. In Section 3 we present details of our SVM formulation. In Section 4 we comment on implementation. Experiments are discussed in Section 5. Results are presented in Section 6. Related work and conclusions are in Section 7 and Section 8, respectively.

2 Background

Basic Concepts Each *fact* in a knowledge graph is represented as a triple, the entries of which are called a *head*, a *relation* and a *tail*. The head and

Proceedings of the 2nd Workshop on Simple and Efficient Natural Language Processing, pages 1–10
November 10, 2021.

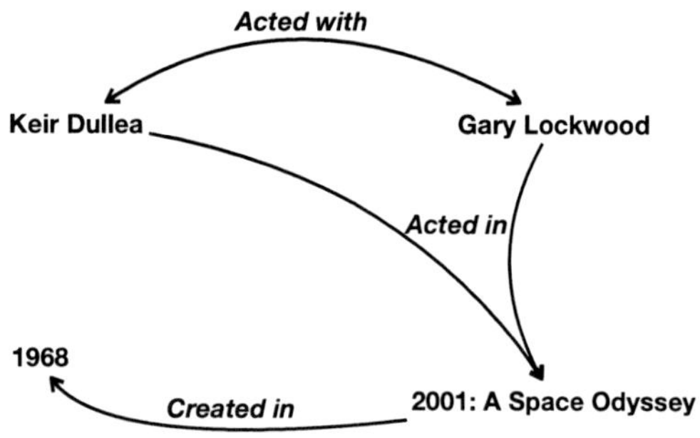

Figure 1: Example of a knowledge graph.

tail belong to a set of *entities*. More formally, given a set of relations R and entities E, the standard representation of a knowledge graph is a set $K \subset E \times R \times E$, and each $(h, r, t) \in K$ is a fact. Figure 1 illustrates a simple knowledge graph having four entities (Keir Dullea, Gary Lockwood, 2001: A Space Odyssey, and 1968) and three relations (Acted with, Acted in, and Created in).

Given a set of entities E and relations R, a knowledge graph embedding (KGE) model embeds the elements of $E \cup R$ as elements in $\mathbb{R}^k$ for a fixed positive integer k. For brevity, we abuse notation and will represent the elements and the embeddings of the elements in E and R with the same symbol. Thus, the expressions $e + r$, αe for any $\alpha \in \mathbb{R}$, and e' are well-defined, and represent component-wise addition, scalar multiplication, and transposition, respectively. Additionally, $\|x\|_p := (\sum |x_i|^p)^{1/p}$. Unless otherwise specified, we assume $p = 2$. For each $(h, r, t) \in K$, we define a set of *corrupted* triples as

$$K^{\dagger}_{(h,r,t)} = \left\{(h, r, t^{\dagger}) : t^{\dagger} \in E\right\} \cup \left\{(h^{\dagger}, r, t) : h^{\dagger} \in E\right\} \setminus K.$$

That is, $K^{\dagger}_{(h,r,t)}$ contains triples where either h or t is replaced by $h^{\dagger} \in E$ or $t^{\dagger} \in E$ so that the new triple is not in K. For ease of notation we will often write corrupted triples as $(h^{\dagger}, r, t^{\dagger}) \in K^{\dagger}_{(h,r,t)}$ (where both $h^{\dagger}$ and $t^{\dagger}$ appear), but it is always the case that precisely one of h or t is replaced, not both.

A link prediction model's *score function* is the function that distinguishes positive triples from corrupted triples. If f is a score function, then a well-performing model satisfies $f(h, r, t) \leq f(h^{\dagger}, r, t^{\dagger})$ when $(h, r, t) \in K$ and $(h^{\dagger}, r, t^{\dagger}) \in K^{\dagger}_{(h,r,t)}$.

TransE Our approach is inspired by the "translational model", TransE, introduced in (Bordes et al., 2013). Despite its age and simplicity, TransE exhibits performance that is often competitive with state-of-the-art techniques, and our SVM-based approach shares several key features with it. The goal of TransE is to make $\|h + r - t\|$ small whenever $(h, r, t) \in K$ and large otherwise. To do this, one minimizes the loss function

$$L_{\text{TransE}} := \sum_{\substack{(h,r,t)\in K \\ (h^{\dagger},r,t^{\dagger})\in K^{\dagger}_{(h,r,t)}}} \tau(h, r, t, h^{\dagger}, t^{\dagger}),$$

where

$$\tau(h, r, t, h^{\dagger}, t^{\dagger}) := \left(\gamma + \|h + r - t\| - \left\|h^{\dagger} + r - t^{\dagger}\right\|\right)_{+},$$

$\gamma \in \mathbb{R}$ is a fixed margin, the norm is either 1-norm or the 2-norm and $(y)_+ := \max\{y, 0\}$. The score function for TransE appears directly in the function L_{TransE}, and is $\|h + r - t\|$. Note that L_{TransE} is not convex due to the term $-\left\|h^{\dagger} + r - t^{\dagger}\right\|$ in the definition of τ.

Support Vector Machines A standard linear SVM, trained on data $x_i \in \mathbb{R}^k$ with labels $y_i = \pm 1$ for $i = 1, \ldots, N$, solves the linearly constrained convex optimization problem,

$$\begin{aligned} \min_{\substack{w\in\mathbb{R}^k \\ \zeta\in\mathbb{R}^N \\ \gamma\in\mathbb{R}}} \ & C\|\zeta\|^2 + \|w\|^2 \\ \text{subject to} \ & y_i\left(w'x_i - \gamma\right) \geq 1 - \zeta_i, (1 \leq i \leq N) \\ & \zeta \geq 0, \end{aligned}$$

where $C > 0$ is a regularization parameter. This constrained program may be rewritten as an equivalent unconstrained problem,

$$\min_{w,\gamma} C\left\|(\mathbf{1} - Y(Xw - \gamma\mathbf{1}))_+\right\|^2 + \|w\|^2,$$

where Y is the diagonal matrix with $Y_{ii} = y_i$ and row i of X is x_i' and $\mathbf{1} = (1, 1, 1, \ldots, 1)$.

Given an optimal solution w of this SVM, the function $\phi : x \mapsto w'x - \gamma$ defines a hyperplane that separates $\mathbb{R}^k$ into two half-spaces, $\{x : w'x - \gamma > 0\}$ and $\{x : w'x - \gamma < 0\}$. If $y_i(w'x_i + \gamma) > 0$, for all $i = 1, \ldots, N$, then the data used to train the SVM are linearly separable The function ϕ is the decision function of the SVM. Classification error is measured by $\|\zeta\|^2$. The term

$\|w\|^2$ maximizes the margin between the bounding planes $w'x = \gamma \pm 1$ (Mangasarian, 2006).

One attractive feature of casting a problem as an SVM is the wide availability of high quality SVM software packages. Such packages are numerically robust, and are capable of rapidly solving problems with massive scale.

3 Formulation

We now describe how to express the link prediction problem as a convex variant of TransE, and then we show how to write this convex problem as an SVM. Recall that our goal is to identify a score function $f : E \times R \times E \to \mathbb{R}$ such that

$$f(h + r - t) \le f(h^\dagger + r - t^\dagger) \qquad (1)$$

for all $(h, r, t) \in K$ and $(h^\dagger, r, t^\dagger) \in K^\dagger_{(h,r,t)}$. We will assume that f has the form,

$$f(h + r - t) = \|M(h + r - t)\|, \qquad (2)$$

where $M \in R^{k\times k}$ is some unknown matrix. Finding M is essentially the main goal of TransE. We now show how, modulo technical artifacts, one may *define* the matrix M (and hence f) as the optimal solution to an SVM.

Substituting the right-hand side of (2) into (1), our problem becomes finding a matrix $M \in \mathbb{R}^{k\times k}$ such that

$$\|M(h + r - t)\| \le \left\|M(h^\dagger + r - t^\dagger)\right\| \qquad (3)$$

whenever $(h, r, t) \in K$ and $(h^\dagger, r, t^\dagger) \in K^\dagger_{(h,r,t)}$.

If we define $B := M'M$, then our problem is equivalent to seeking a positive semi-definite $B \in \mathbb{R}^{k\times k}$ with

$$(h + r - t)'B(h + r - t) \le \\ (h^\dagger + r - t^\dagger)'B(h^\dagger + r - t^\dagger) \qquad (4)$$

It is possible to represent the positive semi-definite condition on B as a convex constraint, but optimizing a loss function with this additional constraint is incompatible with an SVM formulation. Since our main goal is to create a score function, we omit the positive definite constraint from our program.

The inequality expressed in (4) is *quadratic* in the problem data, but *linear* in the unknown, B. Indeed, each side of the inequality (4) expresses a quadratic polynomial in the entries of h, r and t, while both expressions are linear in the entries of B.

To make this more explicit, we introduce notation. Let vec : $\mathbb{R}^{n\times n} \to \mathbb{R}^{n^2}$ denote the invertible linear map that "flattens" an $n \times n$ matrix into a n^2-dimensional vector. Then

$$x'Ay = \left(\text{vec}\, xy'\right)' \text{vec}\, A \qquad (5)$$

for any $x, y \in \mathbb{R}^n$ and $A \in \mathbb{R}^{n\times n}$. When A is a symmetric matrix and $x = y$, then (5) can be adapted to apply to the upper-triangular portions of A and xx'.

Just as vec maps square matrices to vectors, one may define symvec that maps symmetric matrices in $\mathbb{R}^{n\times n}$ to vectors in $\mathbb{R}^{n(n+1)/2}$, and which satisfies

$$x'Ax = \left(\text{symvec}\, xx'\right)' \text{symvec}\, A$$

For brevity, we define

$$\text{S}(h, r, t) := \text{symvec}\,(h + r - t)(h + r - t)' \qquad (6)$$

With notation in hand, initialize the embeddings of h,r and t to be one-hot encoded. Our task is to find $w \in \mathbb{R}^{k(k+1)/2}$ that satisfies

$$w'\text{S}(h, r, t) \le w'\text{S}(h^\dagger, r, t^\dagger),$$

for all $(h, r, t) \in K$ and $(h^\dagger, r, t^\dagger), \in K^\dagger_{(h,r,t)}$. To guarantee that the feasible set of this program is nonempty, we introduce non-negative slack variables ζ_i and minimize the residual.

This construction is similar in nature to the well-known "pair-wise transform" (Herbrich et al., 1999) where the ordinal ranking problem its transformed into a two-class classification problem by considering the difference of all comparable elements.

If we define $x_{(h,r,t),(h^\dagger,r,t^\dagger)} := \text{S}(h^\dagger, r, t^\dagger) - \text{S}(h, r, t)$, then this allows us to concisely express a convex program that is identical to the SVM formulation described above, namely

$$\begin{aligned} \min_{w\in\mathbb{R}^{k(k+1)/2},\zeta} \quad & C\,\|\zeta\|^2 + \|w\|^2 \\ \text{subject to} \quad & w'x_\eta \ge 1 - \zeta_\eta, \\ & \left(\eta \in K_{(h,r,t)} \times K^\dagger_{(h,r,t)}\right) \\ & \zeta \ge 0. \end{aligned}$$

In practice, the term in the objective

$$\|\zeta\|^2 = \sum_i \zeta_i^2$$

is replaced with the weighted sum,

$$\sum_i \rho_i \zeta_i^2,$$

where $\rho \geq 0$ is chosen to normalize for problem parameters. Also, rather than include every $(h^\dagger, r, t^\dagger)$ for a given (h, r, t), a fixed integer N is chosen to specify the number of negative triples per positive triple. Our model has two parameters that impact problem performance: integer N and $C > 0$, which is the standard SVM regularization parameter. Performance generally improves as N increases, and selecting $C = 1$ is, we find empirically, a reasonable default. The normalization weighting we choose is uniform, so that each entry of the weight ρ is $1/N$. Finally, since the SVM solver that we applied to this problem requires both $+1$ and -1 labels be present in the data, we define label y_η as a randomly-selected choice from $\{+1, -1\}$, and then we scale x_η by y_η. This step has no impact on the optimal solution.

Our proposed model has several distinguishing features:

- The program data is extremely sparse, with perhaps 0.0001% or fewer nonzero entries in the problem data.
- Our model aims to define a *symmetric* matrix using the coefficients of a standard SVM. We gain symmetry by virtue of how our problem is constructed. The matrix is usually left implicitly defined, and we have no need to reconstruct it explicitly.
- While SVMs are typically employed for the purpose of binary classification, in our application, we are interested in the *score* attributed to triples, not the classification ability.
- Our problem has just two parameters: an integer N that affects the program size, and a regularization parameter, $C > 0$.
- The program, despite its unusually size and structure, can be solved very quickly, often in under a minute for quite large programs.

input $(h, r, t) \in K, N \in \mathbb{N}$
init $X = [], y = []$
while $\text{len}(X) < N$ **do**
  Choose $\epsilon \in \{\pm 1\}$ with probability 1/2
  Choose $h^\dagger \in E$ s.t. $(h^\dagger, r, t) \notin K$
  Append $\epsilon\,\big(S(h^\dagger, r, t) - S(h, r, t)\big)$ to X
  Append ϵ to y
end while
return X, y

Algorithm 1: Building N samples for the SVM by *corrupting* the head entity.

4 Implementation

We solve our programs using the LinearSVC class from scikit-learn (Pedregosa et al., 2011), which uses liblinear (Fan et al., 2008), NumPy (Harris et al., 2020) and SciPy (Virtanen et al., 2020). In particular we rely heavily on SciPy for its sparse array structures. The primary bottleneck is a one-time cost to build the set of negative triples which, fortunately, is an embarrassingly parallel workload. To reduce the cost in time to build the problem, we leverage the multiprocessing capability of the DataLoader class of PyTorch (Paszke et al., 2019).

One of the two main loops used to construct the data fed into the SVM is presented in Algorithm 1. The loop shown selects the negative triples where the head of a given positive is replaced. A separate, and nearly identical loop, builds the tail-corrupted triples.

The returned values of Algorithm 1 are problem data X with labels y. Since the labels are selected with balanced probability, the expected bias of the optimal solution is 0, and the SVM solver is instructed to set the intercept to 0.

A naive implementation of the program does not scale due to large memory requirements. Several tricks are employed when constructing the SVM data and evaluating metrics.

Each relation and entity is 1-hot encoded as a vector in $k := |E| + |R|$ dimensions, and we seek a symmetric matrix that acts on k-dimensional embeddings; our problem dimension is $k(k+1)/2$. Even for modest values of k, the problems passed to SVM solvers can be quite large (see Table 1). Indeed, the included liblinear Python interface experienced integer overflow errors; however, using liblinear via scikit-learn performed adequately on a single-threaded standard CPU-based architecture that we used to compute the metrics for this paper.[1] While the problems are quite large they are extremely sparse. Indeed, independent of N, there are at most 12 nonzero entries in each row of X, and the memory requirements for the program are $O(N\,|K|)$.

Table 1: Problem size for $N = 100$. Problems are embedded in very high dimension, but the memory requirements are modest due to the extreme sparsity.

	FB15K	WN18	PRM45K
k	16296	40961	2884
ROWS OF X	106 MIL	29.3 MIL	7.26 MIL
COLUMNS OF X	132 MIL	8.39 BIL	4.16 MIL
COMPRESSED	1.4G	406M	84M
UNCOMPRESSED	7.5G	2.0G	332M

We now detail an indexing trick which leverages this sparsity and can be used to improve evaluation of metrics by several orders of magnitude over a naive direct evaluation.

If B is a symmetric matrix, and $w := \operatorname{vec} B$, then the entry of w that corresponds to entry $i \leq j$ of the matrix is

$$\text{ij2idx}(i, j) := \frac{k(k-1)}{2} - \frac{(k-i)(k-i-1)}{2} + j$$

If x and y are one-hot encoded and supported on indices i_x and i_y, then:

$$x'By = B_{i_x i_y} = B_{i_y i_x}$$

where the second equality holds by the assumption that B is symmetric. Then:

$$(h + r - t)'B(h + r - t) = B_{i_h i_h} + B_{i_r i_r} + B_{i_t i_t} + 2B_{i_h i_r} - 2B_{i_h i_t} - 2B_{i_r i_t} \tag{7}$$

This has an equivalent form using the function S, which was defined in (6). In this form that uses S, there is a space-savings gain of 1/2. Additionally, one has the guarantee that the matrix B, when reconstructed from the coefficients of the SVM, is symmetric.

The feature $x := h + r - t$ has at most three nonzero entries and is itself sparse. In practice, it is expensive to evaluate the outer product xx' and project onto the upper-triangular portion millions of times. Instead we simply evaluate the quadratic form directly using (7); at most 6 entries with fixed values are required: three on-diagonal entries and three off-diagonal entries.

With such large investment for performance gains, one may ask whether it is possible to simply take advantage of GPU hardware, and the well-established gains that can be had beyond standard CPU processors. Unfortunately, widely-available GPUs do not effectively leverage sparse data structures for improved performance. Indeed, commercial linear and quadratic solvers, which are commonly employed to solve sparse problems, do not support GPU hardware (Glockner, 2020).

5 Experiments

We use three knowledge graph datasets to benchmark our implementation; two are the standard link prediction benchmark datasets Freebase (Bollacker et al., 2008) and WordNet (Miller, 1995), and one is a new knowledge graph we introduce. We report performance on all three. For Freebase (FB15k) and WordNet (WN18) we use the versions distributed in the software package released by the authors of RotatE (Sun et al., 2019). We now briefly describe the data sets.

WN18 WordNet is a knowledge graph that provides lexical relationships between words (Glorot et al., 2013). It is designed to be machine readable, while being a usable dictionary and thesaurus.

FB15k Freebase is a collaboratively-constructed knowledge graph, containing general facts about the world (Bollacker et al., 2008). The FB15k dataset here is the same subset that was introduced in (Bordes et al., 2013).

PRM45k We introduce the product reference manual knowledge graph. It contains taxonomies, articles, frequently-asked-questions and glossary terms found in an insurance company operating manual intended to be referenced by insurance agents. The entities and relationships come from different source systems, and there is some overlap/redundancy, making this a good candidate for the link prediction task as there are many missing relationships. We have included a release of this dataset with our supplementary materials and plan to make a version of the dataset publicly available at http://anonymous.url. Summary statistics about these data sets appear in Table 2.

Hyperparameters We recommend searching over $N = 10, 50, 100$ and $C = 0.5, 1, 2, 4, 8, 16,$

[1]Despite the large size of the problem, we did not find that floating point errors interfered with overall results. We attribute this to the sparsity and modest parameter values.

Table 2: Benchmark data sets.

	FB15K	WN18	PRM45K
RELATIONS	1,345	18	6
ENTITIES	14,951	40,943	2878
TRIPLES	592,213	151,442	45,384

though we report on several other values of N. We find that performance increases in N and that performance is U-shaped in C, with a small neighborhood of values where all reported metrics are close to optimal. As a rule, fit time increases with the regularization parameter C. Table 3 describes performance and build time as a function of N.

Evaluation metrics The metrics we report here are standard metrics and have been used to compare link prediction model performance for nearly a decade (Bordes et al., 2011). Given a positive triple $(h, r, t) \in K$ we evaluate the score function applied to this triple, and then we evaluate the score function applied to all negative triples $(h^\dagger, r, t^\dagger) \in K^\dagger_{(h,r,t)}$. The scores are sorted in decreasing order and the rank of (h, r, t) is recorded. This process is repeated for all positive triples in whatever data we are evaluating on (e.g. the hold-out validation or test sets). The ranks of the positive triples across the data set are aggregated into mean rank (MR), mean reciprocal rank (MRR), and hits at k (H@k).

We note that while SVMs also have an accuracy score which measures the accuracy of the fitted model as a binary classifier, in the context of our knowledge graph link prediction problem this score is not relevant, and we do not report it.

6 Results

Since the model we use is very similar to that of TransE, we expect similar performance characteristics. Table 3 shows that performance gains taper off rather quickly as N grows.

Table 4 displays timing results for our SVM-based method. It also includes self-reported results of RotatE and estimates based on HolE.

Timings report build times using a 96 CPU core processor on a machine running Ubuntu 18.04. As problem build is highly parallelizable, times are inversely-proportional to the number of available cores. Since the SVM solver we use is single-threaded, the additional cores are not necessary for training; only sufficient memory is necessary. Thus, it makes sense to build the program with a compute-optimized configuration and solve the problem with a memory-optimized configuration. Multiple values of C may be fit simultaneously, provided local memory is sufficient.

Table 5 compares metrics of various state-of-the-art methods to ours. The TransE model is noteworthy for being both simple and easy to train (Nickel et al., 2016). We were unable to find reported training times of TransE, so we report here results using the TransE code that was released by RotatE authors. We allowed the model to run for 50,000 epochs on a NVIDIA Tesla K80 GPU using same parameters the authors reported. Note that 50,000 is significantly less than 150,000 used by RotatE authors. The FB15k model was stopped early by hand, and the WN18 model was still in the process of converging when the maximum iterations were reached, so the value of 2+ is a lower bound.

In the TransE framework, the choice of solver and parameter settings (Minervini et al., 2015) has a dramatic impact on solver performance. Hyper-parameter complexity is in contrast to our use of the default parameter settings of the SVM solver, which we use without modification.

7 Related work

Support vector machines Support vector machines have been around for decades, and have proved remarkably versatile. Our use is not standard, for we are not interested in the capability of the SVM as a binary classifier. Traditionally, SVMs are a supervised learning method useful for classification problems. However, an early and very different approach where the distance to the margin is used as a ranking function is (Joachims, 2002). Our approach is the same in spirit: we are using the coefficients of the SVM to yield an implicit symmetric matrix which we use as a score function. SVMs have been used for the problem of link prediction in (Al Hasan et al., 2006). In that work, the authors treat link prediction as a binary classification problem, and SVMs are one of several binary classifiers they evaluated.

The SVM solver that we use, which was distributed in (Pedregosa et al., 2011), is single-threaded. This, in turn, calls the lower-level library (Chang and Lin, 2011), which is tailored to large-scale and very sparse support vector problems. The developers of the Liblinear solver have invested significant effort over many years to iden-

Table 3: Metrics for $C = 1.0$ for FB15k and PRM45k, and $C = 16.0$ for WN18. The metrics here are reported on the same machine used for Table 5. Information from the rows $N = 50$ and $N = 100$ are duplicated in Table 4 and Table 5 for convenience.

N	FB15K				WN18				PRM45K			
	FIT (SEC)	BUILD (SEC)	MRR	H@10	FIT (SEC)	BUILD (SEC)	MRR	H@10	FIT (SEC)	BUILD (SEC)	MRR	H@10
1	21	21	0.320	0.493	12	6	0.179	0.262	<1	2	0.275	0.44
2	58	28	0.398	0.614	116	8	0.368	0.704	<1	3	0.333	0.516
5	82	53	0.484	0.695	214	15	0.491	0.922	2	7	0.500	0.719
10	115	93	0.530	0.738	273	27	0.500	0.934	1	4	0.437	0.647
50	328	467	0.617	0.799	465	125	0.526	0.942	8	33	0.552	0.758
100	497	902	0.632	0.806	607	250	0.540	0.946	15	58	0.555	0.770

Table 4: Timing. Parameters for SVM are $N = 100$ both data sets, $C = 1.0$ for FB15k and $C = 16.0$ for WN18. The Liblinear software is single-threaded, so the primary constraint is memory. The estimate for HolE is based on 11s per epoch on WN18, and an estimated 200 to 500 epochs required for convergence.

MODEL	FB15K		WN18		PRM45K	
	FIT	BUILD	FIT	BUILD	FIT	BUILD
TRANSE	1 HR		2+ HRS		1 HR	
ROTATE	9 HRS		4 HRS		1 HR	
HOLE			1+ HRS (EST)			
SVM(N=50)	6 MIN	8 MIN	8 MIN	2 MIN	8 SEC	33 SEC
SVM(N=100)	9 MIN	15 MIN	10 MIN	4 MIN	15 SEC	1 MIN

tify and then leverage heuristics that improve convergence times. We note that during November 2020, a multi-core version of this lower-level library was released, and the authors claim substantial reduction in fitting times may be possible.

The soft-margin support vector network that we use was introduced in (Cortes and Vapnik, 1995). The idea of representing data quadratically and training an SVM to derive a symmetric matrix was applied in (Rosales and Fung, 2006) to remove the need to choose a distance function by hand and instead *define* a distance function as the solution to a convex program. In that work, the distance function was the solution to a linear program, and extracting a distance from the solution was made possible by enforcing side condition that guaranteed the resulting set of coefficients satisfied diagonal dominance. This allowed the reconstructed matrix to be positive semidefinite, and the optimal distance could then be extracted using a matrix square root, found through a Cholesky decomposition. In this work, we are representing data quadratically, but we do not have the side condition. A similar, but not quite equivalent idea, is to fit an SVM using a quadratic kernel.

Our SVM program is both sparse and convex. We note that very recent work (Tsai and El Ghaoui, 2020) in the space of extractive text summarization also leverages sparsity and convexity to efficiently solve an optimization program. In our program, when both terms in the objective are the 1-norm, the SVM may be written as a linear program. This is attractive, for linear programs have the theoretical guarantee of a polynomial-time solution.

Knowledge graph link prediction Relational learning and knowledge graph link prediction is a large field of machine learning research. One early model is RESCAL, which is a tensor decomposition method (Nickel et al., 2011) for learning relations in a knowledge graph. The idea of the model is to factorize a tensor into a core tensor multiplied by a matrix along each dimension. The core idea adapts the earlier DEDICOM (Harshman et al., 1982) tensor factorization scheme. This method was notable for scalability and improved training times.

Subsequent to TransE, which was a landmark evolution in the performance of link prediction, there has been much research and analysis into the structure of links in knowledge graphs (Trouillon et al., 2016; Toutanova and Chen, 2015; Guu et al., 2015). Relation paths, which are a compound structure, have also been used to extend the TransE model (Lin et al., 2015). Since its introduction, and

Table 5: Results for TransE(1) are from (Bordes et al., 2013), TransE(2) and HolE are from (Nickel et al., 2016), and RotatE are from (Sun et al., 2019). Parameters for SVM are $C = 1.0$ for FB15k and $C = 16.0$ for WN18. We compute and report metrics for the filtered setting, as described in (Bordes et al., 2013).

MODEL	FB15K				WN18				PRM45K			
	MRR	H@10	H@3	H@1	MRR	H@10	H@3	H@1	MRR	H@10	H@3	H@1
TRANSE(1)		0.471				0.892						
TRANSE(2)	0.463	0.749	0.578	0.297	0.495	0.943	0.888	0.113	0.518	0.680	0.569	0.428
HOLE	0.524	0.739	0.613	0.402	0.938	0.949	0.945	0.930				
ROTATE	0.797	0.884	0.830	0.746	0.949	0.959	0.952	0.944	0.518	0.675	0.565	0.432
SVM(N=50)	0.617	0.799	0.676	0.520	0.526	0.942	0.757	0.271	0.553	0.758	0.632	0.431
SVM(N=100)	0.632	0.806	0.690	0.538	0.539	0.944	0.766	0.289	0.554	0.770	0.634	0.433

partally as a result of this work, limitations of the TransE data model were identifed (Nickel et al., 2016). We expect that the known limitations that impact TransE also affect our approach. Despite these limitations, TransE's performance remains competitive on many real-world and benchmark data sets.

Recently, RotatE (Sun et al., 2019) sought to address a variety of the limitations known about TransE. RotatE embeds entities and relations in complex space and treats relations as rotations in the complex plane; the model achieves improved raw performance on standard benchmarks. It is believed that the additional freedom granted by the complex geometry contributes to the success of RotatE at learning graph structure. The authors also introduce *negative adversarial sampling* for link prediction. The idea of using negative sampling has proven quite effective for both learning knowledge graph embeddings (Trouillon et al., 2016) and word embeddings (Mikolov et al., 2013).

Case-based reasoning for knowledge graph completion was introduced in (Das et al., 2020). The authors show that a k-nearest neighbor (KNN) based approach for can be both efficient and scalable for this application.

8 Conclusion and future work

We demonstrate feasibility of using off-the-shelf SVM libraries to address the knowledge graph link-prediction problem. We present results on standard benchmarks that achieve parity with baseline models, while total wall clock time is measured in minutes rather than hours. The model structure we introduce is closely related to a well-established model with good performance characteristics, and it is elementary. The model we introduce has very few parameters to tune, and default solver settings typically yield satisfactory performance.

With the increasing focus on the large time, cost and energy consumption required to train leading machine learning models, it seems reasonable to ask whether casting nonconvex programs as convex programs could provide a path towards more efficient model training without significant sacrifice in performance.

One benefit of our convex formulation is the ability to add constraints to the program. Future directions could introduce rules about the knowledge graph using this method, as proposed in (Fung et al., 2002). Simple "if P then Q" first order logic propositions, where P and Q are linear predicates (equal, larger that, smaller than) can be represented by polyhedral sets of the form $Ax \leq b$. In this way, conditional information in the form of knowledge sets can be considered during the training process. One could also aim to adapt the model to yield proper embeddings by adding additional constraints such as diagonal dominance to the matrix B rather than just scores.

Another direction we would like to explore is how we can introduce nonlinear data models so our problem does not suffer from the same expressivity limitations as TransE. It may be possible to adapt a model derived from RotatE, for instance.

Finally, the model that we present scales quadratically in the number of entities and relations, and the dimensionality of the representation is a function of the problem. It would be useful to find a representation that has good performance without the quadratic growth in dimension.

References

Mohammad Al Hasan, Vineet Chaoji, Saeed Salem, and Mohammed Zaki. 2006. Link prediction using supervised learning. In *SDM06: workshop on link analysis, counter-terrorism and security*, volume 30, pages 798–805.

Kurt Bollacker, Colin Evans, Praveen Paritosh, Tim Sturge, and Jamie Taylor. 2008. Freebase: A collaboratively created graph database for structuring human knowledge. In *Proceedings of the 2008 ACM SIGMOD International Conference on Management of Data*, SIGMOD '08, page 1247–1250, New York, NY, USA. Association for Computing Machinery.

Antoine Bordes, Nicolas Usunier, Alberto Garcia-Duran, Jason Weston, and Oksana Yakhnenko. 2013. Translating embeddings for modeling multi-relational data. In *Advances in neural information processing systems*, pages 2787–2795.

Antoine Bordes, Jason Weston, Ronan Collobert, and Yoshua Bengio. 2011. Learning structured embeddings of knowledge bases. In *Proceedings of the Twenty-Fifth AAAI Conference on Artificial Intelligence*, AAAI'11, page 301–306. AAAI Press.

Chih-Chung Chang and Chih-Jen Lin. 2011. LIBSVM: A library for support vector machines. *ACM Transactions on Intelligent Systems and Technology*, 2:27:1–27:27. Software available at `http://www.csie.ntu.edu.tw/~cjlin/libsvm`.

Corinna Cortes and Vladimir Vapnik. 1995. Support-vector networks. *Machine learning*, 20(3):273–297.

Rajarshi Das, Ameya Godbole, Nicholas Monath, Manzil Zaheer, and Andrew McCallum. 2020. Probabilistic case-based reasoning for open-world knowledge graph completion. In *Findings of the Association for Computational Linguistics: EMNLP 2020*, pages 4752–4765, Online. Association for Computational Linguistics.

Rong-En Fan, Kai-Wei Chang, Cho-Jui Hsieh, Xiang-Rui Wang, and Chih-Jen Lin. 2008. Liblinear: A library for large linear classification. *J. Mach. Learn. Res.*, 9:1871–1874.

G. Fung, O. Mangasarian, and J. Shavlik. 2002. Knowledge-based support vector machine classifiers. In *NIPS*.

Greg Glockner. 2020. Does gurobi support gpus? `https://support.gurobi.com/hc/en-us/articles/360012237852-Does-Gurobi-support-GPUs-`.

Xavier Glorot, Antoine Bordes, J. Weston, and Yoshua Bengio. 2013. A semantic matching energy function for learning with multi-relational data. *Machine Learning*, 94:233–259.

Kelvin Guu, John Miller, and Percy Liang. 2015. Traversing knowledge graphs in vector space. In *Proceedings of the 2015 Conference on Empirical Methods in Natural Language Processing*, pages 318–327.

Yanchao Hao, Yuanzhe Zhang, Kang Liu, Shizhu He, Zhanyi Liu, Hua Wu, and Jun Zhao. 2017. An end-to-end model for question answering over knowledge base with cross-attention combining global knowledge. In *Proceedings of the 55th Annual Meeting of the Association for Computational Linguistics (Volume 1: Long Papers)*, pages 221–231, Vancouver, Canada. Association for Computational Linguistics.

Charles R. Harris, K. Jarrod Millman, St'efan J. van der Walt, Ralf Gommers, Pauli Virtanen, David Cournapeau, Eric Wieser, Julian Taylor, Sebastian Berg, Nathaniel J. Smith, Robert Kern, Matti Picus, Stephan Hoyer, Marten H. van Kerkwijk, Matthew Brett, Allan Haldane, Jaime Fern'andez del R'ıo, Mark Wiebe, Pearu Peterson, Pierre G'erard-Marchant, Kevin Sheppard, Tyler Reddy, Warren Weckesser, Hameer Abbasi, Christoph Gohlke, and Travis E. Oliphant. 2020. Array programming with NumPy. *Nature*, 585(7825):357–362.

Richard A Harshman, Paul E Green, Yoram Wind, and Margaret E Lundy. 1982. A model for the analysis of asymmetric data in marketing research. *Marketing Science*, 1(2):205–242.

R. Herbrich, T. Graepel, and K. Obermayer. 1999. Support vector learning for ordinal regression. In *1999 Ninth International Conference on Artificial Neural Networks ICANN 99. (Conf. Publ. No. 470)*, volume 1, pages 97–102 vol.1.

Thorsten Joachims. 2002. Optimizing search engines using clickthrough data. In *Proceedings of the Eighth ACM SIGKDD International Conference on Knowledge Discovery and Data Mining*, KDD '02, page 133–142, New York, NY, USA. Association for Computing Machinery.

Yankai Lin, Zhiyuan Liu, Huanbo Luan, Maosong Sun, Siwei Rao, and Song Liu. 2015. Modeling relation paths for representation learning of knowledge bases. In *Proceedings of the 2015 Conference on Empirical Methods in Natural Language Processing*, pages 705–714.

Olvi L. Mangasarian. 2006. Exact 1-norm support vector machines via unconstrained convex differentiable minimization. *J. Mach. Learn. Res.*, 7:1517–1530.

G. Miller. 1995. Wordnet: a lexical database for english. *Commun. ACM*, 38:39–41.

Pasquale Minervini, Nicola Fanizzi, Claudia d'Amato, and Floriana Esposito. 2015. Scalable learning of entity and predicate embeddings for knowledge graph completion. In *2015 IEEE 14th International Conference on Machine Learning and Applications (ICMLA)*, pages 162–167. IEEE.

Maximilian Nickel, Lorenzo Rosasco, and Tomaso Poggio. 2016. Holographic embeddings of knowledge graphs. In *Proceedings of the Thirtieth AAAI Conference on Artificial Intelligence*, AAAI'16, page 1955–1961. AAAI Press.

Maximilian Nickel, Volker Tresp, and Hans-Peter Kriegel. 2011. A three-way model for collective learning on multi-relational data. In *Proceedings of the 28th International Conference on Machine Learning, ICML 2011*, pages 809–816.

Adam Paszke, Sam Gross, Francisco Massa, Adam Lerer, James Bradbury, Gregory Chanan, Trevor Killeen, Zeming Lin, Natalia Gimelshein, Luca Antiga, Alban Desmaison, Andreas Kopf, Edward Yang, Zachary DeVito, Martin Raison, Alykhan Tejani, Sasank Chilamkurthy, Benoit Steiner, Lu Fang, Junjie Bai, and Soumith Chintala. 2019. Pytorch: An imperative style, high-performance deep learning library. In H. Wallach, H. Larochelle, A. Beygelzimer, F. dÁlché-Buc, E. Fox, and R. Garnett, editors, *Advances in Neural Information Processing Systems 32*, pages 8024–8035. Curran Associates, Inc.

F. Pedregosa, G. Varoquaux, A. Gramfort, V. Michel, B. Thirion, O. Grisel, M. Blondel, P. Prettenhofer, R. Weiss, V. Dubourg, J. Vanderplas, A. Passos, D. Cournapeau, M. Brucher, M. Perrot, and E. Duchesnay. 2011. Scikit-learn: Machine learning in Python. *Journal of Machine Learning Research*, 12:2825–2830.

Rómer Rosales and Glenn Fung. 2006. Learning sparse metrics via linear programming. In *Proceedings of the 12th ACM SIGKDD International Conference on Knowledge Discovery and Data Mining*, KDD '06, page 367–373, New York, NY, USA. Association for Computing Machinery.

Zhiqing Sun, Zhi-Hong Deng, Jian-Yun Nie, and Jian Tang. 2019. Rotate: Knowledge graph embedding by relational rotation in complex space. In *International Conference on Learning Representations*.

Kristina Toutanova and Danqi Chen. 2015. Observed versus latent features for knowledge base and text inference. In *Proceedings of the 3rd Workshop on Continuous Vector Space Models and their Compositionality*, pages 57–66.

Théo Trouillon, Johannes Welbl, Sebastian Riedel, Éric Gaussier, and Guillaume Bouchard. 2016. Complex embeddings for simple link prediction. In *Proceedings of the 33rd International Conference on International Conference on Machine Learning-Volume 48*. International Conference on Machine Learning (ICML).

Alicia Tsai and Laurent El Ghaoui. 2020. Sparse optimization for unsupervised extractive summarization of long documents with the frank-wolfe algorithm. In *Proceedings of SustaiNLP: Workshop on Simple and Efficient Natural Language Processing*, pages 54–62, Online. Association for Computational Linguistics.

Pauli Virtanen, Ralf Gommers, Travis E. Oliphant, Matt Haberland, Tyler Reddy, David Cournapeau, Evgeni Burovski, Pearu Peterson, Warren Weckesser, Jonathan Bright, Stéfan J. van der Walt, Matthew Brett, Joshua Wilson, K. Jarrod Millman, Nikolay Mayorov, Andrew R. J. Nelson, Eric Jones, Robert Kern, Eric Larson, C J Carey, İlhan Polat, Yu Feng, Eric W. Moore, Jake VanderPlas, Denis Laxalde, Josef Perktold, Robert Cimrman, Ian Henriksen, E. A. Quintero, Charles R. Harris, Anne M. Archibald, Antônio H. Ribeiro, Fabian Pedregosa, Paul van Mulbregt, and SciPy 1.0 Contributors. 2020. SciPy 1.0: Fundamental Algorithms for Scientific Computing in Python. *Nature Methods*, 17:261–272.

Chenyan Xiong, Russell Power, and Jamie Callan. 2017. Explicit semantic ranking for academic search via knowledge graph embedding. In *Proceedings of the 26th International Conference on World Wide Web*, WWW '17, page 1271–1279, Republic and Canton of Geneva, CHE. International World Wide Web Conferences Steering Committee.

Bishan Yang and Tom Mitchell. 2017. Leveraging knowledge bases in LSTMs for improving machine reading. In *Proceedings of the 55th Annual Meeting of the Association for Computational Linguistics (Volume 1: Long Papers)*, pages 1436–1446, Vancouver, Canada. Association for Computational Linguistics.

Fuzheng Zhang, Nicholas Jing Yuan, Defu Lian, Xing Xie, and Wei-Ying Ma. 2016. Collaborative knowledge base embedding for recommender systems. In *Proceedings of the 22nd ACM SIGKDD International Conference on Knowledge Discovery and Data Mining*, KDD '16, page 353–362, New York, NY, USA. Association for Computing Machinery.

Evaluating the carbon footprint of NLP methods: a survey and analysis of existing tools

Nesrine Bannour
Sahar Ghannay
Aurélie Névéol
Université Paris-Saclay, CNRS,
LISN, Orsay, France

Anne-Laure Ligozat
Université Paris-Saclay, CNRS,
ENSIIE, LISN, Orsay, France
firstname.lastname
@lisn.upsaclay.fr

Abstract

Modern Natural Language Processing (NLP) makes intensive use of deep learning methods because of the accuracy they offer for a variety of applications. Due to the significant environmental impact of deep learning, cost-benefit analysis including carbon footprint as well as accuracy measures has been suggested to better document the use of NLP methods for research or deployment. In this paper, we review the tools that are available to measure energy use and CO_2 emissions of NLP methods. We describe the scope of the measures provided and compare the use of six tools (carbon tracker, experiment impact tracker, green algorithms, ML CO2 impact, energy usage and cumulator) on named entity recognition experiments performed on different computational set-ups (local server vs. computing facility). Based on these findings, we propose actionable recommendations to accurately measure the environmental impact of NLP experiments.

1 Introduction

Modern Natural Language Processing (NLP) makes intensive use of deep learning methods because of the functional performance they offer for a variety of tasks, including text classification or named entity recognition (Tourille et al., 2018).

Deep learning programs can have a high environmental impact in terms of Greenhouse Gas (GHG) emissions due in particular to the energy consumption of the computational facilities used to run them (Strubell et al., 2019). The impact has been increasing over the years (Schwartz et al., 2019) and is affecting populations that can be different from those generating the impact (Bender et al., 2021). In a recent medical imaging study, Selvan (2021) suggests that the increase of large model carbon footprint does not translate into proportional accuracy gains. Measuring this impact is a first step for raising awareness and controlling the impact of NLP experiments and operations. Some guidelines were offered in the SustaiNLP workshop[1] to measure impact, and it was suggested that different methods for measuring environmental impact can lead to different conclusions in terms of algorithm efficiency (Cao et al., 2020).

Our goal is to conduct a systematic review of tools available for measuring the impact of NLP tools and to offer a comparative analysis from the perspective of calculated impact measures and usability. We seek to understand the methods implemented by the tools as well the criteria used to assess impact. The contributions of this study are threefold:

- We identify tools available for measuring the environmental impact of NLP experiments
- We characterize impact measurement tools with respect to scope of the impact information provided and usability
- We apply the tools to assess the impact of named entity recognition experiments in order to compare the measurement obtained in two computational set-ups.

2 Environmental impact due to deep learning programs

As for any Information and Communication Technology (ICT) service, a deep learning program impacts several environmental indicators, among which the Global Warming Potential, expressed in terms of GreenHouse Gases (GHGs) emissions, CO_2 equivalent emissions, or carbon footprint. Other indicators include: abiotic resource depletion, blue water shortage, human toxicity... Existing tools for deep learning programs focus on the carbon footprint only.

The environmental impact in terms of carbon footprint needs to account for the entire lifecycle of

[1] https://sites.google.com/view/sustainlp2020/home

Proceedings of the 2nd Workshop on Simple and Efficient Natural Language Processing, pages 11–21
November 10, 2021. ©201 Association for Computational Linguistics

ICT equipment from production, through use and finally end of life.

Life Cycle Analysis usually allocates part of the GHG emitted during the production of equipment to the use e.g. when running computer programs, since the equipment was partly produced for the purpose of running programs. For ICT equipment, this phase is difficult to assess because data on GHG emissions during production are not always easily available. In the case of Graphical Processing Unit (GPUs) (or Tensor Processing Unit (TPUs) or equivalents), we could not find any publication or site giving an estimate of the GHG emissions due to the production phase. However, it has to be noted that production can account for a significant part of the total GHG emissions: a French study (Berthoud et al., 2020) on a data center (with Central Processing Unit (CPU) servers only) in Grenoble found that around 40% of the total emissions released during one hour of CPU use were due to the production phase (including emissions due to the equipment alone). Similarly, another recent study (Gupta et al., 2021) reports that the hardware manufacturing and infrastructure accounts for the bulk of the environmental impact of mobile and data center computing equipment, while the impact of operational energy consumption is diminishing.

The end-of-life phase is very difficult to assess for ICT due to lack of data.

To summarize, there are at least four sources of CO_2 equivalent emission sources that should be taken into account to assess the environmental impact of computational experiments: 1/ production of hardware equipment: router, PC, server; 2/ idle use of the hardware; 3/ dynamic use of the hardware; and 4/ end of life of equipment.

3 Tools

Our method for identifying tools and characterizing them relied on a recent study conducting a similar review of annotation tools (Neves and Ševa, 2019). In our study, four authors of this paper contributed to the definition of the criteria and evaluation of the tools. They all have a computer science background with programming experience, and were not involved in the development of any of the tools reviewed or selected.

3.1 Selection of tools

We started from a short list of tools identified by a Working group on the environmental impact of AI in the French group EcoInfo [2] (Experiment Impact tracker, Pyjoules, Carbon tracker).

Then we used snowballing to collect articles citing these tools (according to Google Scholar). For articles published in ArXiv, we also reviewed "related papers" when available. We repeated the process for each newly identified tool we selected.

The goal of this study is to survey and analyze tools that are openly available to the scientific community to evaluate the carbon footprint of natural language processing experiments. Therefore, we selected tools that meet the following criteria:

- freely available
- usable in our programming environment (Mac/linux terminal)
- documented in a scientific publication
- suitable to measure the impact of NLP experiments, such as named entity recognition
- providing a CO_2 equivalent measure for experiments

From our initial shortlist, pyJoules is a python library that monitors the energy consumed by specific device of the host machine such as CPU, RAM, GPU. It is part of the PowerAPI toolkit, which offers solution for measuring energy consumption of software in real time (Bourdon et al., 2013). It was excluded because it does not directly supply a CO_2 equivalent value. Other tools under development were also excluded, when they provided no code or online platform: (Zhang et al., 2020; Shaikh et al., 2021).

Figure 1 presents detailed results of our literature search. A total of 94 publications were obtained from Google Scholar and an additional 20 from ArXiv core related papers. After de-duplication, 85 publications were reviewed. We found that many (N=43) offered opinions or discussion of carbon impact measurement in machine learning, NLP and other fields. Another 27 (represented by the orange flow) described studies that measured the environmental impact of experiments using one of the selected tools. Strubell et al. (2019) presented a study measuring the impact of NLP experiments using methods (nvidia and Intel RAPL system management interface) that are now implemented in some of the selected tools.

[2] https://ecoinfo.cnrs.fr/

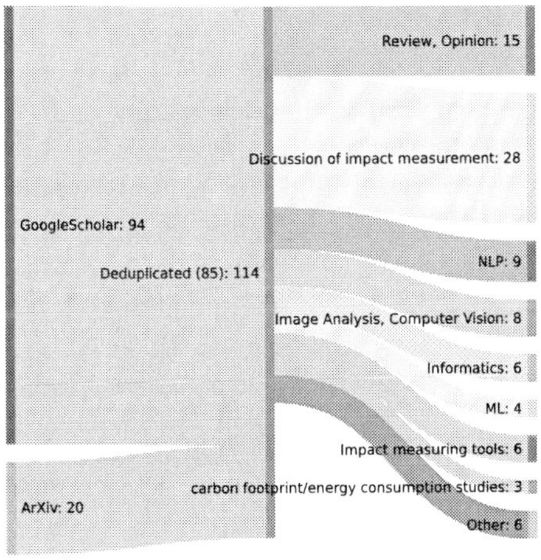

Figure 1: Sankey diagram showing the publications reviewed in our literature search for identifying carbon impact measurement tools.

3.2 List of evaluation criteria

To evaluate the selected impact measurement tools, we defined various criteria to characterize the availability of tools and documentation as well as technical parameters of the tools, including the type of hardware in the scope, the type of measure offered, the detailed information used to assess electricity use by data centers and carbon intensity for electricity production depending on location.

Criteria are split into 4 categories: (a) publication, (b) technical, (c) configuration and (d) functional criteria. Each is presented in detail below.

Publication criteria

P1 - Year of the last publication;

P2 - Citations in Google Scholar (as of 11 May 2021);

P3 - Citations for measuring NLP experiments (as of 11 May 2021).

Technical criteria

T1 - Date of the last version (as of 11 May 2021);

T2 - Availability of the source code;

T3 - Online availability for use;

T4 - Easiness of installation; We evaluated it as "Poor" if we did not manage to install it, "Fair" if we managed to install it but needed system administration access, "Good" if we managed to install it as an ordinary user.

T5 - Quality of the documentation (companion publication or code documentation); We evaluated it as "Poor" if we did not find documentation on the tool, "Fair" if documentation is available, but lacks practical usage details, "Good" if the available documentation addresses usage questions such as parameter settings and country localization.

T6 - Type of license

T7 - Output formats

Configuration criteria

C1 - Local values for carbon intensity: Are local values automatically taken into account or is a global energy mix used?

C2 - Possible (manual) configuration of carbon intensity; Yes if it is possible to configure the carbon intensity without changing the code; No otherwise; We also note whether instructions are provided to the users as to where adequate values can be found.

C3 - Possible (manual) configuration of PUE; Yes if it is possible to configure the PUE without changing the code; No otherwise; We also note whether instructions are provided to the users as to where adequate values can be found.

C4 - Platforms taken into account; which type of equipment is covered by the measurements: PC, server, cloud?

C5 - Other configuration features

Functional criteria

F1 - CO_2 equivalent emission sources taken into account; We consider the following sources, described in section 2: *production*, *idle use*, *dynamic use* and *end of life*.

F2 - Hardware taken into account: does the calculation model account for emissions from data transmission between equipment types as well as from the hardware executing the experiments?

All the tools are supposed to take both CPU and GPU consumption into account, so we did not include this criterion in our analysis.

3.3 List of selected tools

We introduce the selected tools below. Table 1 presents the evaluation of the tools according to the criteria defined in section 3.2.

Green Algorithms (Lannelongue et al., 2021) is an online tool developed by researchers in the UK that calculates the energy consumption and carbon footprint of computer use based on information supplied by the user in a web interface: runtime, number of cores, memory requested, type of platform used (PC, local server, cloud computing), type of cores, location.

ML CO2 Impact (Lacoste et al., 2019) is an online tool developed by researchers in Canada that calculates the energy consumption and carbon footprint of computer use based on user supplied information including hardware, runtime, cloud provider and location of the computing facilities operated. We are aware that a new version of the tool is being developed under the umbrella of the *Code Carbon* [3] initiative. However, it is not yet described in a scientific publication so we have decided to evaluate ML CO2 which has been used by the NLP research community.

Energy Usage (Lottick et al., 2019) was developed by researchers in the United States with the goal of improving accountability in machine learning research. Experiment impact tracker (Henderson et al., 2020) was developed by researchers in north America to assist researchers in measuring and reporting the impact of their machine learning experiments. Carbon tracker (Anthony et al., 2020) was developed by researchers from Denmark for tracking and predicting the energy consumption and carbon footprint of training deep learning models. These three tools are python packages that get the energy consumption of a machine learning program via GPU, CPU and DRAM information.

Cumulator (Tristan Trebaol and Ghadikolaei, 2020) is also a python package developed in Switzerland. Its estimates the energy consumption of computation based on runtime, GPU load and carbon intensity, with a fixed value for consumption of a typical GPU. It also estimates the energy consumption of communication based on the file sizes and the 1 byte model from The Shift Project (The Shift Project, 2018).

[3] `https://codecarbon.io/`

4 Use case: measuring the impact of named entity recognition

In this section, we present experiments for a typical NLP task, named entity recognition (NER). Experiments are conducted on two computational set-ups: (1) the use of a server within the laboratory (equipped with 2 GPUs Nvidia GeForce GTX 1080 Ti) and (2) the use of an external shared computer facility (equipped with 43 GPUs including GPU Nvidia Tesla V100). We hypothesize that this type of set-up can be available to NLP researchers, and that it is relevant to document the implications of choosing one or the other for a set of experiments.

We measure the impact of the experiments using the selected tools and compare the carbon footprint across tools and computational set-ups.

4.1 Named Entity Recognition on QUAERO benchmark corpora

NER methods. Many Named Entity Recognition (NER) models focus on identifying flat entities (Collobert et al., 2011; Lample et al., 2016; Ma and Hovy, 2016; Peters et al., 2018; Luoma and Pyysalo, 2020) based on a sequence labeling approach. However, to address the need for the extraction of nested entities, an increasing number of models do take nested entities into account as well (Alex et al., 2007; Lu and Roth, 2015; Ju et al., 2018; Straková et al., 2019; Yu et al., 2020; Li, 2021). Nested entities are embedded named entities included in other entities. To reflect current needs of entity extraction, we choose to evaluate the energy consumption of two deep learning neuronal models, one that addresses flat entity recognition (Ma and Hovy, 2016) and one that addresses both flat and nested entity recognition, introduced by (Yu et al., 2020). (Yu et al., 2020) adapt the biaffine dependency parsing model of (Dozat and Manning, 2017) to Named Entity Recognition by reformulating this task as the task of identifying start and end indices and associating a category to the span defined by these pairs. The biaffine model is used on top of a multi-layer BiLSTM to assign score to all possibles spans. To reproduce this model, we encode words using the pre-trained Language model CamemBERT$_{\text{BASE}}$ (Martin et al., 2019) provided by the Transformers library[4] from Hugging Face Inc. (Wolf et al., 2020) and we follow the same strategy by using CNN to encode the character-based word embeddings.

[4] https://huggingface.co/transformers/

	Carbon Tracker (Anthony et al., 2020)	**Green Algorithms** (Lannelongue et al., 2021)	**Experiment Impact Tracker** (Henderson et al., 2020)	**ML CO2 Impact** (Lacoste et al., 2019)	**energy usage** (Lottick et al., 2019)	**Cumulator** (Tristan Trebaol and Ghadikolaei, 2020)
P1	2020	2021	2020	2019	2019	2020
P2	18	4	33	35	4	0
P3	1 (Parcollet and Ravanelli, 2021)	1 (Liu et al., 2021)	3 (Cao et al., 2020; Prasanna et al., 2020; Peng et al., 2021)	4 (Sarti, 2020; Selby et al., 2021; Chaudhary et al., 2020; Gencoglu, 2020)	0	0
T1	Dec 8, 2020	Dec 17, 2020	April 29, 2021	May 4, 2021	July 10, 2020	April 29, 2021
T2	Yes	Yes	Yes	Yes	Yes	Yes
T3	No	Yes (online)	No	Yes (online)	No	No
T4	Good	No install needed	Fair	No install needed	Poor	Good
T5	Good	Fair	Fair	Fair	Fair	Good
T6	MIT	CC-BY-4.0	MIT	MIT	Apache	MIT
T7	Generates a statement to report results	Generates a statement to report the results	Generates a statement and graphs to report results	Generates text and LaTeXcode to report the results	Generates text and pdf reports	Generates a text report
C1	Yes: carbon intensity from Energi data service for Denmark, Carbon intensity API for the UK, CO2 signal API otherwise, and European Environment Agency for the default value	Yes, carbon intensity from carbonfootprint	Yes, carbon intensity from electricitymap	Yes, pointers supplied to user, including electricitymap	Yes, carbon intensity from U.S. Energy Information Administration data and U.S. Environmental Protection Agency eGRID data	No
C2	No	No	No	Yes	No	No, but indications are given in the documentation about how to change the default value
C3	No, default value of PUE = 1.67 (2019)	No, default value of PUE = 1.67 (2019)	Yes. Default PUE (1.58) can be adjusted	Partly, for Google, Amazon, Azure cloud providers.	No PUE used but PSU loss can be set	No PUE used
C4	Install dependent	PC, local server, cloud	Install dependent	3 specific providers, private infrastructure	Install dependent	Install dependent
C5	Consumption prediction based on a number of epochs, monitoring of chosen components, conversion to interpretable numbers...	Pragmatic Scaling Factor to take into account the number of experiments, conversion to interpretable numbers, comparison with other locations	Asserting certain hardware	No	Year for the data, comparison with other locations	No
F1	Dynamic use	Dynamic use	Dynamic use	Dynamic use	Dynamic use	Dynamic use
F2	Hardware only	Hardware only	Hardware only	Hardware only	Hardware only	Hardware and communication

Table 1: Evaluation of the tools according to the publication (P), technical (T), configuration (C) and functional (F) criteria.

Experimental set-up. The following configuration is used: 1 core is used; GTX 1080 Ti GPUs are used on the lab server while Tesla V100 GPUs are used on the computing facility; the memory used is 11 GB on the server, and 32GB on the facility; 20 CPUs are used on the facility; the experiments were conducted in France. We documented France as the location for experiments in the impact measurement tools as directed by the tools' documentation.

Datasets. We used two benchmark datasets for Named Entity Recognition in French: the QUAERO Broadcast News Extended Named Entity dataset (Galibert et al., 2010) and the QUAERO French Med dataset (Névéol et al., 2014), which contains the EMEA and MEDLINE subsets. We selected these datasets because they are suitable for the task at hand, illustrate different scales of training data (the Press corpus is much larger than the medical corpus) while remaining of modest size, and are freely available for non-commercial use.

Table 2 presents descriptive statistics including details about nested entities for the datasets.

	QUAERO French News	QUAERO French Med EMEA	QUAERO French Med MEDLINE
Documents	167	38	2,498
Entity Types	5	10	10
Tokens	1,347,368	40,257	31,926
Entities	79,632	7,159	9,074
Unique entities	19,876	1,880	5,895
Nested entities	0	1,009	2,280
% Nested	0 %	14,27 %	25,31 %
Max Depth	1	4	4

Table 2: Corpus Statistics.

4.2 Results

Table 4 presents the results of the experiments, with the CO_2 equivalent measures for training each model. To further understand potential differences in CO_2 measures we also report the corresponding energy consumption in Table 3.

The CO_2 equivalent emissions measured for a same experiment greatly depending on the measuring tool used. We analyzed the computational set-up and tool configurations in an attempt to better understand the observed variations.

Carbon intensity We noticed that carbon tracker used the average carbon intensity for EU-28 in 2017 (294.21 gCO_2eq/kWh) instead of the French value (around 30 to 40 gCO_2eq/kWh according to electricityMap), which overestimates the CO_2 equivalent cost. Green Algorithms, which uses the 2020 values from electricityMap, gives 39 gCO_2eq/kWh. Experiment impact tracker uses the 2018 electricityMap value, which gives a 47.60 gCO_2eq/kWh for France. Energy usage relies on international energy mix data from the U.S. Energy Information Administration data for the year 2016, and assumed carbon equivalencies by energy type. The value for France thus seems to be 424 gCO_2eq/kWh. ML CO2 Impact was used with the default value, 432 gCO_2/kWh. We investigated the data sources provided by the tools to search for a more precise value for France, but the values for Carbon intensity varied a lot: 53 gCO_2/kWh on Carbon footprint when the given link was followed, leading to the 2018 emissions; with the most recent data available, from 2020, the carbon intensity for France is 38,95. On electricityMap, the value at the time of the experiments was 31 gCO_2/kWh. The European Commission link again gives different values, according to the kind of electricity considered, and based on 2013 values.

The carbon intensity values is thus very different even when considering the same country.

Hardware On the computing facility, we used Tesla V100-PCIE-32GB GPUs. However, the hardware options offered by the online algorithms did not exactly correspond to the equipment we used. For example ML CO2 Impact offers only V100-PCIE-16GB or V100-SXM2-32GB, so we reported the results for V100-SXM2-32GB. In Green algorithms, the only GPU option available is Tesla V100. This may lead to a lack of precision on the results.

Green algorithms currently does not enable to input both CPU and GPU usage, although a forthcoming version should include this possibility.

Precision of results The NER experiments conducted were designed to test the impact measurement tools without causing excessive environmental impact. We used modest sized datasets requiring short training times, which posed problems for some tools. For example ML CO2 Impact displayed 0 values for several experiments, so we used the formula provided in the publication to obtain a more precise measurement.

5 Discussion

Measuring carbon footprint is a novel undertaking Table 1 shows that the availability of tools

		CO_2 equivalent (g.)						Runtime (mins.)	NER metrics		
		CT	EIT	EU	Cu	MLCI	GA		P	R	F
NER (Yu et al., 2020)	**French Press**										
	Server	237.96	78	0.496	302	290	350.15	163:39	87.49	74.85	80.68
	Facility	161.16	48	0.979	222	250	260.26	118:04	88.05	74.71	80.83
	EMEA										
	Server	9.70	30	0,00131	19	20	16.67	9:31	73.78	59.74	66.02
	Facility	8.07	1	0,002	13.7	10	14.31	6:51	77.58	58.71	66.84
	MEDLINE										
	Server	13.44	30	0,00128	26.1	20	20.68	11:55	66.62	62.11	64.28
	Facility	10.50	1	0,00259	19.4	20	20.03	9:11	79.73	78.35	78.98
NER (Ma and Hovy, 2016)	**French Press**										
	Server	87.62	12	5.1	100.04	125	104.40	58:30	78.49	69.77	73.87
	Facility	46.43	6	2.87	79.05	99	102.08	46:44	80.75	70.67	75.38
	EMEA										
	Server	2.23	0.004	0.117	4.31	0	3.83	02:14	61.77	50.27	55.43
	Facility	2.28	0	0.151	3.23	0	4.99	02:27	57.46	51.98	54.58
	MEDLINE										
	Server	2.99	0	0.137	5.20	0	5.57	03:11	43.97	41.08	42.47
	Facility	2.74	0	0	0.176	0	5.67	02:58	52.39	36.68	43.15

Table 3: Results of NER experiments. The upper part of the table presents the results obtained with an implementation of the method by (Yu et al., 2020) while the bottom part presents the results obtained with an implementation of the method by (Ma and Hovy, 2016). The CO_2 equivalent measures are reported according to the six selected tools in this study, Carbon Tracker (CT), Green Algorithms (GA), Experiment Impact Tracker (EIT), ML CO2 Impact (MLCI), Energy Use (EU) and Cumulator (Cu).

		Energy consumption (kWh)					
		CT	EIT	EU	Cu	MLCI	GA
NER (Yu et al., 2020)	**French Press**						
	Server	0.809	1.399	0,00117	n/a	0.68	1.38
	Facility	0.548	0.865	0,00231	n/a	0.59	1.03
	EMEA						
	Server	0.033	0.053	0,0000034	n/a	0.04	0.07
	Facility	0.027	0.017	0,0000047	n/a	0.03	0.06
	MEDLINE						
	Server	0.046	0.045	0,0000030	n/a	0.05	0.08
	Facility	0.036	0.021	0,0000061	n/a	0.05	0.08
NER (Ma and Hovy, 2016)	**French Press**						
	Server	0.298	0.209	0.012	n/a	0.29	0.41
	Facility	0.158	0.102	0.0068	n/a	0.23	0.40
	EMEA						
	Server	0.0072	0.007	0.00028	n/a	0.01	0.02
	Facility	0.0078	0.004	0.00036	n/a	0.01	0.02
	MEDLINE						
	Server	0.010	0.007	0.00032	n/a	0.015	0.02
	Facility	0.0094	0.005	0.0004	n/a	0.015	0.02

Table 4: Energy consumption in kWh for each method and experimental condition. The upper part of the table presents the results obtained with an implementation of the method by (Yu et al., 2020) while the bottom part presents the results obtained with an implementation of the method by (Ma and Hovy, 2016). The measures are reported according to the six selected tools in this study, Carbon Tracker (CT), Green Algorithms (GA), Experiment Impact Tracker (EIT), ML CO2 Impact (MLCI), Energy Use (EU) and Cumulator (Cu).

for measuring carbon impact of experiments is quite recent. Furthermore, these tools have been moderately used in the field of NLP (we identified 9 studies in total). However, we can note that the interest in producing impact measures is widespread as the six tools reviewed were developed by researchers in different countries across Europe and North America.

Differences in carbon footprint measurements Miozzo et al. (2021) found the emissions computed by Green algorithms to be higher than those computed by ML CO2 Impact. This is explained by the details of the *functional criteria* reported in table 1, which show that key elements such as carbon intensity values or PUE differ across the tools. The results from table 4 also illustrate the differences.

The CO_2 equivalent emissions obtained from ML CO2 Impact and Green Algorithms are higher than those returned by other tools. This is consistent with our expectation because GA and MLCI do not perform direct measurements of the energy consumption but estimate it based on user supplied information. Carbon Tracker and Experiment Impact Tracker, which are based on the same calculations, produce similar impact measures. We observe that impact measures, in terms of energy consumption as well as CO_2 emissions, are generally lower for the computing facility compared to the local server. This can probably be explained by the difference in equipment (e.g. type of GPUs).

The measures obtained from Energy Usage are much lower than those obtained from the other tools. After investigation, it seems that these results do not take into account the GPU consumption, due to a possible bug in the tool, which was reported to the code authors.

Carbon footprint is underestimated All the tools reviewed in this study only evaluate the carbon footprint of NLP experiments based on energy consumption during the dynamic use phase of equipment. Emissions resulting from the production and end-of-life phases are unaccounted or partially accounted. In addition, we can note that setting up experiments also requires some upstream testing of configurations and model parameters that are often not accounted in the measures. Green Algorithm is the only tool in our selection that brings the users attention to this source of emission with the "pragmatic scaling factor". For these reasons, the measures of CO_2 equivalent obtained with these tools underestimate the actual carbon footprint.

NER performance The performance of the systems in terms of precision, recall and F-measure is above the median and average of participations in the 2016 CLEF eHealth task where the QUAERO French Med dataset was used as a benchmark (Névéol et al., 2016)[5]. As expected, the performance obtained is higher with the more recent nested entity extraction tool (Yu et al., 2020) vs. flat entity extraction tool (Ma and Hovy, 2016). This comes at the cost of higher environmental impact as measured by all tools. We can also note that the state of the art on this dataset remains the low-carbon cost dictionary method submitted to the CLEF eHealth shared task by the Erasmus team (Van Mulligen et al., 2016).

Which tool should be used for measuring carbon footprint of NLP experiments? The online tools (Green Algorithms and ML CO2 impact) are very convenient to use as no installation is necessary. Since they are used separately from running the experiments, an estimate of experiment impact can be obtained after running the experiment. However, some of the information to be supplied is not easy to figure out, such as "memory requirement" (GA) or "carbon intensity" (MLCI). In our experience, the use of the python packages tracking real-time energy usage (Carbon Tracker, Experiment Impact Tracker and Energy Usage) required special permission to read RAPL results, even with through powercap access, so admin assistance was needed to use the tools.

Also, the short training times in the NER experiments yielded impact measures of 0 from some of the tools. This suggests that these tools are not sensitive enough to measure small impacts and may be intended for use on higher impact experiments.

6 Conclusions

In this paper, we have conducted a survey of the literature to identify tools for measuring the environmental impact of NLP experiments. We characterized six tools and evaluated them on a sample named entity recognition task. The measures obtained vary significantly and only account for one in four sources of carbon emissions. More work is needed to better understand the differences in measurement between the tools and to account for sources of carbon emissions other than the dynamic use of hardware equipment: production, idle use, end of life.

[5] We note that while the results of the nested entity extraction tool (Yu et al., 2020) are directly comparable to the shared task results, those of the flat entity extraction tool (Ma and Hovy, 2016) are not because 14-25% of nested entities are not taken into account.

Acknowledgments

The sankey diagram presented in Figure 1 was prepared using `http://www.sankeymatic.com/build/`.

Author contributions

Anne-Laure Ligozat designed the study, developed the list of criteria and wrote a first draft of the manuscript. Aurélie Névéol conducted the literature search and contributed to manuscript drafting. Nesrine Bannour and Sahar Ghannay conducted the NER experiments and impact measurements. All authors contributed to the evaluation of tools.

References

Beatrice Alex, Barry Haddow, and Claire Grover. 2007. Recognising nested named entities in biomedical text. In *Biological, translational, and clinical language processing*, pages 65–72.

Lasse F. Wolff Anthony, Benjamin Kanding, and Raghavendra Selvan. 2020. Carbontracker: Tracking and predicting the carbon footprint of training deep learning models. In *ICML Workshop on "Challenges in Deploying and monitoring Machine Learning Systems"*.

Emily M. Bender, Timnit Gebru, Angelina McMillan-Major, and Shmargaret Shmitchell. 2021. On the dangers of stochastic parrots: Can language models be too big?🦜. In *Proceedings of the 2021 ACM Conference on Fairness, Accountability, and Transparency*, FAccT '21, page 610–623, New York, NY, USA. Association for Computing Machinery.

Francoise Berthoud, Bruno Bzeznik, Nicolas Gibelin, Myriam Laurens, Cyrille Bonamy, Maxence Morel, and Xavier Schwindenhammer. 2020. Estimation de l'empreinte carbone d'une heure.coeur de calcul. Research report, UGA - Université Grenoble Alpes ; CNRS ; INP Grenoble ; INRIA.

Aurélien Bourdon, Adel Noureddine, Romain Rouvoy, and Lionel Seinturier. 2013. PowerAPI: A software library to monitor the energy consumed at the process-level. *ERCIM News*, 2013(92).

Qingqing Cao, Aruna Balasubramanian, and Niranjan Balasubramanian. 2020. Towards accurate and reliable energy measurement of NLP models. In *Proceedings of SustaiNLP: Workshop on Simple and Efficient Natural Language Processing*, pages 141–148, Online. Association for Computational Linguistics.

Yatin Chaudhary, Pankaj Gupta, Khushbu Saxena, Vivek Kulkarni, Thomas Runkler, and Hinrich Schütze. 2020. TopicBERT for energy efficient document classification. In *Findings of the Association for Computational Linguistics: EMNLP 2020*, pages 1682–1690, Online. Association for Computational Linguistics.

Ronan Collobert, Jason Weston, Léon Bottou, Michael Karlen, Koray Kavukcuoglu, and Pavel Kuksa. 2011. Natural language processing (almost) from scratch. *Journal of machine learning research*, 12:2493–2537.

Timothy Dozat and Christopher D Manning. 2017. Deep biaffine attention for neural dependency parsing. In *5th International Conference on Learning Representations, ICLR*.

Olivier Galibert, Ludovic Quintard, Sophie Rosset, Pierre Zweigenbaum, Claire Nédellec, Sophie Aubin, Laurent Gillard, Jean-Pierre Raysz, Delphine Pois, Xavier Tannier, Louise Deléger, and Dominique Laurent. 2010. Named and specific entity detection in varied data: The quæro named entity baseline evaluation. In *Proceedings of the Seventh International Conference on Language Resources and Evaluation (LREC'10)*, Valletta, Malta. European Language Resources Association (ELRA).

Oguzhan Gencoglu. 2020. Large-scale, language-agnostic discourse classification of tweets during covid-19. *Machine Learning and Knowledge Extraction*, 2(4):603–616.

Udit Gupta, Young Geun Kim, Sylvia Lee, Jordan Tse, Hsien-Hsin S. Lee, Gu-Yeon Wei, David Brooks, and Carole-Jean Wu. 2021. Chasing carbon: The elusive environmental footprint of computing. In *IEEE International Symposium on High-Performance Computer Architecture (HPCA 2021)*. IEEE.

Peter Henderson, Jieru Hu, Joshua Romoff, Emma Brunskill, Dan Jurafsky, and Joelle Pineau. 2020. Towards the systematic reporting of the energy and carbon footprints of machine learning. *Journal of Machine Learning Research*, 21(248):1–43.

Meizhi Ju, Makoto Miwa, and Sophia Ananiadou. 2018. A neural layered model for nested named entity recognition. In *Proceedings of the 2018 Conference of the North American Chapter of the Association for Computational Linguistics: Human Language Technologies, Volume 1 (Long Papers)*, pages 1446–1459.

Alexandre Lacoste, Alexandra Luccioni, Victor Schmidt, and Thomas Dandres. 2019. Quantifying the carbon emissions of machine learning. In *Climate Change workshop, NeurIPS 2019*.

Guillaume Lample, Miguel Ballesteros, Sandeep Subramanian, Kazuya Kawakami, and Chris Dyer. 2016. Neural architectures for named entity recognition. In *NAACL*.

Loïc Lannelongue, Jason Grealey, and Michael Inouye. 2021. Green algorithms: Quantifying the carbon footprint of computation. *Advanced Science*, page 2100707.

B. Li. 2021. Named entity recognition in the style of object detection. *ArXiv*, abs/2101.11122.

Leo Z. Liu, Yizhong Wang, Jungo Kasai, Hannaneh Hajishirzi, and Noah A. Smith. 2021. Probing across time: What does roberta know and when? *CoRR*, abs/2104.07885.

Kadan Lottick, Silvia Susai, Sorelle A. Friedler, and Jonathan P. Wilson. 2019. Energy usage reports: Environmental awareness as part of algorithmic accountability. In *Workshop on Tackling Climate Change with Machine Learning at NeurIPS 2019*.

Wei Lu and Dan Roth. 2015. Joint mention extraction and classification with mention hypergraphs. In *Proceedings of the 2015 Conference on Empirical Methods in Natural Language Processing*, pages 857–867.

Jouni Luoma and Sampo Pyysalo. 2020. Exploring Cross-sentence Contexts for Named Entity Recognition with BERT. In *COLING*.

Xuezhe Ma and Eduard Hovy. 2016. End-to-end sequence labeling via bi-directional LSTM-CNNs-CRF. In *Proceedings of the 54th Annual Meeting of the Association for Computational Linguistics (Volume 1: Long Papers)*, pages 1064–1074, Berlin, Germany. Association for Computational Linguistics.

Louis Martin, Benjamin Muller, Pedro Javier Ortiz Suárez, Yoann Dupont, Laurent Romary, Éric Villemonte de la Clergerie, Djamé Seddah, and Benoît Sagot. 2019. CamemBERT: a Tasty French Language Model. In *Proceedings of the 58th Annual Meeting of the Association for Computational Linguistics*, pages 7203–7219. Association for Computational Linguistics.

Marco Miozzo, Zoraze Ali, Lorenza Giupponi, and Paolo Dini. 2021. Distributed and multi-task learning at the edge for energy efficient radio access networks. *IEEE Access*, 9:12491–12505.

Aurélie Névéol, K Bretonnel Cohen, Cyril Grouin, Thierry Hamon, Thomas Lavergne, Liadh Kelly, Lorraine Goeuriot, Grégoire Rey, Aude Robert, Xavier Tannier, and Pierre Zweigenbaum. 2016. Clinical information extraction at the clef ehealth evaluation lab 2016. In *CEUR workshop proceedings*, volume 1609, pages 28–42.

Aurélie Névéol, Cyril Grouin, Jeremy Leixa, Sophie Rosset, and Pierre Zweigenbaum. 2014. The QUAERO French medical corpus: A resource for medical entity recognition and normalization. In *Proc. BioTextM*.

Mariana Neves and Jurica Ševa. 2019. An extensive review of tools for manual annotation of documents. *Briefings in Bioinformatics*, 22(1):146–163.

Titouan Parcollet and Mirco Ravanelli. 2021. The Energy and Carbon Footprint of Training End-to-End Speech Recognizers. Working paper or preprint.

Xutan Peng, Guanyi Chen, Chenghua Lin, and Mark Stevenson. 2021. Highly efficient knowledge graph embedding learning with orthogonal procrustes analysis. In *Proceedings of the Conference of the North American Chapter of the Association for Computational Linguistics*. Association for Computational Linguistics.

Matthew E Peters, Mark Neumann, Mohit Iyyer, Matt Gardner, Christopher Clark, Kenton Lee, and Luke Zettlemoyer. 2018. Deep Contextualized Word Representations. In *Proceedings of the 2018 Conference of the North American Chapter of the Association for Computational Linguistics: Human Language Technologies, Volume 1 (Long Papers)*, pages 2227–2237. Association for Computational Linguistics.

Sai Prasanna, Anna Rogers, and Anna Rumshisky. 2020. When BERT Plays the Lottery, All Tickets Are Winning. In *Proceedings of the 2020 Conference on Empirical Methods in Natural Language Processing (EMNLP)*, pages 3208–3229, Online. Association for Computational Linguistics.

Gabriele Sarti. 2020. Interpreting neural language models for linguistic complexity assessment. Master's thesis, University of Trieste.

Roy Schwartz, Jesse Dodge, Noah A. Smith, and Oren Etzioni. 2019. Green AI. *Communications of the ACM*. Published in 2020.

Kira A. Selby, Yinong Wang, Ruizhe Wang, Peyman Passban, Ahmad Rashid, Mehdi Rezagholizadeh, and Pascal Poupart. 2021. Robust embeddings via distributions. *CoRR*, abs/2104.08420.

Raghavendra Selvan. 2021. Carbon footprint driven deep learning model selection for medical imaging. Https://openreview.net/forum?id=1TPRpNyyj2L.

Omar Shaikh, Jon Saad-Falcon, Austin P Wright, Nilaksh Das, Scott Freitas, Omar Isaac Asensio, and Duen Horng Chau. 2021. Energyvis: Interactively tracking and exploring energy consumption for ml models. *arXiv preprint arXiv:2103.16435*.

Jana Straková, Milan Straka, and Jan Hajič. 2019. Neural architectures for nested NER through linearization. In *Proceedings of the 57th Annual Meeting of the Association for Computational Linguistics*, pages 5326–5331. Association for Computational Linguistics.

Emma Strubell, Ananya Ganesh, and Andrew McCallum. 2019. Energy and policy considerations for deep learning in NLP. In *Proceedings of the 57th Annual Meeting of the Association for Computational Linguistics*, pages 3645–3650, Florence, Italy. Association for Computational Linguistics.

The Shift Project. 2018. Lean ICT: Towards Digital Sobriety. Technical report, The Shift Project. Directed by Hugues Ferreboeuf.

Julien Tourille, Matthieu Doutreligne, Olivier Ferret, Nicolas Paris, Aurélie Névéol, and Xavier Tannier. 2018. Evaluation of a sequence tagging tool for biomedical texts. In *Proceedings of the Ninth International Workshop on Health Text Mining and Information Analysis*, pages 193–203.

Martin Jaggi Tristan Trebaol, Mary-Anne Hartley and Hossein Shokri Ghadikolaei. 2020. A tool to quantify and report the carbon footprint of machine learning computations and communication in academia and healthcare. *Infoscience EPFL: record 278189*.

Erik M Van Mulligen, Zubair Afzal, Saber Akhondi, Dang Vo, and Jan Kors. 2016. Erasmus mc at clef ehealth 2016: Concept recognition and coding in french texts. In *CEUR workshop proceedings*, volume 1609, pages 171–178.

Thomas Wolf, Lysandre Debut, Victor Sanh, Julien Chaumond, Clement Delangue, Anthony Moi, Pierric Cistac, Tim Rault, Rémi Louf, Morgan Funtowicz, Joe Davison, Sam Shleifer, Patrick von Platen, Clara Ma, Yacine Jernite, Julien Plu, Canwen Xu, Teven Le Scao, Sylvain Gugger, Mariama Drame, Quentin Lhoest, and Alexander M. Rush. 2020. Transformers: State-of-the-art natural language processing. In *Proceedings of the 2020 Conference on Empirical Methods in Natural Language Processing: System Demonstrations*, pages 38–45, Online. Association for Computational Linguistics.

Juntao Yu, Bernd Bohnet, and Massimo Poesio. 2020. Named entity recognition as dependency parsing. In *Proceedings of the 58th Annual Meeting of the Association for Computational Linguistics*, pages 6470–6476. Association for Computational Linguistics.

Huaizheng Zhang, Yizheng Huang, Yonggang Wen, Jianxiong Yin, and Kyle Guan. 2020. No more 996: Understanding deep learning inference serving with an automatic benchmarking system. *arXiv preprint arXiv:2011.02327*.

Limitations of Knowledge Distillation for Zero-shot Transfer Learning

Saleh Soltan
Amazon Alexa AI
ssoltan@amazon.com

Haidar Khan
Amazon Alexa AI
khhaida@amazon.com

Wael Hamza
Amazon Alexa AI
waelhamz@amazon.com

Abstract

Pretrained transformer-based encoders such as BERT have been demonstrated to achieve state-of-the-art performance on numerous NLP tasks. Despite their success, BERT style encoders are large in size and have high latency during inference (especially on CPU machines) which make them unappealing for many online applications. Recently introduced compression and distillation methods have provided effective ways to alleviate this shortcoming. However, the focus of these works has been mainly on monolingual encoders. Motivated by recent successes in zero-shot cross-lingual transfer learning using multilingual pretrained encoders such as mBERT, we evaluate the effectiveness of Knowledge Distillation (KD) both during pretraining stage and during fine-tuning stage on multilingual BERT models. We demonstrate that in contradiction to the previous observation in the case of monolingual distillation, in multilingual settings, distillation during pretraining is more effective than distillation during fine-tuning for zero-shot transfer learning. Moreover, we observe that distillation during fine-tuning may hurt zero-shot cross-lingual performance. Finally, we demonstrate that distilling a larger model (BERT Large) results in the strongest distilled model that performs best both on the source language as well as target languages in zero-shot settings.

1 Introduction

Since the introduction of pretrained word embeddings (Mikolov et al., 2013b; Pennington et al., 2014), unsupervised representation learning has become an essential part of Natural Language Processing (NLP). The idea of exploiting unlabeled corpuses to improve performance on downstream NLP tasks has been excelled in recent years by the introduction of contextualized representation learning techniques (Peters et al., 2018) using the Language Modeling (LM) objective. Follow-up works utilized transformer-based architecture (Vaswani et al., 2017) and subword tokenization techniques (Sennrich et al., 2016) to further improve these contextualized representations and achieve state-of-the-art performance on various NLP tasks when fine-tuned on labeled data (Radford et al., 2018; Devlin et al., 2019).

Bidirectional Encoder Representations from Transformers (BERT) (Devlin et al., 2019) has also been successfully pretrained on corpuses from 100+ languages to learn a shared representation among different languages (a.k.a mBERT). mBERT has been demonstrated to be capable of performing cross-lingual zero-shot transfer learning given the labeled data in a single language (e.g., English) without ever seeing a parallel corpus during pretraining (Pires et al., 2019). Moreover, it has been demonstrated that by increasing the size of the encoder and the pretaining corpus, such a multilingual encoder can achieve state-of-the-art cross-lingual zero-shot performance across many tasks (Conneau et al., 2020; Mukherjee and Awadallah, 2020).

Despite their success in many NLP task, BERT encoders are not very attractive for practical applications due to their huge size (often a few Gbs) and their latency (especially on CPU machines). Hence, there has been a great effort in recent years to compress these encoders without a big drop in performance using knowledge distillation (Hinton et al., 2015), network pruning (Li et al., 2020b), and quantization (Zafrir et al., 2019). However, there has been little work on compressing multilingual BERT encoders and evaluating their effectiveness in maintaining their cross-lingual learning capabilities after compression, which is the main focus of our work.

In this work, we focus on Knowledge Distillation (KD) which is an effective approach for reducing both size and latency of a BERT style encoder. In particular, we first pretrain a multilingual BERT base and a multilingual BERT large encoders on

Proceedings of the 2nd Workshop on Simple and Efficient Natural Language Processing, pages 22–31
November 10, 2021. ©201 Association for Computational Linguistics

Wikipedia data of 8 languages (namely mBERT8 and mBERT8$_{\text{Large}}$) and follow (Jiao et al., 2019) to distill them into 4-layer encoders, namely mLeanBERT and mXLeanBERT, respectively (see Table 1). We then compare the zero-shot cross-lingual performance of the student to teacher models on 5 datasets including XNLI, PAWS-X, Wikiann, MultiATIS++, and mTOP (see Table 3) when the models are fine-tuned only on English training data. *We show that mLeanBERT performance degrades by 2-9% on English test sets but by 6-25% on non-English ones (zero-shot) compared to mBERT8. However, mLeanBERT is 0.25-10% better than a similar sized model pretrained with no KD (Vanilla mLeanBERT) on zero-shot performance. Moreover, our results demonstrate that mXLeanBERT (distilled from mBERT8$_{Large}$) performs better than Vanilla mLeanBERT by up to 18% in zero-shot.*

Finally, we study the effectiveness of distillation during fine-tuning and demonstrate that in contrast to previous observations in monolingual settings (Jiao et al., 2019), it can hurt zero-shot cross-lingual performance. *In particular, extra distillation during fine-tuning degrades zero-shot cross-lingual performance of mLeanBERT by up to 2.5% despite improving or not changing its performance on English test set.*

The main contributions of this work are:

- Evaluating state-of-the-art knowledge distillation method on pretrained multilingual BERT Base and Large models and demonstrating its effectiveness (when done during pretraining) in multilingual settings.
- Demonstrating that in contradiction to monolingual settings, knowledge distillation during fine-tuning mostly hurts zero-shot cross-lingual transfer. This argument holds even if knowledge distillation during fine-tuning is the only distillation step (not as a second stage distillation step).
- Pretraining a multilingual BERT large model and utilizing it as the teacher during knowledge distillation to demonstrate that a larger model as teacher results in a stronger distilled model performing better for zero-shot cross-lingual transfer.

2 Related Work

2.1 Cross-lingual Transfer Learning

Transferring a task specific knowledge between different languages has always been an intriguing subject in NLP. Such a transfer is demonstrated to be possible by aligning word embeddings using a limited dictionary of words (Mikolov et al., 2013a; Schuster et al., 2019) or even without a dictionary (Lample et al., 2018). Aligning sentence representations is also demonstrated to be effective for cross-lingual transfer for sentence level tasks such as Natural Langual Inference (NLI) (Conneau et al., 2018).

Despite the success of alignment methods, sharing an encoder for multiple languages is demonstrated to be a more effective way of cross-lingual transfer learning. In particular, (Artetxe and Schwenk, 2019) showed that by sharing an encoder to learn sentence representations for multiple languages for Machine Translation (MT) can outperform previous methods for sentence level tasks. However, BERT-style pretraining tasks (Devlin et al., 2019) on mixed corpus from different languages is shown to be as effective as MT task in cross-lingual transfer without access to any parallel data (Siddhant et al., 2020). Moreover, recent work by (Conneau et al., 2020) demonstrated that by using larger encoders and larger pretraining corpus, BERT-style pretrained encoders (i.e., XLM-R) can outperform all previous methods on various NLP tasks.

Another recently proposed approach for cross-lingual transfer mixes the word alignment approach with encoder sharing to expand a monolingual BERT model to a new language and allow transfer learning (Artetxe et al., 2020; Tran, 2020). The approach is shown to be as effective as joint pretraining on mixed corpus and mixed vocabulary.

Finally, when available, (Lauscher et al., 2020) demonstrated that using a few target language training examples can significantly improve cross-lingual performance of pretrained multilingual models.

2.2 Model Compression and Distillation

Knowledge distillation is widely used to transfer knowledge from large (teacher) models into small (student) models (Ba and Caruana, 2014; Hinton et al., 2015). This type of compression has a number of benefits, including reducing model size/latency, semi-supervised learning, and con-

Model	KD?	#lgs	tokenization	L	H_m	H_{ff}	A	V	#params*
mBERT8$_{\text{Large}}$	no	8	BPE	24	1024	4096	16	120k	302M
mBERT8	no	8	BPE	12	768	3072	12	120k	85M
mBERT	no	104	WordPiece	12	768	3072	12	110k	85M
mXLeanBERT	yes	8	BPE	4	768	1200	12	120k	17M
mLeanBERT	yes	8	BPE	4	768	1200	12	120k	17M
Vanilla mLeanBERT	no	8	BPE	4	768	1200	12	120k	17M

Table 1: List of models. L, H_m, H_{ff}, A and V denote the number of layers, transformer hidden dimension, feed-forward layers' hidden dimension, number of attention heads, and the vocabulary size, respectively. mLeanBERT and mXLeanBERT are distilled (1st stage distillation) from mBERT8 and mBERT8$_{\text{Large}}$, respectively. Vanilla mLeanBERT, however, is pretrained normally with no teachers. The same multilingual data is used to pretrain and distill all the models. *Number of parameters excluding the embeddings.

tinual learning. Previous work has demonstrated successful compression of teachers into students of the same type (Kim and Rush, 2016; Sanh et al., 2019) as well as into students with different model types and architectures (Tang et al., 2019). Depending on the approach, the limits of compression, and the ideal initialization procedure differ substantially (Sanh et al., 2019; Yang et al., 2019b; Turc et al., 2019). The resulting student models are shown to preserve many of the attractive qualities of the teacher model and perform better than training the same models without knowledge distillation. Some distillation approaches jointly train the teacher and student, such as in (Jin et al., 2019), however we consider the common case of a "fixed" teacher at distillation time in this work.

The most common approach to distillation is output matching between the teacher and the student, where the student is trained to minimize two losses during training; the standard cross-entropy loss and the cross-entropy loss between the teacher output and the student output (Hinton et al., 2015). There exists variations of this approach, such as adding loss functions leveraging cues from internal representations of the teacher (Jiao et al., 2019; Sun et al., 2019; Aguilar et al., 2020; Romero et al., 2014).

In the context of pretrained models, distillation can be executed directly after teacher pretraining as in (Sanh et al., 2019), after teacher fine-tuning, or both (Jiao et al., 2019). In an ablation study, (Jiao et al., 2019) found that distillation after teacher finetuning (2nd stage) is more important than distillation after teacher pretraining (1st stage). However, the relative importance of the two stages of distillation remains an open question for distilling multilingual models.

Distillation of multilingual models for NER is explored in (Mukherjee and Awadallah, 2020) in the setting of 2nd stage distillation, i.e. distillation after finetuning, while 1st stage distillation is not considered. In addition, (Mukherjee and Awadallah, 2020) did not investigate the zero-shot performance of the distilled models. In a similar vein, (Tan et al., 2019; Wang et al., 2020b; Reimers and Gurevych, 2020) distill language-specific models into a combined multilingual machine translation model. In a recent parallel work to ours, (Wang et al., 2020a) introduced a new distillation method and demonstrated its effectiveness in multilingual settings. However, they focused on distillation during pretraining and evaluate their model only on XNLI from XTREME benchmarks. Since they used common crawl data for pretraining and a different architecture, their models are not directly comparable to ours.

3 Method

3.1 Pretraining

We pretrain two multilingual BERT models, namely *mBERT8$_{Base}$* and *mBERT8$_{Large}$*, on 8 languages including English, French, German, Japanese, Hindi, Italian, Spanish and Portuguese. For pretraining, we use Wikipedia data of the corresponding languages. For English, we also add Google Billion Words Corpus (Chelba et al., 2014) to the mix. All data are tokenized using a tokenizer that transforms written format to spoken format (e.g., removes casing and punctuation).

We mix and upsample the data following (Conneau and Lample, 2019). In particular, we sample 500M sentences according to a multinomial distri-

Model	perplexity	#epochs
mBERT8$_{\text{Large}}$	5.89	2
mBERT8	6.78	4
mXLeanBERT	9.76	4
mLeanBERT	10.18	4
Vanilla mLeanBERT	9.94	4

Table 2: Models' perplexity on the validation set (comprised of all languages) after pretraining. Epochs denotes the total number of epochs used for pretraining each model.

bution with probabilities $(q_1, q_2, \ldots, q_N)$, where:

$$q_i = \frac{p_i^\alpha}{\sum_{j=1}^N p_j^\alpha}, \; p_i = \frac{n_i}{\sum_{j=1}^N n_j} \quad (1)$$

in which N is the total number of languages and n_i is the total number of sentences in language i (we set $\alpha = 0.5$). Byte Per Encoding (BPE) codes (Sennrich et al., 2016) of size 120k are then learnt from the mixed training set for subword tokenization. For pretraining task, we only use Masked Language Modeling (MLM) (Devlin et al., 2019) without any sentence-level tasks, similar to RoBERTa (Liu et al., Jul. 2019). However, we limit the length of sentences to 256 characters to speedup the pretraining. We pretrain mBERT8$_{\text{Base}}$ and mBERT8$_{\text{Large}}$ for 4 and 2 epochs, respectively. The perplexities (MLM perpelxity) on the validation set after the pretrainings are provided in Table 2.

3.2 Knowledge Distillation (KD)

We distill the pretrained mBERT8 and mBERT8$_{\text{Large}}$ models into the *LeanBERT* architecture, namely a 4 layer, 768 unit, 1200 hidden unit, and 12 attention head transformer. We differentiate between distillation during pretraining of the student model (1st stage), where the learning task is the unsupervised MLM task using dataset described in Section 3.1, and distillation during fine-tuning (2nd stage distillation), where the task is sentence/token level classification or sequence-to-sequence generation.

For 1st stage and 2nd stage distillation, we train the student model with a combination of distillation losses in addition to the standard cross-entropy loss. We follow the distillation losses proposed in (Jiao et al., 2019) that comprise of output/logit based loss functions and intermediate representation loss functions. At the output level, we penalize the student model by the cross-entropy between the student output predictions and the teacher output predictions. Given the student output predictions $\mathbf{z}_s$ and the teacher output predictions $\mathbf{z}_t$, the output layer distillation loss is:

$$\mathcal{L}_{output} = -\mathbf{z}_t \cdot \log \mathbf{z}_s. \quad (2)$$

For intermediate representations, the student model is trained to minimize the L_2 distance to the teacher's corresponding intermediate representation. When the number of layers or units in the teacher and student model do not match, this requires establishing a mapping $g(m)$ between the teacher/student layers and a projection $f(\mathbf{x})$ to match number of units. Given the m-th teacher intermediate representation $\mathbf{x}_{t,m}$ and the corresponding student intermediate representation $\mathbf{x}_{s,g(m)}$, the intermediate layer distillation loss is:

$$\mathcal{L}_{inter} = ||\mathbf{x}_{t,m} - f(\mathbf{x}_{s,g(m)})||_2 \quad (3)$$

Note that this loss function is applied to three types of intermediate representations: embeddings, transformer outputs, and self-attention scores. In our experiments, we adopt the same mapping $g(m)$ as (Jiao et al., 2019), namely that the student model learns from every three layers of the teacher model.

The combinations of these loss functions can be applied to distill the pretrained teacher for 1st stage distillation and to distill the pretrained+fine-tuned teacher for 2nd stage distillation (we refer to this as **ft-distill**).

We refer to the models distilled from mBERT8 and mBERT8$_{\text{Large}}$ during pretraining (1st stage distillation) as *mLeanBERT* and *mXLeanBERT*, respectively (see Table 1). We used all the data as described in Section 3.1 during distillation. For comparison purposes, we also pretrained a *Vanilla mLeanBERT* model with no distillation by following the steps described in the previous subsection. The perplexity of these models after pretraining can be seen in Table 2.

It can be seen that mXLeanBERT which has been distilled from the mBERT8$_{\text{Large}}$ results in the lowest perplexity between the 3 models. However, the Vanilla mLeanBERT results in a lower perplexity compared to mLeanBERT which is distilled from mBERT8 model. *As we demonstrate in the next section, this lower perplexity is not a good predictor for better cross-lingual capability of the Vanilla mLeanBERT model.*

Corpus	Task	|Train|	|Dev|	|Test|	Metric
XNLI	Classification	392,702	2,490	5,010	Acc.
PAWS-X	Classification	49,401	2,000	2,000	Acc.
Wikiann	NER	19,999	9,999	999-9,999	F1
MultiATIS++	IC/NER	4,488	490	~900	Exact Match
mTOP	Semantic Parsing	15,667	1,527	~3,000	Exact Match

Table 3: Characteristics of the datasets.

Model	XNLI	PAWS-X	Wikiann	MultiATIS++	mTOP
mBERT8$_{\text{Large}}$	82.49	92.73	84.21	87.53	82.24
mBERT8	81.67	91.68	83.46	87.98	82.09
mBERT	81.36	93.4	84.85	88.12	81.8
Vanilla mLeanBERT	77.47	85.22	80.47	87.34	80.26
KD during pretraining (1st stage)					
mLeanBERT	77.23	84.21	79.92	86.59	79.85
mXLeanBERT	**78.91**	**88.58**	**80.76**	**87.42**	**81.24**
KD during fine-tuning (2nd stage)					
mLeanBERT (ft-distill)	77.13	87.93	80.28	86.17	79.77
Vanilla mLeanBERT (ft-distill)	77.68	85.73	80.63	86.75	80.44

Table 4: Results on English test set (averaged over 4 seed runs). All models are fine-tuned only on English training data. Bold numbers denote the best score across all LeanBERT sized models.

4 Experimental Results

4.1 Data

We evaluate our models on multiple tasks (summarized in Table 3). We limited our experimentation to these datasets due to the sheer number of required experimentation (9 models, 5 task, and 4 seeds).

XNLI is a Cross-Lingual Natural Language Inference task that asks whether a premise sentence entails, contradicts, or is neutral toward a hypothesis (Conneau et al., 2018).

PAWS-X requires the model to determine whether two sentences are paraphrase of each other (Zhang et al., 2019; Yang et al., 2019a). We obtained the data using XTREME repository code (Hu et al., 2020). However, we downloaded the test sets directly.[1]

Wikiann is a Name Entity Recognition dataset (NER). The data is extracted from Wikipedia in which name entities are tagged as `LOC`, `PER`, and `ORG` (Pan et al., 2017). As in PAWS-X, we obtained the data through XTREME repository but downloaded test sets directly (Pan et al., 2017).

MultiATIS++ is a Natural Language Understanding (NLU) dataset that requires the model to detect the *intent* of an utterance as well as the related *slots*. It is an extension to MultiATIS dataset (Upadhyay et al., 2018) to Spanish, German, Chinese, Japanese, Portuguese, and French languages in addition to English, Hindi, and Turkish (Xu et al., 2020).[2]

mTOP is a multilingual Task Oriented Parsing dataset that covers English, German, French, Spanish, Hindi, and Thai languages (Li et al., 2020a).

4.2 Models

We consider models in Table 1 as introduced in Section 3 and fine-tune them only on the English training data for the tasks described in Section 4.1. Besides these models, we also consider distillation during fine-tuning for mLeanBERT and Vanilla mLeanBERT. In all distillations during fine-tuning,

[1]XTREME code does not download test set on purpose to keep them private for its leaderboard. Although, the test sets are available directly from their original source (Zhang et al., 2019; Yang et al., 2019a).

[2]We noticed that in the test sets of MultiATIS++ there are a few utterances for which number of tags do not match the number of tokens. We removed those instances from the test sets.

Model	XNLI	PAWS-X	Wikiann	MultiATIS++	mTOP
mBERT8$_{\text{Large}}$	72.61	85.69	77.88	46.25	37.41
mBERT8	70.31	83.47	76.73	45.42	34.60
mBERT	67.54	85.18	77.33	35.24	25.80
Vanilla mLeanBERT	64.53	74.06	71.30	34.06	23.74
KD during pretraining (1st stage)					
mLeanBERT	66.09	75.07	71.48	**37.58**	25.96
mXLeanBERT	**67.69**	**80.26**	71.17	37.05	**28.01**
KD during fine-tuning (2nd stage)					
mLeanBERT (ft-distill)	65.52	77.98	**71.62**	36.79	25.33
Vanilla mLeanBERT (ft-distill)	64.97	74.76	71.57	34.01	24.15

Table 5: Average zero-shot results across selected languages (averaged over 4 seed runs). All models are fine-tuned only on English training data. Bold numbers denote the best score across all LeanBERT sized models.

we use mBERT8 as the teacher. For these experiments, the teacher is fine-tuned on the English training data for the task and the same data is used for distillation.

4.3 Experimentations Setup

For all of the tasks except mTOP, we followed the original BERT paper (Devlin et al., 2019) and fine-tuned the encoder on the downstream task with additional output blocks. We also *kept the embedding layers frozen* to prevent the change only in subset of subwords that appear in the training data.

For mTOP, we followed (Rongali et al., 2020) and fine-tuned a seq2seq model with pointers which has been shown to achieve state-of-the-art results on TOP dataset (Gupta et al., 2018). In all experiments, we used the pretrained encoders but randomly initialized a 3-layer decoder with the same hidden dimension and number of heads as the encoder. The feedforward layers in the decoder have the dimension of 512. As in all of the other experiments, we kept the encoder embedding layers frozen during fine-tuning.

4.4 Key Findings

The results on the English test sets and the average zero-shot performance across different languages can be seen in Tables 4 and 5, respectively. Per language performance of different models on XNLI, PAWS-X, Wikiann, MutiATIS++, and mTOP can be seen in Tables 6, 7, 8, 9,10, respectively.

The following subsections describe the key findings from these results.

4.4.1 Stage 1 Distillation is Effective for Multilingual Models

It has been previously demonstrated by (Jiao et al., 2019) that stage 1 distillation is effective in improving performance in monolingual settings. We confirm this finding in our experiments by comparing mBERT8, mLeanBERT, and Vanilla mLeanBERT performances on English test sets in Table 4. Our new finding, however, is that as can be seen in Table 5, mLeanBERT outperforms Vanilla mLeanBERT in all the tasks in zero-shot setting as well. **In particular mLeanBERT outperforms Vanilla mLeanBERT on all the tasks in zero-shot setting (by more that 9% on MultiATIS++ and mTOP).**

Moreover, by comparing mBERT8 and mLeanBERT performances, we can see that despite being 5 times smaller, mLeanBERT performance degrades only by 5.74%, 8.87%, 4.43%, 1.6%, and 2.8% on English test set and by 6.00%, 10.06%, 6.84%, 17.26%, and 24.97% in zero-shot performance on XNLI, PAWS-X, Wikiann, MultiATIS++, and mTOP tasks, respectively. We observe that performance degradation in zero-shot performance is greater than on English which emphasizes the challenges in multilingual distillation.

4.4.2 Stage 2 Distillation Can Hurt Zero-shot Cross-lingual Performance

Another important observation from our experimental results is that in contrast to previous observations by (Jiao et al., 2019) in the monolingual case, 2nd stage distillation may hurt zero-shot cross-lingual performance. In particular, although as can be seen in Tables 4 and 5 ft-distill im-

Model	en	fr	de	es	hi
mBERT8$_{Large}$	82.49	75.71	73.48	76.19	65.07
mBERT8	81.67	73.32	70.70	74.94	62.28
mBERT	81.36	70.32	67.94	73.07	58.82
Vanilla mLeanBERT	77.47	67.80	65.01	68.91	56.4
KD during pretraining (1st stage)					
mLeanBERT	77.23	68.79	66.41	70.25	58.91
mXLeanBERT	**78.90**	**70.37**	**67.85**	**71.51**	**61.04**
KD during fine-tuning (2nd stage)					
mLeanBERT (ft-distill)	77.13	68.85	66.15	69.37	57.71
Vanilla mLeanBERT (ft-distill)	77.68	68.15	65.60	68.92	57.23

Table 6: XNLI results (accuracy) per language (averaged over 4 seed runs). All models are fine-tuned only on English training data. Bold numbers denote the best score across all LeanBERT sized models.

Model	en	fr	de	es	ja*
mBERT8$_{Large}$	92.95	86.15	85.65	85.85	66.8
mBERT8	91.55	84.8	83.65	85.05	62.1
mBERT	93.4	85.35	84.35	85.85	71.8
Vanilla mLeanBERT	82.9	74.43	73.21	74.55	59.18
KD during pretraining (1st stage)					
mLeanBERT	84.21	75.53	73.9	75.77	60.77
mXLeanBERT	**88.58**	**80.52**	**78.67**	**81.6**	**63**
KD during fine-tuning (2nd stage)					
mLeanBERT (ft-distill)	87.93	78.55	76.66	78.75	61.22
Vanilla mLeanBERT (ft-distill)	85.73	75.22	73.78	75.28	61.02

Table 7: PAWS-X results (accuracy) per language (averaged over 4 seed runs). All models are fine-tuned only on English training data. Bold numbers denote the best score across all LeanBERT sized models.*Results on Japanese test set are not included in the average zero-shot performance presented in Table 5. The main reason for that is that the tokenizer we used for Japanese is incompatible with PAWS-X data describing the degradation in accuracy compared to the public mBERT.

Model	en	fr	de	es	pt	it	hi
mBERT8$_{Large}$	84.21	79.65	79.06	75.20	80.01	79.82	73.56
mBERT8	83.47	78.06	78.48	76.90	79.37	78.79	68.77
mBERT	84.85	80	78.18	74.17	81.42	80.89	61.81
Vanilla mLeanBERT	80.47	**73.46**	73.47	73.81	73.82	74.38	58.9
KD during pretraining (1st stage)							
mLeanBERT	79.92	73.33	72.13	70.58	75.02	72.98	64.89
mXLeanBERT	**80.76**	72.24	73.00	69.23	**74.54**	74.17	63.87
KD during fine-tuning (2nd stage)							
mLeanBERT (ft-distill)	80.28	73.34	72.15	70.64	75.00	72.93	**65.67**
Vanilla mLeanBERT (ft-distill)	80.63	73.25	**73.90**	**73.98**	74.29	**74.81**	59.2

Table 8: Wikiann results (F1 scores) per language (averaged over 4 seed runs). All models are fine-tuned only on English training data. Bold numbers denote the best score across all LeanBERT sized models.

Model	en	fr	de	es	pt	hi
mBERT8$_{Large}$	87.54	62.04	61.97	53.29	45.59	8.42
mBERT8	87.99	59.98	59.77	51.32	41.84	14.18
mBERT	88.12	44.37	35.87	43.78	35.76	16.46
Vanilla mLeanBERT	87.35	45.23	45.10	41.79	37.5	3.39
KD during pretraining (1st stage)						
mLeanBERT	86.59	48.13	**53**	39.73	**41.36**	5.71
mXLeanBERT	**87.43**	**52.81**	41.14	**43.53**	41.20	**6.58**
KD during fine-tuning (2nd stage)						
mLeanBERT (ft-distill)	86.17	47.09	51.97	38.75	40.5	5.62
Vanilla mLeanBERT (ft-distill)	86.76	44.16	44.70	40.56	37.70	2.97

Table 9: MultiATIS++ results (Exact Match) per language (averaged over 4 seed runs). All models are fine-tuned only on English training data. Bold numbers denote the best score across all LeanBERT sized models.

Model	en	fr	de	es	hi
mBERT8$_{Large}$	82.25	47.34	40.80	43.12	18.42
mBERT8	82.10	46.98	36.07	39.72	15.65
mBERT	81.8	34.85	28.43	34.75	5.2
Vanilla mLeanBERT	80.26	33.34	24.32	31.98	5.36
KD during pretraining (1st stage)					
mLeanBERT	79.85	34.95	26.59	**33.48**	8.86
mXLeanBERT	**81.24**	**37.85**	**30.43**	33.15	**10.61**
KD during fine-tuning (2nd stage))					
mLeanBERT (ft-distill)	79.77	33.71	26.99	32.4	8.25
Vanilla mLeanBERT (ft-distill)	80.45	33.50	24.79	33.09	5.24

Table 10: mTOP results (Exact Match) per language (averaged over 4 seed runs). All models are fine-tuned only on English training data. Bold numbers denote the best score across all LeanBERT sized models.

proves Vanilla LeanBERT performance (except on MultiATIS++), **ft-distill *degrades* zero-shot performance of mLeanBERT by** 0.86%, 2.1%, **and** 2.43% **on XNLI, MultiATIS++, and mTOP, respectively (see Table 5).**

These mixed results demonstrate that 2nd stage fine-tuning cannot be reliably used to improve cross-lingual performance of multilingual models. We hypothesize that 2nd stage fine-tuning makes multilingual models to overfit to the source language resulting in degradation in cross-lingual performance (i.e., catastrophic forgetting).

4.4.3 Distilling a Larger Model Results in a Stronger Distilled Model

Finally, as has been previously observed by (Li et al., 2020b) in the network pruning context, compressing larger models to the same size results in stronger compressed models. Our results demonstrate the same performance gain both on the English test set and in the zero-shot setting when distilling from BERT8$_{Large}$.

As can be seen in Table 4, **mXLeanBERT performs better than mLeanBERT on all the tasks on English test sets (outperforming it by** 5.2% **on PAWS-X). For zero-shot cross-lingual performance, we also observe the same trend in Table 5. This time mXLeanBERT outperforms mLeanBERT by** 6.46% **on zero-shot cross-lingual performance on PAWS-X and by** 7.31% **on mTOP.** On Wikiann and MultiATIS++ the two models provide a very similar performance (which can be due to instability of exact match metric for NER).

Based on the three observations, we observe that when it comes to distilling multilingual models, pretraining a larger model and then distilling it results in the best distilled multilingual model.

5 Conclusion

In this work, we applied state-of-the-art knowledge distillation methods on multilingual BERT encoders and demonstrated that distillation during pretraining is as effective in multilingual setting. However, in contradiction to previous observations in monolingual settings, we demonstrated that distillation during fine-tuning may degrade zero-shot cross-lingual performance. When it comes to multilingual distillation, we showed that pretraining a larger model and then distilling it results in the best performing distilled model.

References

Gustavo Aguilar, Y. Ling, Y. Zhang, B. Yao, Xing Fan, and Edward Guo. 2020. Knowledge distillation from internal representations. In *Proc. AAAI'20.*

Mikel Artetxe, Sebastian Ruder, and Dani Yogatama. 2020. On the cross-lingual transferability of monolingual representations. In *Proc. ACL'20.*

Mikel Artetxe and Holger Schwenk. 2019. Massively multilingual sentence embeddings for zero-shot cross-lingual transfer and beyond. *TACL*, 7:597–610.

Jimmy Ba and Rich Caruana. 2014. Do deep nets really need to be deep? In *Proc. NeurIPS'14.*

Ciprian Chelba, Tomas Mikolov, Mike Schuster, Qi Ge, Thorsten Brants, Phillipp Koehn, and Tony Robinson. 2014. One billion word benchmark for measuring progress in statistical language modeling. In *Proc. Interspeech'14.*

Alexis Conneau, Kartikay Khandelwal, Naman Goyal, Vishrav Chaudhary, Guillaume Wenzek, Francisco Guzmán, Edouard Grave, Myle Ott, Luke Zettlemoyer, and Veselin Stoyanov. 2020. Unsupervised cross-lingual representation learning at scale. In *Proc. ACL'20.*

Alexis Conneau and Guillaume Lample. 2019. Cross-lingual language model pretraining. In *Proc. NeurIPS'19.*

Alexis Conneau, Ruty Rinott, Guillaume Lample, Adina Williams, Samuel Bowman, Holger Schwenk, and Veselin Stoyanov. 2018. XNLI: Evaluating cross-lingual sentence representations. In *Proc. EMNLP'18.*

Jacob Devlin, Ming-Wei Chang, Kenton Lee, and Kristina Toutanova. 2019. BERT: Pre-training of deep bidirectional transformers for language understanding. In *Proc. NAACL'19.*

Sonal Gupta, Rushin Shah, Mrinal Mohit, Anuj Kumar, and Mike Lewis. 2018. Semantic parsing for task oriented dialog using hierarchical representations. In *Proc. EMNLP'18.*

Geoffrey Hinton, Oriol Vinyals, and Jeff Dean. 2015. Distilling the knowledge in a neural network. *arXiv:1503.02531.*

Junjie Hu, Sebastian Ruder, Aditya Siddhant, Graham Neubig, Orhan Firat, and Melvin Johnson. 2020. XTREME: A massively multilingual multi-task benchmark for evaluating cross-lingual generalization. *arXiv:2003.11080.*

Xiaoqi Jiao, Yichun Yin, Lifeng Shang, Xin Jiang, Xiao Chen, Linlin Li, Fang Wang, and Qun Liu. 2019. Tinybert: Distilling bert for natural language understanding. *arXiv:1909.10351.*

Xiao Jin, Baoyun Peng, Yichao Wu, Yu Liu, Jiaheng Liu, Ding Liang, Junjie Yan, and Xiaolin Hu. 2019. Knowledge distillation via route constrained optimization. In *Proc. IEEE ICCV'19.*

Yoon Kim and Alexander M Rush. 2016. Sequence-level knowledge distillation. In *Proc. EMNLP'16.*

Guillaume Lample, Alexis Conneau, Marc'Aurelio Ranzato, Ludovic Denoyer, and Hervé Jégou. 2018. Word translation without parallel data. In *Proc. ICLR'18.*

Anne Lauscher, Vinit Ravishankar, Ivan Vulić, and Goran Glavaš. 2020. From zero to hero: On the limitations of zero-shot language transfer with multilingual Transformers. In *Proc. EMNLP'20.*

Haoran Li, Abhinav Arora, Shuohui Chen, Anchit Gupta, Sonal Gupta, and Yashar Mehdad. 2020a. MTOP: A comprehensive multilingual task-oriented semantic parsing benchmark. *arXiv:2008.09335.*

Zhuohan Li, Eric Wallace, Sheng Shen, Kevin Lin, Kurt Keutzer, Dan Klein, and Joseph E Gonzalez. 2020b. Train large, then compress: Rethinking model size for efficient training and inference of transformers. *arXiv:2002.11794.*

Yinhan Liu, Myle Ott, Naman Goyal, Jingfei Du, Mandar Joshi, Danqi Chen, Omer Levy, Mike Lewis, Luke Zettlemoyer, and Veselin Stoyanov. Jul. 2019. Roberta: A robustly optimized bert pretraining approach. *arXiv:1907.11692.*

Tomas Mikolov, Quoc V Le, and Ilya Sutskever. 2013a. Exploiting similarities among languages for machine translation. *arXiv:1309.4168.*

Tomas Mikolov, Ilya Sutskever, Kai Chen, Greg S Corrado, and Jeff Dean. 2013b. Distributed representations of words and phrases and their compositionality. In *Proc. NeurIPS'13.*

Subhabrata Mukherjee and Ahmed Hassan Awadallah. 2020. Xtremedistil: Multi-stage distillation for massive multilingual models. In *Proc. ACL'20.*

Xiaoman Pan, Boliang Zhang, Jonathan May, Joel Nothman, Kevin Knight, and Heng Ji. 2017. Cross-lingual name tagging and linking for 282 languages. In *Proc. ACL'17*.

Jeffrey Pennington, Richard Socher, and Christopher D Manning. 2014. Glove: Global vectors for word representation. In *Proc. EMNLP'14*.

Matthew E Peters, Mark Neumann, Mohit Iyyer, Matt Gardner, Christopher Clark, Kenton Lee, and Luke Zettlemoyer. 2018. Deep contextualized word representations. In *Proc. NAACL-HLT'18*.

Telmo Pires, Eva Schlinger, and Dan Garrette. 2019. How multilingual is multilingual bert? In *Proc. ACL'19*.

Alec Radford, Karthik Narasimhan, Tim Salimans, and Ilya Sutskever. 2018. Improving language understanding by generative pre-training.

Nils Reimers and Iryna Gurevych. 2020. Making monolingual sentence embeddings multilingual using knowledge distillation. *arXiv:2004.09813*.

Adriana Romero, Nicolas Ballas, Samira Ebrahimi Kahou, Antoine Chassang, Carlo Gatta, and Yoshua Bengio. 2014. Fitnets: Hints for thin deep nets. *arXiv:1412.6550*.

Subendhu Rongali, Luca Soldaini, Emilio Monti, and Wael Hamza. 2020. Don't parse, generate! a sequence to sequence architecture for task-oriented semantic parsing. In *Proc. WWW'20*.

Victor Sanh, Lysandre Debut, Julien Chaumond, and Thomas Wolf. 2019. Distilbert, a distilled version of bert: smaller, faster, cheaper and lighter. *arXiv:1910.01108*.

Tal Schuster, Ori Ram, Regina Barzilay, and Amir Globerson. 2019. Cross-lingual alignment of contextual word embeddings, with applications to zero-shot dependency parsing. In *Proc. NACL'19*.

Rico Sennrich, Barry Haddow, and Alexandra Birch. 2016. Neural machine translation of rare words with subword units. In *Proc. ACL'16*.

Aditya Siddhant, Melvin Johnson, Henry Tsai, Naveen Ari, Jason Riesa, Ankur Bapna, Orhan Firat, and Karthik Raman. 2020. Evaluating the cross-lingual effectiveness of massively multilingual neural machine translation. In *Proc. AAAI'20*.

Siqi Sun, Yu Cheng, Zhe Gan, and Jingjing Liu. 2019. Patient knowledge distillation for BERT model compression. *arXiv:1908.09355*.

Xu Tan, Yi Ren, Di He, Tao Qin, and Tie-Yan Liu. 2019. Multilingual neural machine translation with knowledge distillation. In *Proc. ICLR'19*.

Raphael Tang, Yao Lu, Linqing Liu, Lili Mou, Olga Vechtomova, and Jimmy Lin. 2019. Distilling task-specific knowledge from bert into simple neural networks. *arXiv:1903.12136*.

Ke Tran. 2020. From english to foreign languages: Transferring pre-trained language models. *arXiv:2002.07306*.

Iulia Turc, Ming-Wei Chang, Kenton Lee, and Kristina Toutanova. 2019. Well-read students learn better: On the importance of pre-training compact models. *arXiv:1908.08962*.

Shyam Upadhyay, Manaal Faruqui, Gokhan Tür, Hakkani-Tür Dilek, and Larry Heck. 2018. (Almost) zero-shot cross-lingual spoken language understanding. In *Proc. IEEE ICASSP'18*.

Ashish Vaswani, Noam Shazeer, Niki Parmar, Jakob Uszkoreit, Llion Jones, Aidan N Gomez, Łukasz Kaiser, and Illia Polosukhin. 2017. Attention is all you need. In *NeurIPS'19*.

Wenhui Wang, Furu Wei, Li Dong, Hangbo Bao, Nan Yang, and Ming Zhou. 2020a. Minilm: Deep self-attention distillation for task-agnostic compression of pre-trained transformers. In *Proc. NeurIPS'20*.

Xinyu Wang, Yong Jiang, Nguyen Bach, Tao Wang, Fei Huang, and Kewei Tu. 2020b. Structure-level knowledge distillation for multilingual sequence labeling. In *Proc. ACL'20*.

Weijia Xu, Batool Haider, and Saab Mansour. 2020. End-to-end slot alignment and recognition for cross-lingual NLU. *arXiv:2004.14353*.

Yinfei Yang, Yuan Zhang, Chris Tar, and Jason Baldridge. 2019a. PAWS-X: A cross-lingual adversarial dataset for paraphrase identification. In *Proc. EMNLP-IJCNLP'19*.

Ze Yang, Linjun Shou, Ming Gong, Wutao Lin, and Daxin Jiang. 2019b. Model compression with multi-task knowledge distillation for web-scale question answering system. *arXiv:1904.09636*.

Ofir Zafrir, Guy Boudoukh, Peter Izsak, and Moshe Wasserblat. 2019. Q8bert: Quantized 8bit bert. *arXiv:1910.06188*.

Yuan Zhang, Jason Baldridge, and Luheng He. 2019. PAWS: Paraphrase adversaries from word scrambling. In *Proc. NAACL'19*.

Countering the Influence of Essay Length in Neural Essay Scoring

Sungho Jeon and **Michael Strube**
Heidelberg Institute for Theoretical Studies gGmbH
{sungho.jeon, michael.strube}@h-its.org

Abstract

Previous work has shown that automated essay scoring systems, in particular machine learning-based systems, are not capable of assessing the quality of essays, but are relying on essay length, a factor irrelevant to writing proficiency. In this work, we first show that state-of-the-art systems, recent neural essay scoring systems, might be also influenced by the correlation between essay length and scores in a standard dataset. In our evaluation, a very simple neural model shows the state-of-the-art performance on the standard dataset. To consider essay content without taking essay length into account, we introduce a simple neural model assessing the similarity of content between an input essay and essays assigned different scores. This neural model achieves performance comparable to the state of the art on a standard dataset as well as on a second dataset. Our findings suggest that neural essay scoring systems should consider the characteristics of datasets to focus on text quality.

1 Introduction

Automated essay scoring (AES) is the task of assigning a score for a given essay, aiming to replicate human scoring results. The public release of a standard dataset from a shared task[1] increased the interest in this task significantly. There have been several systems applied to the standard dataset including machine learning-based systems employing diverse features (Chen and He, 2013; Phandi et al., 2015) and neural essay scoring systems (Taghipour and Ng, 2016; Dong et al., 2017).

Previous work, nevertheless, has shown that AES systems are not capable of assessing the quality of essays (Winerip, 2005; Ben-Simon and Bennett, 2007; Wolfe et al., 2016), but indeed work by adopting shallow heuristics for the majority of training examples. Perelman (2014) argues that machine learning-based systems rely on the factor of essay length, and that the high correlation between essay length and scores in the standard dataset leads to top performance. Following this criticism, AES systems must not rely on essay length, a factor irrelevant to writing proficiency (Madnani and Cahill, 2018).

Recent neural essay scoring systems, which do not employ a feature capturing essay length explicitly, achieve state-of-the-art performance. In this work, however, we first show that even neural essay scoring systems might also be influenced by the correlation between essay length and scores in the standard dataset. To investigate this, we here present a simple neural model manipulating essay length. We notice that averaged RNN outputs are the common component in previous neural models, and we modify this component to manipulate essay length. This simple neural model shows performance comparable to state-of-the-art neural models in the standard dataset. However, this artifact does not hold for a second dataset, the Test of English as a Foreign Language dataset (TOEFL, Blanchard et al. (2013)), which has a lower correlation between essay length and scores.

Second, we demonstrate that considering essay content without taking essay length into account can improve the performance of a neural essay scoring system. We incorporate a feature representing Kullback-Leibler divergence into our first simple model, which measures the difference between probability distributions. The intuition is that this feature lets the model consider essay content by assessing the similarity of the word distributions in an input essay and essays assigned different scores. We demonstrate that this neural model achieves performance comparable to the state of the art on both datasets. Our experiments show that neural essay scoring systems might also be influenced by the characteristics of the standard dataset[2].

[1] https://kaggle.com/c/asap-aes/

[2] https://github.com/sdeva14/sustai21-counter-neural-essay-length

Proceedings of the 2nd Workshop on Simple and Efficient Natural Language Processing, pages 32–38
November 10, 2021. ©201 Association for Computational Linguistics

2 Essay Length and Scores in Datasets

Datasets: We use two essay datasets, the Automated Student Assessment Prize (ASAP) dataset and the TOEFL dataset, respectively. ASAP was introduced in the shared task on evaluating AES systems, measured against human scores. The essays are written by students in grade levels 7 to 10 of US middle schools. Since the shared task, ASAP has been used as a standard dataset for automatic essay scoring. The dataset consists of eight prompts with different linguistic characteristics such as concreteness vs. open-endedness and different scoring ranges. TOEFL is the standard English test for the entrance to colleges and universities for nonnative students. This dataset has not been commonly used for AES, while it has been used as a standard dataset for another shared task, native language identification (Malmasi et al., 2017) (see the supplementary material for details).

Correlation between essay lengths and scores: To uncover relationships between essay length and scores, we check Pearson and Spearman's rank correlation coefficient with p-value < 0.001. In ASAP, all prompts have a high correlation between length and assigned scores: the average of Pearson is 0.702 and the average of Spearman's is 0.707. Only prompt 8 has a rather low correlation between length and the assigned scores. As Perelman (2014) describes, the large range of scores used in prompt 8 (scores range from 1 to 60) causes statistical noise which leads to the low correlation. TOEFL, in general, shows a lower but still high correlation between essay length and scores: the average of Pearson is 0.591 and the average of Spearman's is 0.568.

3 Experimental Setup

Following recent work on ASAP, we evaluate performance at the prompt level in Table 1. We compare with the best performance reported in the literature. Table 2 reports the performance of models on TOEFL achieved by our re-implementations. Our experimental setup is described as follows (see the supplementary material for details).

Implementation Details: While previous neural models deploy pre-trained embeddings for the ASAP dataset (Taghipour and Ng, 2016), our model builds upon Glove, the 100-dimensional pretrained embedding model trained on Google News (Pennington et al., 2014). We use 100-dimensional Glove for all models on TOEFL. All other settings are identical with previous work.

For our models, we test two variations for an RNN module with a Gated Recurrent Unit (GRU, Cho et al., 2014) and a large-scale natural language pretraining model (XLNet, Yang et al., 2019). XLNet not only outperforms BERT (Devlin et al., 2019) which has led to significant improvements in many NLP tasks, but – unlike BERT – XLNet can also handle any input sequence length, required for our datasets. We encode a whole text at once using the pretrained language model.

Evaluation Details: For ASAP, we perform the experiments in line with prior work (Taghipour and Ng, 2016), including the same cross-validation (CV) partitions, the same evaluation measure, Quadratic Weighted Kappa (QWK), which measures agreement between annotators considering the agreement occurring by chance, and the same loss function, mean squared error. We use the ADAM optimizer with a learning rate of 0.001. For TOEFL, we follow the same setup with the setup of ASAP, but we use a different learning rate of 0.003.

For our implementations, the reported results are obtained by the mean of 10 CV runs with different random seeds. We validate statistical significance by a one-sample t-test with p-value < 0.01.

4 Related Work: Essay Scoring Systems

Taghipour and Ng (2016) introduce a model consisting of a convolutional layer, followed by a recurrent layer, and a mean-over-time layer. The recurrent layer encodes the representation of an essay, the mean-over-time layer then averages the RNN outputs to produce an output vector. Dong et al. (2017) replace the mean-over-time layer by the attention mechanism (Bahdanau et al., 2015). Tay et al. (2018) propose a model that consists of a neural coherence feature and temporal mean pooling, representing the flow of the argument and coherence over time, respectively. They mainly discuss their neural coherence feature, which is composed of a parameterized pair of skipped words. Temporal mean pooling averages RNN outputs. Based on Dong et al. (2017), Nadeem et al. (2019) propose a model considering both the word level and the sentence level with attention between adjacent tokens. Interestingly, we notice that averaged RNN

Model	Prompt								Avg QWK
	1	2	3	4	5	6	7	8	
Phandi et al. (2015)	76.1	60.6	62.1	74.2	78.4	77.5	73.0	61.7	70.5
Taghipour and Ng (2016)	82.1	68.8	69.4	80.5	80.7	81.9	80.8	64.4	76.1
Dong et al. (2017)	82.2	68.2	67.2	81.4	80.3	81.1	80.1	70.5	76.4
Tay et al. (2018)	83.2	68.4	69.5	78.8	81.5	81.0	80.0	69.7	76.4
Cozma et al. (2018)	**84.5**	**72.9**	68.4	**82.9**	**83.3**	**83.0**	80.4	72.9	78.5
Averaging-Length-GRU	80.1	67.5	68.0	79.2	80.5	79.9	79.9	53.6	73.6
Manipulating-Length-GRU	83.7	69.6	68.7	79.2	81.1	80.4	79.8	70.6	76.6
Averaging-Length-XLNet	80.7	69.4	65.4	81.5	79.3	80.7	82.2	73.7	76.6
Manipulating-Length-XLNet	80.8	69.4	66.4	81.6	79.2	80.6	82.2	73.5	76.7
Considering-Content-GRU	84.2	70.8	69.0	79.4	81.5	80.9	80.8	71.2	77.2
Considering-Content-XLNet	82.8	70.6	**69.4**	82.7	80.6	82.0	**83.8**	**76.9**	**78.6**

Table 1: ASAP QWK performance comparison

outputs are commonly used in neural essay scoring systems.

In Table 1, Taghipour and Ng (2016) clearly outperform non-neural essay scoring (Phandi et al., 2015), which uses linguistic features in regression-based machine learning (0.761 > 0.705). Though more recent neural systems introduce more complicated models (Dong et al., 2017; Tay et al., 2018), they only modestly improve the performance (0.764 > 0.761). While the performance of recent neural models is plateauing, a non-neural model which combines a string kernel and word embeddings outperforms previous neural models (Cozma et al., 2018).

5 Influence of Essay Length

A neural model manipulating essay length: To investigate the influence of essay length, we present a simple neural model manipulating essay length, which consists of averaged RNN outputs. Instead of normalizing the sum of RNN outputs by the actual length of an essay, we normalize them by the average of essay lengths in a prompt. The intuition is that normalizing by the average of essay lengths penalizes an essay of shorter length. As an essay has a fewer number of tokens, they have a fewer number of RNN outputs while the same denominator is applied for all essays in the same prompt. This allows a simple RNN model to capture the influence of essay length better.

Results: In ASAP, we first evaluate the performance of the model consisting of averaged RNN outputs with actual essay length, which is commonly used in previous neural models (0.736 < 0.764). We then show that our first neural model manipulating essay length with GRU is comparable with the state-of-the-art neural model (0.766 > 0.764). This demonstrates that the simple neural model manipulating essay length is as powerful as state-of-the-art neural models in the standard dataset. In contrast, a simple neural model relying on the pretrained language model not only shows better performance than previous neural models but also show similar performance against the manipulated model using essay length. It supports the claim of the previous work that a large-scale pretrained language model learns linguistic features from input texts (Warstadt et al., 2020).

In TOEFL, in contrast to ASAP, we observe that the simple neural model which manipulates essay length shows lower performance than the state-of-the-art neural model. Since TOEFL has a lower correlation between essay length and scores than ASAP, we view this as evidence that the performance of previous neural models might be influenced by the correlation of essay length and scores in the target dataset.

6 Countering the Influence

A neural model assessing the similarity of essay content: We propose a neural model which considers essay content by assessing the similarity of word distributions in the input essay and essays grouped into three different levels: low, mid, and high. Grouping scores to three levels enables the model to handle the different score ranges of each dataset. KL divergence for an input essay x is then defined as $KL(p_{lvl}, q) = \sum_x p_{lvl}(x) \log \frac{p_{lvl}(x)}{q(x)}$, where p_{lvl} is a word distribution in the essays grouped to level lvl and q is a word distribution in the input essay. In ASAP where prompts have different score ranges, we define the lower 20% of the scores as the low level, the upper 20% of the scores as the high level, and all others as the mid level. In TOEFL, we define three levels corresponding to the

Model	Prompt								Avg Acc (%)
	1	2	3	4	5	6	7	8	
*Dong et al. (2017)	69.3	66.5	65.8	66.4	68.9	64.2	67.1	65.7	66.7
*Nadeem et al. (2019)	58.9	55.8	65.6	61.3	57.8	57.5	52.4	52.8	57.8
Averaging-Length-GRU	65.7	65.0	63.0	62.9	66.5	64.4	63.2	62.6	64.2
Manipulating-Length-GRU	65.7	65.1	62.6	63.3	66.4	63.0	63.2	62.6	64.0
Averaging-Length-XLNet	73.3	73.6	69.1	70.6	74.1	72.3	71.5	70.5	71.9
Manipulating-Length-XLNet	73.3	73.6	69.1	70.6	73.8	71.9	71.5	70.4	71.8
Considering-Content-GRU	69.4	67.5	66.3	65.5	69.4	65.8	67.4	64.0	66.9
Considering-Content-XLNet	**74.4**	**74.2**	**70.4**	**71.9**	**74.6**	**72.5**	**72.6**	**71.8**	**72.8**

Table 2: TOEFL Accuracy performance comparison (*: our re-implementation)

scores in the dataset. Given an essay, we therefore compute three scalar values of KL divergence, and normalize them by the average of KL divergence in the same level. Finally, we concatenate the three scalar values of KL divergence to the vector representing averaged RNN outputs, which is our first simple model.

Results: We evaluate the performance of the model considering essay content using KL divergence. In ASAP, this model with GRU leads to 0.8% QWK improvement compared to the previous neural models (0.772 > 0.764). Finally, this model with XLNet shows performance comparable to the non-neural state of the art (0.786 > 0.785).

We observe a performance gain with the model considering essay content mainly in prompt 7 and 8, while the non-neural state of the art outperforms this model in prompt 4, 5, and 6. We suspect that the different improvements of performance are caused by different linguistic properties in the essays responding to those prompts. The string kernel method is based on character similarity (Cozma et al., 2018). It has an advantage in a task which is similar to extractive summarization such as prompt in 4, 5, and 6. These prompts ask the students to write an essay within a given context. In this case, we suspect that including specific information regarding the given context has more influence to human annotators. In contrast, prompts 7 and 8 do not have a given context. They are open-ended. Our experiments show that considering essay content leads to significant improvement in this case.

In TOEFL, the model considering essay content with GRU shows performance comparable to the state-of-the-art neural models (0.669 > 0.667). Eventually, this model with XLNet outperforms all other models (0.728 > 0.669), and it also leads to a 1.0% improvement compared to the model manipulating essay length. This also supports our finding that considering essay content leads to a performance improvement for neural essay scoring systems. Unlike ASAP, the model considering essay content models on the TOEFL show consistent performance gain regardless of prompts. We believe this is caused by an overall higher quality of TOEFL dataset. The prompts do not vary so much, the student population is more controlled, and the essays have a similar length.

We also compare with the state of the art on TOEFL, Nadeem et al. (2019). We notice that the performance reported in Nadeem et al. (2019) cannot be compared with previous work due to a different experimental setup. They filter out content whose sentence length is longer than 40 words or whose document length is longer than 25 sentences, which results in filtering the more than 7.5% of sentences; they also evaluate performance without CV[3]. To ensure a fair comparison, we only modified the experimental setup in their implementation. The model proposed in Nadeem et al. (2019) shows substantially lower performance than all models in the same experimental setup with previous work.

7 Conclusions

While the recent neural essay scoring systems emphasize novel aspects of the neural architecture, they have neither shown significant improvement nor helped interpreting the scores assigned by humans. We show that recent neural models might also be influenced by characteristics of the standard dataset, a high correlation between essay length and scores. To investigate this, we evaluate models on two datasets, not only the standard dataset, ASAP, but also TOEFL, which has a lower correlation between essay length and scores. Our findings suggest that neural essay scoring systems should focus on text quality, and at the same time, should consider characteristics of the target dataset.

[3]We confirmed this by examining their implementation and emailing the first author.

Acknowledgments

The authors would like to thank the anonymous reviewers for their comments. This work has been funded by the Klaus Tschira Foundation, Heidelberg, Germany. The first author has been supported by a Heidelberg Institute for Theoretical Studies Ph.D. scholarship.

References

Dzmitry Bahdanau, Kyunghyun Cho, and Yoshua Bengio. 2015. Neural machine translation by jointly learning to align and translate. *In Proceedings of the ICLR Conference*.

Anat Ben-Simon and Randy Elliot Bennett. 2007. Toward more substantively meaningful automated essay scoring. *The Journal of Technology, Learning and Assessment*, 6(1).

Daniel Blanchard, Joel Tetreault, Derrick Higgins, Aoife Cahill, and Martin Chodorow. 2013. TOEFL11: A corpus of non-native english. *ETS Research Report Series*, 2013(2):i–15.

Hongbo Chen and Ben He. 2013. Automated essay scoring by maximizing human-machine agreement. In *Proceedings of the 2013 Conference on Empirical Methods in Natural Language Processing*, pages 1741–1752, Seattle, Washington, USA. Association for Computational Linguistics.

Kyunghyun Cho, Bart van Merriënboer, Caglar Gulcehre, Dzmitry Bahdanau, Fethi Bougares, Holger Schwenk, and Yoshua Bengio. 2014. Learning phrase representations using RNN encoder–decoder for statistical machine translation. In *Proceedings of the 2014 Conference on Empirical Methods in Natural Language Processing (EMNLP)*, pages 1724–1734, Doha, Qatar. Association for Computational Linguistics.

Mădălina Cozma, Andrei Butnaru, and Radu Tudor Ionescu. 2018. Automated essay scoring with string kernels and word embeddings. In *Proceedings of the 56th Annual Meeting of the Association for Computational Linguistics (Volume 2: Short Papers)*, pages 503–509, Melbourne, Australia. Association for Computational Linguistics.

Jacob Devlin, Ming-Wei Chang, Kenton Lee, and Kristina Toutanova. 2019. BERT: Pre-training of deep bidirectional transformers for language understanding. In *Proceedings of the 2019 Conference of the North American Chapter of the Association for Computational Linguistics: Human Language Technologies, Volume 1 (Long and Short Papers)*, pages 4171–4186, Minneapolis, Minnesota. Association for Computational Linguistics.

Fei Dong, Yue Zhang, and Jie Yang. 2017. Attention-based recurrent convolutional neural network for automatic essay scoring. In *Proceedings of the 21st Conference on Computational Natural Language Learning (CoNLL 2017)*, pages 153–162, Vancouver, Canada. Association for Computational Linguistics.

Nitin Madnani and Aoife Cahill. 2018. Automated scoring: Beyond natural language processing. In *Proceedings of the 27th International Conference on Computational Linguistics*, pages 1099–1109, Santa Fe, New Mexico, USA. Association for Computational Linguistics.

Shervin Malmasi, Keelan Evanini, Aoife Cahill, Joel Tetreault, Robert Pugh, Christopher Hamill, Diane Napolitano, and Yao Qian. 2017. A report on the 2017 native language identification shared task. In *Proceedings of the 12th Workshop on Innovative Use of NLP for Building Educational Applications*, pages 62–75, Copenhagen, Denmark. Association for Computational Linguistics.

Farah Nadeem, Huy Nguyen, Yang Liu, and Mari Ostendorf. 2019. Automated essay scoring with discourse-aware neural models. In *Proceedings of the Fourteenth Workshop on Innovative Use of NLP for Building Educational Applications*, pages 484–493, Florence, Italy. Association for Computational Linguistics.

Jeffrey Pennington, Richard Socher, and Christopher Manning. 2014. GloVe: Global vectors for word representation. In *Proceedings of the 2014 Conference on Empirical Methods in Natural Language Processing (EMNLP)*, pages 1532–1543, Doha, Qatar. Association for Computational Linguistics.

Les Perelman. 2014. When "the state of the art" is counting words. *Assessing Writing*, 21:104–111.

Peter Phandi, Kian Ming A. Chai, and Hwee Tou Ng. 2015. Flexible domain adaptation for automated essay scoring using correlated linear regression. In *Proceedings of the 2015 Conference on Empirical Methods in Natural Language Processing*, pages 431–439, Lisbon, Portugal. Association for Computational Linguistics.

Kaveh Taghipour and Hwee Tou Ng. 2016. A neural approach to automated essay scoring. In *Proceedings of the 2016 Conference on Empirical Methods in Natural Language Processing*, pages 1882–1891, Austin, Texas. Association for Computational Linguistics.

Yi Tay, Minh C Phan, Luu Anh Tuan, and Siu Cheung Hui. 2018. Skipflow: Incorporating neural coherence features for end-to-end automatic text scoring. In *Thirty-Second AAAI Conference on Artificial Intelligence*.

Alex Warstadt, Yian Zhang, Xiaocheng Li, Haokun Liu, and Samuel R. Bowman. 2020. Learning which features matter: RoBERTa acquires a preference for linguistic generalizations (eventually). In *Proceedings of the 2020 Conference on Empirical Methods* in *Natural Language Processing (EMNLP)*, pages 217–235, Online. Association for Computational Linguistics.

Michael Winerip. 2005. SAT essay test rewards length and ignores errors. *New York Times*, 9.

Edward W. Wolfe, Tian Song, and Hong Jiao. 2016. Features of difficult-to-score essays. *Assessing Writing*, 27:1–10.

Zhilin Yang, Zihang Dai, Yiming Yang, Jaime Carbonell, Russ R. Salakhutdinov, and Quoc V. Le. 2019. XLNet: Generalized autoregressive pretraining for language understanding. In *Advances in Neural Information Processing Systems*, pages 5754–5764.

8 Appendix A. Dataset Details

Table 3 describes statistics on two datasets, GCDC[4] and TOEFL[5]. We use NLTK library to tokenize for models based on GRU, and use XLNet tokenizer for the models based on XLNet. Table 4 describes the topic of each prompt in TOEFL. They are all open-ended tasks, that do not have given context but require students to submit their opinion.

Dataset	#Texts	Avg len (Std)	Max len	Scores
A-P1	1,785	463 (155)	1092	2-12
A-P2	1,800	467 (194)	1337	1-6
A-P3	1,726	135 (67)	452	0-3
A-P4	1,772	114 (64)	451	0-3
A-P5	1,805	153 (73)	520	0-4
A-P6	1,800	187 (69)	545	0-4
A-P7	1,569	223 (119)	878	0-30
A-P8	723	770 (269)	1396	0-60
T-P1	1,656	401 (97)	902	1-3
T-P2	1,562	423 (97)	902	1-3
T-P3	1,396	407 (102)	837	1-3
T-P4	1,509	405 (99)	852	1-3
T-P5	1,648	424 (101)	993	1-3
T-P6	960	425 (101)	925	1-3
T-P7	1,686	396 (87)	755	1-3
T-P8	1,683	407 (92)	795	1-3

Table 3: Dataset statistics on tokenization: each ASAP prompt (A-P) and each TOEFL prompt (T-P).

9 Appendix B. Experimental Setup Details

For ASAP, we perform the experiments in line with prior work (Taghipour and Ng, 2016), including the same cross-validation (CV) partitions, the same evaluation measure, Quadratic Weighted Kappa (QWK), which measures agreement between annotators considering the agreement occurring by chance, and the same loss function, mean squared error. We use the ADAM optimizer with a learning rate of 0.001. We evaluate performance for 50 epochs on the validation set. We evaluate performance on the validation set for every epoch and apply the best model to the test set. We use a mini-batch size of 32 with random-shuffle. For TOEFL, we evaluate performance in accuracy for the three-class classification problem with 5-fold CV. We deploy cross-entropy loss for training. Like ASAP, we evaluate performance on the validation set for every epoch and apply the best model to the test set. We use a mini-batch size of 32 with random-shuffle. We use the ADAM optimizer with a learning rate of 0.003. We use 23GB GPU memory a NVidia P40.

[4]https://github.com/aylai/GCDC-corpus

[5]https://catalog.ldc.upenn.edu/LDC2014T06

A-Prompt 1	The writers had to write a letter to their local newspaper in which they stated their opinion on the effects computers have on people.
A-Prompt 2	The writers had to write a persuasive essay reflecting their views on censorship in libraries.
A-Prompt 3	The writers had to read an extract from Rough Road Ahead: Do Not Exceed Posted Speed Limit by Joe Kurmaskie. They then had to explain how the features of the setting affected the cyclist.
A-Prompt 4	The writers had to read an extract from Winter Hibiscus by Minfong Ho. They then had to explain why the author concludes the story in the way that she did.
A-Prompt 5	The writers had to read an extract from Narciso Rodriguez by Narciso Rodriguez. They then had to describe the mood created by the author with supporting evidence from the extract.
A-Prompt 6	The writers had to read an extract from The Mooring Mast by Marcia Amidon Lusted. They then had to answer a question about the difficulties faced by the builders of the Empire State Building in allowing dirigibles to dock there.
A-Prompt 7	Write a story about a time when you, or someone you know, was patient
A-Prompt 8	Write a story in which laughter plays a part.
T-Prompt 1	Agree or Disagree: It is better to have broad knowledge of many academic subjects than to specialize in one specific subject.
T-Prompt 2	Agree or Disagree: Young people enjoy life more than older people do.
T-Prompt 3	Agree or Disagree: Young people nowadays do not give enough time to helping their communities.
T-Prompt 4	Agree or Disagree: Most advertisements make products seem much better than they really are.
T-Prompt 5	Agree or Disagree: In twenty years, there will be fewer cars in use than there are today.
T-Prompt 6	Agree or Disagree: The best way to travel is in a group led by a tour guide.
T-Prompt 7	Agree or Disagree: It is more important for students to understand ideas and concepts than it is for them to learn facts.
T-Prompt 8	Agree or Disagree: Successful people try new things and take risks rather than only doing what they already know how to do well.

Table 4: Topic description: ASAP (A) and TOEFL (T).

Memory-efficient Transformers via Top-k Attention

Ankit Gupta[1*] **Guy Dar**[2] **Shaya Goodman**[2] **David Ciprut**[2] **Jonathan Berant**[2,3]

[1]IBM Research [2]Tel Aviv University [3]Allen Institute for AI

{ankitgupta.iitkanpur, guyd1995, ishayahu156, davidciprut}@gmail.com, joberant@cs.tau.ac.il

Abstract

Following the success of dot-product attention in Transformers, numerous approximations have been recently proposed to address its quadratic complexity with respect to the input length. While these variants are memory and compute efficient, it is not possible to directly use them with popular pre-trained language models trained using vanilla attention, without an expensive corrective pre-training stage. In this work, we propose a simple yet highly accurate approximation for vanilla attention. We process the queries in chunks, and for each query, compute the top-k scores with respect to the keys. Our approach offers several advantages: (a) its memory usage is linear in the input size, similar to linear attention variants, such as Performer and RFA (b) it is a drop-in replacement for vanilla attention that does not require any corrective pre-training, and (c) it can also lead to significant memory savings in the feed-forward layers after casting them into the familiar query-key-value framework. We evaluate the quality of top-k approximation for multi-head attention layers on the Long Range Arena Benchmark, and for feed-forward layers of T5 and UnifiedQA on multiple QA datasets. We show our approach leads to accuracy that is nearly-identical to vanilla attention in multiple setups including training from scratch, fine-tuning, and zero-shot inference.

1 Introduction

The Transformer architecture (Vaswani et al., 2017) has been successful in a wide range of natural language processing tasks, including machine translation (Edunov et al., 2018), language modeling (Roy et al., 2021), question-answering (Karpukhin et al., 2020), and many more. Transformers pre-trained on large amounts of text with a language modeling (LM) objective, have become the standard in NLP, exhibiting surprising amounts of linguistic and world knowledge (Peters et al., 2018; Devlin et al., 2019; Petroni et al., 2019; Hewitt and Manning, 2019; Roberts et al., 2020).

The contextualizing component of the Transformer is the attention layer where all positions in an input sequence of length L aggregate information from the entire sequence in parallel. At its core, given L query, key, and value vectors Q, K, V respectively, the *dot-product attention* function outputs $\mathrm{softmax}(QK^\top)V$ where the softmax function is applied row-wise on the matrix $QK^\top \in \mathbb{R}^{L\times L}$ of similarity scores of the query-key pairs, leading to an expensive $\Omega(L^2)$ memory requirement.

To alleviate this, past work proposed approximation methods for the computation of $\mathrm{softmax}(QK^\top)$. One major line of research focused on *sparse attention* variants, where only a few similarity scores are computed per query, and the rest are ignored. Methods differ by which query-key pairs are selected (Child et al., 2019; Ye et al., 2019; Qiu et al., 2020; Roy et al., 2021; Kitaev et al., 2020; Beltagy et al., 2020; Gupta and Berant, 2020; Vyas et al., 2020). A second line of research explored *dense* variants (Katharopoulos et al., 2020; Wang et al., 2020; Bello, 2021; Tay et al., 2020a) (cf. (Tay et al., 2020b) for a survey). For example, instead of computing the attention scores exactly for only a small number of query-key pairs, (Choromanski et al., 2021) compute an approximation of scores for all pairs.

In this work, we adopt the sparse attention approach, but rather than *approximating* the k most similar key vectors per query vector, we compute this quantity *exactly*. Specifically, we propose *top-k attention* where, for each query vector, we only keep its k largest similarity scores with respect to the L keys, where $k \ll L$. We show that top-k attention can be implemented in a memory-efficient manner by (a) chunking the query vectors when

*majority of work done while author was part of IBM AI Residency program.

Proceedings of the 2nd Workshop on Simple and Efficient Natural Language Processing, pages 39–52
November 10, 2021. ©201 Association for Computational Linguistics

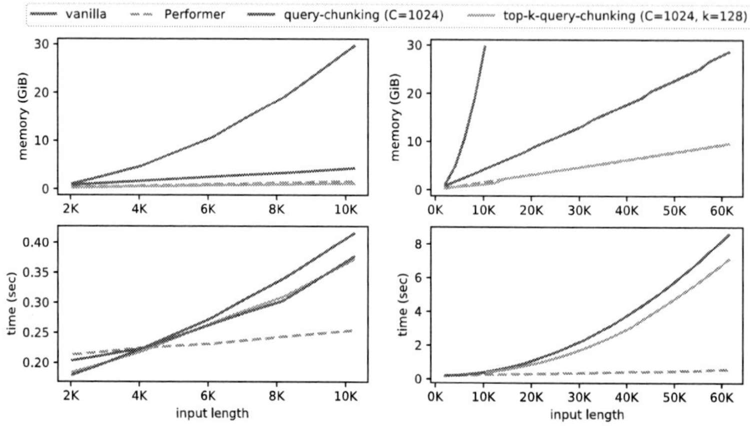

Figure 1: Memory and time required for a forward and backward pass on a single BERT-base multi-head self-attention layer with causal masking on short (left) and long (right) inputs. Details are in §3.

computing the output one chunk at a time, when computing $\mathrm{softmax}(QK^\top)V$, and (b) a custom implementation of the forward and backward pass that does not require caching activations while processing chunks in the forward pass.

Compared to prior methods, top-k attention has multiple attractive properties:

- Top-k attention has the same memory footprint as Performer (Choromanski et al., 2021), a state-of-the-art attention variant with linear time and memory complexity, on very long inputs (orange curve, Fig. 1, top-right), while being as fast as vanilla attention, and even faster than linear variants on inputs of length up to $4K$ (Figure 1, bottom-left). This allows us, e.g., to train a typical 12-layer Transformer decoder over $32K$-long inputs on a 30GiB GPU (Figure 3a).
- Top-k attention also reduces memory consumption in Transformer feed-forward layers, by casting this layer into the familiar query-key-value framework using ReLU instead of the row-wise $\mathrm{softmax}$ (Sukhbaatar et al., 2019). This is specifically appealing in models such as T5 (Raffel et al., 2020) and GPT-3 (Brown et al., 2020), where for short inputs, the memory consumption is dominated by the feed-forward layers, as the number of keys, corresponding to the feed-forward hidden dimension size, is as large as $65K$. Conversely, methods that rely on random feature approximations of attention, such as Performer (Choromanski et al., 2021) and RFA (Peng et al., 2021) do not admit an efficient approximation for the ReLU activation (Yehudai and Shamir, 2019).
- Top-k attention is a highly accurate approximation to vanilla attention and is a *plug-and-play* replacement at both multi-head attention and feed-forward layers of a Transformer. This is unlike past attention variants (Katharopoulos et al., 2020; Choromanski et al., 2021; Peng et al., 2021) that require an expensive corrective pre-training stage to adjust model weights to the new variant, which can be prohibitive for large models. We show top-k attention can replace vanilla attention in a zero-shot inference setup and at fine-tuning time without any corrective pre-training.

We extensively evaluate top-k attention on a wide range of tasks and demonstrate its mentioned advantages. Training from scratch, we show top-k attention performs as well as vanilla self-attention on Long Range Arena, a benchmark dedicated to evaluating the ability of transformers to handle long sequences, and in a language modeling task (WikiText-103). Second, we show top-k attention can be used as a drop-in replacement for vanilla attention at inference time without any additional training at the feed-forward layer of the UnifiedQA model (Khashabi et al., 2020) on 12 different question answering (QA) datasets, reducing the number of keys used per query by more than 99%. Last, we show top-k attention obtains similar performance to vanilla attention on a wide range of QA tasks when fine-tuning T5 (Raffel et al., 2020), without the need for any corrective pre-training.

Overall, our results demonstrate that top-k attention is a simple and effective method for dramatically reducing the memory footprint of Transformers without loss of accuracy that can allow resource-constrained researchers enjoy the benefits of large pre-trained Transformer-based models. Our code is available at `https://github.com/ag1988/top_k_attention`.

2 Efficient Transformer through Top-k Attention

In this section, we briefly review the Transformer architecture, its sparse approximations, and show how to cast the feed-forward layer into the query-key-value framework (§2.1). We then describe top-k attention and our memory-efficient implementation for it (§2.2).

2.1 Attention in Transformers

A Transformer (Vaswani et al., 2017) is a stack of layers each consisting of multi-head attention and feed-forward sub-layers. Its contextualizing component is the multi-head attention defined as follows.

Multi-head Attention Given a query $Q \in \mathbb{R}^{L_Q \times d}$, key $K \in \mathbb{R}^{L_K \times d}$ and value $V \in \mathbb{R}^{L_K \times d}$, the output $\in \mathbb{R}^{L_Q \times d}$ of dot-product attention is defined as:

$$\text{Attention}(Q, K, V) = \text{row-softmax}\left(\frac{QK^\top}{\lambda}\right) V, \tag{1}$$

where λ is an optional temperature typically fixed as $\sqrt{d}$.[1] In multi-head attention, for a given number of heads h, instead of computing a single attention output with d_{model} dimensional queries, keys and values, these are linearly projected down in parallel h times to $d = d_{\text{model}}/h$ dimensions, using different learned projection matrices. Attention is applied to each of the h new queries, keys and values, yielding d dimensional outputs which are concatenated and again projected to obtain a d_{model}-dimensional output.

Sparse approximations The attention function (Eq. 1) requires the computation of $QK^\top$ containing $L_Q \cdot L_K$ entries and can be expensive for long sequences (L_Q and L_K are typically the sequence length). To alleviate this issue, *sparse attention* variants (Child et al., 2019; Qiu et al., 2020; Kitaev et al., 2020; Beltagy et al., 2020; Gupta and Berant, 2020) relax this requirement and compute only a few entries of $QK^\top$, masking out the rest. For a binary mask $B \in \{0, -\infty\}^{L_Q \times L_K}$,

$$\begin{aligned}&\text{SparseAttention}(Q, K, V, B) = \\ &\text{row-softmax}\left(QK^\top + B\right) V.\end{aligned} \tag{2}$$

The sparsity of B can be leveraged via customized implementations of matrix product (Child et al., 2019; Beltagy et al., 2020) and, thus Eq. 2 can be significantly cheaper to compute compared to Eq. 1.

Feed-forward as attention In the feed-forward layer, a 1-hidden layer fully-connected network is applied identically to every input token. As observed in past work (Sukhbaatar et al., 2019; Shazeer, 2020; Geva et al., 2020), a feed-forward layer can be cast into the query-key-value framework as:

$$\text{FF}_{K,V}(Q) = \text{ReLU}\left(QK^\top\right) V. \tag{3}$$

In this case, the queries $Q \in \mathbb{R}^{L_Q \times d_{\text{model}}}$ are the inputs to the layer with L_Q tokens, similar to self-attention. However, the keys $K = W_K \in \mathbb{R}^{L_K \times d_{\text{model}}}$ and values $V = W_V \in \mathbb{R}^{L_K \times d_{\text{model}}}$ are learned parameters that are independent of the input. The number of keys L_K here is known as the *feed-forward dimension* and can be as large as $65K$ for wide models such as T5 (Raffel et al., 2020) and GPT-3 (Brown et al., 2020). In the common case where the input sequences are relatively short, memory consumption is dominated by the feed-forward sub-layer and not the self-attention sub-layer.

Unlike top-k attention, past approaches for approximating attention are incompatible with feed-forward layers. Most approximate attention variants, such as Sparse Transformer (Child et al., 2019), LongFormer (Beltagy et al., 2020), BigBird (Zaheer et al., 2020), Sinkhorn attention (Tay et al., 2020a), rely on a *locality bias* in sequences, where the key vectors indexed close to each other in K are assumed to have similar representations. This is irrelevant for keys in a feed-forward layer, which are permutation-equivariant and do not have any local structure. Dense attention variants relying on random fourier features for approximating the softmax function are also not applicable, since it is known that ReLU cannot be approximated using such features (Yehudai and Shamir, 2019).

2.2 Top-k Attention

In this work we propose top-k attention, where for each query, we mask out all but its k largest dot products with the keys, that is, in each row of $QK^\top$ we only keep its k largest elements and mask out the rest:

$$\begin{aligned}&\text{top-}k\text{-Attention}(Q, K, V) = \\ &\text{activation}\left(\text{top-}k(QK^\top)\right) V,\end{aligned} \tag{4}$$

[1] we omit this in rest of our presentation as Q can be scaled by $1/\lambda$ beforehand.

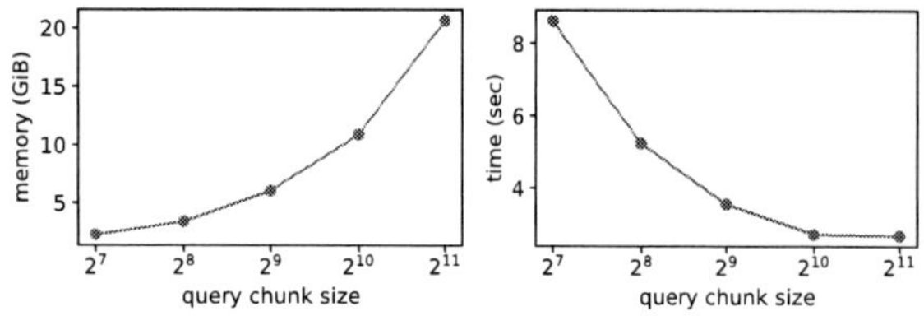

Figure 2: Memory and time required for a forward pass on a single BERT-base multi-head self-attention layer on inputs of length $65,536$.

where activation can be $\mathrm{softmax}$, ReLU, or any other activation, and top-$k(QK^{\top})$ denotes a sparse matrix consisting only of the row-wise top-k elements of $QK^{\top}$. A naïve approach for computing top-$k(QK^{\top})$ would be to first compute $QK^{\top}$ and applying a row-wise top-k operation. Unfortunately, computing $QK^{\top} \in \mathbb{R}^{L_Q \times L_K}$ explicitly would require $\Omega(L_Q \cdot L_K)$ memory. We now describe our approach, which avoids this high cost.

Query chunking A simple way to implement attention and reduce its peak memory consumption is to chunk queries: instead of processing all the queries at once, we partition the queries into chunks and process them sequentially, one chunk at a time. For a chunk size C, the rows of Q are grouped into L_Q/C contiguous chunks of size C and the attention function (Eq. 1, 3, 4) is computed using Q_C, K, V as inputs where Q_C denotes the subset of Q corresponding to chunk $\mathcal{C}$.

During *inference*, once a query chunk is fully processed, the intermediate activations produced during its processing can be discarded and, hence, the peak memory required to process all L_Q queries is bounded by the memory required to process a single chunk. Therefore, modulo the storage required for Q, K, V and the outputs themselves, the peak memory usage reduces from $\Omega(L_Q \cdot L_K)$ to $O(C \cdot L_K)$ which is linear with respect to L_K for a fixed chunk size C.

Chunk size provides a simple way to trade-off between the maximum memory usage and the slowdown due to the sequential processing of chunks. Fig. 2 shows memory and time for different chunk sizes for a single BERT-base self-attention layer over a sequence of length $65,536$. We observe that chunk sizes $2^9, 2^{10}$ yield a good trade-off between time and memory.

Input checkpointing While query chunking provides a straightforward approach for bounding the peak memory usage of attention during *inference*, it is not so straightforward to employ it during *training*. Let $d(A)$ denote the gradient of the loss with respect to a tensor A. For a given query chunk Q_C, the intermediate activations produced during the computation of the output $o_C = \mathrm{Attention}(Q_C, K, V)$ are required for computing $d(Q_C)$ from $d(o_C)$ via backpropagation. Unfortunately, for the above bound on the peak memory usage to hold, we cannot afford to cache these activations for all the chunks, as done by standard automatic differentiation packages.

Taking inspiration from *gradient checkpointing* (Chen et al., 2016), we observe that if the inputs Q_C, K, V are available during the backward pass, we can re-compute o_C and then use the produced intermediate activations to compute $d(Q_C)$ from $d(o_C)$. Once $d(Q_C)$ is computed, we can again discard the intermediate activations and gradients produced during this step and move on to the next chunk. This ensures that the peak memory usage during the backward pass through the attention layer is bounded by the memory required to backpropagate through a single chunk.

To summarize, a customized backward pass allows us to utilize query chunking, both during forward and backward passes, and only requires us to cache the inputs to the attention function. For a stack of N attention layers and fixed d, this reduces the peak memory usage from $\Omega(L_Q \cdot L_K \cdot N)$ to $O((L_Q + L_K) \cdot N + C \cdot L_K)$.

As described above, the combination of query chunking and input checkpointing provides a simple method for reducing the memory-footprint of vanilla attention, independent of top-k attention. Indeed, our benchmarking experiments in §3 demonstrate this. However, a drawback of this approach is that, during the backward pass, an implicit second forward pass is performed to re-compute the intermediate activations as described above. This can potentially increase the compute (FLOPs) required for a combined forward and backward pass by 50%. We now describe how to further improve both compute and memory by combining query chunking and input checkpointing with top-k attention.

Improving efficiency through top-k attention We now show that one can avoid re-computing activations in the case of top-k-$\mathrm{Attention}$ (Eq. 4). At a high level, top-$k(QK^{\top})$ provides a highly compressed but accurate representation of $QK^{\top}$ and requires only $O(L_Q \cdot k)$ storage, compared to $\Omega(L_Q \cdot L_K)$ for $QK^{\top}$, where we assume $k \ll L_K$. Hence, we can cache it in addition to Q, K, V with-

```
1  def forward (Q, K, V, k, activation):
2      # Q: query chunk, K: keys, V: values                  # [C, d], [L_K, d], [L_K, d]
3      dots = matrix_prod(Q, transpose(K))                   # [C, L_K]
4      top_dots, top_indices = row_wise_topk(dots, k)        # [C, k], [C, k]
5      del dots
6      top_actv = activation(top_dots)                       # [C, k]
7      actv = matrix(top_actv, top_indices)
8      out = matrix_prod(actv, V)                            # [C, d]
9      to_cache(Q, K, V, top_dots, top_indices, activation)
10     return out
11
12 def backward(d_out):
13     # d_out: grad of loss w.r.t. out                      # [C, d]
14     Q, K, V, top_dots, top_indices, activation = from_cache()
15     d_top_actv = matrix_prod(d_out, transpose(V), out_indices=top_indices) # [C, k]
16     # did not cache top_actv so re-compute it to backpropagate
17     with compute_grads():
18         top_actv = activation(top_dots)                   # [C, k]
19     d_top_dots = top_actv.backpropagate(d_top_actv)       # [C, k]
20     actv = matrix(top_actv, top_indices)
21     d_V = transpose(matrix_prod(transpose(d_out), actv))# [L_K, d]
22     del actv
23     d_dots = matrix(d_top_dots, top_indices)
24     d_Q = matrix_prod(d_dots, K)                          # [C, d]
25     d_K = transpose(matrix_prod(transpose(Q), d_dots))    # [L_K, d]
26     return d_Q, d_K, d_V
```

out incurring a significant increase in memory usage.

In the pseudo-code above, we show the forward and backward pass for top-k attention over a query chunk with input checkpointing. The steps of the forward pass that we re-compute during the backward pass is the application of activation on the output of top-$k(QK^\top)$ and forming its matrix representation for subsequent operations (compare Lines 6, 7 and Lines 18, 20). Therefore, the number of FLOPs spent on re-computation in our implementation of top-k attention is at most $O(L_Q \cdot (k + L_K) \cdot N)$, typically much lower than $\Omega(L_Q \cdot L_K \cdot d \cdot N)$, as there is no need to re-compute the dot-products.

Moreover, our benchmarking experiments (§3) show that top-k attention leads to improved memory usage compared to query chunking. This is because in vanilla attention (Eq. 1), while performing the re-computation in the backward pass of a query chunk Q_C, we first re-compute $Q_C K^\top$, then apply activation and backpropagate through this operation to compute $d(Q_C K^\top)$. This implies that at this point there are three $C \times L_K$ matrices in memory. In top-k attention, activation is applied only on a $C \times k$ matrix and at any given time during the backward pass shown below there is at most one $C \times L_K$ matrix in memory: either `actv` (Line 20) or `d_dots` (Line 23). As our experiments show, this can lead to a much smaller memory footprint for small values of k, N.

3 Benchmarking

In this section, we benchmark top-k attention in terms of time and memory, and compare it to vanilla attention, query-chunking without the top-k operation, and to Performer (Choromanski et al., 2021), as a representative of state-of-the-art linear attention variants. We separately benchmark (a) a single self-attention layer over long sequences, (b) a single feed-forward layer with a large feed-forward dimension, and (c) a 12-layer Transformer decoder with same architecture as BERT-base (Devlin et al., 2019).

Experimental details For all models, we benchmark by running a forward and backward pass over random inputs. Each measurement is an average over 3 runs on an Nvidia A100 GPU and is discarded if memory usage exceeds 30GiB. We use causal masking for self-attention layers to highlight the simplicity of our approach that can seamlessly handle arbitrary attention masks, unlike other methods (Wang et al., 2020; Katharopoulos et al., 2020;

Choromanski et al., 2021), where implementing causal masking requires customized CUDA implementations. For Performer, we use 256 random features, and the CUDA implementation from (Katharopoulos et al., 2020).

Multi-head attention layer We benchmark a single multi-head attention layer over long sequences in a configuration similar to BERT-base: d_{model} is 768, 12 heads of size 64, and feed-forward dimension 3072. Fig. 1 shows the results when setting k to 128 and the query chunk size to 1024, which was shown to provide a good time-memory trade-off in §2.2.

We observe that top-k attention has the same device-memory usage as the Performer (top) for sequences as long as $65K$ tokens, while being as fast as vanilla attention, and even faster than Performer on inputs of length up to $4K$. With vanilla attention, we cannot fit even a single multi-head attention layer over a sequence of more than $10K$ tokens, while top-k uses less than 10GiB of memory over sequences of length $65K$. Lastly, we observe improvement in both time and memory when comparing top-k attention to query chunking over vanilla attention, where using top-k leads to a $3\times$ memory reduction for sequences of length $65K$.

Feed-forward layer While considerable effort has been dedicated to devising efficient models for long contexts, a large feed-forward dimension is useful for knowledge-intensive tasks such as open-domain QA (Roberts et al., 2020; Brown et al., 2020), and efforts have been made to reduce its complexity (Fedus et al., 2021). We benchmark the resource usage of top-k attention at a single feed-forward layer for different feed-forward dimensions using batch size 512 and input length 512, which results in 2^{18} queries per batch.

Top-k attention (Figure 3b), for $k = 512$ and query chunk size 2^{14}, dramatically improves device-memory usage compared to vanilla attention: it allowed us to use a feed-forward dimension $65K$ with 11GiB, while vanilla attention uses the same amount of memory with a feed-forward dimension $2K$. Fitting a linear curve to the memory usage of vanilla attention and top-k attention, we estimate that top-k attention can handle feed-forward dimension $205K$ compared to $7K$ for vanilla attention on a 30GiB machine. Moreover, comparing top-k attention to query chunking, we again observe a $3\times$ improvement in memory usage when the number of keys is $65K$. Lastly, we observe only a minor slowdown in top-k attention compared to vanilla attention.

12-layer model We benchmark a 12-layer model to examine the cumulative utility of not caching $QK^\top$ in all N layers compared to the Performer. We use the same architecture as BERT-base with batch size 1 and vary the input length. We use a Transformer decoder with top-64 attention and chunk size $1,024$ at the self-attention layers, and simple query chunking with chunk size $4,096$ at the feed-forward layers.

We easily fit a $32K$-long input on a 30GiB GPU, improving memory consumption by more than $8\times$ compared to vanilla Transformer and $2\times$ compared to Performer. Moreover, top-k attention outperforms query chunking in terms of both memory and runtime. As top-k attention targets memory consumption but not runtime, a current limitation is that runtime, unlike Performer, is still quadratic. Thus, running multi-layer models on long sequences is reasonable in a fine-tuning or zero-shot inference setup, but further work is required for training from scratch 12-layer models over large datasets that contain long sequences.

Overall, our benchmarking results over multi-head attention, feed-forward, and multi-layer Transformer establish top-k attention as a strong baseline for future work on efficient Transformers that dramatically improves memory consumption. Next, we evaluate top-k attention on downstream tasks and show that top-k attention can be used as a drop-in replacement for vanilla attention without additional pre-training, which can allow resource-constrained research groups experiment with Transformers over long sequences or models with a large feed-forward dimension.

4 Experimental Evaluation of Top-k Attention

Having established top-k attention as a memory efficient alternative to vanilla attention, we now show that, even for small values of k, top-k attention provides a high-quality approximation of vanilla attention, both at the multi-head attention and feed-forward layers. We empirically show this in a wide range of setups including (a) training from scratch on tasks that require handling long-range dependencies (§4.1) and on language modeling (§4.2), (b) fine-tuning pre-trained language models (T5) on multiple QA datasets (§4.5), and (c) perform-

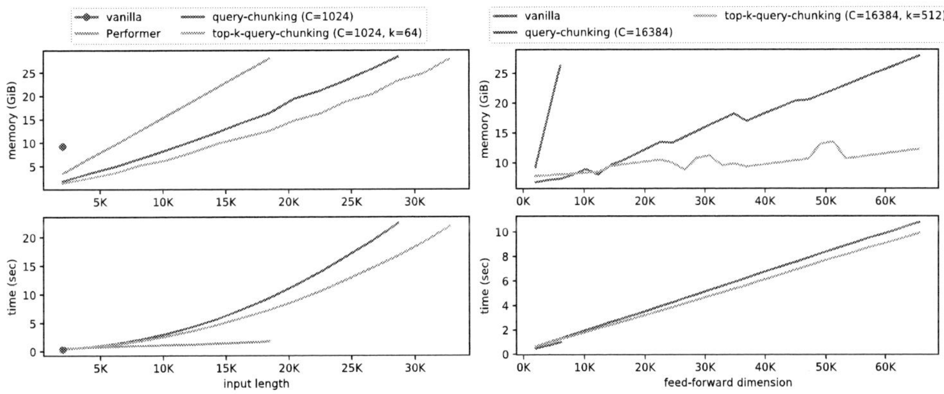

(a) 12-layer "base" Transformer decoder (b) single feed-forward layer

Figure 3: Memory and time required for a combined forward and backward pass (details in §3).

ing zero-shot inference using pre-trained language models (UNIFIEDQA) without any training (§4.3).

4.1 Long Range Arena

Long Range Arena (Tay et al., 2021) is a recently established benchmark for evaluating the ability of Transformer variants to handle long sequences. It comprises of multiple text classification tasks with inputs containing thousands of tokens (Table 1). In ListOps (Nangia and Bowman, 2018), given a sequence of operations on single-digit integers, the model predicts a single-digit solution modeled as 10-way classification. IMDb movie reviews (Maas et al., 2011) is a character-level binary sentiment classification task. Lastly, in the ACL Anthology Network (AAN) (Radev et al., 2013) task, a character-level model classifies if there is a citation between a pair of papers.

For each task, we downloaded and directly used the vanilla Transformer code offered by the authors (Tay et al., 2021) and compared the performance before and after replacing the multi-head attention layers with top-128 attention, using identical hyperparameters for both cases (details in §A.1).[2]

Test accuracy measured at the training checkpoint with the highest accuracy on the development set is reported in Table 1 and the learning curves on the development and test sets are shown in Fig. 5. On IMDb and AAN, the performance of top-128 is comparable or better than vanilla attention. For ListOps, there is a minor drop in performance (1.5 points), but learning curves (Figure 5a) exhibit similar behaviour.

[2] https://github.com/google-research/long-range-arena

Thus, top-k attention, even for k as small as 3% of the number of keys, results in a performance very similar to that of vanilla attention. This shows that an exact and sparse top-k solution is a high-quality approximation for vanilla attention at multi-head attention layers.

	ListOps	IMDb	AAN	mean
input length	$2K$	$1K$	$4K$	
vanilla (reported in (Tay et al., 2021))	36.4	64.3	57.5	52.7
vanilla (our run)	**38.12**	63.66	57.93	53.2
top-128	36.56	**63.72**	**59.14**	53.1

Table 1: Test accuracy for vanilla and top-128 attention on Long Range Arena.

4.2 Language Modeling

We further ascertain the findings of §4.1 via language modeling on WikiText-103 (Merity et al., 2017) using a 6-layer Transformer decoder with 156M parameters. Using an input length of 1024, we trained two models with vanilla and top-64 attentions at the self-attention layers, obtaining test perplexity scores of 30.96 and 30.51 respectively, slightly better in case of top-64 (details in §A.3).

4.3 Zero-shot Inference with UNIFIEDQA

We have established that the performance of top-k attention is comparable to vanilla attention when training the model from scratch. In this set-up, several recently-proposed approaches have also reported competitive performances (Tay et al., 2021). Now, we consider a different and more practical setup, where the starting point is using an already pre-trained language model (Devlin et al., 2019; Raffel et al., 2020). As such models were trained using vanilla attention, replacing it with a new attention variant typically requires a corrective pre-training stage to allow the model weights to adjust

k	AI2 elem.	AI2 mid.	ARC easy	ARC chal.	BoolQ	CSQA	MCTest	NarQA	OBQA	RACE	SQuAD v1	SQuAD 2.0
64	82.9	77.6	79.3	71.6	88.7	72.4	92.8	30.5	77.4	83.5	86.1	82.0
128	87.8	81.6	83.5	72.2	89.7	74.8	**93.1**	31.6	80.0	85.8	86.8	84.3
256	91.1	**84.0**	85.3	75.6	90.0	75.9	92.8	32.1	**85.4**	86.8	86.8	85.7
512	91.1	84.0	85.4	75.9	90.4	77.0	93.1	**32.3**	83.6	87.2	86.9	86.2
1024	**91.9**	83.2	**86.3**	**76.3**	90.7	77.2	93.1	32.3	85.0	87.3	**87.0**	**86.3**
2048	91.9	82.4	85.8	75.9	**90.8**	77.2	93.1	32.3	85.0	87.3	87.0	86.3
4096	91.9	82.4	86.0	75.6	90.8	**77.6**	93.1	32.3	85.2	**87.4**	87.0	86.3
65536 (vanilla)	91.9	82.4	86.0	75.6	90.7	77.5	93.1	32.3	85.2	87.4	87.0	86.3

Table 2: Exact match scores of UNIFIEDQA on development sets with top-k attention at feed-forward layers. *Notation*: AI2 science elementary (AI2 elem.), AI2 science middle (AI2 mid.), ARC challenging (ARC chal.), CommonsenseQA (CSQA), NarrativeQA (NarQA), OpenbookQA (OBQA).

to the new variant, which can be expensive for large models. For example, (Gupta and Berant, 2021; Peng et al., 2021) have shown that using random features *without* corrective pre-training leads to high error rates in a language modeling task. Moreover, as explained in §2.1, most past methods are incompatible with feed-forward layers. In the subsequent experiments we show that it is possible to replace vanilla with top-k attention, at multi-head attention and feed-forward layers, and perform inference and fine-tuning without any need for such correction.

First, we compare the performance of UNIFIEDQA (Khashabi et al., 2020) before and after replacing its feed-forward layers with our implementation of top-k attention and directly performing inference on 12 different question answering (QA) datasets without any training. UNIFIEDQA is a T5-based (Raffel et al., 2020) model with 11B parameters (Raffel et al., 2020), fine-tuned on a weighted mixture of QA datasets. The 12 datasets include diverse domains, such as science questions, factoid questions over Wikipedia, commonsense questions, etc. Details regarding the datasets and metrics can be found in §A.2.

Table 2 shows the results for increasing values of k, where the feed-forward dimension of the model is $65,536$. We observe that already when $k = 256$ and $k = 512$, i.e., less than 1% of the number of keys, performance is comparable to vanilla Transformer. When $k = 4,096$ (6% of the number of keys), performance is equal or better than vanilla Transformer on all tasks. This highlights the plug-and-play property of top-k attention, which can be used without *any* additional training.

4.4 Zero-shot Inference with BERT

To verify that the plug-and-play property of top-k attention also holds at self-attention layers, we downloaded a BERT-large-uncased-whole-word-masking checkpoint (Devlin et al., 2019) already fine-tuned on SQuAD v1 (Rajpurkar et al., 2016) and evaluated its performance on the development set before and after replacing its self-attention layers with top-k attention. For k as low as 16 (4% of input length), we only saw a minor decrease in the exact match scores ($86.9 \rightarrow 86.2$). Moreover, to empirically verify that dense approximations of vanilla attention (Performer, RFA, etc) indeed require corrective pre-training, we repeated the measurement using Performer attention with 256 features, obtaining a score of 0.38.

4.5 T5 Finetuning

Having established the plug-and-play property of top-k attention in zero-shot inference (§4.3, §4.4), we now show the effectiveness of top-k attention when fine-tuning a model, and that there are no unforeseen issues stemming from training under high sprasity. Here, we use T5-base rather than T5-11B and evaluate on five QA datasets (and not 12) due to computational constraints.

Similar to §4.3, we replace the feed-forward layers of T5-base, which has feed-forward dimension 3072, with our implementation of top-256 attention and fine-tuned on multiple QA datasets. As summarized in Table 3, we found that the performance of top-256 attention was again comparable to vanilla attention on BoolQ, CommonsenseQA and ROPES with a minor loss in performance on MCTest ($81.2 \rightarrow 79.4$) and OpenbookQA ($58.8 \rightarrow 58.0$).

	BoolQ	CSQA	MCTest	OBQA	ROPES
T5-base	0.5	35.7	36.6	17.0	21.7
UNIFIEDQA-base	82.0	45.0	85.3	59.6	26.3
T5-base + finetuning	83.3	61.9	81.2	58.8	54.0
T5-base, top-256 + finetuning	83.1	62.0	79.4	58.0	53.8

Table 3: Exact match scores on development sets. "Finetuning" denotes model was finetuned on the dataset, else it was evaluated directly without any training. All models use vanilla feed-forward layers except the ones that say top-256 (§4.5).

To summarize, our experiments in §4.1-§4.5 demonstrated that the performance of vanilla attention and top-k attention is comparable at both multi-head attention (§4.1, §4.4) and feed-forward layers in multiple set-ups including training from scratch (§4.1, §4.2), fine-tuning (§4.5) and zero-shot inference (§4.3, §4.4), while dramatically improving memory usage, as shown in §3.

5 Discussion

Related work Our work follows a long line of works on efficient Transformers (see §1). Our method employs three main ideas: (a) computing the top-k attention scores for each query (b) grouping the queries into chunks and processing these sequentially (c) caching only a part of the activations for the backward pass. Top-k operation was used at self-attention layers by (Zhao et al., 2019) to show improved model performance, attributed to the removal of irrelevant information in the context. We use it to reduce the resource usage of multi-head attention and feed-forward layers. Processing query chunks sequentially was also used in Reformer (Kitaev et al., 2020) as activations are not cached. But in that case, by replacing vanilla residual connections in the Transformer with reversible connections (Gomez et al., 2017). Similar to the explanation provided in §2.2, these require an extra implicit forward pass during the backward pass and do not provide the compute and memory savings we get from our top-k specific backward pass (§2.2). Secondly, replacing residual connections with reversible ones changes the function computed by the model and would require corrective pre-training to be used with BERT, T5, etc (§4.3-§4.5).

Limitations and future work As our method requires computing inner products of all queries and keys, it has a quadratic compute requirement. As seen in our pseudo-code (§2.2), there are *four* matrix products (Lines 8, 15, 21, 25) involving a large sparse matrix and a small dense one. The results presented in the benchmarking section (§3) are based on our implementation that does not leverage this sparsity and hence is as slow as vanilla attention.

Leveraging sparsity of matrices We considered the option of performing matrix products involving large sparse matrices (Lines 8, 15, 21, 25 in our pseudo-code (§2.2)) by representing them in PyTorch's `torch.sparse_coo_tensor` format and using the `torch.sparse` framework to explicitly leverage their sparsity for saving compute. Unfortunately, the results were not encouraging even for $k = 1\%$ of number of keys (Figure 4). While future devices might allow faster sparse-dense products, in the immediate future, one can leverage block-sparse kernels (Child et al., 2019; Tillet et al., 2019) which have been successfully used for such products (Rasley et al., 2020).

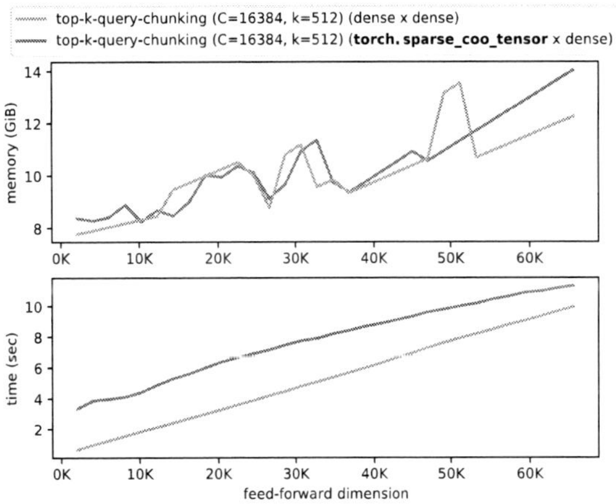

Figure 4: Memory and time required for a combined forward and backward pass on a single feed-forward layer for ***random*** inputs.

Conclusion In this work, we proposed a memory-efficient and accurate sparse approximation of the primary sub-layers of a Transformer, benchmarked the resulting resource savings, and verified its quality and unique advantages, on a wide range of downstream tasks and evaluation set-ups.

Acknowledgments

We thank Achille Fokoue, Maria Chang and Avi Sil for helpful discussions. Most of our experiments were conducted on IBM's Cognitive Computing Cluster with additional resources from Hybrid Cloud Infrastructure Research. This research was partially supported by (1) The Yandex Initiative for Machine Learning, and the European Research Council (ERC) under the European Union Horizons 2020 research and innovation programme (grant ERC DELPHI 802800), and (2) the IBM AI Residency program.

References

Irwan Bello. 2021. Lambdanetworks: Modeling long-range interactions without attention. In *International Conference on Learning Representations*.

Iz Beltagy, Matthew E Peters, and Arman Cohan.

2020. Longformer: The long-document transformer. *arXiv preprint arXiv:2004.05150.*

Tom B. Brown, Benjamin Mann, Nick Ryder, Melanie Subbiah, Jared Kaplan, Prafulla Dhariwal, Arvind Neelakantan, Pranav Shyam, Girish Sastry, Amanda Askell, Sandhini Agarwal, Ariel Herbert-Voss, Gretchen Krueger, Tom Henighan, Rewon Child, Aditya Ramesh, Daniel M. Ziegler, Jeffrey Wu, Clemens Winter, Christopher Hesse, Mark Chen, Eric Sigler, Mateusz Litwin, Scott Gray, Benjamin Chess, Jack Clark, Christopher Berner, Sam McCandlish, Alec Radford, Ilya Sutskever, and Dario Amodei. 2020. Language models are few-shot learners. In *Advances in Neural Information Processing Systems 33: Annual Conference on Neural Information Processing Systems 2020, NeurIPS 2020, December 6-12, 2020, virtual.*

T. Chen, B. Xu, C. Zhang, and Carlos Guestrin. 2016. Training deep nets with sublinear memory cost. *ArXiv*, abs/1604.06174.

Rewon Child, Scott Gray, Alec Radford, and Ilya Sutskever. 2019. Generating long sequences with sparse transformers. *arXiv preprint arXiv:1904.10509.*

Krzysztof Marcin Choromanski, Valerii Likhosherstov, David Dohan, Xingyou Song, Andreea Gane, Tamas Sarlos, Peter Hawkins, Jared Quincy Davis, Afroz Mohiuddin, Lukasz Kaiser, David Benjamin Belanger, Lucy J Colwell, and Adrian Weller. 2021. Rethinking attention with performers. In *International Conference on Learning Representations.*

Christopher Clark, Kenton Lee, Ming-Wei Chang, Tom Kwiatkowski, Michael Collins, and Kristina Toutanova. 2019. BoolQ: Exploring the surprising difficulty of natural yes/no questions. In *Proceedings of the 2019 Conference of the North American Chapter of the Association for Computational Linguistics: Human Language Technologies, Volume 1 (Long and Short Papers)*, pages 2924–2936. Association for Computational Linguistics.

Peter Clark. 2015. Elementary school science and math tests as a driver for AI: take the aristo challenge! In *Proceedings of the Twenty-Ninth AAAI Conference on Artificial Intelligence, January 25-30, 2015, Austin, Texas, USA*, pages 4019–4021. AAAI Press.

Peter Clark, Isaac Cowhey, Oren Etzioni, Tushar Khot, Ashish Sabharwal, Carissa Schoenick, and Oyvind Tafjord. 2018. Think you have solved question answering? try ARC, the AI2 reasoning challenge. *ArXiv*, abs/1803.05457.

Jacob Devlin, Ming-Wei Chang, Kenton Lee, and Kristina Toutanova. 2019. BERT: Pre-training of deep bidirectional transformers for language understanding. In *Proceedings of the 2019 Conference of the North American Chapter of the Association for Computational Linguistics: Human Language Technologies, Volume 1 (Long and Short Papers)*, pages 4171–4186. Association for Computational Linguistics.

Sergey Edunov, Myle Ott, Michael Auli, and David Grangier. 2018. Understanding back-translation at scale. In *Proceedings of the 2018 Conference on Empirical Methods in Natural Language Processing*, pages 489–500. Association for Computational Linguistics.

W. Fedus, Barret Zoph, and Noam M. Shazeer. 2021. Switch transformers: Scaling to trillion parameter models with simple and efficient sparsity. *ArXiv*, abs/2101.03961.

Mor Geva, R. Schuster, Jonathan Berant, and Omer Levy. 2020. Transformer feed-forward layers are key-value memories. *ArXiv*, abs/2012.14913.

Aidan N. Gomez, Mengye Ren, Raquel Urtasun, and Roger B. Grosse. 2017. The reversible residual network: Backpropagation without storing activations. In *Advances in Neural Information Processing Systems 30: Annual Conference on Neural Information Processing Systems 2017, December 4-9, 2017, Long Beach, CA, USA*, pages 2214–2224.

Ankit Gupta and Jonathan Berant. 2020. GMAT: Global memory augmentation for transformers. *arXiv preprint arXiv:2006.03274.*

Ankit Gupta and Jonathan Berant. 2021. Value-aware approximate attention. *ArXiv*, abs/2103.09857.

John Hewitt and Christopher D. Manning. 2019. A structural probe for finding syntax in word representations. In *Proceedings of the 2019 Conference of the North American Chapter of the Association for Computational Linguistics: Human Language Technologies, Volume 1 (Long and Short Papers)*, pages 4129–4138. Association for Computational Linguistics.

Vladimir Karpukhin, Barlas Oguz, Sewon Min, Patrick Lewis, Ledell Wu, Sergey Edunov, Danqi Chen, and Wen-tau Yih. 2020. Dense passage retrieval for open-domain question answering. In *Proceedings of the 2020 Conference on Empirical Methods in Natural Language Processing (EMNLP)*, pages 6769–6781. Association for Computational Linguistics.

Angelos Katharopoulos, Apoorv Vyas, Nikolaos Pappas, and François Fleuret. 2020. Transformers are RNNs: Fast autoregressive transformers with linear attention. In *Proceedings of the 37th International Conference on Machine Learning, ICML 2020, 13-18 July 2020, Virtual Event*, volume 119 of *Proceedings of Machine Learning Research*, pages 5156–5165. PMLR.

Daniel Khashabi, Sewon Min, Tushar Khot, Ashish Sabharwal, Oyvind Tafjord, Peter Clark, and Hannaneh Hajishirzi. 2020. UNIFIEDQA: Crossing format boundaries with a single QA system. In *Findings of the Association for Computational Linguistics: EMNLP 2020*, pages 1896–1907. Association for Computational Linguistics.

Nikita Kitaev, Lukasz Kaiser, and Anselm Levskaya. 2020. Reformer: The efficient transformer. In *8th International Conference on Learning Representations, ICLR 2020, Addis Ababa, Ethiopia, April 26-30, 2020*. OpenReview.net.

Tomáš Kočiský, Jonathan Schwarz, Phil Blunsom, Chris Dyer, Karl Moritz Hermann, Gábor Melis, and Edward Grefenstette. 2018. The NarrativeQA reading comprehension challenge. *Transactions of the Association for Computational Linguistics*, 6:317–328.

Guokun Lai, Qizhe Xie, Hanxiao Liu, Yiming Yang, and Eduard Hovy. 2017. RACE: Large-scale ReAding comprehension dataset from examinations. In *Proceedings of the 2017 Conference on Empirical Methods in Natural Language Processing*, pages 785–794. Association for Computational Linguistics.

Kevin Lin, Oyvind Tafjord, Peter Clark, and Matt Gardner. 2019. Reasoning over paragraph effects in situations. In *Proceedings of the 2nd Workshop on Machine Reading for Question Answering*, pages 58–62. Association for Computational Linguistics.

Andrew L. Maas, Raymond E. Daly, Peter T. Pham, Dan Huang, Andrew Y. Ng, and Christopher Potts. 2011. Learning word vectors for sentiment analysis. In *Proceedings of the 49th Annual Meeting of the Association for Computational Linguistics: Human Language Technologies*, pages 142–150. Association for Computational Linguistics.

Stephen Merity, Caiming Xiong, James Bradbury, and Richard Socher. 2017. Pointer sentinel mixture models. In *5th International Conference on Learning Representations, ICLR 2017, Toulon, France, April 24-26, 2017, Conference Track Proceedings*. OpenReview.net.

Todor Mihaylov, Peter Clark, Tushar Khot, and Ashish Sabharwal. 2018. Can a suit of armor conduct electricity? a new dataset for open book question answering. In *Proceedings of the 2018 Conference on Empirical Methods in Natural Language Processing*, pages 2381–2391. Association for Computational Linguistics.

Nikita Nangia and Samuel Bowman. 2018. ListOps: A diagnostic dataset for latent tree learning. In *Proceedings of the 2018 Conference of the North American Chapter of the Association for Computational Linguistics: Student Research Workshop*, pages 92–99. Association for Computational Linguistics.

Hao Peng, Nikolaos Pappas, Dani Yogatama, Roy Schwartz, Noah Smith, and Lingpeng Kong. 2021. Random feature attention. In *International Conference on Learning Representations*.

Matthew Peters, Mark Neumann, Mohit Iyyer, Matt Gardner, Christopher Clark, Kenton Lee, and Luke Zettlemoyer. 2018. Deep contextualized word representations. In *Proceedings of the 2018 Conference of the North American Chapter of the Association for Computational Linguistics: Human Language Technologies, Volume 1 (Long Papers)*, pages 2227–2237. Association for Computational Linguistics.

Fabio Petroni, Tim Rocktäschel, Sebastian Riedel, Patrick Lewis, Anton Bakhtin, Yuxiang Wu, and Alexander Miller. 2019. Language models as knowledge bases? In *Proceedings of the 2019 Conference on Empirical Methods in Natural Language Processing and the 9th International Joint Conference on Natural Language Processing (EMNLP-IJCNLP)*, pages 2463–2473. Association for Computational Linguistics.

Jiezhong Qiu, Hao Ma, Omer Levy, Wen-tau Yih, Sinong Wang, and Jie Tang. 2020. Blockwise self-attention for long document understanding. In *Findings of the Association for Computational Linguistics: EMNLP 2020*, pages 2555–2565. Association for Computational Linguistics.

Dragomir R. Radev, Pradeep Muthukrishnan, Vahed Qazvinian, and Amjad Abu-Jbara. 2013. The ACL anthology network corpus. *Language Resources and Evaluation*, 47:919–944.

Colin Raffel, Noam Shazeer, Adam Roberts, Katherine Lee, Sharan Narang, Michael Matena, Yanqi Zhou, Wei Li, and Peter J. Liu. 2020. Exploring the limits of transfer learning with a unified text-to-text transformer. *J. Mach. Learn. Res.*, 21:140:1–140:67.

Pranav Rajpurkar, Robin Jia, and Percy Liang. 2018. Know what you don't know: Unanswerable questions for SQuAD. In *Proceedings of the 56th Annual Meeting of the Association for Computational Linguistics (Volume 2: Short Papers)*, pages 784–789. Association for Computational Linguistics.

Pranav Rajpurkar, Jian Zhang, Konstantin Lopyrev, and Percy Liang. 2016. SQuAD: 100,000+ questions for machine comprehension of text. In *Proceedings of the 2016 Conference on Empirical Methods in Natural Language Processing*, pages 2383–2392. Association for Computational Linguistics.

Jeff Rasley, Samyam Rajbhandari, Olatunji Ruwase, and Yuxiong He. 2020. Deepspeed: System optimizations enable training deep learning models with over 100 billion parameters. In *KDD '20: The 26th ACM SIGKDD Conference on Knowledge Discovery and Data Mining, Virtual Event, CA, USA, August 23-27, 2020*, pages 3505–3506. ACM.

Matthew Richardson, Christopher J.C. Burges, and Erin Renshaw. 2013. MCTest: A challenge dataset for the open-domain machine comprehension of text. In *Proceedings of the 2013 Conference on Empirical Methods in Natural Language Processing*, pages 193–203. Association for Computational Linguistics.

Adam Roberts, Colin Raffel, and Noam Shazeer. 2020. How much knowledge can you pack into the parameters of a language model? In *Proceedings of the*

2020 Conference on Empirical Methods in Natural Language Processing (EMNLP)*, pages 5418–5426. Association for Computational Linguistics.

Aurko Roy, Mohammad Saffar, Ashish Vaswani, and David Grangier. 2021. Efficient content-based sparse attention with routing transformers. *Transactions of the Association for Computational Linguistics*, 9:53–68.

Noam M. Shazeer. 2020. GLU variants improve transformer. *ArXiv*, abs/2002.05202.

Sainbayar Sukhbaatar, Edouard Grave, Guillaume Lample, H. Jégou, and Armand Joulin. 2019. Augmenting self-attention with persistent memory. *ArXiv*, abs/1907.01470.

Alon Talmor, Jonathan Herzig, Nicholas Lourie, and Jonathan Berant. 2019. CommonsenseQA: A question answering challenge targeting commonsense knowledge. In *Proceedings of the 2019 Conference of the North American Chapter of the Association for Computational Linguistics: Human Language Technologies, Volume 1 (Long and Short Papers)*, pages 4149–4158. Association for Computational Linguistics.

Yi Tay, Dara Bahri, Liu Yang, Donald Metzler, and Da-Cheng Juan. 2020a. Sparse sinkhorn attention. In *Proceedings of the 37th International Conference on Machine Learning, ICML 2020, 13-18 July 2020, Virtual Event*, volume 119 of *Proceedings of Machine Learning Research*, pages 9438–9447. PMLR.

Yi Tay, M. Dehghani, Dara Bahri, and Donald Metzler. 2020b. Efficient transformers: A survey. *ArXiv*, abs/2009.06732.

Yi Tay, Mostafa Dehghani, Samira Abnar, Yikang Shen, Dara Bahri, Philip Pham, Jinfeng Rao, Liu Yang, Sebastian Ruder, and Donald Metzler. 2021. Long Range Arena : A benchmark for efficient transformers. In *International Conference on Learning Representations*.

Philippe Tillet, H. Kung, and D. Cox. 2019. Triton: an intermediate language and compiler for tiled neural network computations. *Proceedings of the 3rd ACM SIGPLAN International Workshop on Machine Learning and Programming Languages*.

Ashish Vaswani, Noam Shazeer, Niki Parmar, Jakob Uszkoreit, Llion Jones, Aidan N. Gomez, Lukasz Kaiser, and Illia Polosukhin. 2017. Attention is all you need. In *Advances in Neural Information Processing Systems 30: Annual Conference on Neural Information Processing Systems 2017, December 4-9, 2017, Long Beach, CA, USA*, pages 5998–6008.

A. Vyas, A. Katharopoulos, and F. Fleuret. 2020. Fast transformers with clustered attention. In *Proceedings of the International Conference on Neural Information Processing Systems (NeurIPS)*.

Sinong Wang, Belinda Z. Li, Madian Khabsa, Han Fang, and Hao Ma. 2020. Linformer: Self-attention with linear complexity. *ArXiv*, abs/2006.04768.

Thomas Wolf, Lysandre Debut, Victor Sanh, Julien Chaumond, Clement Delangue, Anthony Moi, Pierric Cistac, Tim Rault, R'emi Louf, Morgan Funtowicz, and Jamie Brew. 2019. Huggingface's transformers: State-of-the-art natural language processing. *ArXiv*, abs/1910.03771.

Zihao Ye, Qipeng Guo, Quan Gan, Xipeng Qiu, and Zheng Zhang. 2019. BP-Transformer: Modelling long-range context via binary partitioning. *arXiv preprint arXiv:1911.04070*.

Gilad Yehudai and Ohad Shamir. 2019. On the power and limitations of random features for understanding neural networks. In *Advances in Neural Information Processing Systems 32: Annual Conference on Neural Information Processing Systems 2019, NeurIPS 2019, December 8-14, 2019, Vancouver, BC, Canada*, pages 6594–6604.

Manzil Zaheer, Guru Guruganesh, Kumar Avinava Dubey, Joshua Ainslie, Chris Alberti, Santiago Ontanon, Philip Pham, Anirudh Ravula, Qifan Wang, Li Yang, et al. 2020. Big Bird: Transformers for longer sequences. *Advances in Neural Information Processing Systems*, 33.

Guangxiang Zhao, Junyang Lin, Zhiyuan Zhang, Xuancheng Ren, Qi Su, and X. Sun. 2019. Explicit sparse transformer: Concentrated attention through explicit selection. *ArXiv*, abs/1912.11637.

A Supplemental Material

A.1 Details of Long Range Arena

ListOps (Nangia and Bowman, 2018) aims to diagnose the capability of modelling hierarchically structured data. Given a sequence of operations on single-digit integers, the model predicts the solution, also a single-digit integer modeled as a 10-way classification. Character-level text classification with the IMDb movie review dataset (Maas et al., 2011) is a binary sentiment classification task. In the character-level document retrieval with the ACL Anthology Network (AAN) (Radev et al., 2013), the model classifies if there is a citation between a pair of papers.

We used the code and pre-processed data provided by the authors of Long Range Arena (Tay et al., 2021) and default model configurations. For each task, we used identical hyperparameters for vanilla and top-k attentions (Table 4) and used at most two Nvidia A100 for each run.

Hyperparameter Notation BSZ: effective batch size, SQL: input sequence length, LR: learning rate, WRM: linear LR warm-up steps, STEP: number of gradient updates, EFQ: evaluated every these many steps, NL: number of layers in encoder/decoder, HS: hidden size, FF: feed-forward dimension, NH: number of heads, VOC: vocabulary size, DRP: dropout rate, CLIP: maximum gradient norm.

A.2 Details of UNIFIEDQA inference & T5 finetuning

We used Hugging Face's Transformers library (Wolf et al., 2019) for these experiments. Authors of UNIFIEDQA collected and pre-processed several QA datasets into a common format: "QUESTION \n CHOICES \n CONTEXT". We downloaded this data by following the instructions provided by the authors[3] and used it for the UNIFIEDQA inference experiments (§4.3). Some statistics are shown in Table 5. Longer inputs were truncated to 512 tokens.

Given an instance from the pre-processed data, we computed the exact match score of a prediction with respect to the list of provided answers via the SQuAD v1 evaluation script (Rajpurkar et al., 2016).

For the T5 experiments (§4.5), we used a slightly different input format. Given an instance in the UNIFIEDQA format, we formed the modified instance as "question: QUESTION context: <yes> <no> <No Answer> CHOICES \n CONTEXT".

A.3 Language Modeling on WikiText-103

WikiText-103 is a language modeling task based on English Wikipedia. We used the language modeling framework provided by Faiseq[4] and hyperparameters in Table 7. The details of Adam optimizer are β_1=0.9, β_2=0.98, weight-decay: 0.01, CLIP: none, LR schedule: inverse square root. During evaluation on test set, dataset is chunked into segments of length 1024 and perplexity is computed over each segment normally without access to other segments.

A.4 Benchmarking details

Benchmarking (§3) was done in PyTorch 1.8.1. For each run, we sampled a batch of random 32-bit input vectors and a backward pass was performed using the mean of the output elements as the loss. The part of code that was timed was enclosed within `torch.cuda.synchronize()` to ensure all CUDA threads finished. Memory usage was measured using `torch.cuda.max_memory_reserved()`. On Nvidia A100, any internal casting to TF32 was explicitly disabled.

[3] https://github.com/allenai/unifiedqa

[4] https://github.com/pytorch/fairseq

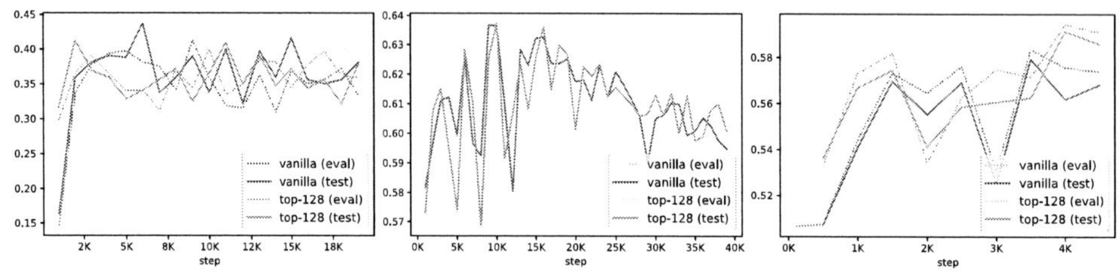

(a) ListOps (b) IMDb (c) AAN

Figure 5: Learning curves of vanilla and top-128 attention on Long Range Arena (§4.1).

task	BSZ	SQL	LR	WRM	STEP	EFQ	NL	HS	FF	NH
ListOps	16	2K	0.02	1K	20K	1K	6	512	2048	8
IMDb	32	1K	0.03	8K	40K	1K	4	256	1024	4
AAN	8	4K	0.05	8K	5K	500	4	128	512	4

Table 4: Hyperparameters for LRA tasks (§4.1). Other hyperparameters were used as provided at `https://github.com/google-research/long-range-arena`.

		training samples	eval samples	T5 tokens per sample (90th percentile)
CSQA	(Talmor et al., 2019)	9741	1221	54
OBQA	(Mihaylov et al., 2018)	4957	500	60
ARC easy	(Clark et al., 2018)	2251	570	90
AI2 elem.	(Clark, 2015)	623	123	96
ARC chal.	(Clark et al., 2018)	1119	299	101
BoolQ	(Clark et al., 2019)	9427	3270	253
SQuAD 2.0	(Rajpurkar et al., 2018)	130124	11873	294
SQuAD v1	(Rajpurkar et al., 2016)	87489	10570	295
ROPES	(Lin et al., 2019)	10924	1688	345
MCTest	(Richardson et al., 2013)	1480	320	435
RACE	(Lai et al., 2017)	87860	4887	568
NarQA	(Kočiský et al., 2018)	65494	6922	1278

Table 5: Statistics of the pre-processed datasets used in §4.3 and §4.5.

dataset	BSZ	LR	STEP	SQL	CLIP
CSQA	576	5e-5	3K	512	1
OBQA	512	5e-5	3K	512	1
BoolQ	80	5e-5	3K	512	1
MCTest	80	5e-5	3K	512	1
ROPES	80	5e-5	3K	512	1

Table 6: Hyperparameters for T5-base finetuning (§4.5). Trainings were performed on a single Nvidia V100 using Adam optimizer with a constant LR and evaluation was done only at end of training.

BSZ	SQL	LR	WRM	STEP	NL	HS	FF	NH	VOC	DRP
64	1024	5e-4	4K	50K	6	512	2048	8	267744	0.1

Table 7: Hyperparameters for WikiText-103 task (§4.2).

BioCopy: A Plug-And-Play Span Copy Mechanism in Seq2Seq Models

Yi Liu [1], Guoan Zhang [2], Puning Yu [3], Jianlin Su [4], Shengfeng Pan [4]
[1] RMIT University, Melbourne, Australia
[2] King's College London, the United Kingdom
[3] South China University of Technology, China
[4] Shenzhen Zhuiyi Technology Co., Ltd., China
yiliumelai@gmail.com, guoan.zhang@kcl.ac.uk,
ypn20010116@163.com, {bojonesu,nickpan}@wezhuiyi.com

Abstract

Copy mechanisms explicitly obtain unchanged tokens from the source (input) sequence to generate the target (output) sequence under the neural seq2seq framework. However, most of the existing copy mechanisms only consider single word copying from the source sentences, which results in losing essential tokens while copying long spans. In this work, we propose a plug-and-play architecture, namely BioCopy, to alleviate the problem aforementioned. Specifically, in the training stage, we construct a BIO tag for each token and train the original model with BIO tags jointly. In the inference stage, the model will firstly predict the BIO tag at each time step, then conduct different mask strategies based on the predicted BIO label to diminish the scope of the probability distributions over the vocabulary list. Experimental results on two separate generative tasks show that they all outperform the baseline models by adding our BioCopy to the original model structure.

1 Introduction

Recent neural seq2seq systems have been successful in various NLP tasks which utilize an encoder to convert a source sentence into a fixed vector, and a decoder to generate a target sentence by using the semantic information amongst the fixed vectors. However, seq2seq suffers from the out-of-vocabulary and rare word problem(Luong et al., 2015; Gulcehre et al., 2016) that words in source sentence are not able to be obtained to generate the target sentence. Due to this problem, (He et al., 2016; Srivastava et al., 2015), propose the so-called 'copy mechanism' where it locates certain words in the input sentence and put these words into the target sequence. In their work, every output word can be generated either by predicting from the vocabulary or copying from the source sequence. Unfortunately, most of them copy the words from the source sentence to the target sentence in a word-by-word manner. However, in many cases, the copied words are generated consecutively from a span in the source sequence.

In this paper, we propose a novel and portable copy mechanism to solve the problem of low accuracy when copying spans in the seq2seq framework. To implement this new copy mechanism, we propose a BIO-tagged strategy that annotates the target sequences with BIO tags by matching the longest common subsequence (LCS) with the source sequence. Therefore, the BIO tags are able to exactly locate the start and end position of every single span in target sequences. In the inference stage, we design a span extractor to determine copying spans from the source sequence. Specifically, the BIO tag is firstly predicted at each time step to indicate the position of the copied span, then we decide a copy algorithm to guide the span extractor by generating the eligible n-gram set.

Since our method does not change the structure of the model itself, this BioCopy can be seen as a plug-and-play component, which is simple and effective enough to transfer and apply to any generative seq2seq framework. The experimental results in generative relation extraction and abstractive summarization tasks indicate the effectiveness of our proposed copy mechanism.

2 Approach

The conventional seq2seq framework generates one token at each time step. Therefore, given the predicted token sequence, the mode decoder predicts the current token by computing the probability distribution over the entire vocabulary list:

$$y_t = p(y_t | y_{<t}, x) \tag{1}$$

In our case, we add an extra sequence prediction task to the model decoder. Specifically, the former decoder just models the distribution on each token, but the current decoder predicts an additional label

Proceedings of the 2nd Workshop on Simple and Efficient Natural Language Processing, pages 53–57
November 10, 2021. ©201 Association for Computational Linguistics

distribution:

$$y_t, z_t = p(y_t, z_t|y_{<t}, x) = p(y_t|y_{<t}, x)p(z_t|y_{<t}, x) \tag{2}$$

where $z \in \{B, I, O\}$. The meaning is as follows:

- **B** indicates the current token is copied from the source sentence.
- **I** indicates the current token is copied and forms a continuous fragment with the previous token from source sentence.
- **O** indicates the current token is not copied, but generated from the vocabulary list.

BIO-tag Building As we mentioned above, we utilize the supervised method to train the BIO tag z. In order to acquire the labels, we compute the longest common subsequence (Paterson and Dancík, 1994) between the source sentence and target sentence. The token will be considered as copied from source sentence as long as it appears in the longest common subsequence, and different tags are assigned according to the specific meaning of BIO. In summary, in the training phase, besides the original token sequence prediction task, we also introduce one more sequence prediction task, of which the tags are all given. It is easy to implement and does not add any extra computational cost. The loss function $\mathcal{L}$ is defined as the following:

$$\mathcal{L} = \frac{1}{NT} \sum^{N} \sum_{i}^{T} y_i^{'} \log y_i + z_i^{'} \log z_i \tag{3}$$

where $y^{'}$ and $z^{'}$ denotes gold label of token sequence and BIO-tag sequence, T is the sequence length and N is the batch size. y and z denotes predicted label.

Inference In the inference stage, at each time step, we first predict the BIO-tag z_t, the result will be one of three circumstances: if $z_t = O$, we do not need to change anything. If $z_t = B$, we mask all the token probability distributions of which they are not in the source sentence. If $z_t = I$, it indicates the token sequence from current token to its nearest token with $z_t = B$ constitutes a consecutive n-gram from source sentence. Therefore, we mask all the tokens in the token probability distribution that cannot constitute the corresponding n-gram in the source sentence. In this way, the model decoder still generates tokens in a step-by-step manner, rather than generating a segment at one time step. According to utilise the mask operation, the tokens where their $z_t = B$ or $z_t = O$ are selected from a segment in the input sentence. A detailed example has been shown in Figure 1 for illustration.

It should be pointed out that the proposed copy mechanism can not only improve the model performance in terms of long-span extraction, but also ensures the consistency between the generated text and the original text, thereby avoiding professional errors, which is quite necessary for practical use.

3 Experiment

3.1 Generative Relation Extraction

Generative relation extraction tackles the conventional relation extraction problem by utilizing the seq2seq framework. At each time step, the model decoder either predicts the relation or copy a token from the input sentence. We focus on the task of extracting multiple tuples from sentences. We choose the New York Times (NYT) corpus(Zeng et al., 2018) for our experiments. The detailed statistics are listed in Table 1. Intuitively, the model capability of extracting long-span entities can be boosted by adding the proposed BioCopy.

	Train	Test
examples	56,000	5,000
triplets	88,366	8,120
2 token	37,352	3,335
3 token	6,362	566
3+ tokens	1,259	112

Table 1: Statistics of train/test split of the NYT. n-token denotes the number of examples that contain n-token entities.

Baselines We compare our model performance with the following state-of-the-art relation extraction models. **Tagging**(Zheng et al., 2017) is a neural sequence labeling model which jointly extracts the entities and relations using an LSTM encoder and an LSTM decoder. **CopyR**(Zeng et al., 2018) uses an encoder-decoder framework to extract entities and relations jointly. **GraphR**(Fu et al., 2019) models each token in a sentence as a node, and edges connecting the nodes as relations between them, they adopt the graph neural network to predict the relation triplets. **Ngram-att** uses an encoder-decoder framework with a n-gram attention layer. The encoder takes source sequence as input and decoder produces entity and relation IDs from Wikidata(Vrandečić and Krötzsch,

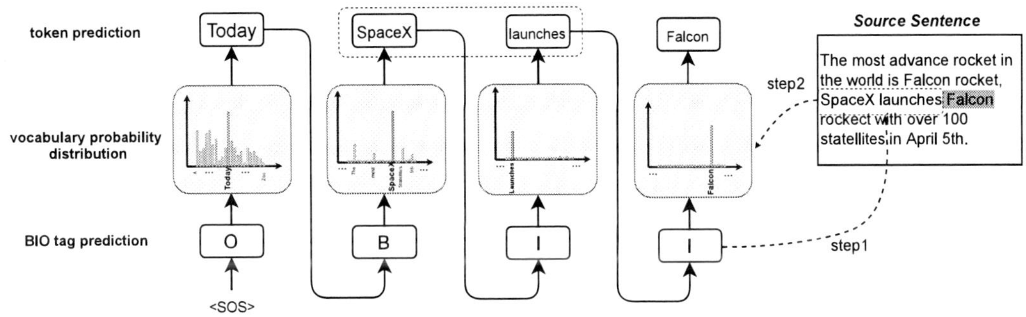

Figure 1: The workflow of model decoder in the inference stage: in order to predict the current token 'Falcon', the model firstly predicts its BIO = I, which indicates the current token constitutes a 3-gram with the predicted tokens 'SpaceX', 'launches'. Then, we search the potential 3-grams from the source sentence, and the 'Falcon' is the only valid candidate. Finally, the token probability distributions except 'Falcon' are all masked as zero.

2014). **WordDec** and **PointerDec** are both originated from (Nayak and Ng, 2020), where they use both word decoder and pointerNet as model decoder.

Model Details Since WordDec (Nayak and Ng, 2020) is the state-of-the-art model on the NYT dataset, thus we select WordDec as our backbone model and all the model details are aligned with the original settings. Concretely, we initialize the word vectors by using Word2Vec(Mikolov et al., 2013). We set the word embedding dimension $d_w = 300$ and relation embedding dimension $d_r = 300$, the hidden dimension d_h of the LSTM cell is set at 300. The model is trained with the mini-batch size of 32 and the network parameters are optimized using Adam(Kingma and Ba, 2015). Dropout layers with a dropout rate fixed at 0.3 are used in our network to avoid overfitting.

Models	Precision	Recall	F1 score
Tagging	62.4%	31.7%	42.0%
CopyR	61.0%	56.6%	58.7%
GraphR	63.9%	60.0%	61.9%
Ngram-att	78.3%	69.8%	73.8%
PointerDec	80.6%	77.3%	78.9%
WordDec	**88.1%**	76.1%	81.7%
Our model	87.7%	**77.7%**	**82.4%**

Table 2: Performance comparison on NYT24 dataset

Result We run the model with the above experimental settings, and we get the result as shown in Table 2. Our model outperforms the state-of-the-art methods 0.4% by recall and 0.7% by F1 score respectively.

To further verify the effectiveness of the proposed BioCopy, We conduct the ablation experiment, and the results are presented in Table 3. To be more specific, we firstly use a raw seq2seq model without any involvement of copy mechanism. Then, we add the *Attention Copy* that has been conducted by WordDec (Nayak and Ng, 2020), i.e., if the predicted token is unknown, we will select the token with the highest attention score from the input sentence . As we can see from Table 3, *raw seq2seq* unsurprisingly turns out to be the lowest performance due to the massive prediction of unknown. Adding *Attention Copy* can alleviate the unknown problem, but it is still a lack of capability of extracting long-span entities. By adding our *BioCopy*, the model performance exceeds the other two since our model is able to not only deal with the unknown problem, but extracting the long-span entities properly.

	Precision	Recall	F1 score
Raw Seq2seq	71.4%	59.6%	65.0%
+ Attention Copy	**88.1%**	76.1%	81.7%
+ BioCopy	87.7%	**77.7%**	**82.4%**

Table 3: Model performance with different settings

Table 3 suggests our approach boosts the model performance to some extent. However, it is still not clear how effectively could our method act on multi-token entity extraction. Since the multi-token entities can be regarded as a long span, we speculate that our method can improve the model capability in terms of tackling the multi-token entities, We conduct an auxiliary experiment to verify this. As shown in Table 4, we can notice that the percentage of error cases, which are caused by incorrectly extracting long-span entities, drop from 49.1% to 18.6% by adding our BioCopy where it strongly verifies that the improvement of the model performance in this task is due to the reduction of long-span copy errors.

	Error Percentage
Raw Seq2seq	49.1%
+ Attention Copy	23.7%
+ BioCopy	18.6%

Table 4: Percentage of error cases of extracting long-span entities.

3.2 Auxiliary Experiment

To verify the robustness of our proposed method, we also conduct an auxiliary experiment on abstractive summarization task. Abstractive summarization task aims to generate a new shorter text that conveys the most critical information from the original long text, where it usually requires to generate much longer text spans from the source sentenc, which can be leveraged to further evaluate our BioCopy.

We conducted our experiment on a Chinese legal summarization dataset (CAIL2020) [1], which contains a large number of legal terms. CAIL2020 dataset has 9,484 sample pairs. Each source text contains an average of 2569 words and each summary text contains 283 words.

Baseline and Metrics Recently, pre-training models have achieved promising results when fine-tuned on several text summarization tasks (Dong et al., 2019a; Lewis et al., 2020). We choose NEZHA (Dong et al., 2019a) as our backbone model, which is a large-scale Chinese pre-trained model and is able to encode the input text with any length. For a fair comparison, we convert the original encoder mask of NEZHA to the seq2seq mask as same as the BERT-UniLM (Dong et al., 2019b) used in Table 5. We use ROUGE scores for evaluation, in which Total is calculated as a weighted average of the above scores.

Result In Table 5, we first compare the model performance with BERT-based models. We can notice that BERT model can achieve a better result by utilizing our BioCopy than by just simply using UniLM (Dong et al., 2019b). Since the dataset is in Chinese, we select NEZHA (Dong et al., 2019a) as our backbone model as it is pre-trained on massive Chinese corpus. The results in Table 5 show that

[1]https://github.com/china-ai-law-challenge/CAIL2020/tree/master/sfzy

Models	Rouge-1	Rouge-2	Rouge-L	Total
LSTM-Seq2seq	46.48	30.48	41.80	38.21
BERT-UniLM	63.83	51.29	59.76	57.19
BERT-BioCopy	64.98	53.92	66.54	61.18
NEZHA	70.93	54.38	69.89	63.89
NEZHA-BioCopy	**71.31**	**54.72**	**70.29**	**64.29**

Table 5: Performance comparison on CAIL2020 dataset

the model can gain 71.31 Rouge-1, 54.72 Rouge-2, 70.29 Rouge-L and 64.29 Total, respectively, where it surpasses all the baseline models.

4 Related Work

Generative relation extraction. (Zeng et al., 2018) proposed CopyRE, a joint model based on a copy mechanism, which transforms the joint extraction task into a generation task.(Nayak and Ng, 2020) propose two different encoders. The word decoder generates multiple triplets in a token-by-token manner, and each triplets is distinguished by the special token, while the pointer decoder simply utilizes pointerNet (Vinyals et al., 2015) to generate start and end indexes for each entity. CopyMTL (Zeng et al., 2019) introduced a multi-task framework with a sequence labeling layer in the encoder, to alleviate the problem that CopyRE can only extract the last token in a multi-token entity.

Abstractive summarization. The previous work mainly leverage an encoder-decoder framework by choosing different model structures. (Zhong et al., 2019) utilize Transformers or graph neural network (Wang et al., 2020) for model encoder. Despite most of the previous work conducting the seq2seq model, some works (Wang et al., 2019) deploy a non-autoregressive model decoder to tackle this task, which also shows great effectiveness.

5 Conclusion

In this paper, we propose BioCopy, a plug-and-play copy mechanism to alleviate the long-span copying problem in generative tasks. By adding an extra sequence prediction layer in the training stage, our proposed approach is able to diminish the scope of probability distribution on each token. Experiments in generative relation extraction and abstractive summarization verifies the model's effectiveness.

References

Li Dong, Nan Yang, Wenhui Wang, Furu Wei, Xiaodong Liu, Yu Wang, Jianfeng Gao, Ming Zhou, and Hsiao-Wuen Hon. 2019a. Unified language model pre-training for natural language understanding and generation. In *Advances in Neural Information Processing Systems 32: Annual Conference on Neural Information Processing Systems 2019, NeurIPS 2019, December 8-14, 2019, Vancouver, BC, Canada*, pages 13042–13054.

Li Dong, Nan Yang, Wenhui Wang, Furu Wei, Xiaodong Liu, Yu Wang, Jianfeng Gao, Ming Zhou, and Hsiao-Wuen Hon. 2019b. Unified language model pre-training for natural language understanding and generation. *arXiv preprint arXiv:1905.03197*.

Tsu-Jui Fu, Peng-Hsuan Li, and Wei-Yun Ma. 2019. Graphrel: Modeling text as relational graphs for joint entity and relation extraction. In *Proceedings of the 57th Annual Meeting of the Association for Computational Linguistics*, pages 1409–1418.

Caglar Gulcehre, Sungjin Ahn, Ramesh Nallapati, Bowen Zhou, and Yoshua Bengio. 2016. Pointing the unknown words. In *Proceedings of the 54th Annual Meeting of the Association for Computational Linguistics (Volume 1: Long Papers)*, pages 140–149, Berlin, Germany. Association for Computational Linguistics.

Kaiming He, Xiangyu Zhang, Shaoqing Ren, and Jian Sun. 2016. Deep residual learning for image recognition. In *2016 IEEE Conference on Computer Vision and Pattern Recognition, CVPR 2016, Las Vegas, NV, USA, June 27-30, 2016*, pages 770–778. IEEE Computer Society.

Diederik P. Kingma and Jimmy Ba. 2015. Adam: A method for stochastic optimization. In *3rd International Conference on Learning Representations, ICLR 2015, San Diego, CA, USA, May 7-9, 2015, Conference Track Proceedings*.

Mike Lewis, Yinhan Liu, Naman Goyal, Marjan Ghazvininejad, Abdelrahman Mohamed, Omer Levy, Veselin Stoyanov, and Luke Zettlemoyer. 2020. BART: Denoising sequence-to-sequence pre-training for natural language generation, translation, and comprehension. In *Proceedings of the 58th Annual Meeting of the Association for Computational Linguistics*, pages 7871–7880, Online. Association for Computational Linguistics.

Thang Luong, Ilya Sutskever, Quoc Le, Oriol Vinyals, and Wojciech Zaremba. 2015. Addressing the rare word problem in neural machine translation. In *Proceedings of the 53rd Annual Meeting of the Association for Computational Linguistics and the 7th International Joint Conference on Natural Language Processing (Volume 1: Long Papers)*, pages 11–19, Beijing, China. Association for Computational Linguistics.

Tomás Mikolov, Ilya Sutskever, Kai Chen, Gregory S. Corrado, and Jeffrey Dean. 2013. Distributed representations of words and phrases and their compositionality. In *Advances in Neural Information Processing Systems 26: 27th Annual Conference on Neural Information Processing Systems 2013. Proceedings of a meeting held December 5-8, 2013, Lake Tahoe, Nevada, United States*, pages 3111–3119.

Tapas Nayak and Hwee Tou Ng. 2020. Effective modeling of encoder-decoder architecture for joint entity and relation extraction. In *Proceedings of the AAAI Conference on Artificial Intelligence*, volume 34, pages 8528–8535.

Mike Paterson and Vlado Dancík. 1994. Longest common subsequences. In *Proceedings of the 19th International Symposium on Mathematical Foundations of Computer Science 1994*, MFCS '94, page 127–142, Berlin, Heidelberg. Springer-Verlag.

Rupesh Kumar Srivastava, Klaus Greff, and Jürgen Schmidhuber. 2015. Highway networks. *CoRR*, abs/1505.00387.

Oriol Vinyals, Meire Fortunato, and Navdeep Jaitly. 2015. Pointer Networks. *arXiv e-prints*, page arXiv:1506.03134.

Denny Vrandečić and Markus Krötzsch. 2014. Wikidata: a free collaborative knowledgebase. *Communications of the ACM*, 57(10):78–85.

Danqing Wang, Pengfei Liu, Yining Zheng, Xipeng Qiu, and Xuanjing Huang. 2020. Heterogeneous graph neural networks for extractive document summarization. *arXiv preprint arXiv:2004.12393*.

Danqing Wang, Pengfei Liu, Ming Zhong, Jie Fu, Xipeng Qiu, and Xuanjing Huang. 2019. Exploring domain shift in extractive text summarization. *arXiv preprint arXiv:1908.11664*.

Daojian Zeng, Ranran Haoran Zhang, and Qianying Liu. 2019. CopyMTL: Copy Mechanism for Joint Extraction of Entities and Relations with Multi-Task Learning. *arXiv e-prints*, page arXiv:1911.10438.

Xiangrong Zeng, Daojian Zeng, Shizhu He, Kang Liu, and Jun Zhao. 2018. Extracting relational facts by an end-to-end neural model with copy mechanism. In *Proceedings of the 56th Annual Meeting of the Association for Computational Linguistics (Volume 1: Long Papers)*, pages 506–514, Melbourne, Australia. Association for Computational Linguistics.

Suncong Zheng, Feng Wang, Hongyun Bao, Yuexing Hao, Peng Zhou, and Bo Xu. 2017. Joint extraction of entities and relations based on a novel tagging scheme. *arXiv preprint arXiv:1706.05075*.

Ming Zhong, Danqing Wang, Pengfei Liu, Xipeng Qiu, and Xuanjing Huang. 2019. A closer look at data bias in neural extractive summarization models. *arXiv preprint arXiv:1909.13705*.

Combining Lexical and Dense Retrieval for Computationally Efficient Multi-hop Question Answering

Georgios Sidiropoulos[1], **Nikos Voskarides**[2*], **Svitlana Vakulenko**[1], **Evangelos Kanoulas**[1]
[1] University of Amsterdam, Amsterdam, The Netherlands
[2] Amazon, Barcelona, Spain
g.sidiropoulos@uva.nl, nvvoskar@amazon.com, s.vakulenko@uva.nl, e.kanoulas@uva.nl

Abstract

In simple open-domain question answering (QA), dense retrieval has become one of the standard approaches for retrieving the relevant passages to infer an answer. Recently, dense retrieval also achieved state-of-the-art results in multi-hop QA, where aggregating information from multiple pieces of information and reasoning over them is required. Despite their success, dense retrieval methods are computationally intensive, requiring multiple GPUs to train. In this work, we introduce a hybrid (lexical and dense) retrieval approach that is highly competitive with the state-of-the-art dense retrieval models, while requiring substantially less computational resources. Additionally, we provide an in-depth evaluation of dense retrieval methods on limited computational resource settings, something that is missing from the current literature.

1 Introduction

Multi-hop QA requires retrieval and reasoning over multiple pieces of information (Yang et al., 2018). For instance, consider the multi-hop question: "Where is the multinational company founded by Robert Smith headquartered?". To answer this question we first need to retrieve the passage about Robert Smith in order to find the name of the company he founded (General Mills), and subsequently retrieve the passage about General Mills, which contains the answer the question (Golden Valley, Minnesota). Even though multi-hop QA requires multiple retrieval hops, it is fundamentally different from session search (Yang et al., 2015; Levine et al., 2017) and conversational search (Dalton et al., 2019; Voskarides et al., 2020; Vakulenko et al., 2021), since in multi-hop QA the information need of the user is expressed in a single question, thus not requiring multiple turns of interaction.

QA systems typically consist of (i) a retriever that identifies the passage/document in the underlying collection that contains the answer to the user's question, and (ii) a reader that extracts or generates the answer from the identified passage (Chen et al., 2017). Given that often the answer cannot be found in the top-ranked passage, inference follows a standard beam-search procedure, where top-k passages are retrieved and the reader scores are computed for all k passages (Lee et al., 2019). However, readers are very sensitive to noise in the top-k passages, thus making the performance of the retriever critical for the performance of QA systems (Yang et al., 2019). This is further amplified in multi-hop QA, where multiple retrieval hops are performed; potential retrieval errors get propagated across hops and thus severely harm QA performance.

The majority of current approaches to multi-hop QA use either traditional IR methods (TF-IDF, BM25) (Qi et al., 2019) or graph-based methods for the retriever (Nie et al., 2019; Asai et al., 2020). However, those approaches have serious limitations. The former approaches require high lexical overlap between questions and relevant passages, while the latter rely on an interlinked underlying corpus, which is not always the case. Recently, Xiong et al. (2021) introduced a dense multi-hop passage retrieval model that constructs a new query representation based on the question and previously retrieved passages and subsequently uses the new representation to retrieve the next set of relevant passages. This model achieved state-of-the-art results while not relying on an interlinked underlying corpus.

Even though dense retrieval models achieve state-of-the-art results on multi-hop QA, they are computationally intensive, requiring multiple GPUs to train. Existing work only reports results for the cases where such resources are available; therefore providing no answer on how feasible is to train such models on a low resource setting. In this

[*] Research conducted when the author was at the University of Amsterdam.

Proceedings of the 2nd Workshop on Simple and Efficient Natural Language Processing, pages 58–63
November 10, 2021.

paper, we focus on developing an efficient retriever for multi-hop QA that can be trained effectively in a low computational resource setting. We aim to answer the following research questions:

RQ1 How does the performance of dense retrieval compare to lexical and hybrid approaches?

RQ2 How does the performance degrade in the low computational resource settings?

Our main contributions are the following: (i) we propose a hybrid (lexical and dense) retrieval model which is competitive against its fully dense competitors while requiring eight times less computational power and (ii) we perform a thorough analysis on the performance of dense passage retrieval models on the task of multi-hop QA.[1]

2 Task Description

Let $p \in \mathcal{C}$ denote a passage within a passage collection $\mathcal{C}$, and q a multi-hop question. Given q and $\mathcal{C}$ the task is to retrieve a set of relevant passages $\mathcal{P} = \{p_1, p_2, \ldots, p_n\}$, where $p_i \in \mathcal{C}$. In the multi-hop scenario we consider here, not all relevant passages can be retrieved using the input question q alone. This is due to the fact that there is a low lexical overlap or semantic relationship between question q and one or more of the relevant passages in $\mathcal{P}$. In this case, information from one of the relevant passages p_i is needed to retrieve another relevant passage p_j, where p_j may be lexically/semantically different from question q.

3 Experimental Setup

In this section, we describe the dataset used in our experiments, the metrics we use to answer our research questions and the models we compare against.

3.1 Dataset

For our experiments, we focus on the HotpotQA dataset and particularly the full-wiki setting (Yang et al., 2018). HotpotQA is a large-scale 2-hop QA dataset where the answers to questions must be found in the context of the entire Wikipedia. Questions in HotpotQA fall into one of the following categories: bridge or comparison. In *bridge* questions, the bridge entity that connects the two relevant passages is missing; e.g., 'When did the show that Skeet Ulrich is currently starring in premiere?", where the bridge entity "Riverdale (2017 TV series)" is missing. In *comparison* questions the main two entities (of the two relevant passages) are both mentioned and compared; e.g., "Which has smaller flowers, Campsis or Kalmiopsis?".

3.2 Metrics

Following previous work (Yang et al., 2018; Xiong et al., 2021), we report passage Exact Match (EM) to measure the overall retrieval performance. Exact Match is a metric that evaluates whether both of the ground-truth passages for each question are included in the retrieved passages (then EM=1 otherwise EM=0). Note that metrics such as EM and F1 w.r.t question's answer (Ans) and supporting facts on sentence-level (Sup) do not fit in our experimental setup since we focus on the retrieval part of the pipeline and not on the reading.

3.3 Models

In this section, we describe the models we experiment with.

3.3.1 Single-hop models

Given a question, single-hop models retrieve a ranked list of passages. Thus, they are not aware of the multi-hop nature of the task.

BM25 is a standard lexical retrieval model. We use the default Anserini parameters (Yang et al., 2017).

Rerank is a standard two-stage retrieval model that first retrieves passages with BM25 and then uses BERT to rerank the top-k passages (Nogueira and Cho, 2019). The BERT (base) classifier was trained with a point-wise loss (Nogueira and Cho, 2019). It was fine-tuned on the train split of HotpotQA for 2 epochs. Training took 5 hours with batch size of 8 using a single 12GB GPU. We experimented with k=100 and k=1000, and found that k=100 results in a better reranking performance at the top positions.

DPR is a dense passage retrieval model for simple questions (Karpukhin et al., 2020). Given a question q, a relevant passage p^+ and a set of irrelevant passages $\{p_1^-, p_2^-, \ldots, p_m^-\}$, the model learns to rank p^+ higher via the optimization of the negative log likelihood of the relevant passage. To train DPR on HotpotQA, a multi-hop QA dataset, we follow the procedure described in (Xiong et al., 2021). This model was trained for 25 epochs ($\sim$ 2 days)

[1] Our trained models and data are available at https://github.com/GSidiropoulos/hybrid_retrieval_for_efficient_qa.

on a single 12GB GPU, using a RoBERTa-based encoder.

3.3.2 Multi-hop models

These models are aware of the multi-hop nature of the task. They recursively retrieve new information at each hop by conditioning the question on information retrieved on previous hops (Xiong et al., 2021). In practice, at each hop t the question q and the passage retrieved in the previous hop p_{t-1} gets encoded as the new query $q_t = h(q, p_{t-1})$, where $h(\cdot)$ the question encoder, to retrieve the next relevant passage; when $t = 1$ then we have just the question. Differently from single-hop models, at inference time, given a question, beam search is used to obtain the top-k passage pair candidates. The candidates to beam search at each hop are generated by a similarity function using the query representation at hop t, and the beams are scored by the sum of the individual similarity scores.

MDR is a state-of-the-art dense retriever for multi-hop questions (Xiong et al., 2021). It extends DPR in an iterative fashion by encoding the question and passages retrieved in previous hops as the new query to retrieve the next relevant passages. This model was trained for 25 epochs ($\sim$ 3 days) on a single 12GB GPU, using a RoBERTa-based encoder, without the memory bank mechanism (Wu et al., 2018). The memory bank mechanism is dropped since it is very expensive to compute and its contribution to retrieval performance is limited.

MDR (full) is MDR with the additional memory bank mechanism, trained for 50 epochs on 8×32GB GPUs by Xiong et al. (2021).

Rerank + DPR$_2$ is a hybrid model we propose in this paper. Specifically, for the first hop we rely on the BERT-based re-ranking model described in Section 3.3.1 (Rerank), while for the second hop we train a DPR only on second hop questions (DPR$_2$). To train the latter, we build a variation of HotpotQA where the question gets concatenated with the ground truth passage of the first hop, and the second hop ground truth passage is the only relevant passage to be retrieved. DPR$_2$ was trained for 25 epochs ($\sim$ 1 day) on a single 12GB GPU, using a RoBERTa-based encoder.

4 Results

In this section, we present our experimental results that answer our research questions.

Model	EM@2	EM@10	EM@20
BM25	0.127	0.320	0.395
Rerank	0.314	0.476	0.517
DPR	0.116	0.275	0.336
MDR	0.440	0.581	0.619
Rerank+DPR$_2$	0.599	0.732	0.762
MDR (full)	**0.677**	**0.772**	**0.793**

Table 1: Overall retrieval performance. In the first group we show single-hop models, while in the second group we show multi-hop models.

4.1 Overall performance

Here we aim to answer **RQ1** by comparing the retrieval performance of the models we consider. In Table 1, we observe that the single-hop models perform much worse than the multi-hop models. This is expected since single-hop models are not aware of the multi-hop nature of the task.

As for the multi-hop models, we observe that MDR (full) achieves the best performance at the higher positions in the ranking. It is important to underline here that MDR (full) uses considerably more resources than Rerank+DPR$_2$ and MDR. The last two use relatively limited computational resources and a comparison between them is more fair (see Section 3.3).[2] We observe that our Rerank+DPR$_2$ outperforms MDR on all metrics while is also competitive against MDR (full), especially w.r.t EM@10 and EM@20. This is due to the fact that often questions and their relevant passages are not only semantically related, but also have high lexical overlap. This is also highlighted by Karpukhin et al. (2020), who reported that dense retrieval has performance issues when the question has high lexical overlap with the passages.

4.2 Performance for limited resources

In this section, we answer **RQ2** by comparing the retrieval performance of MDR and DPR as provided in (Xiong et al., 2021), against the same models trained with limited computational resources.

In Table 2 we see that performance drops significantly as we limit resources for both DPR and MDR. This is a result of the training scheme that is used in (Karpukhin et al., 2020) and (Xiong et al.,

[2]Even though the memory bank mechanism is omitted from MDR, the comparison of Rerank+DPR$_2$ and MDR remains fair since this particular mechanism can also be potentially applied to Rerank+DPR$_2$ (in the DPR part).

Model	Encoder	# GPU	# Epochs	Batch size	# Gradient acc. steps	EM@2	EM@10	EM@20
MDR (full)	RoBERTa	8 × 32GB	50	150	1	0.677	0.772	0.793
MDR	RoBERTa	8 × 32GB	50	150	1	0.637	0.742	0.772
	RoBERTa	4 × 24GB	50	28	1	0.606	0.711	0.735
	RoBERTa	4 × 24GB	25	28	1	0.550	0.668	0.698
	RoBERTa	4 × 24GB	20	28	1	0.537	0.659	0.687
	RoBERTa	1 × 12GB	25	4	32	0.440	0.581	0.619
	BERT	1 × 12GB	25	4	32	0.421	0.560	0.597
DPR	RoBERTa	8 × 32GB	50	256	1	0.252	0.454	0.521
	RoBERTa	4 × 24GB	25	128	1	0.223	0.427	0.487
	RoBERTa	1 × 12GB	25	8	32	0.116	0.275	0.336

Table 2: Analysis of how computational resources affect the performance of MDR and DPR. The MDR(full) configuration is provided by (Xiong et al., 2021). Different beam size can slightly change the results from what was originally reported. MDR and DPR, both trained trained on 8 GPUs, are not available and therefore we report the results as they were reported in (Xiong et al., 2021).

2021). More specifically, DPR and MDR rely on using in-batch negatives both for decreasing the training time (positive passages of a question are reused as negative passages for the rest of the questions in the batch, instead of having to sample new ones beforehand), and for improving accuracy (bigger batch size will produce more in-batch negatives, thus increasing the number of training samples). When we have limited resources, training time gets significantly longer (since we use fewer GPUs), and therefore we have to compromise for fewer training epochs while the batch size is restricted by the GPU memory size. For instance, training for 50 epochs takes ~1 day on 8×32GB GPUs, while it takes ~6 days on a single 12GB GPU.

In addition, when comparing MDR trained on 4×24GB GPUs against MDR trained on a single 12GB GPU, for 25 epochs each, we observe that even though we can simulate bigger batch sizes by using gradient accumulation,[3] we do not observe an increase in performance. This is a consequence of the fact that the number of in-batch negatives is limited by the real batch size. Note that we also observe a similar trend for DPR.

In summary, computational resources are of vital importance for multi-hop dense retrieval models. Hence, in the case where only limited resources are available, following a hybrid (lexical and dense) approach such as our proposed Rerank+DPR_2 seems to be a good choice. As we showed in Tables 1 and 2, Rerank+DPR_2 (trained on a single GPU) performs similarly to MDR trained on 4 GPUs and is competitive against MDR trained on 8 GPUs.

4.3 Error Analysis

We perform qualitative analysis to gain further insights into where the models succeed or fail. More specifically, we compare specific cases where our hybrid model (Rerank+DPR_2) retrieves both relevant passages successfully while MDR fails and vice versa. For our analysis we focus on bridge questions since comparison questions are more straightforward to retrieve.

Table 3 shows two typical examples of questions for which Rerank+DPR_2 retrieves both relevant passages at the top positions while MDR fails to do so. When there is a high lexical overlap between the question and a relevant passage, our hybrid model can capture this exact n-gram match and improve the performance. In contrast, fully dense models seem incapable of capturing this. In particular, this lexical overlap can be between the question and both relevant passages for the case of comparison questions, or between the question and the first relevant passage for bridge questions.

In bridge questions if the lexical overlap is between the question and the second passage then our hybrid model favors passages in which this phrase appears, and therefore it retrieves an irrelevant first passage; leading to an irrelevant second passage as well. MDR on the other hand manages to retrieve both relevant passages at the top positions. Those are the cases where the lexical overlap is used in the given question in order to disambiguate the final answer. Examples can be found in Table 4.

In the first example, "Golden Globe Award" is

[3]Gradient accumulation is a mechanism that accumulates the gradients and the losses over consecutive batches for a specific number of steps (without updating the parameters), and then updates the parameters based on the cumulative gradient (Mnih et al., 2016).

	q **[bridge]: Who was the defense counsel of a German woman who underwent Catholic exorcism rites during the year before her death?**
Rerank+DPR$_2$	**Anneliese Michel**: Anneliese Michel] (21 September 1952 – 1 July 1976) was a German woman who underwent Catholic exorcism rites during the year before her death. Later investigation determined that she was malnourished and dehydrated... **Erich Schmidt-Leichner**: Erich Schmidt-Leichner (14 October 1910 – 17 March 1983) was a German lawyer who made a name as a distinguished defense counsel at the Nuremberg Trials (1945 - 1946). In 1978, he was a defense counsel in the "Klingenberg Case" (Anneliese Michel)...
MDR	**Maria Pauer**: Maria Pauer (October 1734/36 – 1750 in Salzburg), was an alleged Austrian witch. She was the last person to be executed for witchcraft in Austria. **Franz Burkard (died 1539)**: Franz Burkard (died 1539) was a canon lawyer in Ingoldstadt who opposed Lutheranism, particularly in the trial of Andreas Seehofer.
•	q **[bridge]: The astronomer who formulated the theory of stellar nucleosynthesis co-authored what landmark paper?**
Rerank+DPR$_2$	**Fred Hoyle**: Sir Fred Hoyle FRS (24 June 1915 – 20 August 2001) was an English astronomer who formulated the theory of stellar nucleosynthesis ... **B2FH paper**: The BFH paper, named after the initials of the authors of the paper, Margaret Burbidge, Geoffrey Burbidge, William Fowler, and Fred Hoyle, is a landmark paper of stellar physics published in "Reviews of Modern Physics" in 1957 ...
MDR	**Sequence hypothesis**: The sequence hypothesis was first formally proposed in the review "On Protein Synthesis" by Francis Crick in 1958 ... **Francis Crick**: Francis Harry Compton Crick (8 June 1916 – 28 July 2004) was a British molecular biologist, biophysicist, and neuroscientist, most noted for being a co-discoverer of the structure of the DNA molecule in ...

Table 3: Two example bridge questions for which Rerank+DPR$_2$ retrieves both relevant passages at the top positions while MDR fails to do so. Lexical overlap is indicated with underlined text while the answer to the question is highlighted.

	q **[bridge]: What Golden Globe Award actor starred in the film Little Fugitive?**
Rerank+DPR$_2$	**Ali MacGraw:** Elizabeth Alice "Ali" MacGraw (born April 1, 1939) is an American actress, model, author, and animal rights activist. She first gained attention with her role in the 1969 film "Goodbye, Columbus", for which she won the Golden Globe Award for Most Promising Newcomer. She reached international fame in 1970's "Love Story", for which she was nominated for an Academy Award for Best Actress and won the Golden Globe Award for Best Actress in a Motion Picture – Drama ... **Little Fugitive**: Little Fugitive (1953) is an American film written and directed by Raymond Abrashkin (as "Ray Ashley"), Morris Engel and Ruth Orkin, that tells the story of a child alone in Coney Island.
MDR	**Little Fugitive (2006 film)**: Little Fugitive is a 2006 remake of the film of the same name. It was directed by Joanna Lipper and produced by Nicholas Paleologos. The film is set in present day Brooklyn and tells the story of 11-year-old Lenny (Nicolas Martí Salgado) who must take care of his 7-year-old brother, Joey (David Castro), while their father (Peter Dinklage) is in jail and their mother work long hours a nursing home ... **Peter Dinklage**: Peter Hayden Dinklage (, born June 11, 1969) is an American actor and film producer. He has received numerous accolades, including a Golden Globe Award and two Primetime Emmy Awards.
	q **[bridge]:Which American professional poker player also starred in the 2015 movie "Extraction"?**
Rerank+DPR$_2$	**Allen Cunningham**: Allen Cunningham (born March 28, 1977) is an American professional poker player who has won five World Series of Poker bracelets. **Extraction (film)**: Extraction is a 2015 American action-thriller film directed by Steven C. Miller and written by Umair Aleem. The film stars Kellan Lutz, Bruce Willis, Gina Carano, D. B. Sweeney, Dan Bilzerian and Steve Coulter ...
MDR	**Extraction (film)**: Extraction is a 2015 American action-thriller film directed by Steven C. Miller and written by Umair Aleem. The film stars Kellan Lutz, Bruce Willis, Gina Carano, D. B. Sweeney, Dan Bilzerian and Steve Coulter ... **Dan Bilzerian**: Dan Brandon Bilzerian (born December 7, 1980) is an American professional poker player.

Table 4: Two example bridge questions for which MDR retrieves both relevant passages at the top positions while Rerank+DPR$_2$ fails to do so. The answer to the question is highlighted.

used in the given question in order to disambiguate the final answer, since in the film "Little Fugitive" there is more than one actor involved. Therefore, "Golden Globe Award" must be used to assist the retrieval of the second passage. Since Rerank+DPR$_2$ builds on top of BM25, it favors passages in which this phrase appears, and therefore it retrieves an irrelevant first passage leading to an irrelevant second passage as well. On the other hand, MDR manages to retrieve both relevant passages at the top positions. Similarly, for the second example, "American professional poker player" is used to specify the actor that starred in the "Extraction" movie, hence supporting the retrieval of the second relevant passage.

5 Conclusion

In this work, we provided insights on the performance of state-of-the-art dense retrieval for multi-hop questions. We showed that Rerank+DPR$_2$ (our hybrid model) outperforms MDR (the state-of-the-art multi-hop dense retrieval model) in the low resource setting, and it is competitive with MDR in the setting where MDR uses considerably more computational resources. Finally, we highlighted that fully dense retrieval models get harmed when using limited computational resources. For future work, we plan to build on our insights to improve the performance of multi-hop models by combining the strengths of lexical and dense retrieval. Also, we aim to develop less computationally expensive multi-hop retrieval models.

Acknowledgements

This research was supported by the NWO Innovational Research Incentives Scheme Vidi (016.Vidi.189.039), the NWO Smart Culture - Big Data / Digital Humanities (314-99-301), the H2020-EU.3.4. - SOCIETAL CHALLENGES - Smart, Green And Integrated Transport (814961). All content represents the opinion of the authors, which is not necessarily shared or endorsed by their respective employers and/or sponsors.

References

Akari Asai, Kazuma Hashimoto, Hannaneh Hajishirzi, Richard Socher, and Caiming Xiong. 2020. Learning to retrieve reasoning paths over wikipedia graph for question answering. In *8th International Conference on Learning Representations, ICLR 2020, Addis Ababa, Ethiopia, April 26-30, 2020*.

Danqi Chen, Adam Fisch, Jason Weston, and Antoine Bordes. 2017. Reading wikipedia to answer open-domain questions. In *Proceedings of the 55th Annual Meeting of the Association for Computational Linguistics, ACL 2017, Vancouver, Canada, July 30 - August 4, Volume 1: Long Papers*, pages 1870–1879. Association for Computational Linguistics.

Jeffrey Dalton, Chenyan Xiong, and Jamie Callan. 2019. Trec cast 2019: The conversational assistance track overview. *Proceedings of the Twenty-Eighth Text REtrieval Conference, TREC*.

Vladimir Karpukhin, Barlas Oguz, Sewon Min, Patrick Lewis, Ledell Wu, Sergey Edunov, Danqi Chen, and Wen-tau Yih. 2020. Dense passage retrieval for open-domain question answering. In *Proceedings of the 2020 Conference on Empirical Methods in Natural Language Processing (EMNLP)*, pages 6769–6781.

Kenton Lee, Ming-Wei Chang, and Kristina Toutanova. 2019. Latent retrieval for weakly supervised open domain question answering. In *Proceedings of the 57th Annual Meeting of the Association for Computational Linguistics*, pages 6086–6096.

Nir Levine, Haggai Roitman, and Doron Cohen. 2017. An extended relevance model for session search. In *Proceedings of the 40th International ACM SIGIR Conference on Research and Development in Information Retrieval*, pages 865–868.

Volodymyr Mnih, Adria Puigdomenech Badia, Mehdi Mirza, Alex Graves, Timothy Lillicrap, Tim Harley, David Silver, and Koray Kavukcuoglu. 2016. Asynchronous methods for deep reinforcement learning. In *International conference on machine learning*, pages 1928–1937. PMLR.

Yixin Nie, Songhe Wang, and Mohit Bansal. 2019. Revealing the importance of semantic retrieval for machine reading at scale. In *Proceedings of the 2019 Conference on Empirical Methods in Natural Language Processing and the 9th International Joint Conference on Natural Language Processing, EMNLP-IJCNLP 2019, Hong Kong, China, November 3-7, 2019*, pages 2553–2566.

Rodrigo Nogueira and Kyunghyun Cho. 2019. Passage re-ranking with BERT. *CoRR*, abs/1901.04085.

Peng Qi, Xiaowen Lin, Leo Mehr, Zijian Wang, and Christopher D. Manning. 2019. Answering complex open-domain questions through iterative query generation. In *2019 Conference on Empirical Methods in Natural Language Processing and 9th International Joint Conference on Natural Language Processing (EMNLP-IJCNLP)*.

Svitlana Vakulenko, Shayne Longpre, Zhucheng Tu, and Raviteja Anantha. 2021. Question rewriting for conversational question answering. In *Proceedings of the 14th ACM International Conference on Web Search and Data Mining*, pages 355–363.

Nikos Voskarides, Dan Li, Pengjie Ren, Evangelos Kanoulas, and Maarten de Rijke. 2020. Query resolution for conversational search with limited supervision. In *Proceedings of the 43rd International ACM SIGIR Conference on Research and Development in Information Retrieval*, pages 921–930.

Zhirong Wu, Yuanjun Xiong, Stella X Yu, and Dahua Lin. 2018. Unsupervised feature learning via non-parametric instance discrimination. In *Proceedings of the IEEE Conference on Computer Vision and Pattern Recognition*, pages 3733–3742.

Wenhan Xiong, Xiang Lorraine Li, Srini Iyer, Jingfei Du, Patrick Lewis, William Yang Wang, Yashar Mehdad, Wen-tau Yih, Sebastian Riedel, Douwe Kiela, et al. 2021. Answering complex open-domain questions with multi-hop dense retrieval. In *Proceedings of the 9th International Conference on Learning Representations (ICLR)*.

Hui Yang, Dongyi Guan, and Sicong Zhang. 2015. The query change model: Modeling session search as a markov decision process. *ACM Transactions on Information Systems (TOIS)*, 33(4):1–33.

Peilin Yang, Hui Fang, and Jimmy Lin. 2017. Anserini: Enabling the use of lucene for information retrieval research. In *Proceedings of the 40th International ACM SIGIR Conference on Research and Development in Information Retrieval*, pages 1253–1256.

Wei Yang, Yuqing Xie, Aileen Lin, Xingyu Li, Luchen Tan, Kun Xiong, Ming Li, and Jimmy Lin. 2019. End-to-end open-domain question answering with bertserini. In *Proceedings of the 2019 Conference of the North American Chapter of the Association for Computational Linguistics: Human Language Technologies, NAACL-HLT 2019, Minneapolis, MN, USA, June 2-7, 2019, Demonstrations*, pages 72–77. Association for Computational Linguistics.

Zhilin Yang, Peng Qi, Saizheng Zhang, Yoshua Bengio, William Cohen, Ruslan Salakhutdinov, and Christopher D Manning. 2018. Hotpotqa: A dataset for diverse, explainable multi-hop question answering. In *Proceedings of the 2018 Conference on Empirical Methods in Natural Language Processing*, pages 2369–2380.

Learning to Rank in the Age of Muppets: Effectiveness–Efficiency Tradeoffs in Multi-Stage Ranking

Yue Zhang,[1*] **Chengcheng Hu,**[2*] **Yuqi Liu,**[2*] **Hui Fang,**[1] **Jimmy Lin**[2]

[1] Department of Electrical and Computer Engineering, University of Delaware
[2] David R. Cheriton School of Computer Science, University of Waterloo

{zhangyue, hfang}@udel.edu, {c45hu, y899liu, jimmylin}@uwaterloo.ca

Abstract

It is well known that rerankers built on pretrained transformer models such as BERT have dramatically improved retrieval effectiveness in many tasks. However, these gains have come at substantial costs in terms of efficiency, as noted by many researchers. In this work, we show that it is possible to retain the benefits of transformer-based rerankers in a multi-stage reranking pipeline by first using feature-based learning-to-rank techniques to reduce the number of candidate documents under consideration without adversely affecting their quality in terms of recall. Applied to the MS MARCO passage and document ranking tasks, we are able to achieve the same level of effectiveness, but with up to 18× increase in efficiency. Furthermore, our techniques are orthogonal to other methods focused on accelerating transformer inference, and thus can be combined for even greater efficiency gains. A higher-level message from our work is that, even though pretrained transformers dominate the modern IR landscape, there are still important roles for "traditional" LTR techniques, and that we should not forget history.

1 Introduction

Pretrained transformers such as BERT (Devlin et al., 2019) have dramatically increased retrieval effectiveness in many tasks across a multitude of domains (Lin et al., 2020a). Nevertheless, in a standard "retrieve-then-rerank" setup, the application of pretrained transformer-based rerankers incurs large computational costs and long query latencies, making those rerankers unrealistic for many real-world applications. For example, according to the ColBERT paper (Khattab and Zaharia, 2020), reranking 1000 hits from the MS MARCO passage dataset takes 32.9 seconds per query. Other researchers have noted the computational costs of transformer-based rankers (Hofstätter and Hanbury, 2019), and this realization has compelled the field to explore other approaches, for example, simplified models (Hofstätter et al., 2020; Soldaini and Moschitti, 2020; Mitra et al., 2020; MacAvaney et al., 2020; Gao et al., 2020; Jiang et al., 2020) and learned dense representations (Xiong et al., 2020; Lin et al., 2020b).

We are also motivated by the desire to reduce the computational costs of ranking with transformers, but from a different perspective. Based on the observation that neural networks in general (and transformers in particular) have largely supplanted feature-based learning to rank (LTR) in modern information retrieval, we ask the question: What, if anything, does "traditional" feature-based learning to rank have to offer in the age of muppets?[1] The subtext of this question is that we, as a field, should not forget our own history.

There are two obvious approaches to try and answer this question. The first is to simply consider transformer-based features (e.g., BERT score, ColBERT score, etc.) as yet another feature within a learning-to-rank framework—for example, with gradient boosted decision trees (Wang et al., 2020). This is not the route that we take, because this approach has less bearing on our desire to increase the efficiency of transformer-based models. Instead, we take the alternative approach of using learning-to-rank techniques as a "filtering" stage in a multi-stage ranking architecture to reduce the number of candidates under consideration by BERT. More concretely, we find that a design based on this idea achieves the same level of effectiveness as a standard retrieve-and-rerank approach using BERT, but is up to 18× faster. Other effectiveness–efficiency tradeoffs are possible, giving developers a rich design space to build systems tailored to different application scenarios.

The contribution of this work is to demon-

* Equal contribution

[1]Muppets being a whimsical way to refer to BERT and related transformer models.

Proceedings of the 2nd Workshop on Simple and Efficient Natural Language Processing, pages 64–73
November 10, 2021. ©201 Association for Computational Linguistics

strate that by inserting a "filtering" learning-to-rank stage prior to BERT-based reranking, we can control effectiveness–efficiency tradeoffs in a manner that makes deployments in real-world applications more practical. We emphasize that this work is orthogonal to other methods that directly attempt to accelerate inference, e.g., via knowledge distillation, early exits, model simplifications, etc. It is likely that our gains are cumulative with respect to these enhancements.

2 Methods

2.1 Multi-Stage Ranking

We adopt a standard formulation of multi-stage ranking, which comprises a candidate generation stage H_0 (also called first-stage retrieval), followed by a pipeline of rerankers, denoted H_1 to H_N. Candidate generation is typically accomplished via keyword search against an inverted index, which retrieves k_0 hits from the corpus. Each subsequent stage H_n receives a ranked list R_{n-1} comprising k_{n-1} candidates from the previous stage, reranks these candidates, and then passes the results to the next stage. The output of the last stage serves as the final ranked list, e.g., to be shown to the user or to be evaluated using standard tools.

In this work, we compare two designs of multi-stage ranking architectures:

BoW + BERT As a baseline, we consider the retrieve-and-rerank approach originally proposed by Nogueira and Cho (2019), which has emerged as the standard architecture for applying pretrained transformers to ranking. We notate a specific configuration of this design as BoW(k_0) + BERT, where k_0 denotes the number of candidates from bag-of-words retrieval that are then reranked by BERT. A commonly used default is BoW(1000) + BERT (Nogueira and Cho, 2019).

In addition, we also examine the docTTTTTquery document expansion technique (Nogueira et al., 2019b; Nogueira and Lin, 2019) based on predicting queries for which a text would be relevant (henceforth, just d2q for short). The predicted queries are concatenated to the end of the original text; this greatly improves BoW retrieval. We call this variant BoW_{d2q} and denote the corresponding pipeline BoW_{d2q}(1000) + BERT.

BoW + LTR + BERT This represents our proposed design of introducing a filtering stage before BERT to reduce the number of candidates under consideration. We notate a specific configuration of this design as BoW(k_0) + LTR(k_1) + BERT, where k_0 denotes the number of candidates from bag-of-words retrieval. Our LTR stage then reranks these k_0 hits to generate a new ranking of k_1 hits that are passed to the BERT stage. Similar to BoW_{d2q}, the LTR variant that extracts features from the document expansions is called LTR_{d2q}.

Given this setup, our research question then becomes an effectiveness–efficiency exploration of BoW + BERT vs. BoW + LTR + BERT (including d2q variants). We want to know, given effectiveness parity as a requirement, what degree of latency reduction we can achieve. To answer this question, we adopt the standard setting of LTR as supervised machine learning, where our objective is to maximize recall. We use features extracted from our LTR module to train a model and then apply inference on candidates from the BoW stage, passing on only the most promising ones for (expensive) neural reranking.

2.2 Learning-to-Rank Features

Our LTR features fall into four categories: term-based, score-based, proximity-based, and translation-based. These features are inspired by previous studies on LTR (Qin and Liu, 2013; Gallagher et al., 2020) and summarized in Table 1. An enumeration of all features is presented in Appendix A.

Term-based features Following previous work, we compute different term statistics including term frequency (TF), inverse document frequency (IDF), log term probability, and inverse collection term frequency. Furthermore, existing retrieval models such as BM25 are used to compute the relevance score of a term, and these scores can also be used as term-based features combining different types of statistics. To aggregate term-based statistics for all terms in a query, a number of different aggregation functions are used, e.g., max, min, sum, mean, median, and the ratio between max and min.

Score-based features Term-based statistics are not sufficient as document-level statistics such as document length are also crucial for retrieval effectiveness. Traditional BoW retrieval models (e.g., BM25, Query Likelihood, Divergence From Randomness) have proposed effective ways of combining term-based and document-based statistics, so we also include the retrieval scores of these models

Feature Category	#	Examples
Term-based	54	Max of IDF, Max of TF
Score-based	14	BM25, DFR
Proximity-based	15	Co-occurrences, BM25-TP
Translation-based	4	translation probability

Table 1: Summary of LTR features.

as features. Note that when we use sum as the aggregation function for term-based statistics, we are essentially computing the retrieval model score.

Proximity-based features Traditional retrieval models assume terms are independent and ignore their relationships, but the proximity among query terms often serves as an important relevance signal. Thus, we include features that directly capture the proximity of query terms, such as the counts of ordered and unordered co-occurrence of bigrams within different window sizes. We compute the scores of proximity-based retrieval functions, such as SDM (Metzler and Croft, 2005; Gallagher et al., 2020) and BM25-TP (Lu et al., 2015; Gallagher et al., 2020), as our features.

Translation-based features Capturing semantic relationships between a query and a document is also crucial to improving retrieval accuracy. To incorporate such features, we can use a translation model (Boytsov and Nyberg, 2020; Boytsov and Kolter, 2021) to measure the log translation probability between queries and documents. The conditional probability we need $p(q|d_n)$ is generated by the IBM Model 1 translation model, and the final query–document feature is the sum of all individual conditional query probabilities.

The extraction of all LTR features is performed at the level of tokens. In particular, both queries and documents are tokenized into a multi-field representation. They include: (1) the *raw* field, which consists of the original tokens; (2) the *stemmed* field, which includes the stemmed tokens; (3) the *subword* field, which breaks tokens into subwords; and (4) the *d2q* field, which includes the stemmed tokens from the concatenated docTTTTTquery predictions (for the d2q variants). For each query–document pair, feature extraction is repeated over all applicable fields. In total, there are 83 different features (per field) plus four translation-based features that are only available in the *raw* and *subword* fields. Table 1 summarizes our features and provides examples for each feature category.

3 Experimental Setup

Data We use the MS MARCO passage ranking dataset (Bajaj et al., 2018) for training and testing. The training set contains ~500K queries while the development and test sets contain ~7K queries each. On average, each query has only one positive example; negative examples are taken from BM25 results that are not otherwise judged as relevant. Since it is inefficient to use all the negative samples, we downsample to 20 negative examples per query and combine them with all the positive examples to arrive at the training data.

We additionally test on the MS MARCO document ranking task (Bajaj et al., 2018) in a zero-shot manner. For this, we segment each document into multiple passages as the neural models cannot process long documents. Specifically, we use the sliding window strategy of Pradeep et al. (2021), where the window length is ten sentences with a stride of five sentences. Retrieval is performed at the passage level, and the document score is computed based on the highest relevance score among its passages.

Implementation We use Anserini (Yang et al., 2018), an open-source IR toolkit built on Lucene, to build the indexes and retrieve top-ranked candidate passages. For first-stage retrieval, we use BM25, with parameters ($k_1 = 0.82$ and $b = 0.68$) based on the authors' recommendations to optimize for recall@1000. The retrieved candidate passages are then sent to feature extraction through Anserini's Python interface, Pyserini (Lin et al., 2021).[2]

For our LTR module, we use the LambdaMART algorithm implemented in LightGBM[3] as our model. The hyperparameters are tuned to achieve the highest recall@200 on the development set. Specifically, num_leaves is 200, learning_rate is 0.1, min_data_in_leaf is 50, max_bin is 255. We fix early stopping patience to 200 and use up to 1000 trees. Finally, we utilize batch processing and multi-threading to accelerate the processing. This helps us leverage contemporary multi-core CPUs.

For the final-stage neural reranker, we experiment with BERT-large and T5-base in the PyGaggle library fine-tuned on the MS MARCO passage data.[4] We simply use checkpoints provided by the library, as our work is not specifically focused

[2] https://github.com/castorini/pyserini
[3] https://github.com/microsoft/LightGBM
[4] https://github.com/castorini/pygaggle

Configuration	N	MRR@10	NDCG@10	Latency	
BoW(1k) + BERT	1000	0.379	0.441	9.63s	
BoW(10k) + LTR(100) + BERT	100	0.381	0.443	1.32s	(7×)
BoW(10k) + LTR$_{d2q}$(20)+ BERT	20	0.382	0.442	0.53s	(18×)
BoW(1k) + T5	1000	0.380	0.443	5.60s	
BoW(10k) + LTR(100) + T5	100	0.382	0.445	0.92s	(6×)
BoW(10k) + LTR$_{d2q}$(20) + T5	20	0.382	0.444	0.46s	(12×)
BoW$_{d2q}$(1k) + BERT	1000	0.389	0.454	9.63s	
BoW$_{d2q}$(10k) + LTR$_{d2q}$(50) + BERT	50	0.389	0.454	0.83s	(12×)
BoW$_{d2q}$(1k) + T5	1000	0.386	0.453	5.60s	
BoW$_{d2q}$(10k) + LTR$_{d2q}$(50) + T5	50	0.388	0.454	0.63s	(9×)

Table 2: The effectiveness and efficiency of different pipeline configurations on the MS MARCO passage ranking task. The effectiveness of the pipelines with additional LTR modules are statistically indistinguishable from the baselines without the LTR modules.

on final-stage neural reranking. Previous evaluations (Nogueira and Cho, 2019; Nogueira et al., 2020; Pradeep et al., 2021) have already verified that these two models serve as competitive baselines. We pad all the token sequences in the batch to have the same length and truncate them if their lengths exceed 512 tokens.

Latency Measurements When measuring latency, we used two different servers. The latency of first-stage retrieval and the LTR filtering module is measured on a server equipped with 2 Intel Xeon Platinum 8160 CPUs. The index is located on a local SSD partition. The neural model latency is measured using a 6 core server with a single Tesla V100 GPU. All latency measurements exclude the time to load data and models. Component results are summed to yield end-to-end query latency, which we normalize into a speedup value when comparing different conditions.

4 Results and Analysis

4.1 Results on Passage Ranking

Evaluation results on MS MARCO passage ranking are shown in Table 2 for the various pipeline configurations based on the notation introduced in Section 2. N represents the number of candidates reranked by the final neural reranker, which consumes most of the query time. Note that in these experiments, our goal is to obtain effectiveness parity (i.e., same level of effectiveness) while accelerating inference (i.e., reducing query latency).

The first row in each block of the table represents a baseline configuration, with N set to the common value of 1000. We present six LTR pipelines, where we choose the smallest N (and different k's) that can reach MRR@10 parity with the baseline. We conduct two-tailed paired t-tests to confirm that there are no significant effectiveness differences between results before and after inserting LTR as the filtering stage. Depending on the pipeline setup, we only need to perform neural inference on 20 to 100 candidates—precisely because of our LTR filtering. We report the per-query latency for each configuration and compute a speedup by normalizing against the latency of each baseline. Based on which neural model we use and whether we use d2q, we observe speedups ranging from 6× to 18×. That is, we can achieve comparable effectiveness with these increases in speed. Note that our baseline BoW + BERT latency is already more than 3× faster than the values reported by Khattab and Zaharia (2020) (∼33s) using the same configuration, primarily due to batch tokenization and other engineering optimizations, so the LTR pipelines are compared against a well-optimized baseline.

Table 3 shows the query latency breakdown for a few representative models. Note that latency is dominated by final-stage neural reranking latency, which scales linearly, so smaller N values (in Table 2) are more desirable. However, this is balanced by the introduction of LTR overhead, both feature extraction as well as the prediction latency itself. Nevertheless, this is a worthwhile tradeoff as we observe large speedups overall. Since T5-base is faster than BERT-large, the effect of the LTR overhead is relatively larger and thus the speedup is lower. We can see that increasing the initial k_0 for BoW from 1k to 10k is acceptable as LTR overhead remains modest.

The most time-consuming step in LTR is feature extraction, and within that, loading the forward in-

Model	Retrieval	Feature Extraction	LTR Prediction	Neural Reranking	**Total**
BoW(1k) + BERT	15	-	-	9610	**9630**
BoW(10k) + LTR(100) + BERT	120	180	40	980	**1320**
BoW(1k) + T5	15	-	-	5580	**5600**
BoW(10k) + LTR(100) + T5	120	180	40	584	**920**

Table 3: Detailed breakdown of latency (ms/query) for a few representative pipeline configurations on the MS MARCO passage ranking task.

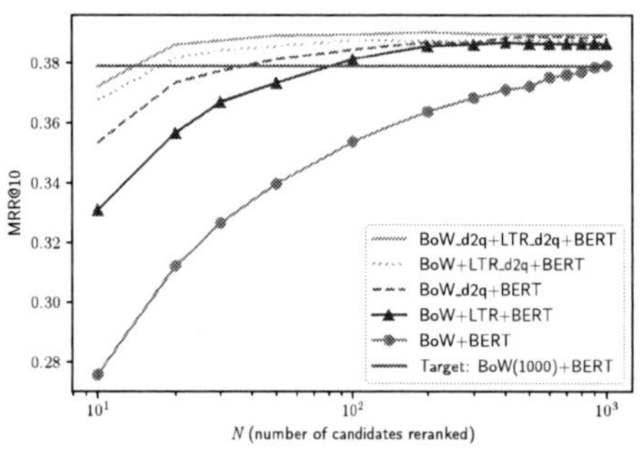

Figure 1: MRR@10 as a function of N, the number of candidates reranked by the final neural reranker, on the MS MARCO passage ranking task.

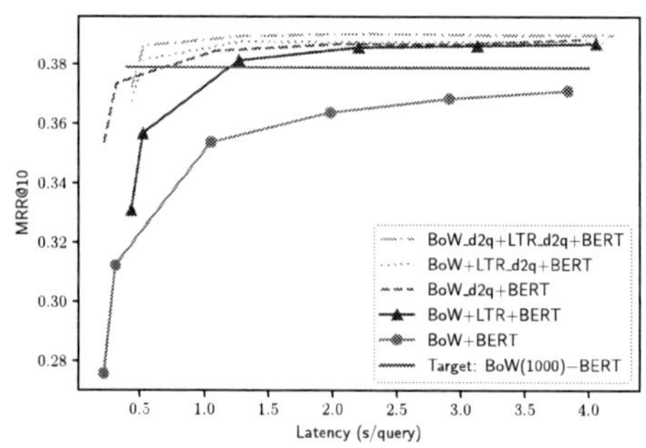

Figure 2: MRR@10 vs. reranking latency on the MS MARCO passage ranking task.

dex for each document is the most expensive single step. Our experiments show that the number of features does not affect latency substantially because we only need to load the document once; once in cache, individual feature extraction is very fast. Note that we have not spent much effort optimizing feature extraction (which is relatively inefficient Java code) and that more engineering effort, for example, optimizations proposed by Asadi and Lin (2013), are likely to further increase speedups.

Figure 1 shows the MRR@10 for our five models as a function of N (number of candidates reranked by the final neural reranker), shown on the x-axis (log scale). Effectiveness of the BoW + BERT baseline at $N = 1000$ is represented as the horizontal line—the effectiveness level we are targeting. Note that for some configurations, we needed to adjust the k_1 for the LTR stage in order to meet the desired N. We can see that our pipelines reach the target MRR@10 with much smaller values of N; reducing expensive neural reranking is where most of our speedups come from. After adding d2q predictions, we are able to achieve our target MRR@10 with an even smaller value of N.

Figure 2 shows the trade-offs between MRR@10 and query latency (the x-axis). Each curve represents a sweep over N values; we only focus on the case when N is relatively small (< 300). We can see that BoW + LTR + BERT is not helpful if the desired per-query latency is less than 0.5s, because the LTR system itself introduces overhead and leaves little time for neural reranking. For reference, without neural reranking, BoW + LTR only reaches 0.25 MRR@10 while consuming 0.34s; in contrast, spending 0.43s with BoW + BERT achieves 0.28 MRR@10. Between 0.5s and 2s, the effectiveness gap between BoW + BERT and BoW + LTR + BERT increases.

Until now, we have focused on targeting effectiveness parity. What if we're willing to sacrifice effectiveness? Figure 3 uses the BoW + LTR + BERT configuration as an example to show possible speedups and corresponding MRR@10 values if we accept lower effectiveness. We use the latency of BoW(1000) + BERT as our reference point to calculate speedups. For example, in one setting, we can achieve 0.36 MRR@10 using only 20 candidates ($N = 20$) and enjoy 17× speedup without using d2q (see Table 2).

We also conduct ablation experiments to investigate the importance of the four feature categories used in our LTR module. We use BoW(10k) + LTR(100) + BERT as our base model and assess

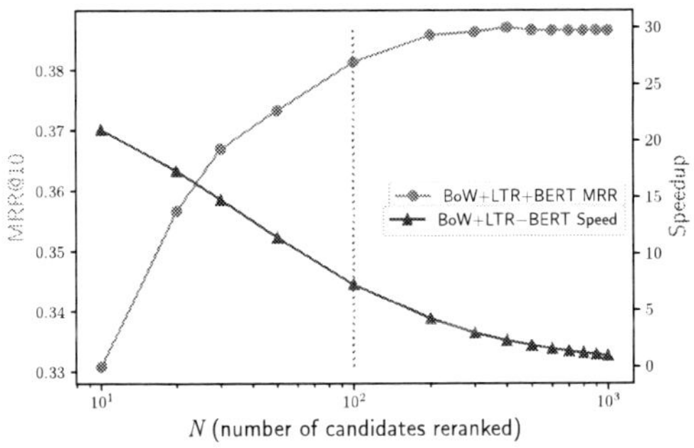

Figure 3: MRR@10 vs. speedup for different N, the number of candidates reranked by the final neural reranker, on the MS MARCO passage ranking task.

Configuration	Recall@100	MRR@10
Full Model	0.781	0.382
– Score-based	0.780 (−0.09%)	0.381 (−0.24%)
– Term-based	0.771 (−1.27%)	0.379 (−0.74%)
– Proximity-based	0.767 (−1.76%)	0.379 (−0.96%)
– Translation-based	0.743 (−4.82%)	0.371 (−3.01%)

Table 4: Feature importance ablation results on the MS MARCO passage ranking task.

feature importance by removing each category of features from the LTR module and measuring the effectiveness of the ablated reranker. Table 4 shows the absolute scores and relative differences in terms of recall@100 and MRR@10.

From these results, we can see that the score-based features appear to be the least important category of features in our model, likely because there is a lot of redundant information between score-based and term-based features. They use different arithmetic formulas to manipulate the same raw signals: term frequency, document frequency, etc. Compared with term-based features, score-based features are fewer in number. Removing score-based features has much less impact than removing term-based features.

Translation-based features appear to be the most important feature category: they make the biggest difference in effectiveness with the smallest number of features. The translation model bridges the query–document gap by modeling alternative expressions of query terms and enables a document to match query terms that are not present in the document (i.e., semantic matching).

We also evaluate each feature's importance by the total number of splits and the total gain of splits using a built-in feature in the LightGBM library. We find that all translation-based features rank in the top 10 features with the highest number of splits. This again confirms that matching alternative expressions is an important factor of why our method works. The GL2 model from the Divergence From Randomness family of scoring functions ranks first in terms of total gain of splits, suggesting that traditional bag-of-words retrieval models still form the backbone of learning to rank.

4.2 Results on Document Ranking

To explore the generality of our LTR approach, we also conduct experiments on the MS MARCO document ranking task. We emphasize here that all experiments are conducted in a zero-shot manner, over paragraph extracts from the collection, what is commonly known as the MaxP approach (Bendersky and Kurland, 2009; Dai and Callan, 2019; Akkalyoncu Yilmaz et al., 2019; Sheetrit et al., 2020). Both the final-stage neural reranker and our LTR module are trained on MS MARCO *passage* data only. However, comparing our effectiveness results with the official leaderboard reveals that our configurations are competitive compared to other single-stage rerankers.

Results are shown in Table 5, organized in the same manner as Table 2. Recall again that the goal here is also to retain effectiveness parity with respect to the reference reranker (T5 in this case). We conduct two-tailed paired t-tests to confirm that there are no statistically significant effectiveness differences between all model configurations. We see that in a zero-shot setting, speedups of nearly $3\times$ can be observed.

We have a few explanations of why the speedups here are not as impressive as in the passage ranking case. First, because we are not training a corpus-specific model, the power of the LTR module is weaker, and hence the pipeline needs to consider more candidates—larger N means more time in final-stage neural reranking, and hence less savings. Additionally, input to the neural models are on average much longer than the candidates from the passage corpus. This means that there is more text and richer signals for the transformers to extract, which correspondingly means that LTR is more impoverished. Furthermore, longer documents translate into more time spent on feature extraction in LTR. Taken together, all of these issues result in smaller speedups.

Configurlation	N	MRR@100	NDCG@10	Latency	
BoW(1k) + T5	1000	0.405	0.470	18.2s	
BoW(10k) + LTR(550) + T5	550	0.406	0.474	10.0s	(1.8×)
BoW(10k) + LTR_{d2q}(750)+ T5	750	0.405	0.470	13.7s	(1.4×)
BoW_{d2q}(1k) + T5	1000	0.409	0.476	18.2s	
BoW_{d2q}(1k) + LTR_{d2q}(350)+ T5	350	0.409	0.476	6.4s	(2.8×)

Table 5: The effectiveness and efficiency of different pipeline configurations on the MS MARCO document ranking task. The effectiveness of the pipelines with additional LTR modules are statistically indistinguishable from the baselines without the LTR modules.

5 Related Work

At a high level, the entire premise of our work *is* the point of multi-stage ranking, in that the architecture evolved to achieve a good balance between effectiveness and efficiency in end-to-end retrieval. Motivated by the observation, dating back more than a decade, that effective techniques are often computationally expensive, multi-stage retrieval architectures control latency by applying expensive techniques over only the most promising candidates (Wang et al., 2011). This is often operationalized as optimizing for recall in the earlier stages of the pipeline. Specifically in the context of transformers, multi-stage neural pipelines have been explored in the past by many researchers (Nogueira et al., 2019a; Soldaini and Moschitti, 2020; Matsubara et al., 2020; Pradeep et al., 2021). The key difference in our work is the (re-)introduction of "traditional" feature-based learning-to-rank approaches alongside neural models. This aligns with our broader goal of investigating how learning to rank might contribute to modern retrieval approaches dominated by neural models.

The computational costs associated with ranking using pretrained transformers can be reduced in various ways. We can accelerate inference using smaller or simpler models. Gao et al. (2020) use distillation to transfer knowledge captured in a larger model into a smaller model, achieving substantial speedups with minimal effectiveness loss. Hofstätter et al. (2020) propose a simpler transformer model to capture contextual information that trades effectiveness for much faster inference. Additional examples of this approach include Mitra et al. (2020) and MacAvaney et al. (2020). An alternative is to introduce early-exit optimizations, as in Soldaini and Moschitti (2020) and Xin et al. (2020). Further speedups can be gained by making modifications to the backbone transformer model, as in Sanh et al. (2020). The key point is that our proposed LTR filtering module achieves speedups in a manner that is orthogonal to the methods discussed here, which focus on directly accelerating transformer inference. Thus, these approaches can be combined with our method for even greater efficiency gains.

6 Conclusions

The "retrieve-then-rerank" approach with transformers has been demonstrated to be effective in many IR tasks, but poor efficiency makes it less attractive for real-world applications. Our goal is to increase the efficiency of the entire pipeline but at the same time maintain the same level of effectiveness: this is achieved by a feature-based learning-to-rank module that filters candidates prior to neural reranking. On the MS MARCO passage ranking task, we observe up to 18× speedup without degradation in terms of MRR@10. In a zero-shot setting on the MS MARCO document ranking task, we can achieve 3× speedup. These results demonstrate that in this age of muppets dominated by transformers and other neural models, learning-to-rank techniques can still be useful. Despite LTR "falling out of fashion", we should not "throw the baby out with the bath water".

One key point that bears emphasis, and one promising direction for future research is that our work can be combined with other approaches that directly accelerate inference in neural models. We expect speedups to be cumulative since we tackle efficiency issues from an orthogonal perspective.

Acknowledgements

The research conducted at the University of Waterloo was supported in part by the Canada First Research Excellence Fund and the Natural Sciences and Engineering Research Council (NSERC) of Canada; computational resources were provided by Compute Canada. The research conducted at the University of Delaware was supported as part of the Center for Plastics Innovation, an Energy Frontier Research Center, funded by the U.S. Department of Energy (DOE), Office of Science, Basic Energy Sciences (BES), under Award Number DE-SC0021166.

References

Zeynep Akkalyoncu Yilmaz, Wei Yang, Haotian Zhang, and Jimmy Lin. 2019. Cross-domain modeling of sentence-level evidence for document retrieval. In *Proceedings of the 2019 Conference on Empirical Methods in Natural Language Processing and the 9th International Joint Conference on Natural Language Processing (EMNLP-IJCNLP)*, pages 3490–3496, Hong Kong, China.

Nima Asadi and Jimmy Lin. 2013. Document vector representations for feature extraction in multi-stage document ranking. *Information Retrieval*, 16(6):747–768.

Payal Bajaj, Daniel Campos, Nick Craswell, Li Deng, Jianfeng Gao, Xiaodong Liu, Rangan Majumder, Andrew McNamara, Bhaskar Mitra, Tri Nguyen, Mir Rosenberg, Xia Song, Alina Stoica, Saurabh Tiwary, and Tong Wang. 2018. MS MARCO: A Human Generated MAchine Reading COmprehension Dataset. *arXiv:1611.09268v3*.

Michael Bendersky and Oren Kurland. 2009. Utilizing passage-based language models for ad hoc document retrieval. *Information Retrieval*, 13:157–187.

Leonid Boytsov and Zico Kolter. 2021. Exploring classic and neural lexical translation models for information retrieval: Interpretability, effectiveness, and efficiency benefits. *arXiv:2102.06815*.

Leonid Boytsov and Eric Nyberg. 2020. Flexible retrieval with NMSLIB and FlexNeuART. *arXiv:2010.14848*.

Zhuyun Dai and Jamie Callan. 2019. Deeper text understanding for IR with contextual neural language modeling. In *Proceedings of the 42nd Annual International ACM SIGIR Conference on Research and Development in Information Retrieval (SIGIR 2019)*, pages 985–988, Paris, France.

Jacob Devlin, Ming-Wei Chang, Kenton Lee, and Kristina Toutanova. 2019. BERT: Pre-training of deep bidirectional transformers for language understanding. In *Proceedings of the 2019 Conference of the North American Chapter of the Association for Computational Linguistics: Human Language Technologies, Volume 1 (Long and Short Papers)*, pages 4171–4186, Minneapolis, Minnesota.

Luke Gallagher, Antonio Mallia, J. Shane Culpepper, Torsten Suel, and B. Barla Cambazoglu. 2020. Feature extraction for large-scale text collections. In *Proceedings of the 29th ACM International Conference on Information and Knowledge Management*, pages 3015–3022.

Luyu Gao, Zhuyun Dai, and Jamie Callan. 2020. Understanding BERT rankers under distillation. In *Proceedings of the 2020 ACM SIGIR International Conference on Theory of Information Retrieval (ICTIR 2020)*.

Sebastian Hofstätter and Allan Hanbury. 2019. Let's measure run time! Extending the IR replicability infrastructure to include performance aspects. In *Proceedings of the Open-Source IR Replicability Challenge (OSIRRC 2019): CEUR Workshop Proceedings Vol-2409*, pages 12–16, Paris, France.

Sebastian Hofstätter, Markus Zlabinger, and Allan Hanbury. 2020. Interpretable & time-budget-constrained contextualization for re-ranking. In *Proceedings of the 24th European Conference on Artificial Intelligence (ECAI 2020)*, Santiago de Compostela, Spain.

Jyun-Yu Jiang, Chenyan Xiong, Chia-Jung Lee, and Wei Wang. 2020. Long document ranking with query-directed sparse transformer. In *Findings of the Association for Computational Linguistics: EMNLP 2020*, pages 4594–4605.

Omar Khattab and Matei Zaharia. 2020. ColBERT: Efficient and effective passage search via contextualized late interaction over BERT. In *Proceedings of the 43rd International ACM SIGIR Conference on Research and Development in Information Retrieval (SIGIR 2020)*, pages 39–48.

Jimmy Lin, Xueguang Ma, Sheng-Chieh Lin, Jheng-Hong Yang, Ronak Pradeep, and Rodrigo Nogueira. 2021. Pyserini: A Python toolkit for reproducible information retrieval research with sparse and dense representations. In *Proceedings of the 44th Annual International ACM SIGIR Conference on Research and Development in Information Retrieval (SIGIR 2021)*, pages 2356–2362.

Jimmy Lin, Rodrigo Nogueira, and Andrew Yates. 2020a. Pretrained transformers for text ranking: BERT and beyond. *arXiv:2010.06467*.

Sheng-Chieh Lin, Jheng-Hong Yang, and Jimmy Lin. 2020b. Distilling dense representations for ranking using tightly-coupled teachers. *arXiv:2010.11386*.

Xiaolu Lu, Alistair Moffat, and J. Shane Culpepper. 2015. On the cost of extracting proximity features for term-dependency models. In *Proceedings of the 24th ACM International on Conference on Information and Knowledge Management*, pages 293–302.

Sean MacAvaney, Franco Maria Nardini, Raffaele Perego, Nicola Tonellotto, Nazli Goharian, and Ophir Frieder. 2020. Efficient document re-ranking for transformers by precomputing term representations. In *Proceedings of the 43rd International ACM SIGIR Conference on Research and Development in Information Retrieval (SIGIR 2020)*, pages 49–58.

Yoshitomo Matsubara, Thuy Vu, and Alessandro Moschitti. 2020. Reranking for efficient transformer-based answer selection. In *Proceedings of the 43rd International ACM SIGIR Conference on Research and Development in Information Retrieval (SIGIR 2020)*, pages 1577–1580.

Donald Metzler and W. Bruce Croft. 2005. A Markov random field model for term dependencies. In *Proceedings of the 28th Annual International ACM SIGIR Conference on Research and Development in Information Retrieval (SIGIR 2005)*, pages 472–479, Salvador, Brazil.

Bhaskar Mitra, Sebastian Hofstätter, Hamed Zamani, and Nick Craswell. 2020. Conformer-kernel with query term independence for document retrieval. *arXiv:2007.10434*.

Rodrigo Nogueira and Kyunghyun Cho. 2019. Passage re-ranking with BERT. *arXiv:1901.04085*.

Rodrigo Nogueira, Zhiying Jiang, Ronak Pradeep, and Jimmy Lin. 2020. Document ranking with a pre-trained sequence-to-sequence model. In *Findings of the Association for Computational Linguistics: EMNLP 2020*, pages 708–718.

Rodrigo Nogueira and Jimmy Lin. 2019. From doc2query to docTTTTTquery.

Rodrigo Nogueira, Wei Yang, Kyunghyun Cho, and Jimmy Lin. 2019a. Multi-stage document ranking with BERT. *arXiv:1910.14424*.

Rodrigo Nogueira, Wei Yang, Jimmy Lin, and Kyunghyun Cho. 2019b. Document expansion by query prediction. *arXiv:1904.08375*.

Ronak Pradeep, Rodrigo Nogueira, and Jimmy Lin. 2021. The expando-mono-duo design pattern for text ranking with pretrained sequence-to-sequence models. *arXiv:2101.05667*.

Tao Qin and Tie-Yan Liu. 2013. Introducing LETOR 4.0 datasets. *arXiv:1306.2597*.

Victor Sanh, Lysandre Debut, Julien Chaumond, and Thomas Wolf. 2020. DistilBERT, a distilled version of BERT: Smaller, faster, cheaper and lighter. In *Proceedings of the 5th Workshop on Energy Efficient Machine Learning and Cognitive Computing at NeurIPS 2019*, Vancouver, British Columbia, Canada.

Eilon Sheetrit, Anna Shtok, and Oren Kurland. 2020. A passage-based approach to learning to rank documents. *Information Retrieval Journal*, 23:159–186.

Luca Soldaini and Alessandro Moschitti. 2020. The cascade transformer: An application for efficient answer sentence selection. In *Proceedings of the 58th Annual Meeting of the Association for Computational Linguistics*, pages 5697–5708.

Lidan Wang, Jimmy Lin, and Donald Metzler. 2011. A cascade ranking model for efficient ranked retrieval. In *Proceedings of the 34th Annual International ACM SIGIR Conference on Research and Development in Information Retrieval (SIGIR 2011)*, pages 105–114, Beijing, China.

Xiao Wang, Yaxiong Wu, Xi Wang, Craig Macdonald, and Iadh Ounis. 2020. University of Glasgow Terrier team at the TREC 2020 deep learning track. In *Proceedings of the Twenty-Ninth Text REtrieval Conference (TREC 2020)*.

Ji Xin, Rodrigo Nogueira, Yaoliang Yu, and Jimmy Lin. 2020. Early exiting BERT for efficient document ranking. In *Proceedings of SustaiNLP: Workshop on Simple and Efficient Natural Language Processing*, pages 83–88.

Lee Xiong, Chenyan Xiong, Ye Li, Kwok-Fung Tang, Jialin Liu, Paul Bennett, Junaid Ahmed, and Arnold Overwijk. 2020. Approximate nearest neighbor negative contrastive learning for dense text retrieval. *arXiv:2007.00808*.

Peilin Yang, Hui Fang, and Jimmy Lin. 2018. Anserini: Reproducible ranking baselines using Lucene. *Journal of Data and Information Quality*, 10(4):1–20.

A Appendix

A.1 Full List of LTR Features

Term-based				
				Sum of ICTF
Average of BM25	Average of DFR_GL2	Average of DFR_in_expB2	Average of DPH	Average of ICTF
Median of BM25	Median of DFR_GL2	Median of DFR_in_expB2	Median of DPH	Median of ICTF
Max of BM25	Max of DFR_GL2	Max of DFR_in_expB2	Max of DPH	Max of ICTF
Min of BM25	Min of DFR_GL2	Min of DFR_in_expB2	Min of DPH	Min of ICTF
MaxMinRatio of BM25	MaxMinRatio of DFR_GL2	MaxMinRatio of DFR_in_expB2	MaxMinRatio of DPH	MaxMinRatio of ICTF
Sum of IDF		Sum of Normalized TF	Sum of TF	
Average of IDF	Average of LMDir	Average of Normalized TF	Average of TF	Average of TFIDF
Median of IDF	Median of LMDir	Median of Normalized TF	Median of TF	Median of TFIDF
Max of IDF	Max of LMDir	Max of Normalized TF	Max of TF	Max of TFIDF
Min of IDF	Min of LMDir	Min of Normalized TF	Min of TF	Min of TFIDF
MaxMinRatio of IDF	MaxMinRatio of LMDir	MaxMinRatio of Normalized TF	MaxMinRatio of TF	MaxMinRatio of TFIDF
Score-based				
SCS	Probablity Sum	Doc Size	Query Length	Query Coverage Ratio
Unique Term Count in Query	Matching Term Count	Normalized TFIDF	BM25	LMDir
DFR_GL2	DFR_in_expB2	DPH	TFIDF	
Proximity-based				
UnorderedSequentialPairs with gap 3	OrderedSequentialPairs with gap 3	UnorderedQueryPairs with gap 3	OrderedQueryPairs with gap 3	BM25-TP
UnorderedSequentialPairs with gap 8	OrderedSequentialPairs with gap 8	UnorderedQueryPairs with gap 8	OrderedQueryPairs with gap 8	Proximity
UnorderedSequentialPairs with gap 15	OrderedSequentialPairs with gap 15	UnorderedQueryPairs with gap 15	OrderedQueryPairs with gap 15	TP distance
Translation-based				
title IBM Model1(*raw* field)	url IBM Model1(*raw* field)	body IBM Model1(*raw* field)	body IBM Model (*subword* field)	

Improving Synonym Recommendation Using Sentence Context

Maria Glenski
Pacific Northwest National Laboratory
Maria.Glenski@pnnl.gov

William Sealy
Georgia Institute of Technology
william.sealy@gatech.edu

Kate Miller
Pacific Northwest National Laboratory
Kate.Miller@pnnl.gov

Dustin Arendt
Pacific Northwest National Laboratory
Dustin.Arendt@pnnl.gov

Abstract

Traditional synonym recommendations often include ill-suited suggestions for writer's specific contexts. We propose a simple approach for contextual synonym recommendation by combining existing human-curated thesauri, e.g. WordNet, with pre-trained language models. We evaluate our technique by curating a set of word-sentence pairs balanced across corpora and parts of speech, then annotating each word-sentence pair with the contextually appropriate set of synonyms. We found that basic language model approaches have higher precision. Approaches leveraging sentence context have higher recall. Overall, the latter contextual approach had the highest F-score.

1 Introduction

Writers often rely on thesauri to recommend synonyms to replace a given word. Though many provide usages of synonyms within example contexts, they cannot account for the specific context of the word "live", i.e., in a writer's specific context. Thus many synonym recommendations are inappropriate, leading writers to reject most synonyms proffered. We propose and evaluate a simple technique to address this problem by combining large scale pre-trained language models and hand-curated thesauri to improve the precision of synonym recommendations in context.

Early research on synonyms and semantic analysis began in the early 1960s and 1970s (Katz and Fodor, 1963) and semantic network representations were popularized by Quillian (Quillian, 1967), Collins (Collins and Quillian, 1969), Woods (Woods, 1975), Brachman (Brachman, 1979) and others. Simplifying these earlier theoretical concepts, the Princeton WordNet was created (Miller et al., 1990). WordNet is a online reference system constructed of synonym sets (synsets) which utilize semantic inheritance to describe word relations. It has served as a widely-adopted baseline tool for synonym retrieval and synset creation.

The NLP community has since developed language models, e.g., Word2Vec (Mikolov et al., 2013), BERT (Devlin et al., 2018) where nearest neighbors in these models' embedding spaces are often synonyms. However, large scale language models have been recently criticized for their complexity, bias, and high energy consumption of training on large-scale web crawls (Bender et al., 2021). Fortunately, pre-trained versions of large scale language models are conveniently available, e.g., SentenceTransformers[1]. This allows researchers or practitioners to use and extend these models for a variety of applications, helping to amortize some costs incurred during training of large scale models.

In addressing the challenges of synonym recommendation and sustainable NLP, this paper makes three contributions: (1) a simple NLP technique using pre-trained language models for contextual synonym recommendation; (2) an approach for producing effective evaluation datasets for this task; and (3) a set of human annotations for the above dataset for our current and future evaluations.

2 Methodology

We identified two baseline synonym tools that rely on token-based lookups — *WordNet* (Miller, 1995) synsets (using the NLTK[2] package (Bird et al., 2009)) and *PyDictionary*[3] (using results from synonym.com) — and an existing counterfactual generative model, PolyJuice (Wu et al., 2021), to provide a baseline comparison for our novel contextual synonym models. Both WordNet and PyDictionary are freely available without API restrictions and commonly used NLP tools, while PolyJuice is a recently released GPT-2 (Radford et al., 2019) model fine-tuned for counterfactual generation.

Two of PolyJuice transformations were relevant: *lexical* and *resemantic* replacement. Lexical re-

[1] https://www.sbert.net
[2] https://www.nltk.org/
[3] pypi.org/project/PyDictionary/

Proceedings of the 2nd Workshop on Simple and Efficient Natural Language Processing, pages 74–78
November 10, 2021.

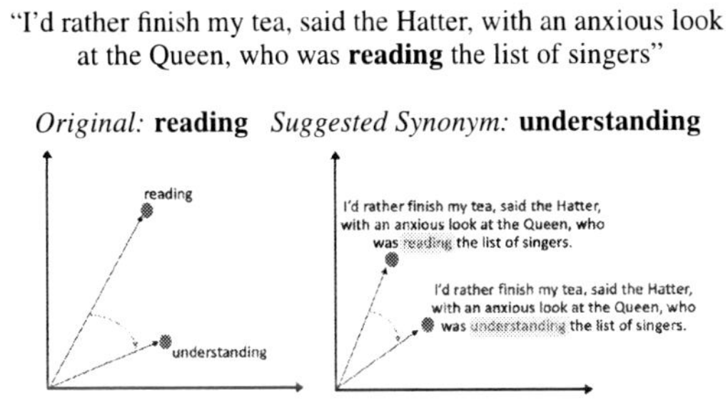

Figure 1: Illustration of the difference calculating cosine similarity between embedding vectors used to filter synonyms for the basic (general) context wrapper (left) and the sentence context wrapper (right) that considers the practical usage in context of the target sentence.

placements suggest alternatives to single words or noun chunks, without altering the part of speech. Resemantic replacements generate replacement phrases that do not alter the dependency tree.

We introduce two novel semantic context wrapper models that leverage pre-trained embeddings to identify synonyms of best fit in context of use. In the *basic context* model, we leverage the general similarity of contextual token embeddings of suggested synonyms to original tokens. This allows us to separate general but unlikely synonyms, edge cases, or noise from the base thesaurus suggestions from those that are generally appropriate in practical use. For example, this is particularly advantageous for tokens that can be used as multiple parts of speech such as "address" or "lead". Our second contextual model, *sentence context*, relies on the distance from the original sentence when the suggested synonym is used in replacement. Both models require a base thesaurus (*e.g.,* WordNet), and we evaluate the performance of three base thesauri: the WordNet and PyDictionary baselines individually, and the union of WordNet and PyDictionary suggestions.

We illustrate the difference in calculating the similarity in the embedding space between the basic (or general) context and sentence context wrappers in Figure 1 for an example sentence: *"I'd rather finish my tea, said the Hatter, with an anxious look at the Queen, who was* ***reading*** *the list of singers*". For both wrappers, we use the same pre-trained sentence-level embedding model, "msmarco-distilroberta-base-v2"[4] using the implementation provided by the sentence_transformers package[5] (Reimers and Gurevych, 2019). The similarity threshold used to exclude unrelated or impractical synonym suggestions is a tunable parameter in our wrapper models, so we establish a high threshold (similarity ≥ 0.3 for basic, 0.9 for sentence context) and low threshold (similarity ≥ 0.25 for basic, 0.8 for sentence context) for each, where thresholds were identified in preliminary experiments that identified tipping points in trade-offs between recall and precision.

3 Evaluation

We curated a balanced annotated dataset of synonyms in context using a vocabulary of candidate synonyms from existing datasets used for synonym research. Our dataset includes examples of their usage in sentences taken from open source datasets covering literary, news, and technical writing.

3.1 Data Preparation

We merged three existing synonym evaluation datasets (SimVerb-3500 (Gerz et al., 2016), SimLex-999 (Hill et al., 2015), and MEN (Bruni et al., 2014)) to build our vocabulary of candidate synonyms. We then identified candidate sentences containing these across our text corpora: *Alice's Adventures in Wonderland* and *The Adventures of Sherlock Holmes*, available from Project Gutenberg[6]; *BBC News*[7], and *NeurIPS* abstracts[8].

We removed candidate words whose synonym sets were smaller than 5 words or greater than 15 then removed words in the bottom 5% and top 95% of the term frequency distribution of the vocabulary. We also excluded sentences with fewer than 80 characters or more than 250 characters, and sentences where spaCy[9] named entity recognition indicated the tagged word for replacement was an entity. This resulted in 735 candidate words across 22,632 candidate sentences.

We ranked candidate words by the total number of different parts of speech (POS) observed across all corpora, and selected the top 35 candidate words. We then randomly selected one sentence from each corpus for each observed POS for a total of 229 sentences to annotate, summarized in Table 1.

[4] https://huggingface.co/sentence-transformers/msmarco-distilroberta-base-v2

[5] https://www.sbert.net/

[6] https://www.gutenberg.org/

[7] http://mlg.ucd.ie/datasets/bbc.html

[8] www.kaggle.com/benhamner/nips-papers

[9] https://spacy.io/

ADJ	ADV	NOUN	VERB	
		x	x	address (6); call (7); care (7); claim (6); drive (6); fall (7); follow (6); hold (8); line (6); map (6); mind (7); note (6); promise (6); reading (7); rise (6); sign (6); stand (6); step (6); stop (7); wait (6); watch (6)
	x	x	x	advance (7)
x			x	narrow (6)
x		x	x	bottom (7); break (7); delay (7); hurt (6); mean (8); post (6); sketch (7); snap (6)
x	x			sure (6); wide (6)
x	x		x	direct (7)
x	x	x	x	lead (9)

Table 1: An overview of the dataset for annotation, where an 'x' indicates the parts of speech observed for the words in their sentence contexts. Parentheses contain the number of sentences the word occurs in.

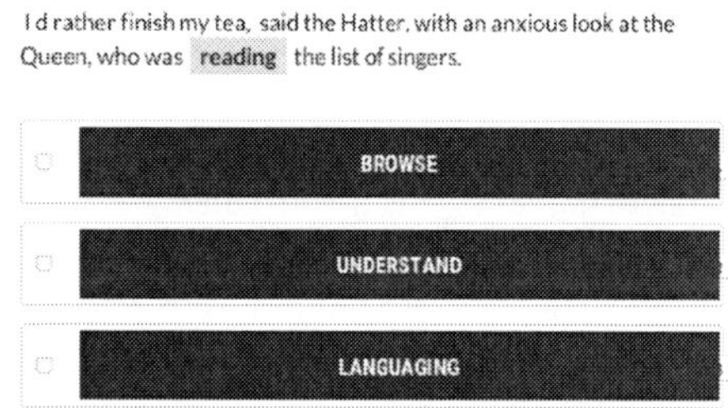

Figure 2: Screen capture of the interface used to collect annotations on synonyms in context. For space, the image has been truncated after the first three synonyms.

3.2 Annotation Protocol

For each sentence, the outputs of our models were merged into a list of synonyms. A Prodigy[10] "text classification recipe" was extended to allow annotators to mark all synonyms that were correct substitutions in the context of the sentence for the given/highlighted word. Figure 2 shows an example of the interface used for annotation.

Authors of this paper were the annotators, so annotation was conducted without indication of which model(s) provided suggestions to avoid bias. We developed and followed the guidelines below:

- Accept if direct substitution of the synonym with the word is appropriate.
- Maintaining syntactic correctness after substitution is not required.
- Given synonyms with different stems, accept only the one with the best substitution.
- Accept synonyms that would be appropriate if they replaced a phrase containing the word.
- Reject words that were part of technical or proper noun phrases.

Overall annotator agreement was high, and annotators took approximately 2 hours to complete the task. We measured agreement by counting the number of annotators who either accepted or rejected a synonym (per word, per context). Annotators "agreed" if the majority of annotators accepted a synonym, or all annotators rejected a synonym. Averaged across all 3911 synonyms, annotators agreed 91% of the time. Averaged across the 782 synonyms where at least one annotator accepted a word, annotators agreed 54% of the time.

3.3 Results

We evaluated model effectiveness using precision, recall, and F-score (F1) calculated per sentence (comparing the set of synonyms produced by the model to those accepted by a majority of annotators), then averaged across sentences. The performance of PolyJuice was very low (F1 < 0.003) relative to the other models, so we omitted it from subsequent analysis and discussion. Figure 3 shows the average precision versus recall. Despite comparable F1, "basic context" had higher precision, outperforming the baselines and other approaches in this dimension, while "sentence context" had higher recall and similarly outperformed the baselines and other approaches. High versus low thresholds affect model performance slightly for basic context, and not at all for sentence context models. Combining WordNet and PyDictionary improved model F1 by greatly improving recall for sentence context models and modestly improved recall for basic context, but did so at the cost of precision.

We also explored whether overall performance was consistent within corpora, show in Fig. 4. These plots reveal that model performance in literary corpora (Alice and Sherlock) was less consistent than the others. Models sHwp and sLwp were within the top three models in each case, only outperformed by bLwp in Sherlock and NeurIPS.

Figure 5 compares the precision and recall of the two model approaches at the individual word level, and shows the same trends seen on aggregate. In cases where the basic context model has non-

[10] `https://prodi.gy`

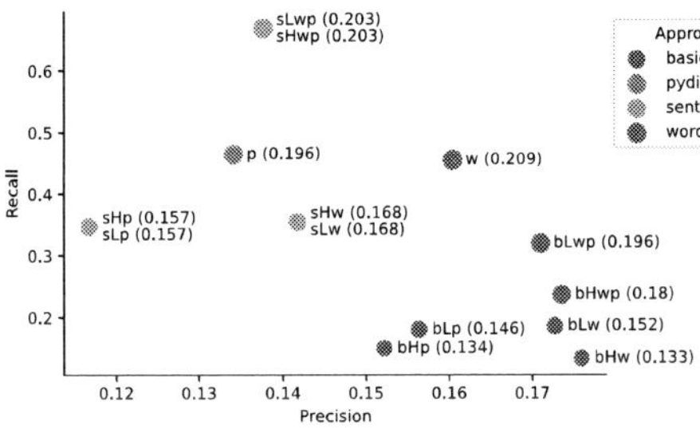

Figure 3: Average Precision versus Recall for top models, colored by model. F-score is shown in parentheses. Model names are abbreviated according to basic versus sentence context, High vs Low threshold, and the combination of WordNet and PyDictionary base.

zero precision/recall, the sentence context model achieves higher recall at the expense of some precision. More often, however, the sentence context model has non-zero precision/recall compared to zero precision/recall for the basic context model.

4 Conclusions and Future Work

Our main finding was that sentence context-based models improve overall performance by trading off a small loss in precision for a large gain in recall. As both techniques were nearest neighbor based, the sentence context approach allowed acceptable synonyms to be identified for the specified context that were less applicable in a general context (i.e., farther away in the word embedding used by the basic context model). An interpretation of this is that pure word embedding techniques will be most effective for the most frequently used synonyms, but sentence context techniques perform better to identify synonyms in less common usage. This is also an area where there is the greatest potential impact for contextual synonym approaches over traditional thesauri or synsets.

We note that overall F-scores were low, indicating the task was challenging and has room for model improvements. For example, a limitation of our approach is the reliance on hand curated synsets or thesauri, i.e., WordNet and PyDictionary. The model's true recall is bounded by the recall of these thesauri. During annotation, there were several cases where none of the recommendations were appropriate, but the annotators remarked they could recall acceptable synonyms. Using proprietary thesauri could be used to improve model performance, e.g., the Miriam-Webster API[11] provides synonyms

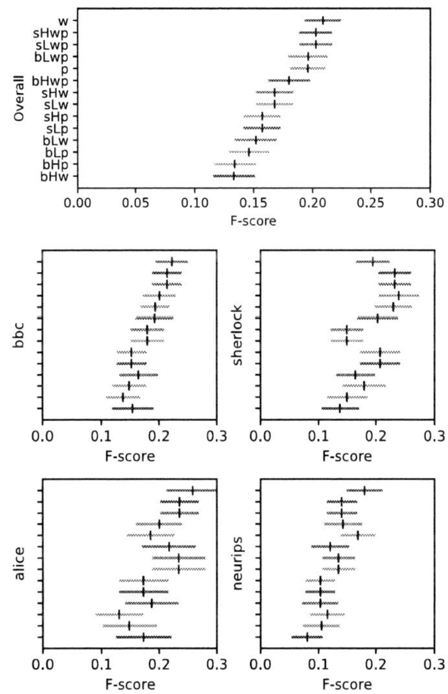

Figure 4: Model performance (F1) overall and within corpora. Error bars show standard error of the mean.

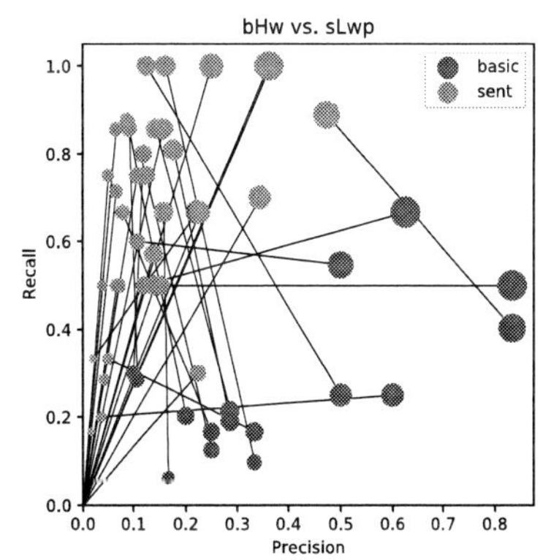

Figure 5: Word-level precision vs. recall for the top models. Lines connect the same word across models.

faceted by verb case as well as contextual sentence examples. Furthermore, limiting context to phrases between the entire sentence and a single word level could further improve performance by eliminating irrelevant sentence context.

Beyond synonym recommendation for end users, our technique could be used to perturb model input to help quantify model robustness, for counterfactual explanations, or for query rewriting.

[11] https://dictionaryapi.com

Acknowledgements

Any opinions, findings, and conclusions or recommendations expressed in this material are those of the author(s) and do not necessarily reflect the views of the United States Government or any agency thereof.

References

Emily M Bender, Timnit Gebru, Angelina McMillan-Major, and Shmargaret Shmitchell. 2021. On the dangers of stochastic parrots: Can language models be too big? In *Proceedings of the 2021 ACM Conference on Fairness, Accountability, and Transparency*, pages 610–623.

Steven Bird, Ewan Klein, and Edward Loper. 2009. *Natural language processing with Python: analyzing text with the natural language toolkit.* " O'Reilly Media, Inc.".

Ronald J Brachman. 1979. On the epistemological status of semantic networks. In *Associative networks*, pages 3–50. Elsevier.

Elia Bruni, Nam-Khanh Tran, and Marco Baroni. 2014. Multimodal distributional semantics. *Journal of artificial intelligence research*, 49:1–47.

Allan M. Collins and M. Ross Quillian. 1969. Retrieval time from semantic memory. *Journal of Verbal Learning and Verbal Behavior*, 8(2):240–247.

Jacob Devlin, Ming-Wei Chang, Kenton Lee, and Kristina Toutanova. 2018. Bert: Pre-training of deep bidirectional transformers for language understanding. *arXiv preprint arXiv:1810.04805.*

Daniela Gerz, Ivan Vulić, Felix Hill, Roi Reichart, and Anna Korhonen. 2016. Simverb-3500: A large-scale evaluation set of verb similarity. In *Proceedings of the 2016 Conference on Empirical Methods in Natural Language Processing*, pages 2173–2182.

Felix Hill, Roi Reichart, and Anna Korhonen. 2015. Simlex-999: Evaluating semantic models with (genuine) similarity estimation. *Computational Linguistics*, 41(4):665–695.

Jerrold J Katz and Jerry A Fodor. 1963. The structure of a semantic theory. *language*, 39(2):170–210.

Tomas Mikolov, Ilya Sutskever, Kai Chen, Greg S Corrado, and Jeff Dean. 2013. Distributed representations of words and phrases and their compositionality. In *Advances in neural information processing systems*, pages 3111–3119.

George A Miller. 1995. Wordnet: a lexical database for english. *Communications of the ACM*, 38(11):39–41.

George A Miller, Richard Beckwith, Christiane Fellbaum, Derek Gross, and Katherine J Miller. 1990. Introduction to wordnet: An on-line lexical database. *International journal of lexicography*, 3(4):235–244.

M. Ross Quillian. 1967. Word concepts: A theory and simulation of some basic semantic capabilities. *Behavioral Science*, 12(5):410–430.

Alec Radford, Jeffrey Wu, Rewon Child, David Luan, Dario Amodei, Ilya Sutskever, et al. 2019. Language models are unsupervised multitask learners. *OpenAI blog*, 1(8):9.

Nils Reimers and Iryna Gurevych. 2019. Sentence-bert: Sentence embeddings using siamese bert-networks. In *Proceedings of the 2019 Conference on Empirical Methods in Natural Language Processing*. Association for Computational Linguistics.

William A Woods. 1975. What's in a link: Foundations for semantic networks. In *Representation and understanding*, pages 35–82. Elsevier.

Tongshuang Wu, Marco Tulio Ribeiro, Jeffrey Heer, and Daniel S Weld. 2021. Polyjuice: Generating counterfactuals for explaining, evaluating, and improving models. In *Proceedings of the 59th Annual Meeting of the Association for Computational Linguistics*.

Semantic Categorization of Social Knowledge for Commonsense Question Answering

Gengyu Wang[1] Xiaochen Hou[2]
Diyi Yang[3] Kathleen McKeown[1] Jing Huang[2]
[1]Columbia University, New York, NY
[2]JD AI Research, Mountain View, CA
[3]Georgia Institute of Technology, Atlanta, GA
gengyu.wang@columbia.edu, houxiaochen1994@hotmail.com
diyi.yang@cc.gatech.edu, kathy@cs.columbia.edu, jing.huang@jd.com

Abstract

Large pre-trained language models (PLMs) have led to great success on various commonsense question answering (QA) tasks in an end-to-end fashion. However, little attention has been paid to what commonsense knowledge is needed to deeply characterize these QA tasks. In this work, we proposed to categorize the semantics needed for these tasks using the SocialIQA as an example. Building upon our labeled social knowledge categories dataset on top of SocialIQA, we further train neural QA models to incorporate such social knowledge categories and relation information from a knowledge base. Unlike previous work, we observe our models with semantic categorizations of social knowledge can achieve comparable performance with a relatively simple model and smaller size compared to other complex approaches.

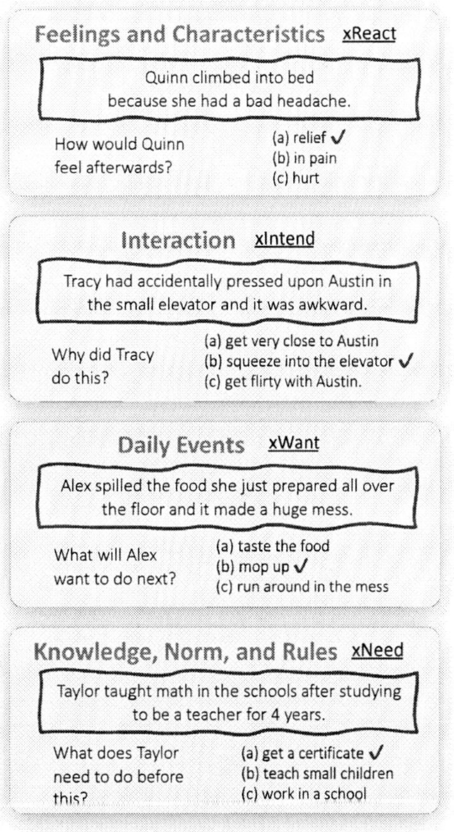

Figure 1: SocialIQA Examples for Social Knowledge Categories and **Question Relation Type**

1 Introduction

Recently, large pre-trained language models (PLMs) (Devlin et al., 2019; Raffel et al., 2019; Liu et al., 2019) have been widely used on various commonsense QA tasks such as CommonsenseQA (Malaviya et al., 2020), SocialIQA (Sap et al., 2019b), and Mostafazadeh et al. (2016); Huang et al. (2019); Boratko et al. (2020); Levesque et al. (2012); Roemmele et al. (2011). One line of work (Khashabi et al., 2020) improved the performances of these QA tasks by aggregating more QA data and using even bigger PLM T5 (Raffel et al., 2019). Other line of work tried to supplement the question context with retrieval of related knowledge from external knowledge bases (KB), or re-trained PLMs under the guidance of KBs (Shen et al., 2020; Shwartz et al., 2020; Mitra et al., 2019; Ji et al., 2020a,b).

However, very little past research has paid attention to the specific question/context knowledge types that are needed for these commonsense QA tasks. Therefore, in this paper, we go deeper into the QA task context and take a closer look at the semantics on what additional information can be inferred from the given question-answer context in order to answer a question. Using SocialIQA as an example, we propose to add two new context types (See Figure 1) into the neural QA model: one on question relation type derived from ATOMIC (which was used to create SocialIQA), and another knowledge category type from our own constructed social knowledge taxonomy. While the question

Proceedings of the 2nd Workshop on Simple and Efficient Natural Language Processing, pages 79–85
November 10, 2021. ©201 Association for Computational Linguistics

relation type derived from ATOMIC is restricted on ATOMIC related datasets, our constructed social knowledge category type has the potential be generally applied to other social knowledge related tasks.

To fully utilize these two new types of context information, we adopt a simple yet effective way of integrating this information to help in the neural QA model. Specifically, we concatenate each QA pair with its assigned question relation type or its social knowledge category as the input to a PLM (say RoBERTa (Liu et al., 2019)), and fine tune the RoBERTa model for the SocialIQA task. Our experimental results show that this simple and interpretable method not only outperforms the RoBERTa baseline model, but also achieves comparable performances as that of previous work, which adopted much more complex models to encode external knowledge or re-train large language models.

In terms of creating efficient and sustainable models for QA tasks, our work illustrates the importance of deep understanding of what knowledge is required for the specific commonsense tasks. Our constructed social knowledge category, along with experiment code and human annotations on some of the SocialIQA data, are released to the research community.[1]

2 Related Work

SocialIQA Task Most previous works on SocialIQA task involve either large size of pre-trained models, and datasets (Khashabi et al., 2020; Lourie et al., 2021) or complicated models that heavily rely on external knowledge bases (Shen et al., 2020; Shwartz et al., 2020; Mitra et al., 2019; Ji et al., 2020a,b; Chang et al., 2020). Among them, UnifiedQA (Khashabi et al., 2020) achieved impressive performance by fine-tuning 11B T5 model (Raffel et al., 2019) with 17 existing QA datasets. Unlike previous efforts, our work achieves comparable performance with a relatively small model and simple knowledge extraction method that does not rely on knowledge bases nor require additional pretraining.

Commonsense Categorization in NLP LoBue and Yates (2011) proposed form-based and content-based categories for commonsense knowledge that is involved in recognizing textual entailment. Boratko et al. (2018) refined the categorization method for knowledge and reasoning proposed for a QA dataset ARC (Clark et al., 2018). The human-annotated relevant sentences was used only for improving the retrieval model, not for the ARC task. In summary none of these work had attempted to leverage such categories in the intended task.

Social Knowledge Categorization Kiesler (1983) proposed a taxonomy for two-dimensional interpersonal behavior, which consists of 16 segments and 128 subclasses. Cowen and Keltner (2017) identified 27 distinct varieties of human emotion, such as anger, excitement, relief, etc. Recently, Forbes et al. (2020) introduced a formalism to study people's social and moral norms over daily life situations, which includes 12 different dimensions of people's judgments. Motivated by these prior work that covered different aspects of knowledge of daily events and social interactions, our work provides a comprehensive overview of social knowledge needed by the SocialIQA task.

3 Methodology

This section presents two approaches to model the underlying semantics and knowledge of the SocialIQA task, together with a simple yet effective method that leverages these knowledge types to improve QA models.

3.1 Question Relation Type

The SocialIQA dataset was derived from the ATOMIC (Sap et al., 2019a). ATOMIC is a knowledge base that focuses on everyday social commonsense knowledge organized as ten types of if-then relations. Based on this observation, we tag each question in SocialIQA according to its relation types in ATOMIC by conducting rule-based mapping between them. Specifically, we match keywords in the questions and use the Spacy model (Honnibal et al., 2020) to detect subjective and objective in context sentences. [2]

Once the mapped types are obtained for each SocialIQA question, we transfer such information to QA models by simply concatenating the tags to original QA examples in the format of $[Context, \text{SEP}, Question, \underline{Tag}, Answer]$ as input to a PLM for fine-tuning. [3] Although we

[1]https://github.com/posuer/social-commonsense-knolwedge

[2]Take the fourth instance in Figure 1 as an example; we firstly match the word "need" in question to the "Need" relation, then detect the name "Taylor" is subjective in the context, so we assign "xNeed" to this question.

[3]All the tags are added into the model's vocabulary as spe-

use RoBERTa model in this work, our method is generic and can be applied to any PLMs.

3.2 Social Knowledge Categorization

Although utilizing ATOMIC to obtain relation type is straightforward and simple, it is restricted to datasets derived from ATOMIC. Inspired by previous work around emotion and social interactions in psychology (Kiesler, 1983; Cowen and Keltner, 2017; Forbes et al., 2020), we propose a taxonomy to categorize social commonsense knowledge into types, which can be generally applied to other social commonsense reasoning related tasks. As shown in Figure 1, this taxonomy includes four categories as follows:

Feelings and Characteristics involves personal feelings and characteristics. Specifically, it includes the development of subsequent feelings and emotions, and events triggered by personal feelings, emotions or characteristics; the feelings and emotions caused by a certain event; and the personal characteristics reflected by a particular event.

Interaction includes events, daily life habits and experiences caused by interactions or emotions among two or more people, as well as interactions and possible responsibilities and obligations between individuals and groups.

Daily Events deal with relationships between daily events, habits, and life experiences. In this category, most situations only involve individuals. Even if multiple people are involved, the focus is on the event itself rather than on the interaction between people. For example, in such a scenario, "Two people went to the hair salon together, what will they do next?", it will be classified into this category even though it involves two persons.

Knowledge, Norm, and Rules Unlike daily events, the events included in this category usually involve social or scientific knowledge and rules that are written in documents or books. The knowledge and rules here may pertain to various topics such as legislation, law, career development, social identity, and medical care.

3.3 SocialIQA-Category Dataset

We manually annotate some of the SocialIQA data with our proposed four social knowledge categories.

cial tokens, for instance $[xNeed]$, and they are concatenated to QA examples in text form.

Model	Dev	Test
RoBERTa large	77.4	77.0
+ **Question Relation**	79.0	78.3
+ **Social Knowledge Cat**egory	79.4	78.5
+ **Question Relation + Social Knowledge Cat**	79.8	78.5
Knowledge Source (Mitra et al., 2019)	79.5	78.0
GLM (Shen et al., 2020)	79.6	78.6
Ablation Study:		
+ Question Relation **(Random)**	77.6	75.3
+ Social Knowledge Category **(Random)**	77.6	76.4

Table 1: Accuracy on SocialIQA test set

Among the total 800 examples in this dataset, 600 training examples are selected from SocialIQA training data, and 200 dev examples are selected from SocialIQA dev data.

Dataset Creation Since the annotation requires fully understanding the social knowledge category, two listed authors annotate two rounds of 50 examples, discuss the disagreements in the middle. The percentage of agreement on the second round is higher than 95%, which indicates that these categories are well-defined. Then each of the two annotators is responsible for another 350 examples separately.

Knowledge Category Prediction We fine-tune RoBERTa large model with the SocialIQA-Category training set and achieve up to 80% accuracy on the dev set for this four-category classification task. The trained model is used to assign category labels to the whole SocialIQA dataset automatically. Follow the same method in section 3.1, the obtained category labels are concatenated to original examples in the format of $[Context, \underline{label}, \text{SEP}, Question, Answer]$ to train and test the QA model.

4 Experiments and Results

We use the SocialIQA data set for our experiments. SocialIQA contains 33, 410 training examples, 1, 954 dev examples and 2, 224 test examples.

Models & Baselines We employ the RoBERTa-large model as baseline. Our proposed method uses RoBERTa-large models in the same way of the baseline, except concatenating the tags or labels to original QA examples (described in Section 3.1 and 3.3). We also compare our methods with the following published models on SocialIQA: *GLM* (Shen et al., 2020) re-trains the RoBERTa

Model	xIntent	xNeed	xAttr	xReact	xWant	xEffect	oReact	oWant	oEffect	Other
RoBERTa-large	0.20	0.22	0.26	0.24	0.26	0.24	0.23	0.23	0.28	0.21
+ Question Relation	**0.19**↓	**0.19**↓	**0.24**↓	**0.23**↓	**0.24**↓	**0.21**↓	0.23	**0.20**↓	**0.26**↓	**0.13**↓
+ Question Relation + Social Knowledge Cat.	0.22	0.23	**0.21**↓	**0.21**↓	**0.21**↓	0.21	0.23	**0.18**↓	**0.25**↓	0.17

Table 2: Error Rate Distribution of *Question Relation* model on SocialIQA Dev Set

Model	Feelings and Characteristics	Interaction	Daily Events	Knowledge, Norm, and Rules
RoBERTa-large	0.25	0.21	0.24	0.21
+Social Knowledge Category	**0.21**↓	**0.19**↓	**0.20**↓	0.22
+ Question Relation + Soc. Knowl. Cat.	0.21	**0.16**↓	0.20	0.26

Table 3: Error Rate Distribution of *Social Knowledge Category* model on SocialIQA-Category Dev Set

model by injecting structured knowledge from the knowledge graph. *Knowledge Source* (Mitra et al., 2019) concatenates the question, answer, and the context as the query to retrieve and re-rank the top ten sentences from ATOMIC, and then fuses them into the QA model to select the right answer.

Training Setup The hyperparameters are selected based on the best performing model on the dev set. We use grid search to fine-tune the model, and select select the learning rate from $\{1e-5, 2e-5\}$, batch size from $\{4, 8\}$ and gradient accumulation from $\{4, 8, 16\}$. The model is trained up to 4 epochs. [4]

Results We report the accuracy results on the SocialIQA test set in Table 1.

- Both ways of using knowledge type information outperform the RoBERTa baseline models. The paired t-test shows that *Social Knowledge Category* achieves significant gains over the RoBERTa model with $p < 0.05$, and *Question Relation* is a little short of significance on test set ($p = 0.06$).
- Compared with *GLM* and *Knowledge Source* that require large amounts of engineering work to explore external knowledge from ATOMIC, our simple and direct utilization of the ATOMIC relations and social knowledge categorization achieves competitive performances.
- The naive combination of question relation type and social knowledge category shows no gains over any single model. One reason may be that these two types of relations are not entirely orthogonal to each other.

[4]Details about the experiment setting is in Appendix.

Error Analysis We conduct detailed error analysis to examine the performance gains from *Question Relation* and *Social Knowledge Category* models. The results are presented in Table 2 and 3.

For the *Question Relation* model, we present the error rate under different relations on the socialIQA dev set. As we can see, the *Question Relation* model achieves consistent improvements on almost all relations, which proves the effectiveness of incorporating the logical relation type.

We also compare the error rate of the *Social Knowledge Category* and the *RoBERTa-large* on the manually annotated dev set with 200 examples. We observe performance gains on all categories except the Knowledge, Norm and Rules category. This suggests that current QA models still struggle with questions involving knowledge and norms, calling for more sophisticated techniques to reason over these social and scientific knowledge. [5]

Ablation Study We conduct the ablation study for our proposed method described in Section 3.1 and 3.3. While training and testing, the mapped relation type tag or predicted knowledge category label is replaced by a randomly chosen tag or label. The experiment result presented in Table 1 shows that the randomly chosen tags or labels could not help the QA models. The performance gains from knowledge of Question Relation or Social Knowledge Category are indeed valid.

5 Conclusion

In this work, using the SocialIQA task as an example, we integrate two different knowledge types into the QA model training: one based on question relations, and the other is our own defined social knowledge category. Experimental results demonstrated that incorporating semantic categorizations of social knowledge into QA models helps boost performances on the social commonsense QA task. The proposed simply ways of incorporating knowledge into the model also achieved comparable performances to these much complicated models.

[5]More examples and error analyses on these two types of relations can be found in Appendix.

6 Ethics

We create a dataset, SocialIQA-Category, by annotating part of the SocialIQA dataset (Sap et al., 2019a). SocialIQA dataset is accessible to the public and can be downloaded from an open URL. All the annotations are done by the listed authors of this paper. The annotations only include the aforementioned relation type and social knowledge category. Our work focuses on QA tasks, specifically the SocialIQA task. Neural models that are created for this task are not supposed to solve any real-world problem. In terms of environmental consequences, all of our experiments are done with the RoBERTa model. Models training for SocialIQA is usually done within 1 hour on a single GPU.

References

Michael Boratko, Xiang Li, Tim O'Gorman, Rajarshi Das, Dan Le, and Andrew McCallum. 2020. ProtoQA: A question answering dataset for prototypical common-sense reasoning. In *Proceedings of the 2020 Conference on Empirical Methods in Natural Language Processing (EMNLP)*, pages 1122–1136, Online. Association for Computational Linguistics.

Michael Boratko, Harshit Padigela, Divyendra Mikkilineni, Pritish Yuvraj, Rajarshi Das, Andrew McCallum, Maria Chang, Achille Fokoue-Nkoutche, Pavan Kapanipathi, Nicholas Mattei, Ryan Musa, Kartik Talamadupula, and Michael Witbrock. 2018. A systematic classification of knowledge, reasoning, and context within the ARC dataset. In *Proceedings of the Workshop on Machine Reading for Question Answering*, pages 60–70, Melbourne, Australia. Association for Computational Linguistics.

Ting-Yun Chang, Yang Liu, Karthik Gopalakrishnan, Behnam Hedayatnia, Pei Zhou, and Dilek Hakkani-Tur. 2020. Incorporating commonsense knowledge graph in pretrained models for social commonsense tasks. In *Proceedings of Deep Learning Inside Out (DeeLIO): The First Workshop on Knowledge Extraction and Integration for Deep Learning Architectures*, pages 74–79.

Peter Clark, Isaac Cowhey, Oren Etzioni, Tushar Khot, Ashish Sabharwal, Carissa Schoenick, and Oyvind Tafjord. 2018. Think you have solved question answering? try arc, the ai2 reasoning challenge. *arXiv preprint arXiv:1803.05457*.

Alan S. Cowen and Dacher Keltner. 2017. Self-report captures 27 distinct categories of emotion bridged by continuous gradients. *Proceedings of the National Academy of Sciences*, 114(38):E7900–E7909.

Jacob Devlin, Ming-Wei Chang, Kenton Lee, and Kristina Toutanova. 2019. BERT: Pre-training of deep bidirectional transformers for language understanding. In *Proceedings of the 2019 Conference of the North American Chapter of the Association for Computational Linguistics: Human Language Technologies, Volume 1 (Long and Short Papers)*, pages 4171–4186, Minneapolis, Minnesota. Association for Computational Linguistics.

Maxwell Forbes, Jena D. Hwang, Vered Shwartz, Maarten Sap, and Yejin Choi. 2020. Social chemistry 101: Learning to reason about social and moral norms. In *Proceedings of the 2020 Conference on Empirical Methods in Natural Language Processing (EMNLP)*, pages 653–670, Online. Association for Computational Linguistics.

Matthew Honnibal, Ines Montani, Sofie Van Landeghem, and Adriane Boyd. 2020. spaCy: Industrial-strength Natural Language Processing in Python.

Lifu Huang, Ronan Le Bras, Chandra Bhagavatula, and Yejin Choi. 2019. Cosmos qa: Machine reading comprehension with contextual commonsense reasoning. *arXiv preprint arXiv:1909.00277*.

Haozhe Ji, Pei Ke, Shaohan Huang, Furu Wei, and Minlie Huang. 2020a. Generating commonsense explanation by extracting bridge concepts from reasoning paths. *arXiv preprint arXiv:2009.11753*.

Haozhe Ji, Pei Ke, Shaohan Huang, Furu Wei, Xiaoyan Zhu, and Minlie Huang. 2020b. Language generation with multi-hop reasoning on commonsense knowledge graph. *arXiv preprint arXiv:2009.11692*.

Daniel Khashabi, Tushar Khot, Ashish Sabharwal, Oyvind Tafjord, Peter Clark, and Hannaneh Hajishirzi. 2020. Unifiedqa: Crossing format boundaries with a single qa system. *arXiv preprint arXiv:2005.00700*.

Donald J Kiesler. 1983. The 1982 interpersonal circle: A taxonomy for complementarity in human transactions. *Psychological review*, 90(3):185.

Hector Levesque, Ernest Davis, and Leora Morgenstern. 2012. The winograd schema challenge. In *Thirteenth International Conference on the Principles of Knowledge Representation and Reasoning*. Citeseer.

Yinhan Liu, Myle Ott, Naman Goyal, Jingfei Du, Mandar Joshi, Danqi Chen, Omer Levy, Mike Lewis, Luke Zettlemoyer, and Veselin Stoyanov. 2019. Roberta: A robustly optimized bert pretraining approach. *arXiv preprint arXiv:1907.11692*.

Peter LoBue and Alexander Yates. 2011. Types of common-sense knowledge needed for recognizing textual entailment. In *ACL-HLT 2011 - Proceedings of the 49th Annual Meeting of the Association for Computational Linguistics: Human Language Technologies*, volume 2, pages 329–334.

Nicholas Lourie, Ronan Le Bras, Chandra Bhagavatula, and Yejin Choi. 2021. Unicorn on rainbow: A universal commonsense reasoning model on a new multitask benchmark. *arXiv preprint arXiv:2103.13009*.

Chaitanya Malaviya, Chandra Bhagavatula, Antoine Bosselut, and Yejin Choi. 2020. Commonsense knowledge base completion with structural and semantic context. In *Proceedings of the AAAI Conference on Artificial Intelligence*, volume 34, pages 2925–2933.

Arindam Mitra, Pratyay Banerjee, Kuntal Kumar Pal, Swaroop Mishra, and Chitta Baral. 2019. How additional knowledge can improve natural language commonsense question answering? *arXiv preprint arXiv:1909.08855*.

Nasrin Mostafazadeh, Nathanael Chambers, Xiaodong He, Devi Parikh, Dhruv Batra, Lucy Vanderwende, Pushmeet Kohli, and James Allen. 2016. A corpus and evaluation framework for deeper understanding of commonsense stories. *arXiv preprint arXiv:1604.01696*.

Colin Raffel, Noam Shazeer, Adam Roberts, Katherine Lee, Sharan Narang, Michael Matena, Yanqi Zhou, Wei Li, and Peter J Liu. 2019. Exploring the limits of transfer learning with a unified text-to-text transformer. *arXiv preprint arXiv:1910.10683*.

Melissa Roemmele, Cosmin Adrian Bejan, and Andrew S Gordon. 2011. Choice of plausible alternatives: An evaluation of commonsense causal reasoning. In *AAAI Spring Symposium: Logical Formalizations of Commonsense Reasoning*, pages 90–95.

Maarten Sap, Ronan Le Bras, Emily Allaway, Chandra Bhagavatula, Nicholas Lourie, Hannah Rashkin, Brendan Roof, Noah A Smith, and Yejin Choi. 2019a. Atomic: An atlas of machine commonsense for if-then reasoning. In *Proceedings of the AAAI Conference on Artificial Intelligence*, volume 33, pages 3027–3035.

Maarten Sap, Hannah Rashkin, Derek Chen, Ronan LeBras, and Yejin Choi. 2019b. Socialiqa: Commonsense reasoning about social interactions. *arXiv preprint arXiv:1904.09728*.

Tao Shen, Yi Mao, Pengcheng He, Guodong Long, Adam Trischler, and Weizhu Chen. 2020. Exploiting structured knowledge in text via graph-guided representation learning. In *Proceedings of the 2020 Conference on Empirical Methods in Natural Language Processing (EMNLP)*, pages 8980–8994.

Vered Shwartz, Peter West, Ronan Le Bras, Chandra Bhagavatula, and Yejin Choi. 2020. Unsupervised commonsense question answering with self-talk. *arXiv preprint arXiv:2004.05483*.

A Appendix: Experiment Setting

The number of hyperparameter search trials is 12 for each model. During training, each epoch takes about 30 mins on average. The hyperparameter configurations for best-performing models are listed as below.

Model	Learning Rate	Batch Size	Gradient Accumulation
RoBERTa Large	$1e-5$	8	8
+Question Relation	$1e-5$	8	8
+Social Knowkedge Cat	$1e-5$	8	4
+Question Relation + Social Knowledge Cat	$1e-5$	8	16

B Appendix: Case Study

We conduct a case study to understand how the two types of categorical information help the QA task. The examples are listed in Table 4, 5.

Question Relation Type: **xNeed**
Riley told Austin's landlord that Austin was making a lot of noise at late hours.
What does Riley need to do before this?
(a) potentially call the police (b) document incidents ✓ | **Question Relation** (c) follow up with the landlord | **RoBERTa**

Table 4: Case Study for Question Relation (✓: golden label)

Social Knowledge Category: **Feelings and Characteristics**
Austin was taking a test and found it difficult at first.
How would you describe Austin?
(a) student | **RoBERTa** (b) stupid (c) overwhelmed ✓ | **Social Knowledge Category**

Table 5: Case Study for Social Knowledge Category (✓: golden label)

B.1 Question Relation Type

Table 4 refers to an example that is predicted correctly by the *Question Relation* model but wrongly by the RoBERTa model. The RoBERTa model mistakenly selects the answer describing an event that could happen after the noise complaint. However, the question is asking possible events before it. The question type "xNeed" exactly provides such signal and indicates that the right answer should happen before the given context, and thus helps the QA model choose the right answer.

B.2 Social Knowledge Category

In Table 5, although the RoBERTa model selects the reasonable answer "student" to describe Austin, it fails to infer more in-depth semantic information embedded in the context. The actual focus is that Austin found the test challenging and was overwhelmed. Our social knowledge taxonomy assigns this example to the "Feelings and Characteristics" category. It enables the QA model to pay more attention to candidates that emphasize a kind of personal feeling.

Speeding Up Transformer Training By Using Dataset Subsampling - An Exploratory Analysis

Lovre Torbarina[†] **Velimir Mihelcic, Bruno Sarlija, Lukasz Roguski, Zeljko Kraljevic**[†]
doXray B.V., Neede, Netherlands
{lovre.torbarina, velimir.mihelcic, bruno.sarlija,
lukasz.roguski, zeljko.kraljevic}@doxray.com

Abstract

Transformer-based models have greatly advanced the progress in the field of the natural language processing and while they achieve state-of-the-art results on a wide range of tasks, they are cumbersome in parameter size. Subsequently, even when pre-trained transformer models are used for fine-tuning on a given task, if the dataset is large, it may still not be feasible to fine-tune the model within a reasonable time. For this reason, we empirically test 8 subsampling methods for reducing the dataset size on text classification task and report the trade-off between metric score and training time. 7 out of 8 methods are simple methods, while the last one is CRAIG, a method for coreset construction for data-efficient model training. We obtain the best result with the CRAIG method, offering an average decrease of 0.03 points in f-score on test set while speeding up the training time on average by 63.93%, relative to the score and time obtained by using the full dataset. Lastly, we show the trade-off between speed and performance for all sampling methods on three different datasets.

1 Introduction

In recent years, a great progress has been observed in the field of natural language processing thanks to use of deep neural network models and, most notably, Transformer (Vaswani et al., 2017) architecture-based models, such as BERT (Devlin et al., 2019). While transformer-based models achieve state-of-the-art results on a wide range of benchmarks (Wang et al., 2018, 2019), they are cumbersome in the number of parameters. Consequently, computers with large amounts of RAM memory and specialized hardware, such as multiple GPU or TPU devices, are required to train the models in reasonable time. As a result, such vast computational requirements put constraints on what can be done in smaller research teams, both in academia and in industry.

As one of the approaches to alleviate this problem, an extensive research has been conducted on methods for model compression, such as, model pruning, quantization, knowledge distillation, parameter sharing and others (Gupta and Agrawal, 2021). Although model compression methods can produce models characterising with low-latency and low-memory footprint for transfer learning, e.g. DistilBERT (Sanh et al., 2020), but if the dataset is significantly large, it may still be not feasible to fine-tune the model within a reasonable time. Therefore, if the model's size can't be further reduced without sacrificing its generalization performance, reducing the dataset is a task worth considering to further reduce training resource requirements.

The challenge of reducing dataset size while trying to preserving model's performance is the main focus of this paper. Previous research conducted on this topic mainly focuses on computer vision or traditional machine learning domain. Pruning the dataset by removing noisy examples to improve model's performance was done in Angelova et al. (2005), while Lapedriza et al. (2013) ranks examples by how *valuable* they are and takes the top ones in a greedy fashion w.r.t. the rankings. In instance selection methods, only the informative examples are selected prior to model training (Olvera-López et al., 2010). Similarly, a coreset (or weighted subset) construction was done in Tsang et al. (2005); Bachem et al. (2017) for specific traditional ML models while Mirzasoleiman et al. (2020) introduced a general approach applicable also to neural network models. In Wang et al. (2020); Sucholutsky and Schonlau (2020), the idea of knowledge distillation was used to distill a dataset to a small set of synthetic examples. To the best of our knowledge, there is no previous work on reducing the train set size for lowering the time

[†]Corresponding authors.

Proceedings of the 2nd Workshop on Simple and Efficient Natural Language Processing, pages 86–95
November 10, 2021.

and resource requirements for transformer-based model training.

In this paper, we applied a general method for coreset construction described in Mirzasoleiman et al. (2020) to a transformer model. We empirically compared its performance against simpler subsampling approaches across 3 text classification datasets. The rest of the paper is organized as follows. In section 2, we describe methodology, including construction of the datasets, description of the sampling methods and experiment set up. In section 3, we show the performance across the datasets. And finally, in section 4, we discuss the results together with our outlook for future work.

2 Methods

2.1 Datasets

In our experiments we used 3 datasets for text classification where texts are sorted over time and partitioned (or segmented) by e.g. months, based on their corresponding timestamp. We chose this data ordering because it simulates a typical real-world problem in which new data arrives over time. An overview of the dataset properties is presented in Table 1. Texts that don't have a timestamp have been discarded from each dataset. All of the datasets have a non-uniform distribution of examples over classes. In the rest of the paper we use the terms *classes* and *categories* interchangeably.

AG's news corpus (AGNC). The news articles corpus was introduced by Antonio Gulli's group[1]. We took 4 largest classes from the corpus and used the title, and description fields as the article's text, similarly as in Zhang et al. (2015). We used weeks as time segments (Appendix. Figure 3 b)).

Multi-Domain Sentiment Dataset (MDSD). Dataset consist of product reviews taken from Amazon.com and was introduced in Blitzer et al. (2007) for solving sentiment classification task. We chose an updated version of the dataset avaliable on the web[2], provided by the same authors. Instead of trying to solve sentiment classification task, we used product type information as a target class for the product review. We used months as time segments (Appendix. Figure 3 c)).

Text Classification Dataset (TCD). Our private real-world dataset for text classification. We used months as time segments (Figure 1).

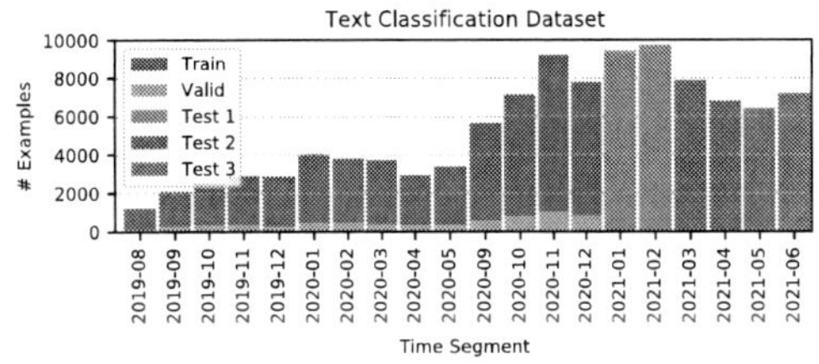

Figure 1: Number of examples per time segment and data split information for Text Classification Dataset. Test 1, 2 and 3 are subsets of the full test set.

2.2 Sampling Methods

We used 8 sampling methods to subsample the dataset. Methods 1) to 7) were used as a data preprocessing step prior to model optimization while method 8) is used after each epoch as part of the model optimization procedure. In the rest of the paper, sampling methods are also called as samplers. Samplers have a hyper-parameter called *sampling ratio* which is used to determine *sample size*, where *sampling ratio* $\in [0, 1]$. When saying at random, we mean uniformly at random unless otherwise stated. A description of the sampling methods used in the experiments is as follows (the implementation for methods 1) to 7) is available in the supplementary materials).

1) Full Dataset Sampler (FDS) takes all the examples, i.e. samples the dataset with *sampling ratio* of 1.0.

2) Latest Examples Sampler (LES) samples portion of the temporally most recent examples per each category proportional to sampling ratio. In a corner case, such that when there are more examples in a time segment than it is needed to satisfy the sample size, the examples are picked at random.

3) Random Sampler (RS) samples the portion of

Dataset	AGNC	MDSD	TCD
Classes	4	25	221
Time Segments	6	35	20
Train	46111	16517	59104
Valid	5124	1833	6563
Test 1	9026	4224	19185
Test 2	8520	7294	14635
Test 3	3249	6444	13576
Test Full	20795	17962	47396

Table 1: An overview of dataset properties. AGNC, MDSD and TCD are abbreviations for AG's news corpus, Multi-Domain Sentiment Dataset and Text Classification Dataset, respectively.

[1] http://groups.di.unipi.it/~gulli/AG_corpus_of_news_articles.html

[2] http://www.cs.jhu.edu/~mdredze/datasets/sentiment/

examples per each category proportional to sampling ratio at random and independently of the time segments.

Samplers 4) to 7) are clustering-based approaches for subsampling the dataset inspired by previous work of Li et al. (2011); Agrawal et al. (2015); Arafat et al. (2017). However, we didn't balance the distribution of examples over classes, but kept the same ratio of examples per category as it is prior to sampling. We did this because the cited methods are not directly applicable or practical to be used with transformers-based models so we only followed the subsampling approaches which by themselves do not balance distribution. For each clustering method we used *k-means++* (Arthur and Vassilvitskii, 2007).

4) Clustering C1 samples portion of the examples per each category proportional to sampling ratio and independently of the time segments, as follows. First, it clusters the category to partition the example space. Then, at random selects from which cluster to take the example from, repeating the sampling procedure *sample size* times. After this step, the number of examples that sampler needs to pick from each cluster is known. Finally, sampler picks determined number of examples from each cluster at random. For representing the examples as a continuous vector we apply TF-IDF.

5) Clustering C2 is same as the **C1** but samples from a non-uniform distribution, by which we model the dependence of the examples on the time segment. In short, the most recent examples and clusters containing these are more likely to be picked (Appendix. A.2).

6) Clustering C3 is the same as **C1** and **7) Clustering C4** is the same as **C2** but both use DistilBERT model to calculate vector representations.

8) CRAIG is a method proposed by Mirzasoleiman et al. (2020). We used the provided implementation by the authors[3], but adjusted it to work for the transformer-based model for text classification.

2.3 Experiments

Dataset Splits. Split statistics are shown in Table 1. Additionally, we show the splits for TCD in Figure 1 with more details in Appendix Figure 3.

Neural Net Architecture. We chose DistilBERT (Sanh et al., 2020) to simulate the use of a compressed model while we want to reduce the dataset.

Metrics. For measuring the model performance we used f1 micro score. Training times are measured against a wall clock, while we treat a total training time as a sum of the sampling time and the training time without evaluation on the validation set.

Training and Evaluation Procedure. For each sampler we trained the model for 10 epochs on the sampled training set and picked the model that achieved the best f-score on the validation set. Then, for each sampler, we evaluated the selected model on the full test set as well as on 3 test subsets. We get the 3 subsets by dividing the test set over time into 3 buckets, the main goal being to additionally test model performance for examples that are near/far in time from the train set. Each model starts from the same initial weights and uses the same hyperparameters (Appendix. A.3). What changes across the experiments is the training subset provided by each of the samplers.

3 Results

We report the mean and standard deviation over sampler's f1 scores on the full test set (Figure 2 a)) as well as the training times (Figure 2 b)), both relative to the full dataset sampler. Exact values are shown in Table 2, with additional information for the 3 test subsets. Detailed results with actual training times can be found in the supplementary materials. Secondly, we report results for the top 4 samplers w.r.t. f1 score but with condition of 0.7, 0.5 and 0.3 on the maximum training time (Table 3), where measures are relative to the full dataset sampler.

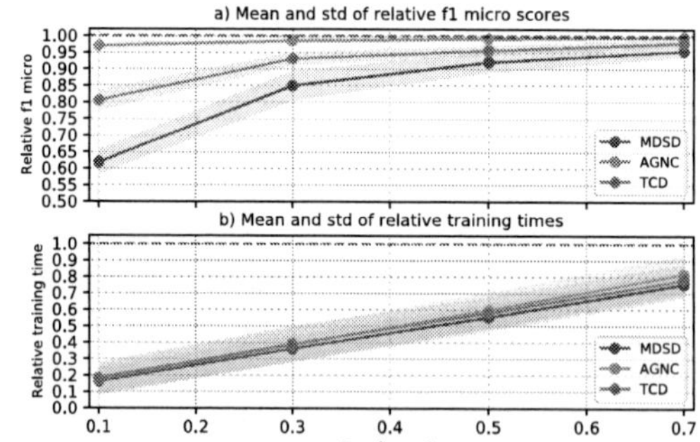

Figure 2: Samplers average f1 scores on full test set and training times, both relative to the full dataset sampler.

4 Discussion

As seen in Figure 2, on average and relative to the full dataset sampler, f-score and training time

[3]https://github.com/baharanm/craig

Samp. Ratio	Dataset	Rel. F1				Rel. Train Time
		Full	Test 1	Test 2	Test 3	
		mean ± std				mean ± std
0.3	AGNC	0.99 ± 0.01	0.98 ± 0.01	0.99 ± 0.01	0.99 ± 0.01	0.39 ± 0.10
	TCD	0.93 ± 0.02	0.94 ± 0.02	0.93 ± 0.02	0.93 ± 0.02	0.39 ± 0.10
	MDSD	0.85 ± 0.04	**0.88 ± 0.03**	**0.84 ± 0.05**	**0.84 ± 0.05**	0.36 ± 0.08
0.1	AGNC	**0.97 ± 0.01**	0.97 ± 0.01	0.97 ± 0.01	0.97 ± 0.01	0.17 ± 0.09
	TCD	**0.81 ± 0.03**	0.81 ± 0.03	0.80 ± 0.03	0.80 ± 0.03	0.18 ± 0.09
	MDSD	**0.62 ± 0.03**	**0.69 ± 0.03**	**0.57 ± 0.04**	**0.62 ± 0.04**	0.16 ± 0.08

Table 2: Training time and f-score on test sets, averaged over all samplers. Measures are relative to the full dataset sampler. Results in bold indicate when a significant drop in f-score happened w.r.t. sampling ratio.

Max Rel. Train Time	Sampler	Samp. ratio	Rel. F1	Rel. Train Time	Rel. Loss
			mean ± std	mean ± std	mean ± std
1.0	Full data	1.0	1.00 ± 0.00	1.00 ± 0.00	1.00 ± 0.00
0.7	CRAIG	0.3	**0.97 ± 0.02**	0.61 ± 0.03	**0.99 ± 0.04**
	Clustering C2	0.5	0.96 ± 0.03	0.56 ± 0.01	1.18 ± 0.21
	Clustering C4	0.5	0.96 ± 0.03	0.58 ± 0.02	1.18 ± 0.18
	Latest Examples	0.5	0.95 ± 0.02	**0.50 ± 0.02**	1.19 ± 0.19
0.5	Latest Examples	0.3	**0.93 ± 0.04**	**0.31 ± 0.01**	1.27 ± 0.19
	Random	0.3	0.92 ± 0.05	**0.31 ± 0.01**	1.26 ± 0.21
	Clustering C4	0.3	0.92 ± 0.05	0.37 ± 0.01	**1.18 ± 0.06**
	Clustering C2	0.3	0.92 ± 0.05	0.36 ± 0.01	1.29 ± 0.21
0.3	Latest Examples	0.1	**0.82 ± 0.11**	**0.10 ± 0.00**	**1.50 ± 0.12**
	Clustering C4	0.1	**0.82 ± 0.11**	0.17 ± 0.01	1.63 ± 0.45
	Random	0.1	0.81 ± 0.13	**0.10 ± 0.00**	1.55 ± 0.27
	Clustering C1	0.1	0.81 ± 0.12	0.15 ± 0.01	1.52 ± 0.18

Table 3: Results of top 4 samplers over datasets w.r.t. f-score per condition on the maximum train time. Measures are relative to the full dataset sampler. Results in bold indicate the best score per maximum train time condition.

decline almost linearly by reducing the sampling ratio from 0.7 up to 0.3. Reducing the sampling ratio below 0.3, causes a significant non-linear drop in f-score. More precisely, focusing on the sampling ratio interval from 0.3 to 0.1, we have a drop on average of 0.2, 0.12 and 0.23 points in relative f-score for all the datasets, respectively. We assume that after discarding certain portion of the examples, we can not reduce it more without removing good representative examples from each category, i.e. there are less redundant examples to discard. Additionally, we measured relative f-score on each test subset to see if and when the drop in performance might happen, as this simulates use cases where new data arrives over time. On MDSD dataset we observed that performance drops as we try to predict further in time, when sampling ratio is 0.3 or lower (Table 2). Specifically, f-score drops from 0.69 to 0.57 and then raise to 0.62 as we go through Test 1, 2 and 3, respectively. This is likely related to the number of classes and examples per class, we leave it for further investigation.

We further discuss the effect of conditioning on the maximum allowed training time (Table 3). We chose values for maximum relative training time (Table 3, column 1) based on the Figure 2, with intention to cover the different situations regarding picked sampling ratio. With a condition of a maximum relative training time of 0.7, CRAIG achieves the best results, on average, with decrease of 0.03 points in f1 score while speeding up the training time by 63.93%, relative to the score and time obtained by using the full dataset. As we reduce the condition value below 0.5 we are left only with data preprocessing samplers. In this case, the top performing sampler w.r.t. f-score is LES. Interestingly, LES was ranked in top 4 samplers for each condition on the maximum relative training time. We assume this might be the case because we sorted the data by their timestamp and partitioned into time segments. It might be that the most recent time segments contain more representative examples for the test set as they are closer in time. Next, we compare clustering samplers. We observed that C2 and C4, the ones which apply bigger weights for more recent examples while sampling, outperformed C1 and C3, the ones that use uniform weights. This aligns with our previous assumption that the recent examples give more information for predicting on the future time segments. Additionally, C4, on average, outperformed C2, which may indicate that clustering transformer embeddings instead of using

TF-IDF vectors might provide more representative examples for model training.

Finally, for the completeness of comparison, we tested the samplers on the same datasets but without preserving temporal information. Only samplers which do not require temporal information to work were taken into account. Again, we obtained top results by using CRAIG sampler (Appendix Table 6). The samplers, on average, performed similarly w.r.t sampling ratios as on datasets with temporal information (Appendix Figure 4 and Table 7). The samplers, on average, achieved slightly better results on datasets without temporal information (Appendix Table 6). Interestingly, after setting the time condition equal to 0.7 or less, samplers are not performing better than random sampler besides CRAIG, hence we leave the topic for future investigation. As datasets without temporal information are not our primary focus, we include additional information in Appendix C about the results and the methodology used.

Conclusion. Fine-tuning a compressed transformer model can still take significant amount of time if the dataset is large. We empirically compared 8 sampling methods for reducing train set on 3 datasets and reported trade-offs between f1 score and training time.

References

Astha Agrawal, Herna L. Viktor, and Eric Paquet. 2015. SCUT: Multi-class imbalanced data classification using SMOTE and cluster-based undersampling. In *2015 7th International Joint Conference on Knowledge Discovery, Knowledge Engineering and Knowledge Management (IC3K)*, volume 01, pages 226–234.

A. Angelova, Y. Abu-Mostafam, and P. Perona. 2005. Pruning training sets for learning of object categories. In *2005 IEEE Computer Society Conference on Computer Vision and Pattern Recognition (CVPR'05)*, volume 1, pages 494–501 vol. 1. ISSN: 1063-6919.

Md. Yasir Arafat, Sabera Hoque, and Dewan Md. Farid. 2017. Cluster-based under-sampling with random forest for multi-class imbalanced classification. In *2017 11th International Conference on Software, Knowledge, Information Management and Applications (SKIMA)*, pages 1–6. ISSN: 2573-3214.

David Arthur and Sergei Vassilvitskii. 2007. k-means++: the advantages of careful seeding. In *Proceedings of the eighteenth annual ACM-SIAM symposium on Discrete algorithms*, SODA '07, pages 1027–1035, USA. Society for Industrial and Applied Mathematics.

Olivier Bachem, Mario Lucic, and Andreas Krause. 2017. Practical Coreset Constructions for Machine Learning. *arXiv:1703.06476 [stat]*. ArXiv: 1703.06476.

John Blitzer, Mark Dredze, and Fernando Pereira. 2007. Biographies, Bollywood, boom-boxes and blenders: Domain adaptation for sentiment classification. In *Proceedings of the 45th Annual Meeting of the Association of Computational Linguistics*, pages 440–447, Prague, Czech Republic. Association for Computational Linguistics.

Jacob Devlin, Ming-Wei Chang, Kenton Lee, and Kristina Toutanova. 2019. *BERT: Pre-training of Deep Bidirectional Transformers for Language Understanding*, pages 4171–4186. Association for Computational Linguistics, Minneapolis, Minnesota.

Manish Gupta and Puneet Agrawal. 2021. Compression of Deep Learning Models for Text: A Survey. *arXiv:2008.05221 [cs]*. ArXiv: 2008.05221.

Agata Lapedriza, Hamed Pirsiavash, Zoya Bylinskii, and Antonio Torralba. 2013. Are all training examples equally valuable? *arXiv:1311.6510 [cs, stat]*. ArXiv: 1311.6510.

Shoushan Li, Guodong Zhou, Zhongqing Wang, Sophia Lee, and Rangyang Wang. 2011. Imbalanced sentiment classification. pages 2469–2472.

Baharan Mirzasoleiman, Jeff Bilmes, and Jure Leskovec. 2020. Coresets for Data-efficient Training of Machine Learning Models. *arXiv:1906.01827 [cs, stat]*. ArXiv: 1906.01827.

J. Arturo Olvera-López, J. Ariel Carrasco-Ochoa, J. Francisco Martínez-Trinidad, and Josef Kittler. 2010. A review of instance selection methods. *Artificial Intelligence Review*, 34(2):133–143.

Victor Sanh, Lysandre Debut, Julien Chaumond, and Thomas Wolf. 2020. DistilBERT, a distilled version of BERT: smaller, faster, cheaper and lighter. *arXiv:1910.01108 [cs]*. ArXiv: 1910.01108.

Ilia Sucholutsky and Matthias Schonlau. 2020. Soft-Label Dataset Distillation and Text Dataset Distillation. *arXiv:1910.02551 [cs, stat]*. ArXiv: 1910.02551.

Ivor W. Tsang, James T. Kwok, and Pak-Ming Cheung. 2005. Core Vector Machines: Fast SVM Training on Very Large Data Sets. *Journal of Machine Learning Research*, 6(13):363–392.

Ashish Vaswani, Noam Shazeer, Niki Parmar, Jakob Uszkoreit, Llion Jones, Aidan N. Gomez, Łukasz Kaiser, and Illia Polosukhin. 2017. Attention is all you need. In *Proceedings of the 31st International Conference on Neural Information Processing Systems*, NIPS'17, pages 6000–6010, Red Hook, NY, USA. Curran Associates Inc.

Alex Wang, Yada Pruksachatkun, Nikita Nangia, Amanpreet Singh, Julian Michael, Felix Hill, Omer Levy, and Samuel R. Bowman. 2019. SuperGLUE: A stickier benchmark for general-purpose language understanding systems. *Advances in Neural Information Processing Systems*, 32.

Alex Wang, Amanpreet Singh, Julian Michael, Felix Hill, Omer Levy, and Samuel Bowman. 2018. GLUE: A Multi-Task Benchmark and Analysis Platform for Natural Language Understanding. In *Proceedings of the 2018 EMNLP Workshop BlackboxNLP: Analyzing and Interpreting Neural Networks for NLP*, pages 353–355, Brussels, Belgium. Association for Computational Linguistics.

Tongzhou Wang, Jun-Yan Zhu, Antonio Torralba, and Alexei A. Efros. 2020. Dataset Distillation. *arXiv:1811.10959 [cs, stat]*. ArXiv: 1811.10959.

Xiang Zhang, Junbo Zhao, and Yann LeCun. 2015. Character-level convolutional networks for text classification. In *Proceedings of the 28th International Conference on Neural Information Processing Systems - Volume 1*, NIPS'15, pages 649–657, Cambridge, MA, USA. MIT Press.

A Additional Methods Details

A.1 Dataset Splits

We created training, validation and test sets for each of the datasets described in Subsection 2.1. First, we created full test set by taking 6 most recent time segments. Then, in order to get test sets 1, 2 and 3, we divided the test set over time into 3 buckets, each containing two time segments. Thirdly, in train set are all examples from time segments older than test set 1. Finally, we created validation set by sampling 10% of the train set while keeping example ratio per category the same between the splits. The splits are fixed and do not change across experiments. Data splits for each dataset are shown in Figure 3 and split statistics are given in Table 1.

A.2 Sampling Distribution Calculation

We calculated the distributions by using weights w_i assigned to each example e_i where $i \in 1, 2, ..., |TrainSet|$. Each dataset has n train time segments T, known after segmentation and dataset split is done (Figure 3). Each time segment T has index j, where the most recent segment in time has index $j = 1$, the second most recent has index $j = 2$ and so on up to the last index $j = n$. Every example e_i belongs to one of the time segments T_j so we define membership function to get index of the segment in which example belongs to, as follows:

$$\mu_T(e_i) = \begin{cases} j & \text{if } e_i \in T_j \\ 0, & \text{otherwise} \end{cases}, j \in \{1, ..., n\} \quad (1)$$

Note that $\mu_T(e_i)$ will never be 0 as every example belongs to one of the segments. We chose linear decay function f_w to assign weight w_i to example e_i w.r.t. index j of the segment T_j to which the example e_i belongs. Function f_w is defined as follows:

$$w_i = f_w(e_i) = \frac{1}{\mu_T(e_i)} \quad (2)$$

where the weight w_i has the highest value for examples from the most recent segments and decreases linearly as the segments get older. After performing clustering we obtained m clusters. For a cluster weight c_k, we averaged weights w_i of all examples e_i which belong to the cluster k. We did this for each cluster. To determine distribution for sampling which cluster to take the example from, we calculated cluster probability p_k as follows:

$$p_k = \frac{c_k}{\sum_{l=1}^{m} c_l}, k \in \{1, ..., m\} \quad (3)$$

$$\sum_{k=1}^{m} p_k = 1 \quad (4)$$

To determine distribution for sampling examples within cluster C_k, we calculate example probability p'_i per cluster C_k, $k = 1, ..., m$, as follows:

$$p'_i = \frac{w_i}{\sum_{l=1}^{|S_k|} w_l}, l, i \in S_k \quad (5)$$

$$\sum_{i=1}^{|S_k|} p'_i = 1 \quad (6)$$

where S_k is a set of indexes of examples e_i that belongs to a cluster C_k.

A.3 Neural Network Training Info

Transformer's maximum sequence length used was 512 and we used batch size of 32. We used Adam optimizer with initial learning rate of $3e^{-5}$.

B Additional Discussion Remarks

B.1 CRAIG Remarks

In Table 5, we ranked the samplers w.r.t. relative f-score over the datasets, setting no condition on max rel. time. Top f-score performance on average is achieved by CRAIG, but if we look at the average and standard deviation of the relative training time we see that by sampling the data with ratio of 0.7 the model training was slower than on the full dataset. This is because the time needed for selecting the subsets creates the time overhead if sampling ratio is not small enough.

C Case Without Temporal Information

C.1 Dataset Splits

We created datasets without temporal information as follows. For TCD and MDSD we took splits with temporal information, merged them and discarded the time information. Subsequently, we shuffled the data and randomly split it in 8:1:1 ratio to create the training, validation and test sets. For AGNC we took the same training and test splits as in Zhang et al. (2015), and did not discard articles that do not have timestamp. Hence we could have

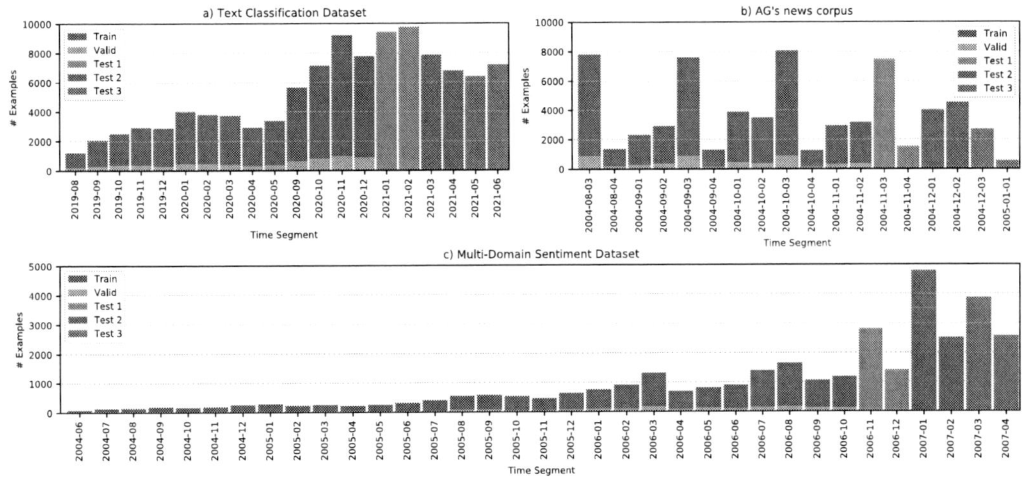

Figure 3: Number of examples per time segments together with dataset split information for each used dataset.

Samp. Ratio	Dataset	Rel. F1				Rel. Train Time
		Full	Test 1	Test 2	Test 3	
		mean ± std				mean ± std
1.0	Every	1.00 ± 0.00	1.00 ± 0.00	1.00 ± 0.00	1.00 ± 0.00	1.00 ± 0.00
0.7	AGNC	1.00 ± 0.00	0.99 ± 0.00	1.00 ± 0.00	1.00 ± 0.00	0.82 ± 0.11
	TCD	0.98 ± 0.01	0.98 ± 0.01	0.98 ± 0.02	0.98 ± 0.01	0.78 ± 0.09
	MDSD	0.96 ± 0.02	0.96 ± 0.01	0.96 ± 0.02	0.95 ± 0.02	0.76 ± 0.08
0.5	AGNC	0.99 ± 0.00	0.99 ± 0.00	0.99 ± 0.00	0.99 ± 0.00	0.60 ± 0.11
	TCD	0.96 ± 0.01	0.96 ± 0.01	0.96 ± 0.02	0.96 ± 0.02	0.58 ± 0.09
	MDSD	0.92 ± 0.03	0.93 ± 0.03	0.92 ± 0.03	0.92 ± 0.03	0.55 ± 0.08
0.3	AGNC	0.99 ± 0.01	0.98 ± 0.01	0.99 ± 0.01	0.99 ± 0.01	0.39 ± 0.10
	TCD	0.93 ± 0.02	0.94 ± 0.02	0.93 ± 0.02	0.93 ± 0.02	0.39 ± 0.10
	MDSD	0.85 ± 0.04	$\mathbf{0.88 \pm 0.03}$	$\mathbf{0.84 \pm 0.05}$	$\mathbf{0.84 \pm 0.05}$	0.36 ± 0.08
0.1	AGNC	$\mathbf{0.97 \pm 0.01}$	0.97 ± 0.01	0.97 ± 0.01	0.97 ± 0.01	0.17 ± 0.09
	TCD	$\mathbf{0.81 \pm 0.03}$	0.81 ± 0.03	0.80 ± 0.03	0.80 ± 0.03	0.18 ± 0.09
	MDSD	$\mathbf{0.62 \pm 0.03}$	$\mathbf{0.69 \pm 0.03}$	$\mathbf{0.57 \pm 0.04}$	$\mathbf{0.62 \pm 0.04}$	0.16 ± 0.08

Table 4: Average f1 scores and training times on test sets for each sampler, both relative to the full dataset sampler. Results in bold signal when a significant drop in f-score happened w.r.t. sampling ratio.

one dataset that is often used as a benchmark for text classification. To create AGNC validation set we randomly sampled 10% of the AGNC training set. We kept the same ratio of examples per categories across splits for each dataset. The splits statistics are presented in Table 8.

C.2 Results

We report the mean and standard deviation over samplers f1 scores on the test set (Figure 4 a)) and the training times (Figure 4 b)), both relative to the full dataset sampler. Exact values are shown in Table 7. Detailed results with measured training times are in the supplementary materials. Next, we report results for the top 4 samplers w.r.t. f1 score but with condition of 0.7, 0.5 and 0.3 on the maximum training time (Table 6), where measures are relative to the full dataset sampler.

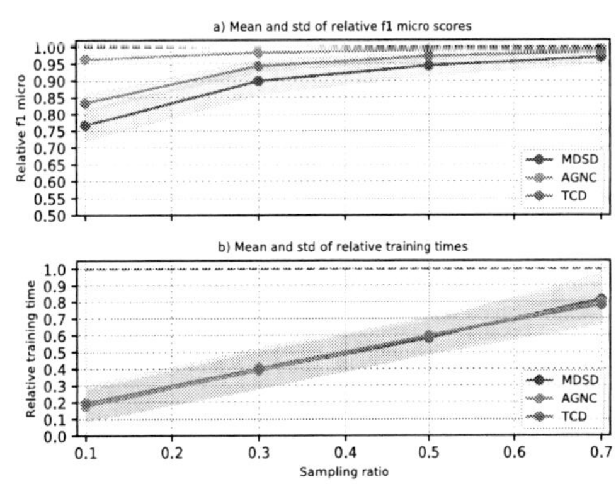

Figure 4: Samplers average f1 scores on test set and training times on datasets without time dimension, both relative to the full dataset sampler.

Max Rel. Train Time	Sampler	Samp. ratio	Rel. F1 mean ± std	Rel. Train Time mean ± std	Rel. Loss mean ± std
1.0	Full data	1.0	1.00 ± 0.00	1.00 ± 0.00	1.00 ± 0.00
inf	CRAIG	0.7	$\mathbf{1.00 \pm 0.00}$	1.00 ± 0.05	$\mathbf{1.01 \pm 0.08}$
inf	CRAIG	0.5	0.99 ± 0.00	0.79 ± 0.04	1.04 ± 0.12
inf	Latest Examples	0.7	0.98 ± 0.01	$\mathbf{0.70 \pm 0.03}$	1.05 ± 0.11
inf	Clustering C4	0.7	0.98 ± 0.01	0.77 ± 0.01	1.10 ± 0.17
0.7	CRAIG	0.3	$\mathbf{0.97 \pm 0.02}$	0.61 ± 0.03	$\mathbf{0.99 \pm 0.04}$
0.7	Clustering C2	0.5	0.96 ± 0.03	0.56 ± 0.01	1.18 ± 0.21
0.7	Clustering C4	0.5	0.96 ± 0.03	0.58 ± 0.02	1.18 ± 0.18
0.7	Latest Examples	0.5	0.95 ± 0.02	$\mathbf{0.50 \pm 0.02}$	1.19 ± 0.19
0.5	Latest Examples	0.3	$\mathbf{0.93 \pm 0.04}$	$\mathbf{0.31 \pm 0.01}$	1.27 ± 0.19
0.5	Random	0.3	0.92 ± 0.05	$\mathbf{0.31 \pm 0.01}$	1.26 ± 0.21
0.5	Clustering C4	0.3	0.92 ± 0.05	0.37 ± 0.01	$\mathbf{1.18 \pm 0.06}$
0.5	Clustering C2	0.3	0.92 ± 0.05	0.36 ± 0.01	1.29 ± 0.21
0.3	Latest Examples	0.1	$\mathbf{0.82 \pm 0.11}$	$\mathbf{0.10 \pm 0.00}$	$\mathbf{1.50 \pm 0.12}$
0.3	Clustering C4	0.1	$\mathbf{0.82 \pm 0.11}$	0.17 ± 0.01	1.63 ± 0.45
0.3	Random	0.1	0.81 ± 0.13	$\mathbf{0.10 \pm 0.00}$	1.55 ± 0.27
0.3	Clustering C1	0.1	0.81 ± 0.12	0.15 ± 0.01	1.52 ± 0.18

Table 5: Results of top 4 samplers on average over datasets w.r.t. relative f1 micro scores with condition on the maximum relative training time. Results in bold indicate the best scores for specific condition on the maximum training time. inf condition represents no limit on the maximum training time.

Max Rel. Train Time	Sampler	Samp. ratio	Rel. F1 mean ± std	Rel. Train Time mean ± std	Rel. Loss mean ± std
1.0	Full data	1.0	1.00 ± 0.00	1.00 ± 0.00	1.00 ± 0.00
inf	CRAIG	0.7	$\mathbf{0.99 \pm 0.01}$	0.95 ± 0.09	1.09 ± 0.16
inf	CRAIG	0.5	0.99 ± 0.00	0.77 ± 0.01	$\mathbf{0.92 \pm 0.36}$
inf	Clustering C3	0.7	0.98 ± 0.01	0.77 ± 0.01	1.02 ± 0.40
inf	Clustering C1	0.7	0.98 ± 0.01	$\mathbf{0.75 \pm 0.03}$	0.94 ± 0.35
0.7	CRAIG	0.3	$\mathbf{0.98 \pm 0.01}$	0.59 ± 0.02	1.01 ± 0.10
0.7	Random	0.5	0.97 ± 0.02	$\mathbf{0.50 \pm 0.01}$	$\mathbf{0.98 \pm 0.36}$
0.7	Clustering C3	0.5	0.97 ± 0.02	0.55 ± 0.00	1.34 ± 3.52
0.7	Clustering C1	0.5	0.96 ± 0.02	0.55 ± 0.01	1.14 ± 0.49
0.5	Random	0.3	$\mathbf{0.95 \pm 0.04}$	0.30 ± 0.00	$\mathbf{1.07 \pm 0.41}$
0.5	Clustering C3	0.3	0.94 ± 0.04	0.35 ± 0.00	1.10 ± 0.43
0.5	Clustering C1	0.3	0.94 ± 0.03	0.34 ± 0.02	1.08 ± 0.41
0.5	Random	0.1	0.87 ± 0.07	$\mathbf{0.10 \pm 0.00}$	1.40 ± 0.59
0.3	Random	0.1	$\mathbf{0.87 \pm 0.07}$	$\mathbf{0.10 \pm 0.00}$	1.40 ± 0.59
0.3	Clustering C3	0.1	0.86 ± 0.07	0.15 ± 0.00	1.40 ± 0.58
0.3	Clustering C1	0.1	0.86 ± 0.07	0.14 ± 0.02	$\mathbf{1.34 \pm 0.53}$

Table 6: Results of top 4 samplers on average over datasets w.r.t. relative f1 micro scores with condition on the maximum relative training time. Results in bold indicate the best scores for specific condition on the maximum training time. inf condition represents no limit on the maximum training time. Datasets have no time dimension.

Samp. Ratio	Dataset	Rel. F1 Test mean ± std	Rel. Train Time mean ± std
1.0	Every	1.00 ± 0.00	1.00 ± 0.00
0.7	AGNC	0.99 ± 0.00	0.80 ± 0.13
	TCD	0.98 ± 0.00	0.78 ± 0.06
	MDSD	0.97 ± 0.02	0.82 ± 0.16
0.5	AGNC	0.99 ± 0.00	0.60 ± 0.11
	TCD	0.97 ± 0.01	0.60 ± 0.10
	MDSD	0.94 ± 0.03	0.58 ± 0.10
0.3	AGNC	0.98 ± 0.00	0.39 ± 0.11
	TCD	0.94 ± 0.02	0.41 ± 0.12
	MDSD	0.90 ± 0.04	0.39 ± 0.11
0.1	AGNC	0.96 ± 0.01	0.18 ± 0.10
	TCD	0.83 ± 0.03	0.20 ± 0.10
	MDSD	0.77 ± 0.05	0.18 ± 0.09

Table 7: Average f1 scores and training times on test sets for each sampler, both relative to the full dataset sampler. Datasets have no time dimension.

Dataset	AGNC	MDSD	TCD
Classes	4	25	221
Train	108000	29049	90450
Valid	12000	3631	11306
Test	7600	3632	11307

Table 8: An overview of dataset properties where time dimension is excluded. AGNC, MDSD and TCD are abbreviations for AG's news corpus, Multi-Domain Sentiment Dataset and Text Classification Dataset, respectively.

Hyperparameter Power Impact in Transformer Language Model Training

Lucas Høyberg Puvis de Chavannes 🌱
IT University of Copenhagen
M47 Labs
lucas.puvis@m47labs.com

Mads Kongsbak 🌱
IT University of Copenhagen
mkon@itu.dk

Timmie Mikkel Rantzau Lagermann 🌱
IT University of Copenhagen
timn@itu.dk

Leon Derczynski
IT University of Copenhagen
ld@itu.dk

Abstract

Training large language models can consume a large amount of energy. We hypothesize that the language model's configuration impacts its energy consumption, and that there is room for power consumption optimisation in modern large language models. To investigate these claims, we introduce a power consumption factor to the objective function, and explore the range of models and hyperparameter configurations that affect power. We identify multiple configuration factors that can reduce power consumption during language model training while retaining model quality.

1 Introduction

Large language models have pushed the boundaries of accuracy and performance in various NLP tasks, at the cost of energy efficiency. This is due to the increasing amount of compute time and power needed to train these models (Amodei, 2018), thus increasing the amount of energy the computers training the models need to consume.

The Robustly Optimized BERT approach (RoBERTa) (Liu et al., 2019) achieved this by improving the Bidirectional Encoder Representations from Transformers (BERT) (Devlin et al., 2019) in multiple ways, such as increasing the training time through more epochs and a larger amount of data, with BERT already requiring 1507 kWh of electricity and emitting 652 kg of CO_2. Other strategies, such as NAS, an English to German machine translation model, consumed 656,347 kWh of electricity, corresponding to 248,019 kg of CO_2 (Strubell et al., 2019). While these models show great potential, it comes at the cost of high CO_2 emissions. The core issue is that the electricity consumed is not guaranteed to be environmentally friendly, and often comes from sources such as coal or gas. According to Strubell et al. (2019), we must cut CO_2 emissions by half to slow natural disasters. However, much research in the field ignores the perspective of energy efficiency. When looking at papers from three top AI conferences, namely ACL, NeurIPS, and CVPR, work tends to focus on accuracy rather than efficiency, or a mixture (Schwartz et al., 2019).

An added benefit to developing more energy-efficient models is a reduced barrier of entry to NLP research. Researchers with good ideas may not be able to execute those ideas, given that state-of-the-art results are locked behind large-scale compute (Strubell et al., 2019; Bender et al., 2021).

This study investigates how to reduce power consumption in training transformer language models. We seek to address the issue of high-power models by analysing the resulting models' hyperparameters, energy consumption, and perplexity and providing initial parameter guidelines for low-power, high-performance transformers, and an opening into the research of low-power transformers.

Our research question is: How can we reduce the energy consumption of models to both lower the barrier of entry and reduce CO2 emissions, while still keeping an effective model?

Following Strubell et al. (2019), a possible approach to this problem could be the use of *Bayesian hyperparameter search.* Throughout our work, we managed to identify hyperparameter configurations that provide strong entries for both perplexity and energy consumption. These configurations were found through our methodology utilising Bayesian optimisation, by combining the libraries Hyperopt and PyTorch. The optimal configurations collectively spanned the identified Pareto frontier.

2 Related Work

There is a body of work on making language models and transformers efficient, for varying definitions of efficiency, but we're not aware of any that algo-

🌱: These authors contributed to the paper equally.

Proceedings of the 2nd Workshop on Simple and Efficient Natural Language Processing, pages 96–118
November 10, 2021.

rithmically integrate power consumption into the loss function or architecture search.

The closest related work is that on task-specific network reduction and on low-power language processing. The former can be achieved through distillation, pruning, quantisation, or all of the above. For example, Wasserblat et al. (2020) reduce trained BERT models in size by orders of magnitude while retaining task performance. Similarly, Kim et al. (2019) present highly efficient networks that as a result can process translations very quickly. However, all these techniques require the training of a large network first, thus only offering power savings at inference time. Furthermore, Kaplan et al. (2020) presents scaling laws for neural language models, which can assist in more efficient training when applied.

3 Method

Our general approach is as follows. We specify a dataset, task, objective function, and hyperparameter space. We then explore hyperparameter space, repeatedly training models over the same data and evaluating them in terms of task performance and power consumption. This exploration optimises for good task performance and low power consumption, but is limited to a certain volume of model configurations. Once complete, we analyse these model configurations further, investigating per-epoch performance, and common factors in high and low power consumption and task performance.

3.1 Data

The dataset chosen is the `CC-News` dataset (Mackenzie et al., 2020). This is a subset of the English-language portion of the entire `CC-News` dataset. This specific set of data was chosen due to it being partially what RoBERTa was trained on, and having the longer document length typical to the news genre. Only the first 100 000 examples are used as train, primarily chosen in an attempt to keep the energy consumption of the trained models to a minimum. Each document comes with multiple data fields, with only the `text` field being used for training. The reduced amount of data introduces an assumption that these results will scale, which we address later in the paper when investigating common factors in efficient and inefficient models.

3.2 Task: Language modelling

The task used for this paper is *Masked Language Modelling*, also referred to as Masked LM or MLM. The procedure is very simple: mask some words in the input sentences with the token (`[MASK]`), and then attempt to predict what these words are. An example of such a sentence is "The borders of Paris are [MASK]", where [MASK] is the word to be predicted. Perplexity is a widely used metric for the evaluation of language models. Low perplexity means better performance, which makes it a useful metric to evaluate language models in general. We use perplexity as defined by huggingface, as the exponentiated average negative log-likelihood of a sequence (HuggingFace, 2021).

3.3 Perplexity-Energy Product

We used a simple multiplication of the total perplexity and energy consumption of a model, $m_{perplexity}, m_{energy}$ to act as the return value, Perplexity-Energy Product (PEP), to be reduced:

$$PEP = m_{perplexity} \cdot m_{energy} \quad (1)$$

Where $m_{perplexity}$ is the perplexity of the trained LM, and m_{energy} is the energy consumption for training the LM measured by Carbontracker (Anthony et al., 2020). We chose to call this return value, PEP, as shown in the equation . The reason for using a composite expression of both perplexity and energy is to make the optimization focus on parameters that affect both of these. We chose to multiply the two values as we hypothesised it would punish high values a lot more since multiplication is a lot more violent than addition. An issue with this is that as soon as either value is below 1, the loss is simply a linearly scaled-down expression of the other number. A worst-case scenario would be that Hyperopt would prioritise optimising one value and neglect the other, but the resulting loss would still be acceptable for the optimiser. A lower PEP value is better, since the aim is to minimize the energy cost and the perplexity.

There are underlying issues with assessing both the quality and efficiency of models in a single metric. One of the issues is that when efficiency is below one kilowatt-hour, the resulting PEP value will essentially be a scaled-down perplexity. So potentially, a model with a good balance between efficiency and quality would have a higher PEP value than a model that is very efficient, but lacking in quality. Additionally, using a single metric of the

Parameter	Interval
vocab_size	[1,30522]
hidden_size_multiplier	[1,100]
num_hidden_layers	[1,12]
num_attention_heads	[1,18]
intermediate_size	[1,3072]
hidden_act	(relu, silu, gelu, gelu_new)
hidden_dropout_prob	[0.1,1]
attention_probs_dropout_prog	[0.1,1]
max_position_embeddings	[512,512]
type_vocab_size	[1,1]
initializer_range	[0.02,0.02]
layer_norm_eps	[1.00E-12,1.00E-12]
position_embedding_type	(absolute, relative_key, relative_key_query)

Table 1: Hyperopt parameter search space

product of cost and quality makes an assumption - that changes in either component have a linear impact. This could be regulated by adding a weight to both the metrics in order to regulate the difference of change within the respective metric.

3.4 Hardware

The experiment platform was V100 GPUs on i7 CPUs running over a SLURM service. As stated by (Lasse, 2021), Carbontracker also works slurm, only measuring GPU devices available for the given job, so the reported consumption figures are consistent but could be slight underestimates.

3.5 Hyperparameters

To investigate hyperparameter impact on Transformer model power use, we chose to specifically look at the parameters related to its size, such as the number of its hidden layers or number of attention heads, alongside a few key parameters such as the type of positional encoding, activation functions and dropout probabilities. The parameters picked were chosen on the assumption that they were the ones most likely to affect both model perplexity, and model energy consumption during training.

Table 1 shows our final search space and parameter value intervals. Please note that the *hidden_size* of the model is given as:

$$h_{size} = h_{size\_mult} \cdot \#A_{heads} \tag{2}$$

Where h_{size} is hidden size, h_{size_mult} is hidden size multiplier and $\#A_{heads}$ is number of attention heads. This is due to the constraint that the hidden size of the model has to be a multiple of the number attention heads in the model (Vaswani et al., 2017). This leaves a parameter space of size *1026* between $[1, 1800]$, most of which are centred around the lower end of the interval.

3.6 Search algorithm

We use Bayesian optimisation to traverse hyperparameter space in search of low-power transformer training configurations. Bayesian optimisation is suited to cases where one wishes to find optimal parameter configurations, for some definition of optimal, but individual trials can be expensive. This makes it a good match for transformer hyperparameter tuning. Search is executed in parallel over multiple GPUs and GPU hosts. As noted in (Bergstra et al., 2011), *"The consequence of parallelization is that each proposal x^* is based on less feedback. This makes search less efficient, though faster in terms of wall time"*. Research indicates Bayesian hyperparameter search techniques are more efficient than brute force techniques (Strubell et al., 2019), such as grid search; this family is often the least efficient in terms of time-to-viable-solutions. Further, our general focus on energy efficiency motivates choosing efficient search algorithms.

Samples follow a uniform distribution. This was a deliberate choice, as we have no knowledge over which parameters would perform best. We hypothesised giving a uniform distribution for all parameters would yield the best results. The specific algorithm used to minimise the loss is the *Tree of Parzen Estimators* (TPE) (Bergstra et al., 2013).

3.7 Model Selection and Per-epoch Measurements

Hyperopt was left to run over the data and hyperparameters for a fixed number of days. Models were trained with a batch size of 2, over 3 epochs. The batch size was chosen due to stability, as the relatively low number of epochs could make the results unstable. According to Masters and Luschi (2018), the most stable and best generalization results have been obtained with a batch size of 32 or smaller, but the best results were with batch sizes as low as 2. We also logged all of the parameter configurations alongside the energy consumption and perplexity of each model. The result was 154 different hyperparameter configurations.

We then retrained the 154 hyperparameter configurations we found over 10 epochs to see a further evaluation of how each model would evolve per epoch in terms of power consumption and performance. For each model, a callback implementing Carbontracker was used to gather data about the energy consumption after each epoch, and the same callback was used to log the perplexity of each model. Another callback was created to save a model for each epoch, resulting in *1540* different models being saved. Each model was trained on a single Tesla V100 32GB graphics card.

4 Results

4.1 Correlation Matrices

The majority of the result section is going to utilise correlation matrices to analyse the data. We have two categorical data entries, namely the activation function and the position embedding type. For this, we use categorical correlation to showcase both the activation function and the position embedding type alongside the rest of the data. The primary reason for using correlation matrices is its ability to quickly visualise and pinpoint patterns in the data. We have three different ways of evaluating the different hyperparameters, namely with (i) energy consumption, (ii) perplexity, and (iii) PEP value, and therefore correlation matrices make it easy to visualise the hyperparameters. In general, the primary concern is to see correlations between the evaluation methods and hyperparameters.

4.2 PEP

Table 2 contain overviews of the best 15% of models and worst 15% of models, for PEP value, with regard to average parameter size. A count of what position embedding type and activation function was used can be found in table 3 The models were sorted by lowest PEP value, and the best 15% and worst 15% were chosen. Table 2 presents an overview of average energy consumption and perplexity of the best 15% of models, to compare with the worst 15% of models in terms of PEP value.

The data of the best 15% of models is introduced to analyse tendencies that provide the PEP values. The data of the worst 15% of models is introduced to analyse what *not* to do when choosing parameters for a new model. Three different correlation matrices, for all models, for the best and worst 15% of models are given in Appendix A.

5 Energy

The data here is presented in the same format as the previous section. The table 4 show findings of the best 15% models in terms of low energy consumption, and the worst 15%, alongside several correlation matrices in appendix B. Furthermore,

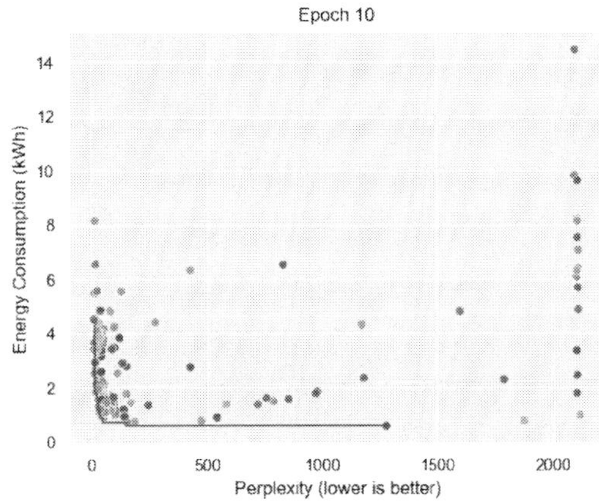

Figure 1: The Pareto curve for epoch 10. An animated visualisation of all 10 epochs can be found at this link.

As these results are extracted from models that have been trained through hyperopt with a specific loss function, the resulting parameters are not chosen to achieve the lowest energy consumption possible, but rather the lowest *PEP*-value. These results can then possibly indicate which parameters can be tweaked to reduce energy consumption specifically, while retaining some performance.

5.1 Identifying optimal models

While PEP is a suitable metric, we also want to be able to identify models which can't be optimised further with respect to perplexity or energy consumption without a penalty in the other. Therefore we identified the Pareto-optimal models.

The next graphs, Figure 1 showcases energy consumption related to perplexity for each model evolving over the 10 epochs. The colour of each dot represents a specific model throughout all the models, hence it is possible to see how each model progresses throughout the graphs. Besides a visualisation of how each model evolves, the graph also highlights the Pareto curve for each epoch, which is an indicator of the best-performing models for each epoch. While some of these best models might not have a particularly good PEP value, they are still a part of the Pareto curve, and thus can't improve either perplexity or energy consumption without a decrease in the other.

Furthermore, as can be seen in figure 1, there are a few models which permanently reside at 2000 perplexity. These are all models which have low vocab size, high dropout probabilities, low hidden size, or a combination of the three. This, combined with a relatively high number of hidden layers and

	Best 15% Mean	Best 15% Std. Dev	Worst 15% Mean	Worst 15% Std. Dev
vocab_size	19458.52	5741.79	16072.78	9451.63
actual_hidden_size	273.17	101.14	670.52	468.80
num_hidden_layers	1.91	0.92	6.52	3.24
num_attention_heads	8.17	4.13	10.47	4.70
intermediate_size	716.17	531.30	1237.08	581.32
hidden_dropout_prob	0.18	0.06	0.52	0.24
attention_probs_dropout_prog	0.25	0.10	0.46	0.26
energy comsumption	1.70	0.51	5.70	3.11
perplexity	27.23	7.80	1809.32	501.77

Table 2: Mean and standard deviation of hyperparameters for the best 15% and worst 15% of models wrt: PEP value.

	Best 15% Count	Worst 15% Count
relative_key_query	20	7
relative_key	0	8
absolute	3	8
GELU	14	8
GELU_new	2	7
ReLU	1	5
SiLU	6	3

Table 3: Count of activation functions and position embedding types wrt: PEP value.

attention heads result in models which have a hard time learning.

6 Analysis

For the analysis, we start with the most trivial optimisation steps and progress towards less trivial ones.

6.1 Parameter correlations

When looking at the best 15% models in terms of low PEP value, analysing the resulting correlation matrix given in Figure 3 in appendix A can give us insight into whether our approach has resulted in a good balance between energy consumption and perplexity. It can also give clues as to what parameter values can be chosen to reduce a models energy consumption without affecting perplexity. Additionally, we define a good balance for a hyperparameter between energy consumption and perplexity as the absolute value of the correlation one parameter to perplexity roughly equalling the absolute value of the correlation between the same parameter and energy consumption. Specifically:

$$|corr_{param_n,PPL}| \approx |corr_{param_n,energy}|$$

The correlation between perplexity and energy consumption is at -0.88, which indicates that the use of hyperopt and our PEP loss function has given a good balance between the quality and energy use during optimisation. The three key parameters appear to be the number of hidden layers, the hidden activation function and the position embedding type. Hidden layer count has a correlation of 0.71 and -0.64 between energy consumption and perplexity respectively, this being the hyperparameter with the greatest impact on both of these values. Activation function also has a high impact, again with -0.63 and 0.68 with energy consumption and perplexity respectively (Derczynski, 2020). Lastly, the positional embedding is at 0.49 and -0.65 respectively. As in Table 2 and 3, the optimal number of hidden layers averaged out at 1.91. The most used activation functions and positional encodings are GELU and relative_key_query and 14 and 20 appearances. It is important to note that as the positional encoding defines the way attention is calculated, there may be an underlying link between the number of attention heads and encoding choice.

It is important to note that correlation is a useful tool to find linear tendencies. While a correlation close to negative and positive indicates a correlation between the two values, a value of zero doesn't guarantee a lack of correlation since there could still exist a non-linear correlation.

6.2 What predicts a good or bad model?

Looking at Table 2, the overall tendency is that the models, on average, are much smaller than the config of $RoBERTa_{BASE}$ (Liu et al., 2019). The number of hidden layers in our best models in terms of PEP value is on average 2, down from 12. With hidden layers having a correlation of 0.71 with energy consumption and -0.64 with perplexity, as seen in Figure 3, it is by far one of the most volatile parameters to adjust. Increasing the number of hid-

	Best 15% Mean	Best 15% Std. Dev	Worst 15% Mean	Worst 15% Std. Dev
vocab_size	21187.73	6426.71	18545.04	9141.88
actual_hidden_size	116.43	84.20	727.78	27.33
num_hidden_layers	1.52	0.77	7.82	3.26
num_attention_heads	8.08	5.27	12.78	4.48
intermediate_size	890.47	554.19	1149.65	739.19
hidden_dropout_prob	0.37	0.23	0.40	0.15
attention_probs_dropout_prog	0.28	0.14	0.47	0.28
energy comsumption	0.99	0.17	6.18	1.93
perplexity	338.51	576.74	1236.04	962.74

Table 4: Mean and standard deviation of hyperparameters for the best 15% and worst 15% of models wrt: energy consumption.

	Best 15% Count	Worst 15% Count
relative_key_query	15	14
relative_key	4	6
absolute	4	3
GELU	3	11
GELU_new	3	5
ReLU	6	3
SiLU	11	4

Table 5: Count of activation functions and position embedding types wrt: energy consumption.

den layers will increase energy consumption, but decrease perplexity. Interestingly, with it having a correlation of 0.056 to PEP value, it could suggest that hyperopt has found a good compromise in the number of hidden layers that gives a good balance between low energy consumption and perplexity.

The number of attention heads is at 8, which is higher than what our initial assumption was, but with a deviation of 4.13, it varies a lot from model to model. It is important to note that this parameter is dependent on the type of positional embedding used, as the way attention is calculated is heavily dependent on it.

While these models have good performance, with the energy consumption averaging at 1.70 and perplexity at 27.23, it is important to note that these two metrics have a negative correlation with each other of -0.88. If one is reduced, the other one increases. This could suggest that we have hit a point where we can no longer make our models smaller without severely affecting our end performance. RoBERTa reported perplexities between 3.68 and 3.99 in table 3 in (Liu et al., 2019). While our perplexities on average are roughly 7.4 times higher, both our amount of training data and model size are vastly smaller by a factor of 10, thus probably leading to a shorter downstream task fine-tuning time, and as a result, lower energy consumption.

On the opposite end of the spectrum are the worst 15% of the models in terms of PEP value. We assume that these models would be bigger, both in terms of hidden layers, their hidden size, and intermediate size, as these would most likely result in longer training times than smaller ones, thus consuming more energy. Comparing Table 2 to the best 15% supports this analysis. The number of hidden layers has increased from an average of 1.91 to 6.52, hidden size from 273 to 670, and intermediate size from 716 to 1237. The energy consumption is indeed also higher, as it has gone from 1.7 kWh to 5.7 kWh. The perplexity is also very bad, being at an average of 1809.

6.3 Reducing LLM training power consumption without reducing quality

There is also a slight correlation between hidden dropout probability and perplexity, but there is almost no correlation between that probability and energy consumption. These correlations suggest that a low hidden dropout probability results in a lower perplexity, without impacting the energy consumption of the models.

The top 15% of models at $\eta = 10$ (Figure 3) indicate interesting correlations. This matrix suggests a stronger negative correlation between energy consumption and perplexity. These results indicate that it is hard to reduce both perplexity and energy consumption at the same time, since lowering one tends to increase the other - a trade-off. This could be because the models are already performing decently well and have reached the point where subsequent iterations bring diminishing returns in perplexity, while still incurring a linear increase in energy consumption. Looking at the models, 10 of the 23 models in the best 15% appear on the Pareto-optimal curve as seen in Figure 1. This suggests that the remaining 13 models are very close to being optimal, whereas the 10 models which appear on the Pareto curve already are. The same trend happens in the number of hidden layers, where the correlations indicate that increasing the number of hidden layers will also increase energy consumption, but will decrease perplexity. Interestingly, the correlation previously seen with the hidden dropout probability has disappeared. This indicates that the best-performing models already have a low enough hidden dropout probability for this correlation to no longer be the case. When looking at the data, the entire dataset features an average hidden dropout probability of 0.385, where the best 15% of models have an average of 0.189, which supports the previous indication.

6.4 Different parameters have different effects in different realms

Most of our well-performing models – no matter if looking only at energy, perplexity, or PEP value – use the relative key query positional embedding. While this is a slightly more complex calculation for self-attention, this suggests that it doesn't have a huge impact on energy consumption, while it has a noticeable impact on perplexity. Relative key query introduces another 143K parameters but is relatively insignificant when compared to the 103M BERT already has (Huang et al., 2020). While our dataset contains 107 models with "relative key query" as the positional embedding type, when looking at the worst-performing models, the distribution looks close to uniform, at least when looking at perplexity and PEP. Furthermore, Table 13 shows the distribution in the first cluster, which features 94 out of the 107 models with relative key query, further strengthening the claim.

A similar trend appears for the choice of activation functions, with GELU being the best-performing activation function for our best models in terms of perplexity and energy loss. If one wants an activation function purely for energy efficiency, SiLU is the most prevalent activation function among the models with the lowest power consumption. When looking at Table 13, it's seen that GELU and SiLU appear the most frequent, but ReLU is still close behind, in line with previous results (Derczynski, 2020).

Our findings were focused on hyperparameter optimization, and no compression of the LMs at all. Jacobsen et al. (2021) provide methods for measuring model size. Li et al. (2020) show that training larger models for longer times and then compressing them leads to more efficient training. Though the previous analysis on layers and attention heads is less relevant for this approach, our findings regarding loss functions and embedding types should hold if choosing to train a larger model and then compress.

	Energy Consumption
Hyperopt (1 Epoch)	50.53 kWh
Hyperopt (3 Epochs)	187.57 kWh
10 Epochs	393.56 kWh
Ad-hoc tests	62.42 kWh
Total	**694.10 kWh**

Table 6: Energy consumption for this work

6.5 Our energy consumption

This paper investigates alternatives to high-performance, high-energy consumption top-of-the-line models by showing that other approaches can provide acceptable performance while cutting the size and training time. As this topic is relevant due to the environmental impact it can have, such as accelerating rising sea levels (Veng and Andersen, 2020), and as training NLP models has an actual impact on the environment due to high energy usage, reducing their consumption is, as a topic, both important and very unexplored. This also means that we, as the authors, have to stress the importance of noting that this is not a complete guide on how to create low-power, low-perplexity transformer models. As an example, reducing the number of hidden layers might have a positive effect in certain models, but not necessarily in others - one has to look at all the model parameters together.

Table 6 shows the total amount of energy we've spent training our various models. As the price of 1 kWh in Denmark is roughly €0.28 (Eurostat, 2021), the total amount of money we spent training all of our models totals roughly €195 in electricity. While not a lot in comparison to the models presented in table 3 in Strubell et al. (2019), our models are also trained on a smaller dataset, and some of them have a configuration that slims down their size. In terms of watt-hour usage, the number of models we trained consumed half the amount of energy that the BERT base did. As a comparison, 700 kWh can power a Tesla Model 3 for a whole 4337 kilometres (standard range of 16kWh per 100 kilometres (Wikipedia, 2021)), which is roughly from Copenhagen to Barcelona and back.

6.6 Limitations

In this subsection, we discuss possible limitations of our study and indicate where future work could explore further.

Given the fact that this work was done on a small subset of the CC-News dataset, the best performing models may be smaller models where the small amount of data is not a downside. If the size of the corpus is increased, it would give space for the larger models to learn more, and maybe perform better than the smaller models deemed as the most efficient. Even though other efficient models might be uncovered, this will not change the correlation between the number of hidden layers and efficiency. There is also a small possibility that perplexity scores are inflated, as CC-News was used to pre-train RoBERTa (Liu et al., 2019), and this could occur non-linearly across hyperparameter configurations – but we expect the relations between network architecture components, power consumption, and performance to hold relative to each other overall.

We also note that this work was monolingual and focused on English, to the exclusion of other languages (Bender, 2019). While transformer-based LLMs seem to exhibit some properties in common across natural languages, there are also many language-specific considerations (e.g. for Finnish, Virtanen et al. (2019)). Our results cannot be guaranteed to generalise across other natural languages.

Given the fact that a heterogeneous cluster was utilized for training all of the models, there is no guarantee that the precise hardware configuration was used to train all 154 models. All compute nodes have the same type of graphics card but contain different server-grade CPUs. Since CPU and DRAM contribute to power consumption (Anthony et al., 2020), the variations in clock speed and core count could potentially have a small effect on the final energy consumption.

We used a relatively low epoch count for the search of hyperparameter space. This might not reflect high-epoch hyperparameter optima, and so the relations between perplexity scores are at best advisory. However, power consumption tends to be stable per epoch, and so this component of the function performs well.

We evaluate using perplexity, which has its own issues and is unlikely to approximate many NLU metrics. However, it does lend itself well to our exploratory compound loss function, retains agnosticity regarding the many possible NLU tasks (such as those in SuperGLUE). The correlations between evaluated language model performance and their final performance are not of maximum certainty; however, these results can guide hyperparameter search/tuning in terms of good balances, and we hope to see much more research in this area of transformer efficiency and quality/energy use trade-off.

We fixed the epoch count for studies. An alternative would be to fix the FLOPS available. Gordon et al. (2018) present a regulariser that optimises FLOPS usage. Because perplexity tends to be asymptotic with zero for useful models, making absolute differences between model scores tend to be smaller as time goes on. This makes the metric a little noisy and differences hard to note. Fixed FLOPS allowances will lead to high epoch counts for smaller models, increasing the risk of model performances being hard to tease apart. Thus, fixing epochs instead of FLOPS during exploration gives finer granularity for very small, or very efficient models, though FLOPS is a closer approximation to power consumption.

As NVIDIA (2021) highlights, some size multipliers are more efficient when it comes to matrix-matrix multiplication. Allowing the search space as denoted on table 1 to take non-efficient values can affect reproducibility because of hardware idiosyncrasies. While general trends can be extracted, precise figures might not generalise well beyond the test setup.

7 Conclusion

We investigated how hyperparameters affected the power consumption and model quality of transformer-based language models. This paper has presented a method for low-power investigation of hyperparameter tuning, integrating power consumption measurement. We identified factors that increase power without giving quality and identified factors that increase quality without taking power. There are many possible extensions to this work and it is our hope that power consumption measurement will be improved and will be integrated with more architecture searches during model training.

References

Dario Amodei. 2018. AI and Compute. https://openai.com/blog/ai-and-compute/.

Lasse F. Wolff Anthony, Benjamin Kanding, and Raghavendra Selvan. 2020. Carbontracker: Tracking and Predicting the Carbon Footprint of Training Deep Learning Models. *arXiv:2007.03051 [cs, eess, stat]*. ArXiv: 2007.03051.

Emily M Bender. 2019. The #benderrule: On naming the languages we study and why it matters. *The Gradient*, 14.

Emily M. Bender, Timnit Gebru, Angelina McMillan-Major, and Shmargaret Shmitchell. 2021. On the dangers of stochastic parrots: Can language models be too big?. In *Proceedings of the 2021 ACM Conference on Fairness, Accountability, and Transparency*, FAccT '21, page 610–623, New York, NY, USA. Association for Computing Machinery.

James Bergstra, Rémi Bardenet, Yoshua Bengio, and Balázs Kégl. 2011. Algorithms for hyper-parameter optimization. In *Proceedings of the 24th International Conference on Neural Information Processing Systems*, NIPS'11, page 2546–2554, Red Hook, NY, USA. Curran Associates Inc.

James Bergstra, Daniel Yamins, and David Cox. 2013. Making a science of model search: Hyperparameter optimization in hundreds of dimensions for vision architectures. In *International conference on machine learning*, pages 115–123. PMLR.

Leon Derczynski. 2020. Power consumption variation over activation functions. *arXiv preprint arXiv:2006.07237*.

Jacob Devlin, Ming-Wei Chang, Kenton Lee, and Kristina Toutanova. 2019. BERT: Pre-training of Deep Bidirectional Transformers for Language Understanding. *arXiv:1810.04805 [cs]*. ArXiv: 1810.04805.

Eurostat. 2021. Electricity price statistics.

Ariel Gordon, Elad Eban, Ofir Nachum, Bo Chen, Hao Wu, Tien-Ju Yang, and Edward Choi. 2018. Morphnet: Fast & simple resource-constrained structure learning of deep networks. In *Proceedings of the IEEE conference on computer vision and pattern recognition*, pages 1586–1595.

Zhiheng Huang, Davis Liang, Peng Xu, and Bing Xiang. 2020. Improve Transformer Models with Better Relative Position Embeddings. *arXiv:2009.13658 [cs]*. ArXiv: 2009.13658.

HuggingFace. 2021. Perplexity of fixed-length models.

Magnus Jacobsen, Mikkel H Sørensen, and Leon Derczynski. 2021. Optimal size-performance tradeoffs: Weighing PoS tagger models. *arXiv preprint arXiv:2104.07951*.

Jared Kaplan, Sam McCandlish, Tom Henighan, Tom B. Brown, Benjamin Chess, Rewon Child, Scott Gray, Alec Radford, Jeffrey Wu, and Dario Amodei. 2020. Scaling Laws for Neural Language Models. *arXiv:2001.08361 [cs, stat]*. ArXiv: 2001.08361.

Young Jin Kim, Marcin Junczys-Dowmunt, Hany Hassan, Alham Fikri Aji, Kenneth Heafield, Roman Grundkiewicz, and Nikolay Bogoychev. 2019. From research to production and back: Ludicrously fast neural machine translation. In *Proceedings of the 3rd Workshop on Neural Generation and Translation*, pages 280–288.

Lasse. 2021. lfwa/carbontracker. Original-date: 2020-04-21T12:01:38Z.

Zhuohan Li, Eric Wallace, Sheng Shen, Kevin Lin, Kurt Keutzer, Dan Klein, and Joseph E. Gonzalez. 2020. Train Large, Then Compress: Rethinking Model Size for Efficient Training and Inference of Transformers. *arXiv:2002.11794 [cs]*. ArXiv: 2002.11794.

Yinhan Liu, Myle Ott, Naman Goyal, Jingfei Du, Mandar Joshi, Danqi Chen, Omer Levy, Mike Lewis, Luke Zettlemoyer, and Veselin Stoyanov. 2019. RoBERTa: A Robustly Optimized BERT Pretraining Approach. *arXiv:1907.11692 [cs]*. ArXiv: 1907.11692.

J. Sander M. Ester, H. P. Kriegel and X. Xu. 1996. A density-based algorithm for discovering clusters in large spatial databases with noise.

Joel Mackenzie, Rodger Benham, Matthias Petri, Johanne R Trippas, J Shane Culpepper, and Alistair Moffat. 2020. CC-News-En: A large English news corpus. In *Proceedings of the 29th ACM International Conference on Information & Knowledge Management*, pages 3077–3084.

Dominic Masters and Carlo Luschi. 2018. Revisiting Small Batch Training for Deep Neural Networks. *arXiv:1804.07612 [cs, stat]*. ArXiv: 1804.07612.

NVIDIA. 2021. Dl performance matrix multiplication.

Roy Schwartz, Jesse Dodge, Noah A. Smith, and Oren Etzioni. 2019. Green AI. *arXiv:1907.10597 [cs, stat]*. ArXiv: 1907.10597.

Emma Strubell, Ananya Ganesh, and Andrew McCallum. 2019. Energy and Policy Considerations for Deep Learning in NLP. In *Proceedings of the 57th Annual Meeting of the Association for Computational Linguistics*, pages 3645–3650, Florence, Italy. Association for Computational Linguistics.

Ashish Vaswani, Noam Shazeer, Niki Parmar, Jakob Uszkoreit, Llion Jones, Aidan N. Gomez, Lukasz Kaiser, and Illia Polosukhin. 2017. Attention Is All You Need. *arXiv:1706.03762 [cs]*. ArXiv: 1706.03762.

Tadea Veng and Ole Andersen. 2020. Consolidating sea level acceleration estimates from satellite altimetry. *Advances in Space Research*.

Antti Virtanen, Jenna Kanerva, Rami Ilo, Jouni Luoma, Juhani Luotolahti, Tapio Salakoski, Filip Ginter, and Sampo Pyysalo. 2019. Multilingual is not enough: Bert for finnish. *arXiv preprint arXiv:1912.07076*.

Moshe Wasserblat, Oren Pereg, and Peter Izsak. 2020. Exploring the boundaries of low-resource bert distillation. In *Proceedings of SustaiNLP: Workshop on Simple and Efficient Natural Language Processing*, pages 35–40.

Wikipedia. 2021. Tesla Model 3. Page Version ID: 1024502085.

A PEP

Figure 2, 3, and 4 showcase the correlation matrices of the 154 trained models, the best 15% of models with regard to PEP value, and the worst 15% of models with regard to PEP value respectively. These correlation matrices are used to find relationships between different hyperparamters and PEP, in order to figure out which hyperparameters have a huge effect on PEP, and which do not have an effect.

B Energy

Figure 5, and 6 showcase the correlation matrices for the best 15% of models with regard to energy consumption, and the worst 15% of models with regard to energy consumption respectively. Having a correlation matrix over all 154 models would produce an identical result to Figure 2, so that's not included here. These correlation matrices are primarily used to find hyperparamters which greatly affect energy consumption, or which hyperparameters barely affect energy consumption. Both of these can be used to find hyperparamters which need to be tuned, and to find hyperparamters which can be tuned with regard to perplexity, given they do not affect energy consumption.

C Early optimisation results

In this section, we will present the preliminary result after the hyperparameter tuning done with hyperopt. This includes some of the first observable tendencies and was used to start the analytical process.

The loss saved from each model produced by hyperopt is the average overall three epoch, instead of the actual loss at the end of the third epoch. This results in difficulty calculating perplexity, as the loss is now skewed heavily towards the mean, and in return also results in energy loss not being comparable to other parts of the project. Energy consumption has been logged after the end of the third epoch, and can therefore still be compared to the rest of the project. Furthermore, it's not possible to try and calculate what the actual perplexity is, given that there is no real relation between perplexity and the number of epochs. The data will still be presented, but given the fact that the data collection has been different from the rest of the project, it will mostly not be compared or analysed further.

After hyperopt training all 154 models on 3 epochs was done, an analysis of the different model configurations was performed in order to spot early trends in the data. A correlation matrix was constructed for all variable parameters, and compared to energy consumption, perplexity, and energy loss, as can be seen in Figure 7. When speaking about energy consumption, hyperparameters such as the number of hidden layers and the size of said hidden layers plays a big role. As either the number of hidden layers or their size increases, so does the energy consumption needed to train the model. Furthermore, when looking at perplexity, there are no correlations that are as strong as there were for energy consumption. The biggest thing to note here is that there is a positive correlation between hidden layer dropout probability and perplexity. The same goes for hidden layers and hidden size, although this correlation is not as strong as with energy consumption.

The last interesting thing to note here is that there is a positive correlation between energy consumption and perplexity. If one looks at the correlation between energy consumption and energy loss, or perplexity and energy loss, you see a closer correlation between those two parameters, which indicates that the ratio between energy consumption and perplexity, albeit a positive one, is a weaker correlation than the others. There are multiple explanations for this. It could be that this correlation shows that models can be improved in either department without sacrificing the other metric when looking at all models as a whole. It could also be that the aforementioned outliers are having an effect on the data. Following this, the correlation matrix for the best 15% of our models was constructed, as can be seen in Figure 8. When filtering for the best performing models, the strongest correlation is between energy consumption and perplexity, with a correlation of -0.86. This indicates that as energy consumption goes higher perplexity will go lower, and the other way around.

D Perplexity

As with the previous section where we went through the models sorted by the best and worst 15% in terms of energy consumption, this section will do the same but in terms of perplexity instead. By analysing the parameters, we might be able to find a relation between certain of these that can cause both low energy consumption and perplexity, thus reducing the model size without affecting performance.

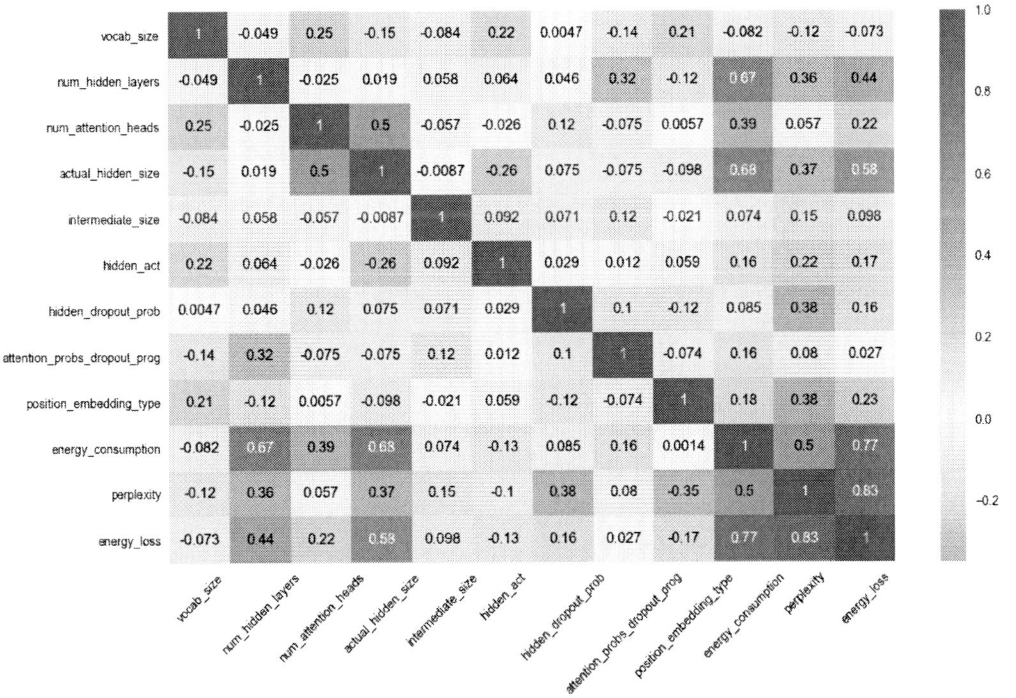

Figure 2: Correlation matrix over hyperparameters for 10 epochs.

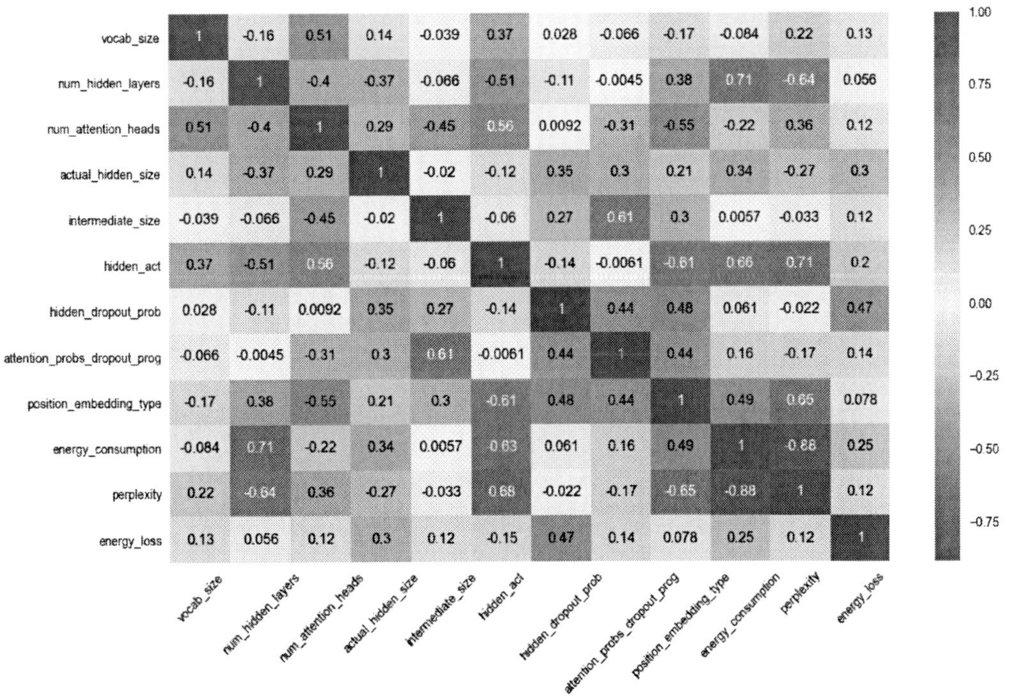

Figure 3: Correlation matrix over hyperparameters for the best 15% of models for 10 epochs.

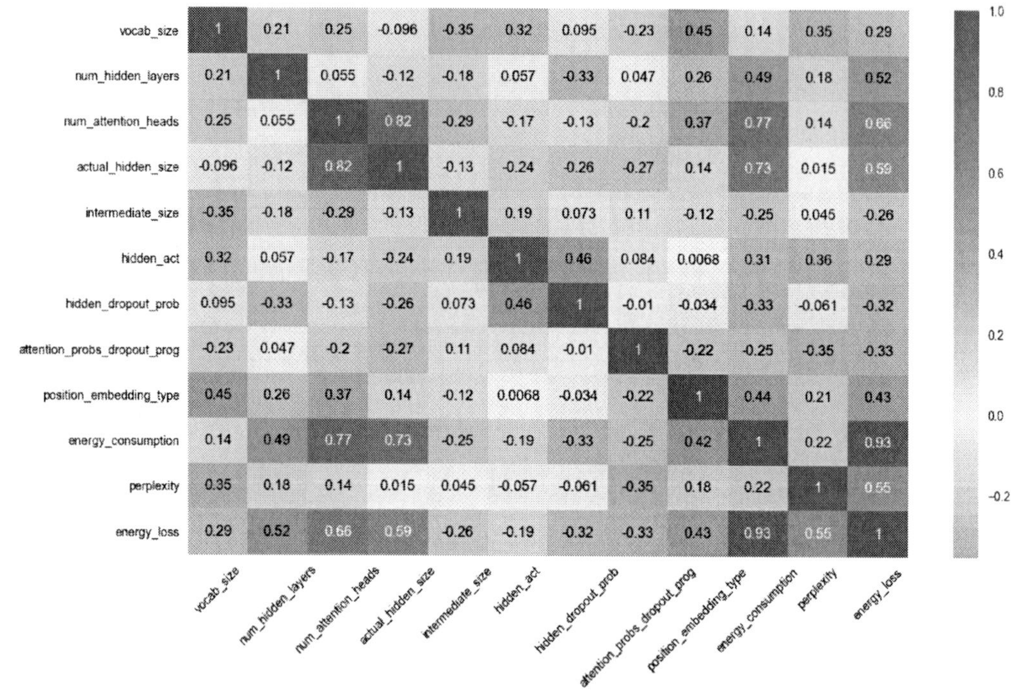

Figure 4: Correlation matrix over hyperparameters for the worst 15% of models for 10 epochs.

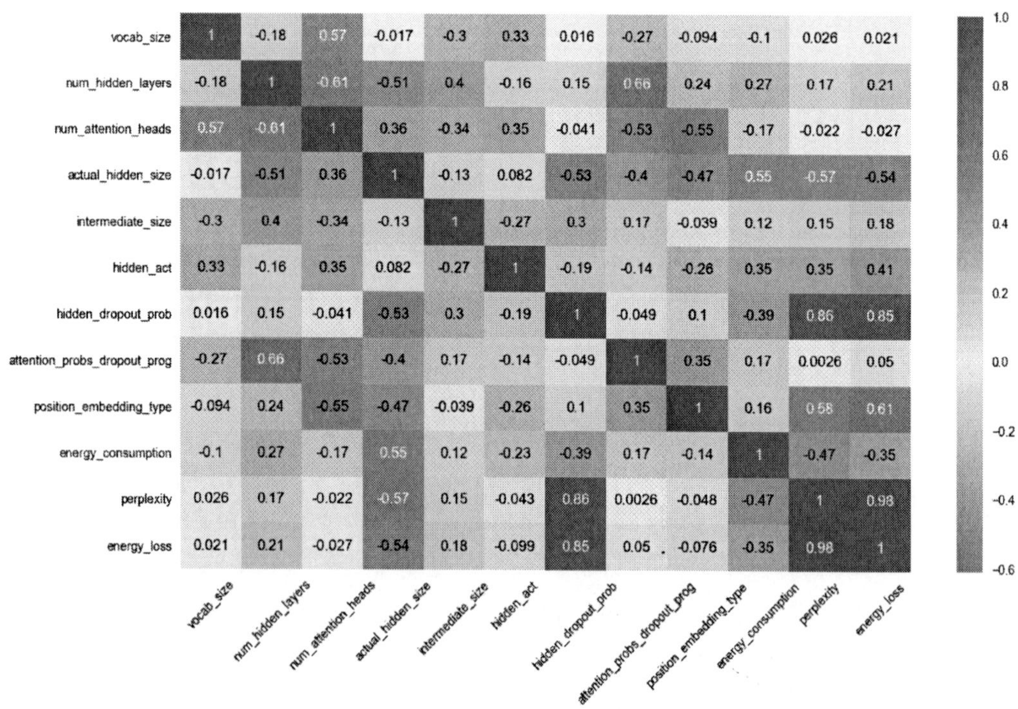

Figure 5: Correlation matrix of the best 15% of models wrt. power consumption.

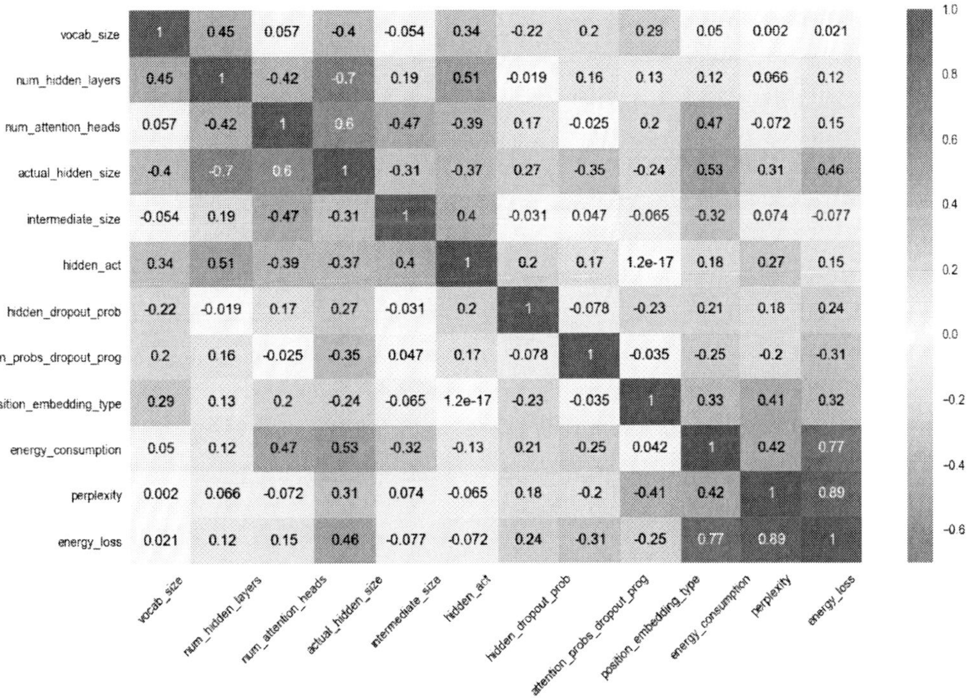

Figure 6: Correlation matrix of the most power-hungry 15% of models.

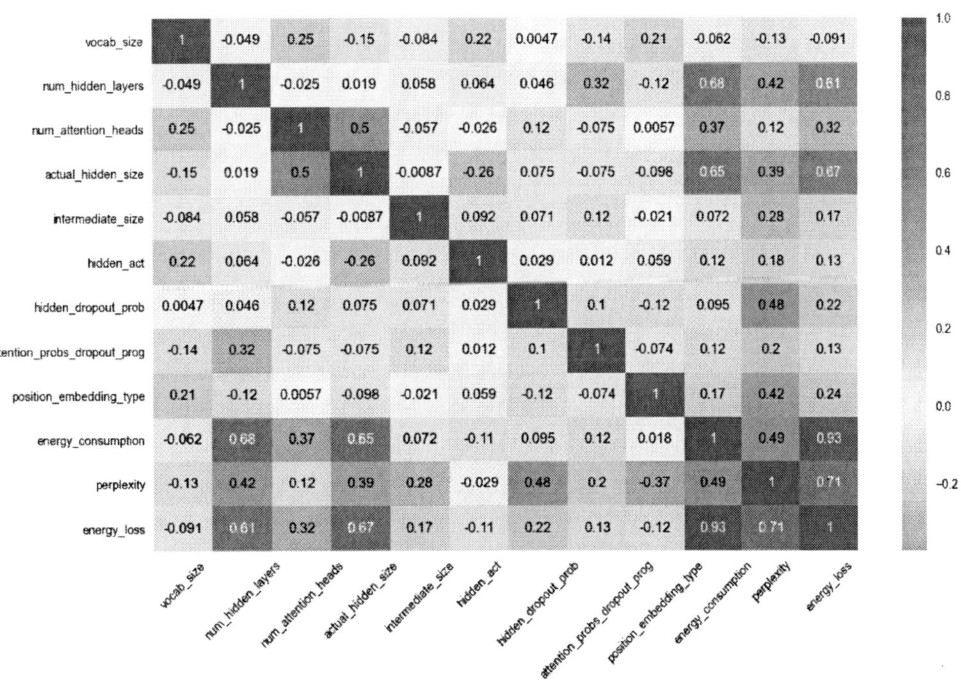

Figure 7: Correlation matrix over hyperparameters for 3 epochs of training.

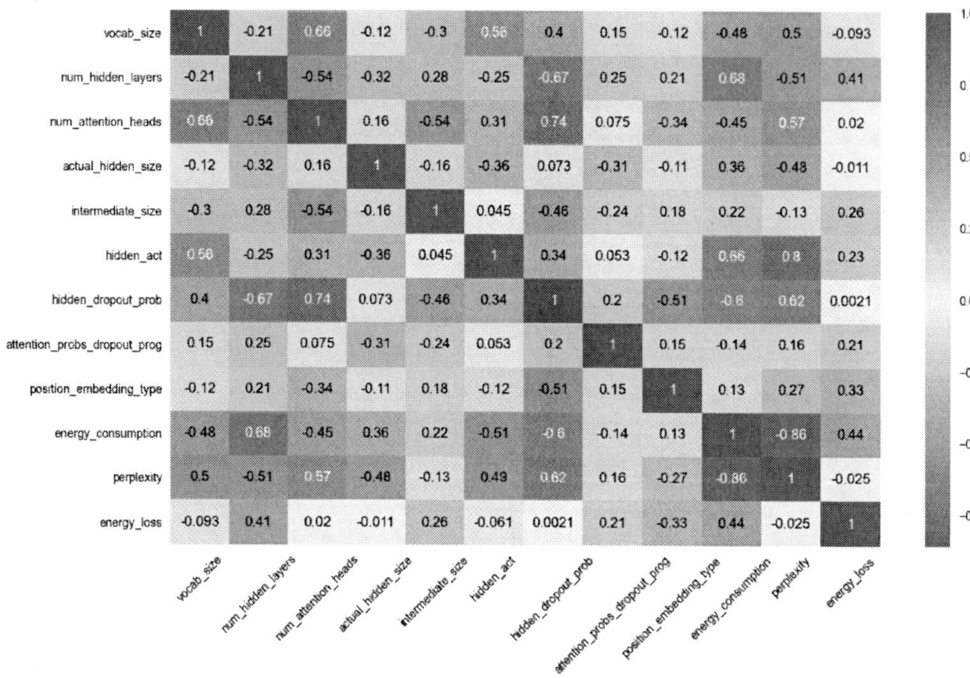

Figure 8: Correlation matrix over hyperparameters for the best 15% of models for 3 epochs of training.

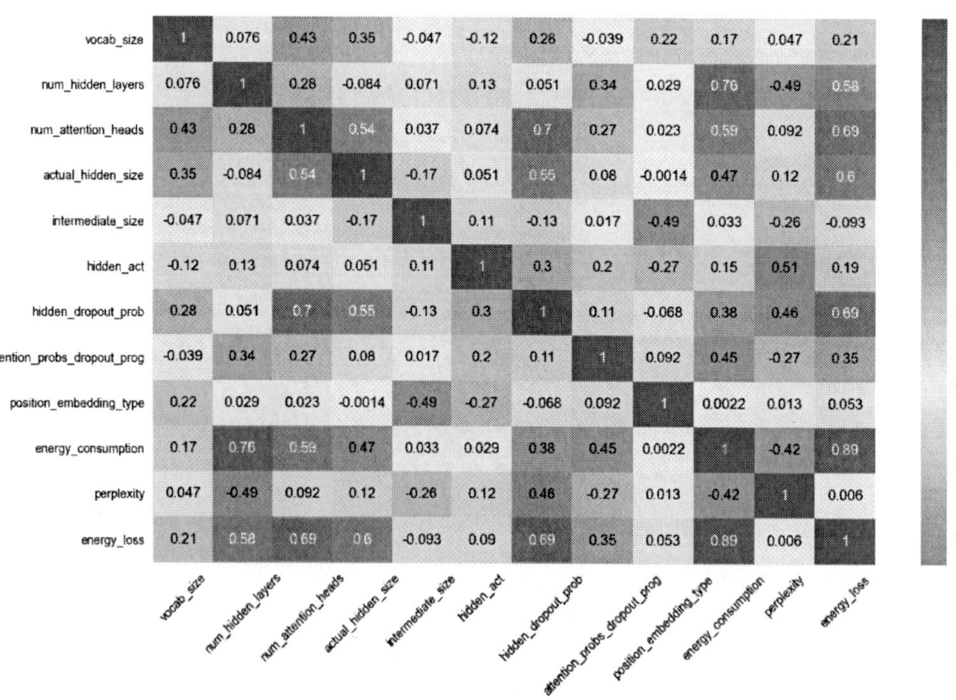

Figure 9: A correlation matrix of the best 15% of models with regard to perplexity.

	Average	Std. Deviation
vocab_size	18002.17	7986.21
actual_hidden_size	404.91	231.93
num_hidden_layers	3.69	2.09
num_attention_heads	10.34	4.62
intermediate_size	851.47	531.30
hidden_dropout_prob	0.21	0.08
attention_dropout_prob	0.37	0.24
energy consumption	3.40	1.58
perplexity	18.79	3.82

Table 7: Table with average hyperparameters of the best 15% of models wrt: perplexity.

The general point with the best-performing models in terms of perplexity is that they are slightly larger than both the best performing energy loss, and energy only models, as can be seen on Table 7. More hidden layers, more attention heads, bigger feed forward neural networks. A lot of these parameters do have a high standard deviation compared to their averages, such as the intermediate size and the number of hidden layers, meaning that there is room for reduction to reduce energy consumption through lower training times. What is interesting to point out is that while the models are slightly bigger, both their average perplexity and energy consumption are vastly better than the worst models in regard to energy consumption. It is possible that our best-performing perplexity models can, due to a slimmer size, reach good performance more easily than compared with the bigger models of the worst energy consumption. This energy consumption is still on average 2.4 kWh higher than our best performing models in terms of energy consumption, being at 1 kWh, but with a vastly better perplexity. It could suggest that energy loss, as a value to minimise for hyperopt, has been effective in finding compromises between performance and energy consumption. As can be seen on the corresponding correlation matrix for the best perplexity models, Figure 9, there is a negative correlation between energy consumption and perplexity of -0.42. This means that reducing one increases the other, which also suggests that hyperopt has found a compromise between the two. This matrix also shows a very high correlation between both energy consumption, perplexity, and the number of hidden layers. For energy consumption, it is 0.76, and for perplexity, it is -0.49. Increasing the hidden layers will drastically increase energy consumption, but it will also lower perplexity a lot. As mentioned earlier, since this adds extra training time to the model, it will automatically increase energy consumption. This could possibly suggest that the number of hidden layers has a direct effect on how well a model performs.

	Appearances
relative_key_query	21
relative_key	2
absolute	0
GELU	11
GELU_new	5
ReLU	3
SiLU	4

Table 8: Count of activation functions and position embedding types in the best 15% of models with regard to perplexity.

Interestingly, as can be observed in Table 8, the distribution over positional embedding and activation function resembles the distribution of the ones sorted by energy loss a lot more than the ones sorted by energy consumption only, with some slight variations. They almost exclusively use relative key query positional embedding and rely more on a GELU activation function.

	Average	Std. Deviation
vocab_size	17920.60	8478.86
actual_hidden_size	569.26	441.47
num_hidden_layers	6.21	3.32
num_attention_heads	10	4.45
intermediate_size	1190.04	587.58
hidden_dropout_prob	0.54	0.26
attention_dropout_prob	0.43	0.26
energy consumption	5.20	3.40
perplexity	1891.61	364.25

Table 9: Table with average hyperparameters of the worst 15% of models wrt: perplexity.

The primary assumption with the models that perform terribly in terms of perplexity is that they are big, and thus have not had enough training time to fully develop. When comparing Figure 1 to Table 9, there are a couple of models that follow this trend, with one taking a significant leap down in perplexity between epoch 8 to 9. As that model follows the trend of badly performing models that are right on top of each other in terms of perplexity, it could be assumed that more epochs are what is needed for perplexity to drop. When looking at the general trend of the parameters, both the hidden size, number of hidden layers, attention heads and intermediate size are higher compared to the mod-

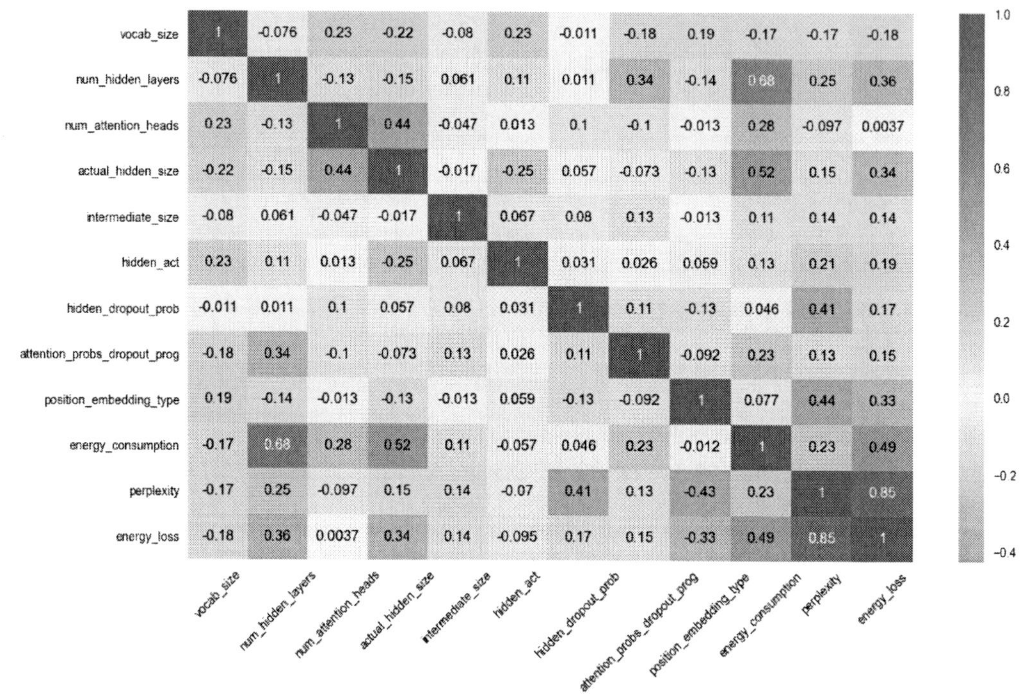

Figure 10: A correlation matrix of the worst 15% of models with regard to perplexity.

els that perform well in terms of perplexity. When looking at Table 9, the parameters for the models in the top 15% worst percentage are definitely larger than those in the top 15% best percentage for perplexity in most aspects. Hidden size and layers are much increased, the same with the intermediate size. All dropout probabilities are also higher, which could be a reason as to why some of these models keep performing terribly - whatever they learn, they end up forgetting, thus making it harder to train a bigger model.

	Appearances
relative_key_query	8
relative_key	7
absolute	8
GELU	7
GELU_new	7
ReLU	5
SiLU	4

Table 10: Count of activation functions and position embedding types in the worst 15% of models wrt: perplexity.

When looking at Figure 10, the activation function has a negligible effect on both perplexity and power consumption in terms of its correlation, but the positional embedding type has a significant impact on perplexity, with a correlation of -0.43. Looking at the difference between the choice of these between the best and worst models in terms of perplexity from Table 10 and Table 8, the better models all tend to use relative key query, whereas the distribution for the worse performing models is more uniform over the three choices. As most of the best models in terms of energy consumption and energy loss primarily use relative key query, the results suggest that there is little to no reason to use another type.

E Clustering

In this section, the data will be clustered in order to find commonalities among the different models, and group them into the three found clusters. Those clusters will then be described in detail, pointing out interesting characteristics in each one.

The data were clustered using DBSCAN algorithm, which is a density-based clustering algorithm designed to do spatial clustering with handling of noise (M. Ester and Xu, 1996). The density-based clustering method that is DBSCAN does not handle varying axis ranges well, and given that energy consumption ranges from $[0.529478; 12.986432]$ and perplexity ranges from $[15.14847702; 2021.91427]$, normalization has to be done. The intent for this normalization is to have both axes have a mean of 0 and a standard deviation of 1. One of the consequences of doing this is that the distance used to specify clusters loses some of its intuitive understanding of what distance is now that both axes have been normalised. While this is true, the distance can now be used to properly be used to identify clusters for both metrics, rather than constraining the perplexity to the range of energy consumption. This enables us to find more than just vertical clusters.

For the actual clustering, a distance of 0.4 was chosen with the requirement of needing 5 samples to form a cluster. The clustering showcases the aforementioned outliers which ended at around 2000 perplexity but also finds another cluster close to our primary cluster, as well as 20 different outliers who were unable to be clustered, marked as black dots on Figure 11.

The exact distribution of the clusters can be seen here on Table 11. It's interesting to note that had the minimum samples been a little higher, cluster 3 would not have existed.

	Number of Models
Cluster 1	118
Cluster 2	10
Cluster 3	6
Outliers	20

Table 11: Table showcasing the three cluster distributions and outliers for the DBSCAN clustering

Given that these three clusters were found by our algorithm, it's only right to analyse those clusters further by constructing correlation matrices for each cluster. The first cluster, which can be seen in Figure 12, is the cluster featuring all the best performing models, and also subsequently the biggest cluster out of the three. The trends for this cluster are similar to what has been previously seen - the correlation matrix indicates that the number of hidden layers and energy consumption have a strong correlation, and the same goes for hidden size to a much lesser degree. Furthermore, the hidden size has a negative correlation with perplexity, and the hidden dropout probability has a correlation with perplexity. This indicates the higher the hidden size, the lower the perplexity, and the lower the hidden dropout probability, the lower the perplexity. Interestingly, energy consumption and perplexity has a negative correlation, but it is incredibly weak, and therefore not indicative of anything. Most of our Pareto entries are in this cluster, which contributes to the negative correlation, but given that there are 118 entries here, as seen on Table 11, it indicates that a predominant amount of the models can still be optimised on both parameters.

When looking at the average parameters for the first cluster, it's decently similar to that of the best 15% of models, as seen in Table 2 in section 4.2. Mostly all parameters follow an increasing trend compared to the other table, except for the actual hidden size, which remains slightly lower than when looking at the best 15% of models. As can visually be seen in Figure 11, this cluster features predominantly low perplexity, at an average of 56.28, whereas the energy consumption is slightly higher, sitting at an average of 2.34.

	Average	Std. Deviation
vocab_size	20491.32	7580.56
actual_hidden_size	263.55	208.74
num_hidden_layers	3.34	2.68
num_attention_heads	9.16	4.87
intermediate_size	891.15	730.67
hidden_dropout_prob	0.33	0.16
attention_dropout_prob	0.36	0.20

Table 12: Table with average hyperparameters of the top 15% of models in cluster 1.

Furthermore, it's also seen that there is a heavy bias towards the position embedding type relative_key_query, which was also the case among our best 15% of models. The activation function remains slightly more spread out, with GELU and SiLU being the predominant activation functions, followed closely by ReLU. Among the best 15% of models, GELU was the predominant function, with SiLU at half of the occurrences, as can be seen on Table 2

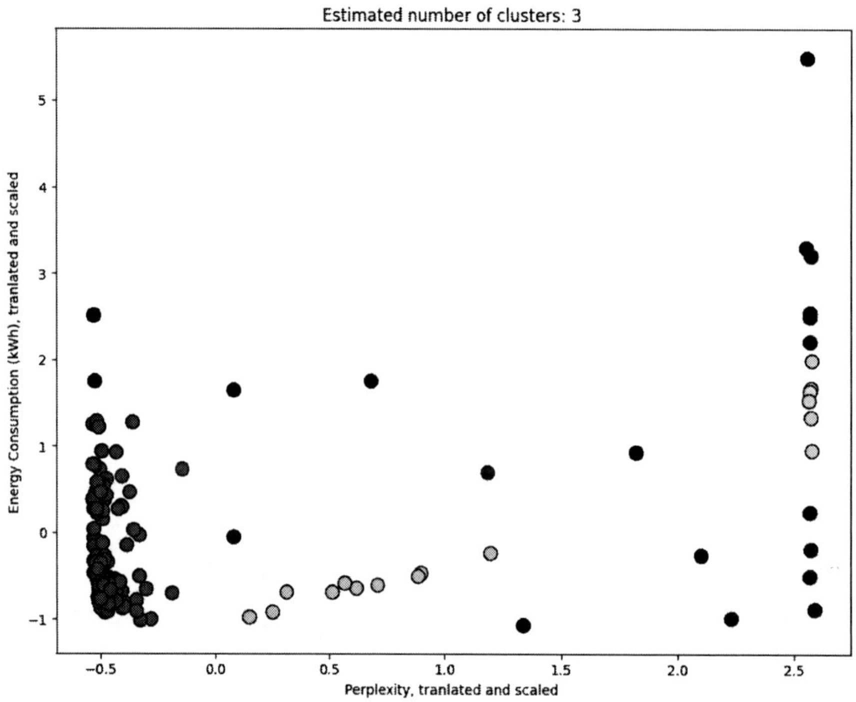

Figure 11: The data clustered using DBSCAN with axes scaled and translated for a mean of 0 and a standard deviation of 1.

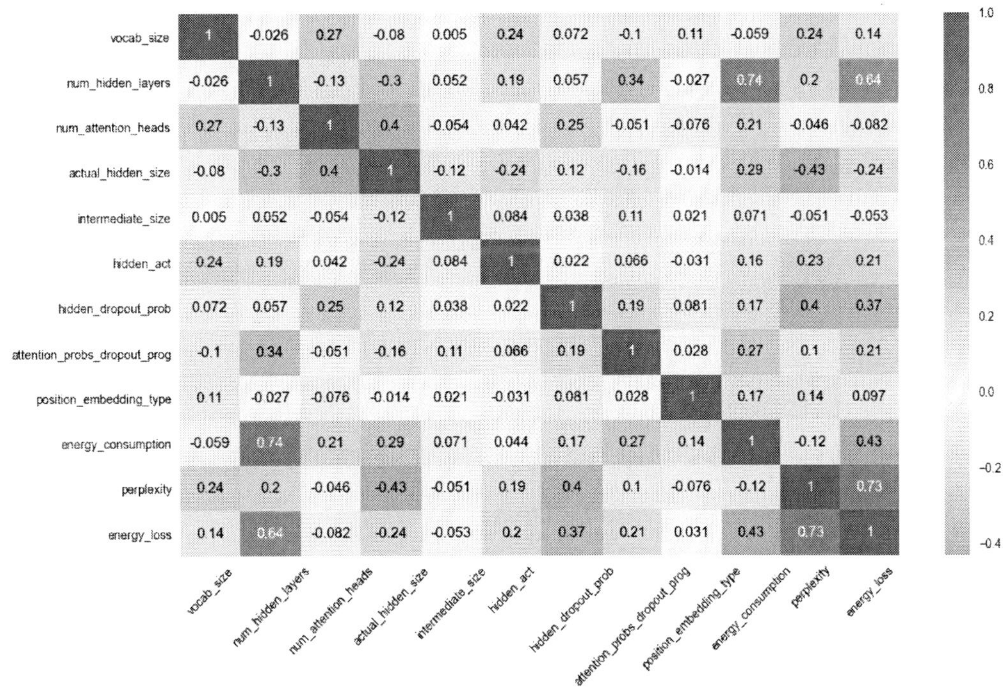

Figure 12: The correlation matrix for the first cluster

	Appearances
relative_key_query	94
relative_key	12
absolute	12
GELU	37
GELU_new	15
ReLU	29
SiLU	37

Table 13: Count of activation functions and position embedding types for the first cluster.

When looking at the second cluster on Figure 11, it can already be seen from this figure that there might be some linear tendencies in the models from this cluster. And as can be seen in Figure 13, energy consumption, perplexity, and energy loss all have a correlation close to 1, which indicates this to be the case. The correlation matrix also indicates linearity in the parameters, given that all parameters have very close correlation ratios between energy consumption, perplexity, and energy loss.

Because of the previously explained linear tendency, a linear regression was done on the models in cluster 2 as can be seen in Figure 14. If one extends beyond the scope of the cluster, it's possible that optimal models which decrease in both energy consumption and perplexity, which also lay on this line. Given that our hyperopt optimization was done on a limited scope, it's not possible to see if this is the case, although this linear regression strongly indicates that there are more models along this line that have not been explored.

The third cluster, being the cluster with all of the detected high perplexity models, can be seen in Figure 15. It features two strong correlations between the number of attention heads and energy consumption, as well as the hidden layer size and energy consumption. This indicates that the high amount of attention heads and hidden layer size have a strong influence on the increase of energy consumption. If one looks at the specific models of this cluster, it can be seen that they on average have 9.5 attention heads and a hidden size of 620.5. If one compares it to the results seen in Table 2, the average number of attention heads increases by approximately 1.5 and the average hidden size by 350. There is also a strong correlation between position embedding type and perplexity with 0.98, which strongly indicates that the position embedding type is tied to an increase in perplexity. Looking at the models in the cluster, it's seen that there's a uniform

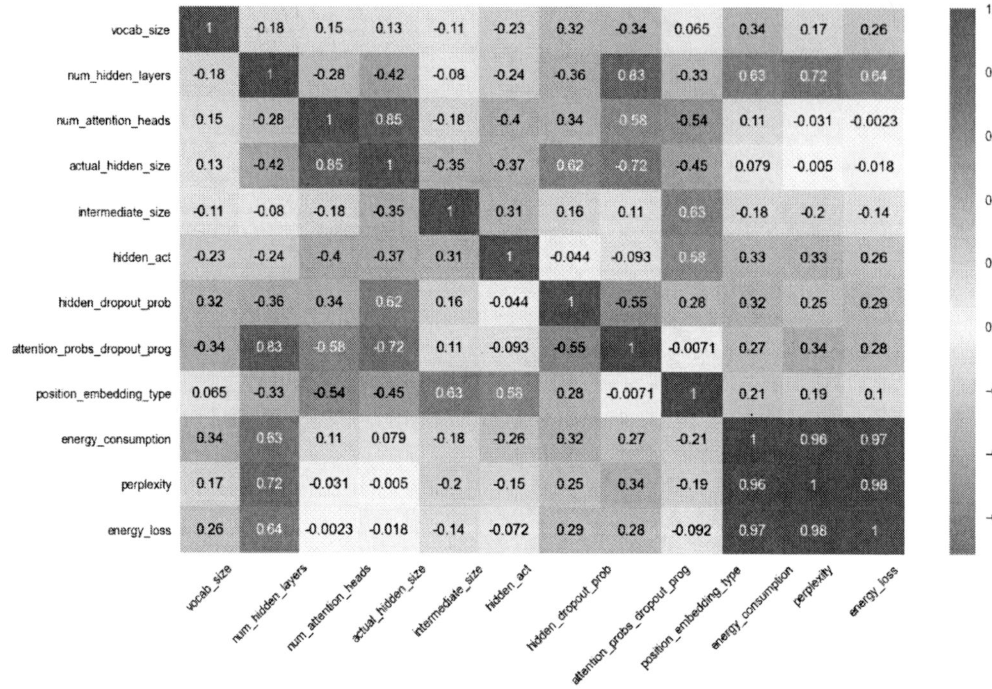

Figure 13: The correlation matrix for the second cluster

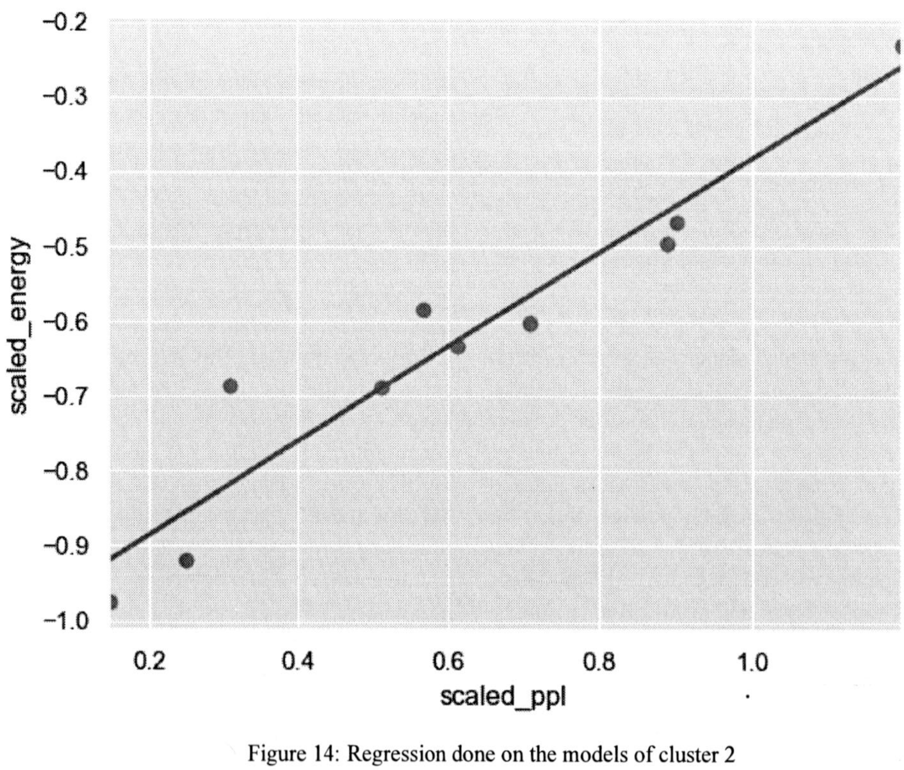

Figure 14: Regression done on the models of cluster 2

distribution between the three-position embedding types in the 6 models in the cluster. When referring back to Figure 10 it is seen that when looking at the 15% worst models with regard to perplexity, the correlation is still there, but not nearly as strong. Furthermore, the same uniform distribution of position embedding types can be seen on Table 10, which indicates that there are too few models to say anything about this correlation.

In Table 14 the 19 models situated on the Pareto curves through all 10 epochs are summarised along with the frequencies of occurrences, and for which epochs they occurred on the Pareto curve. Furthermore, the results with regard to energy consumption and perplexity are also showcased for the models after the 10th epoch, regardless of whether the model was a part of the Pareto curve at this point. Continuing on this point it is also important to note that towards the end of the Pareto curve, that the models most likely won't be the most effective models. This is for example the case with model number 103, which is a part of the Pareto curve for the 10th epoch, but with a perplexity of 1274.87. Model number 103 will probably not be a model you would want to focus on(especially since it was trained over 10 epochs) but can be used as a boundary to attempt to narrow down the search space, and thus still provide valuable information. Similarly, a model such as number 25, has a really strong score with regard to perplexity, but there is a number of models with similar perplexity scores while still having a much lower energy consumption. An important note here is to mention the possibility of training some of the low-cost models for even more epochs, to fairly compare their energy consumption vs perplexity with those of similar models. The reasoning here is if a low-cost model, such as model 103, would be comparable in perplexity to some of the other models after say 20 or 30 epochs, its energy consumption might still be in a relatively comfortable spot compared to another model with an energy consumption similar to that of model 25. The reasoning behind this argument comes from the linear cost of energy consumption for each epoch, such that even after 30 epochs of training, assuming a continuously linear tendency for the following epochs, model number 103 would have an approximate energy consumption of 0.58(the energy consumption for model 103 after 10 epochs) times 3 (to go from 10 to 30 epochs) would be $0.58 \cdot 3 \approx 1.76$.

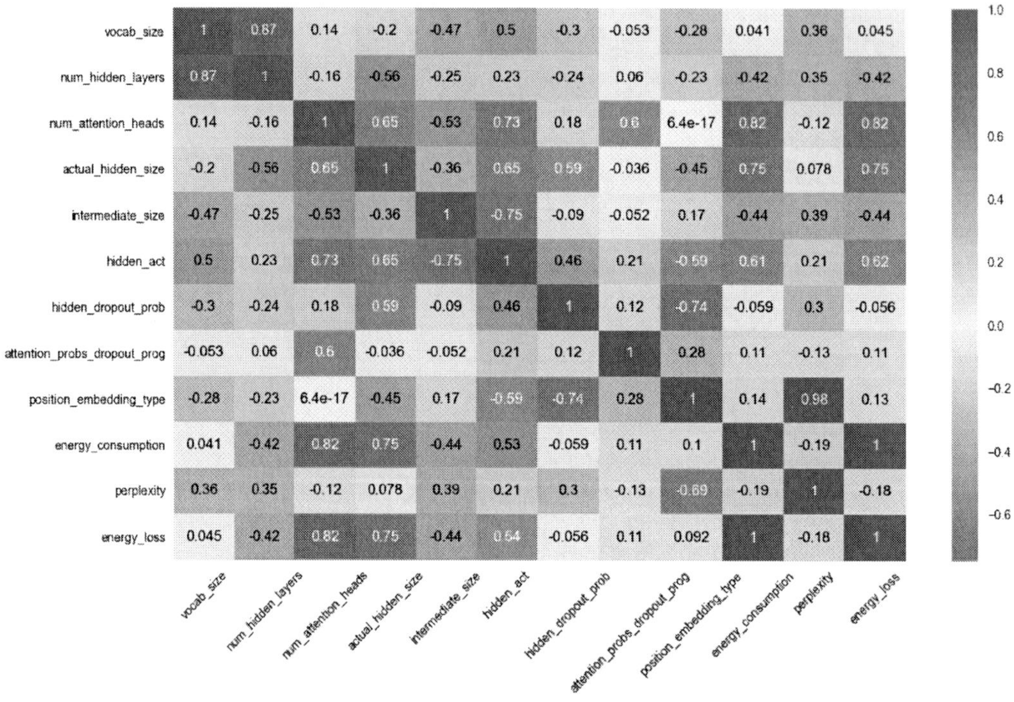

Figure 15: The correlation matrix for the third cluster

id	energy_epoch_10	PPL_epoch_10	occurrence	Epoch Occurrence
10	1.73 kWh	23.66	10	1,2,3,4,5,6,7,8,9,10
25	3.63 kWh	14.31	10	1,2,3,4,5,6,7,8,9,10
29	1.86 kWh	17.61	10	1,2,3,4,5,6,7,8,9,10
81	0.72 kWh	151.56	10	1,2,3,4,5,6,7,8,9,10
97	1.15 kWh	31.77	10	1,2,3,4,5,6,7,8,9,10
103	0.58 kWh	1274.87	10	1,2,3,4,5,6,7,8,9,10
48	0.90 kWh	46.47	9	2,3,4,5,6,7,8,9,10
62	2.52 kWh	15.71	9	2,3,4,5,6,7,8,9,10
88	1 kWh	37.25	9	2,3,4,5,6,7,8,9,10
106	1.26 kWh	29	7	4,5,6,7,8,9,10
111	1.59 kWh	29.27	7	1,2,3,4,5,6,7
58	1.63 kWh	27.19	6	4,6,7,8,9,10
136	1.78 kWh	19.38	6	1,2,3,6,9,10
87	3.66 kWh	13.65	5	6,7,8,9,10
133	4.52 kWh	13.12	5	6,7,8,9,10
147	1.28 kWh	30.43	4	1,2,3,4
114	3.42 kWh	15.51	3	8,9,10
24	1.80 kWh	23.48	2	9,10
99	0.94 kWh	54.87	2	1,2

Table 14: Table over pareto entries, featuring energy consumption and perplexity at 10 epochs, the number of occurrences in the pareto curves of each epoch, and the specific epochs at which it occurs on the pareto curve.

Distiller: A Systematic Study of Model Distillation Methods in Natural Language Processing

Haoyu He[1]*, Xingjian Shi[2], Jonas Mueller[2], Sheng Zha[2], Mu Li[2], and George Karypis[2]
[1]Northeastern University [2]Amazon Web Services
he.haoy@northeastern.edu
{xjshi,jonasmue,zhasheng,mli,gkarypis}@amazon.com

Abstract

Knowledge Distillation (KD) offers a natural way to reduce the latency and memory/energy usage of massive pretrained models that have come to dominate Natural Language Processing (NLP) in recent years. While numerous sophisticated variants of KD algorithms have been proposed for NLP applications, the key factors underpinning the optimal distillation performance are often confounded and remain unclear. We aim to identify how different components in the KD pipeline affect the resulting performance and how much the optimal KD pipeline varies across different datasets/tasks, such as the data augmentation policy, the loss function, and the intermediate representation for transferring the knowledge between teacher and student. To tease apart their effects, we propose Distiller, a meta KD framework that systematically combines a broad range of techniques across different stages of the KD pipeline, which enables us to quantify each component's contribution. Within Distiller, we unify commonly used objectives for distillation of intermediate representations under a universal mutual information (MI) objective and propose a class of *MI-α* objective functions with better bias/variance trade-off for estimating the MI between the teacher and the student. On a diverse set of NLP datasets, the best *Distiller* configurations are identified via large-scale hyper-parameter optimization. Our experiments reveal the following: 1) the approach used to distill the intermediate representations is the most important factor in KD performance, 2) among different objectives for intermediate distillation, MI-α performs the best, and 3) data augmentation provides a large boost for small training datasets or small student networks. Moreover, we find that different datasets/tasks prefer different KD algorithms, and thus propose a simple *AutoDistiller* algorithm that can recommend a good KD pipeline for a new dataset.

*Work done while being an intern at Amazon Web Services.

1 Introduction

Recent advancements in Natural Language Processing (NLP) such as BERT (Devlin et al., 2019), RoBERTa (Liu et al., 2019), and ELECTRA (Clark et al., 2020) have demonstrated the effectiveness of Transformer models in generating transferable language representations. Pretraining over a massive unlabeled corpus and then fine-tuning over labeled data for the task of interest has become the state-of-the-art paradigm for solving diverse NLP problems ranging from sentence classification to question answering (Raffel et al., 2019). Scaling up the size of these networks has led to rapid NLP improvements. However, these improvements have come at the expense of significant increase of memory for their many parameters and compute to produce predictions (Brown et al., 2020; Kaplan et al., 2020). This prevents these models from being deployed on resource-constrained devices such as smart phones and browsers, or for latency-constrained applications such as click-through-rate prediction. There is great demand for models that are smaller in size, yet still retain similar accuracy as those having a large number of parameters.

To reduce the model size while preserving accuracy, various model compression techniques have been proposed such as: pruning, quantization, and Knowledge Distillation (KD) (Gupta and Agrawal, 2020). Among these methods, *task-aware* KD is a popular and particularly promising approach for compressing Transformer-based models (Gupta and Agrawal, 2020). The general idea is to first fine-tune a large model (namely the *teacher* model) based on the task's labeled data, and then train a separate network that has significantly fewer parameters (namely the *student* model) than the original model to mimic the predictions of the original large model. A large number of task-aware KD algorithms have been proposed in the NLP regime, e.g., DistillBERT (Sanh et al., 2019), BERT-PKD (Sun

Proceedings of the 2nd Workshop on Simple and Efficient Natural Language Processing, pages 119–133
November 10, 2021. ©201 Association for Computational Linguistics

et al., 2019), BERT-EMD (Li et al., 2020), TinyBERT (Jiao et al., 2020), DynaBERT (Hou et al., 2020), and AdaBERT (Chen et al., 2020), some of which can compress the teacher network by 10× without significant accuracy loss on certain datasets.

Innovations in KD for NLP generally involve improvements in one of the following aspects: 1) the loss function for gauging the discrepancy between student and teacher predictions (Kim et al., 2021), 2) the method for transferring intermediate network representations between teacher and student (Sun et al., 2019; Li et al., 2020; Yang et al., 2021), 3) the use of data augmentation during student training (Jiao et al., 2020), and 4) multiple stages of distillation (Chen et al., 2020; Mirzadeh et al., 2020). Many research proposals have simultaneously introduced new variations of more than one of these components, which confounds the impact of each component on the final performance of the distillation algorithm. In addition, it is often unclear whether a proposed distillation pipeline will generalize to a new dataset or task, making automated KD challenging. For example, MixKD (Liang et al., 2021) has only been evaluated on classification problems and it is unclear if the method will be effective for question answering.

To understand the importance of different components in KD, we undertake a systematic study of KD algorithms in NLP. Our study is conducted using a meta-distillation pipeline we call *Distiller* that contains multiple configurable components. All candidate algorithms in the search space of *Distiller* work for two types of NLP tasks: text classification and sentence tagging. Distiller unifies existing techniques for knowledge transfer from intermediate layers of the teacher network to the student network (i.e. *intermediate distillation*) as special cases of maximizing (bounds on) the Mutual Information (MI) between teacher and student representations. Based on this unification and recent progress in variational bounds of MI (Poole et al., 2019), we propose a new intermediate distillation objective called MI-α that uses a scalar α to control the bias-variance trade-off of MI estimation. Including MI-α in the search space of *Distiller*, we run extensive hyper-parameter tuning algorithms to search for the best *Distiller*-configuration choices over GLUE (Wang et al., 2019b) and SQuAD (Rajpurkar et al., 2016). This search helps us identify the best distillation pipelines and understand what impact different KD modules have on student performance in NLP. Using the observations of this large-scale study, we train a *AutoDistiller* model to predict the *distillation ratio*, which is defined as the fraction of the teacher's performance achieved by the student, based on KD pipeline choices and characteristics of a dataset. Leave-one-out cross validation evaluation of *AutoDistiller* demonstrates that it is able to reliably prioritize high-performing KD configurations in most folds, and is able to suggest good distillation pipelines on two new datasets.

The main contributions of this work include:

- The meta KD pipeline *Distiller* used to systematically study the impact of different components in KD, including the: 1) data augmentation policy, 2) loss function for transferring intermediate representations, 3) layer mapping strategies for intermediate representations, 4) loss function for transferring outputs, as well as what role the task/dataset play.
- Unification of existing objectives for distilling intermediate representations as instances of maximizing bounds of the mutual information between teacher and student representations. This leads us to propose the MI-α objective that outperforms the existing objectives.
- Using the results collected from our systematic *Distiller* study, we fit a model that automatically predicts the best distillation strategy for a new dataset. On a never-seen dataset "BoolQ"(Wang et al., 2019a), predicted strategies achieve 1.002 distillation ratios (fraction of the student's and the teacher's performance) on average, outperforming random selected strategies with mean of 0.960. To the best of our knowledge, this is the first attempt towards automated KD in NLP.

2 Related Work

Knowledge Distillation. The general KD framework was popularized by Buciluă et al. (2006); Hinton et al. (2014), aiming to transfer knowledge from an accurate but cumbersome teacher model to a compact student model by matching the class probabilities produced by the teacher and the student. Focusing on AutoML settings with tabular data, Fakoor et al. (2020) proposed a general KD algorithm for different classical ML models and ensembles thereof. Also hoping to identify good choices in the KD pipeline like our work, Kim et al. (2021) compared Kullback-Leibler divergence and mean squared error objectives in KD for image classification models, finding that mean squared error performs better.

Recent KD research in the domain of NLP has investigated how to efficiently transfer knowledge from pretrained Transformer models. Sun et al. (2019) proposed BERT-PKD that transfers the knowledge from both the final layer and intermediate layers of the teacher network. Jiao et al. (2020) proposed the TinyBERT model that first distills the general knowledge of the teacher by minimizing the Masked Language Model (MLM) objective (Devlin et al., 2019), with subsequent task-specific distillation. Li et al. (2020) proposed a many-to-many layer mapping function leveraging the Earth Mover's Distance to transfer intermediate knowledge. Our paper differs from the existing work in that we provide a systematic analysis of the different components in single-stage task-aware KD algorithms in NLP and propose the first automated KD algorithm in this area.

Mutual Information Estimation. Mutual Information (MI) measures the degree of statistical dependence between random variables. Given random variables A and B, the MI between them, $I(A, B)$, can be understood as how much knowing A will reduce the uncertainty of B or vice versa. For distributions that do not have analytical forms, maximizing MI directly is often intractable. To overcome this difficulty, recent work resorts to variational bounds (Donsker and Varadhan, 1975; Blei et al., 2017; Nguyen et al., 2010) and deep learning (Oord et al., 2018) to estimate MI. These works utilize flexible parametric distributions or *critics* that are parameterized neural networks (NNs) to approximate unknown densities that appear in MI calcuations. Poole et al. (2019) provides a review of existing MI estimators and proposes novel bounds that trade-off bias and variance. Kong et al. (2020) unified language representation learning objective functions from the MI maximization perspective.

Data Augmentation in NLP. Data Augmentation (DA) is an effective technique for improving the accuracy of text classification models (Wei and Zou, 2019) and has also been shown to boost the performance of KD for NLP algorithms (Jiao et al., 2020) as well as KD in models for tabular data (Fakoor et al., 2020). Wei and Zou (2019) proposed the Easy Data Augmentation (EDA) technique that randomly replaces synonyms, inserts, swaps and deletes characters in the sentence. Jiao et al. (2020) proposed to utilize the pretrained BERT model and GloVe word embeddings (Pennington et al., 2014) to augment the input sentence via random word-level replacement. MixKD (Liang et al., 2021) adopts mixup (Zhang et al., 2018) and backtranslation (Edunov et al., 2018) in augmenting the text data to boost the performance of sentence classification models. Unlike these papers, we propose a novel search space for DA policies that supports stacking elementary augmentation operations such as EDA, mixup, and backtranslation. Thus, our considered DA module is similar to AutoAugment (Cubuk et al., 2019), except it is used for KD in NLP with different elementary operators.

3 Methodology

Our study is structured around a configurable meta-distillation pipeline called *Distiller*. Distiller contains four configurable components, namely: a data augmentation policy $a(\cdot,\cdot)$, a layer mapping configuration of intermediate distillation $\{m_{i,j}\}$, an intermediate distillation objective $l^{\text{inter}}(\cdot,\cdot)$, and a prediction layer distillation objective $l^{\text{pred}}(\cdot,\cdot)$. Assume the teacher network f^T has M layers and the student network f^S has N layers. Then for a given data/label pair (x, y) sampled from the dataset $\mathcal{D}$, the student acquires knowledge from the teacher by minimizing the following objective:

$$\begin{aligned}\mathcal{L} = \mathbb{E}_{\hat{x},\hat{y}\sim a(x,y);x,y\sim\mathcal{D}} \sum_{i=1}^{M}\sum_{j=1}^{N} m_{i,j} l_{i,j}^{\text{inter}}(H_i^{\text{T}}, H_j^{\text{S}}) \\ + \beta_1 l^{\text{pred}}(f^T(x), f^S(x)) + \gamma_1 l^{\text{pred}}(y, f^S(x)) \\ + \beta_2 l^{\text{pred}}(f^T(\hat{x}), f^S(\hat{x})) + \gamma_2 l^{\text{pred}}(\hat{y}, f^S(\hat{x})),\end{aligned} \tag{1}$$

Here $m_{i,j} \in [0, 1]$ represents the layer mapping weight between the i-th teacher layer and j-th student layer, $H_i^{\text{T}}, H_j^{\text{S}}$ are the i-th and the j-th hidden states of the teacher and the student (i.e. their intermediate representations at layers i and j), β_1, β_2 control the strength of distilling from class probabilities produced by the teacher, and γ_1 and γ_2 control the strength of learning from ground truth data (x, y) and synthesized (augmented) data $(\hat{x}, \hat{y})$. In Appendix, we illustrated how previous model distillation algorithms (Jiao et al., 2020; Li et al., 2020; Liang et al., 2021) can be encompassed in the Distiller framework.

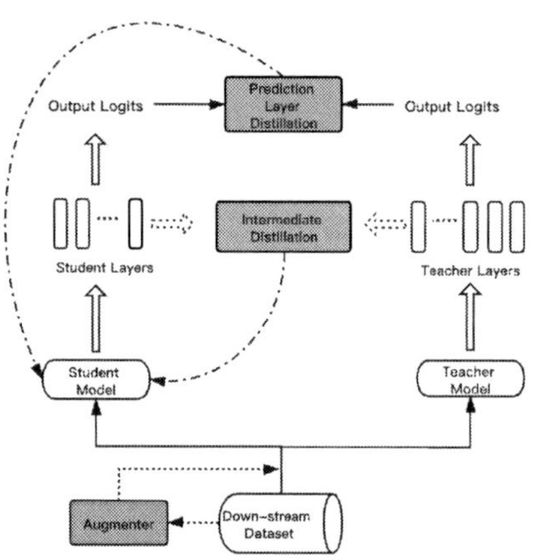

Figure 1: Overview of the *Distiller* pipeline. All configurable components are colored.

Algorithm 1: Data Augmentation Policy

Params: A sequence of elementary data augmentation operations $\mathcal{G}$, $\forall \mathcal{G}_j \in \{CA, RA, BT, Mixup\}$.
Input: Training Dataset $\mathcal{D}_{\text{train}}$
Output: Augmented dataset $\mathcal{D}_{\text{synthesize}}$

Initialize $\mathcal{D}_{\text{synthesize}} \leftarrow \{\}$
foreach $\{x_i, y_i\} \in \mathcal{D}_{train}$ **do**
  for $j \leftarrow 1$ *to len*($\mathcal{G}$) **do**
    $\hat{x}_i, \hat{y}_i = \mathcal{G}_j(x_i, y_i)$;
    $x_i, y_i \leftarrow \hat{x}_i, \hat{y}_i$;
  end
  $\mathcal{D}_{\text{synthesize}} \leftarrow \mathcal{D}_{\text{synthesize}} \cup \{x_i, y_i\}$
end

3.1 Data Augmentation Policy

A key challenge is the limited data available to train students in KD. This can be mitigated via Data Augmentation (DA) to generate additional data samples. Unlike in supervised learning, where labels for synthetic augmented data may be unclear unless the augmentation is limited to truly benign perturbations, the labels for augmented data in KD are simply provided by the teacher which allows for more aggressive augmentation (Fakoor et al., 2020). Denoting the set of training samples of the down-stream task as $\mathcal{D}_{\text{train}}$, the augmenter $a(\cdot, \cdot)$ will stretch the distribution from $E_{x,y \sim \mathcal{D}_{\text{train}}}$ to $E_{\hat{x},\hat{y} \sim a(x,y), x,y \sim \mathcal{D}_{\text{train}}}$. We consider various elementary DA operations including: 1) MLM-based contextual augmentation (CA) , 2) random augmentation (RA), 3) backtranslation (BT) and 4) mixup. The search space of possible augmentations in *Distiller* is constructed by stacking these four elementary operations in an arbitrary order, as detailed in Algorithm 1.

For contextual augmentation, we use the pre-trained BERT model to do word level replacement by filling in randomly masked tokens. As in EDA (Wei and Zou, 2019), our random augmentation randomly swaps words in the sentence or replaces words with their synonyms. For backtranslation, we translate the sentence from one language (in this paper, English) to another language (in this paper, German) and then translate it back. Additionally, mixup can be used to synthesize augmented training samples. First proposed for image classification (Zhang et al., 2018), mixup constructs a synthetic training example via the weighted average of two samples (including the labels) drawn at random from the training data. To use it in NLP, Guo et al. (2019); Liang et al. (2021) applied mixup on the word embeddings at each sentence position $x_{i,t}$ with $\lambda \in [0, 1]$ as the mixing-ratio for a particular pair of examples x_i, x_j:

$$\hat{x}_{i,t} = \lambda x_{i,t} + (1 - \lambda)x_{j,t},\ \hat{y}_i = \lambda y_i + (1 - \lambda)y_j,$$

Here λ is typically randomly drawn from a *Uniform* or *Beta* distribution for each pair, y_i, y_j are labels in one-hot vector format, and $(\hat{x}_i, \hat{y}_i)$ denotes the new augmented sample. To apply mixup for sentence tagging tasks, in which each token has its own label, we propose calculating the weighted combination of the ground-truth target at each location t as the new target:

$$\hat{x}_{i,t} = \lambda x_{i,t} + (1-\lambda)x_{j,t},\ \hat{y}_{i,t} = \lambda y_{i,t} + (1-\lambda)y_{j,t},$$

3.2 Prediction Layer Distillation

In traditional KD, the student network learns from the output logits of the teacher network, adopting these as soft labels for the student's training data (Hinton et al., 2014). Here we penalize the discrepancy between the outputs of student vs. teacher via:

$$\mathcal{L}_{\text{pred}} = l^{\text{pred}}(f^T(x), f^S(x)), \tag{2}$$

where $l^{\text{pred}}(\cdot, \cdot)$ is the KD loss component whose search space in this work includes either: softmax Cross-Entropy (CE) or Mean Squared Error (MSE).

3.3 Intermediate Representation Distillation

To ensure knowledge is sufficiently transferred, we can allow the student to learn from intermediate layers of the teacher rather than only the latter's output predictions by minimizing discrepancies between selected layers from the teacher and the student. These high-dimensional intermediate layer representations constitute a much richer information-dense signal than is available in the low-dimensional predictions from the output layer. As teacher and student usually have different number of layers and hidden-state dimensionalities, it is not clear how to map teacher layers to student layers ($m_{i,j}$) and how to measure the discrepancy between their hidden states ($l_{i,j}^{\text{inter}}$). Previous works proposed various discrepancy measures (or loss functions) for intermediate distillation, including: Cross-Entropy (CE), Mean Squared Error (MSE), L2 distance, Cosine Similarity (Cos), and Patient Knowledge Distillation (PKD) (Sun et al., 2019). For these objectives, we establish the following result (the proof is relegated to the Appendix).

Theorem 3.1 *Minimizing MSE, L2, or PKD loss, and maximizing cosine similarity between two random variables X, Y are equivalent to maximizing lower bounds of the mutual information $I(X;Y)$.*

In our KD setting, X and Y correspond to the hidden state representations of our student and teacher model (for random training examples), respectively. Inspired by this result, we can use any lower bounds of MI as an intermediate objective function in KD. In particular, we consider the multisample MI lower bound of Poole et al. (2019), which estimates $I(X;Y)$ given the sample x, y from $p(x, y)$ and another K additional IID samples $z_{1:K}$ that are drawn from a distribution independent from X and Y:

$$\begin{aligned} I(X;Y) \geq\ & E_{p(x,z_{1:K})p(y|x)}\left[\log \frac{e^{f(x,y)}}{\alpha m(y;x,z_{1:K}) + (1-\alpha)q(y)}\right] \\ & - E_{p(x,z_{1:K})p(y)}\left[\log \frac{e^{f(x,y)}}{\alpha m(y;x,z_{1:K}) + (1-\alpha)q(y)}\right] + 1 \\ \triangleq\ & I_\alpha. \end{aligned} \tag{3}$$

In I_α, $f(\cdot,\cdot)$ and $q(\cdot)$ are critic functions for approximating unknown densities and $m(\cdot,\cdot)$ is a Monte-Carlo estimate of the partition function that appears in MI calculations. Typically, the space z and the sample x, y are from the same minibatch while training, that is $K+1$ equals to the minibatch size. I_α can flexibly trade off bias and variance, since increasing $\alpha \in [0, 1]$ will reduce the variance of the estimator while increasing its bias. We propose to use I_α as an objective for intermediate distillation and call it MI-α. Our implementation leverages a Transformer encoder (Vaswani et al., 2017) to learn $f(\cdot,\cdot)$ and $q(\cdot)$. To our knowledge, this is the first attempt to utilize complex NN architectures for critic functions in MI estimation; typically only shallow multilayer perceptrons (MLPs) are used (Tschannen et al., 2020). Our experiments (Table 4 in Appendix) reveal that Transformer produces a better critic function than MLP.

Note that for intermediate distillation, objectives like MSE attempt to ensure the teacher and student representations take matching values, whereas objectives like MI (and tighter bounds thereof) merely attempt to ensure the information in the teacher representation is also captured in the student representation. The latter aim is conceptually better suited for KD, particularly in settings where the student's architecture differs from the teacher (e.g. it is more compact), in which case forcing intermediate student representations to take the exact same values as teacher representations seems overly stringent and unnecessary for a good student (it may even be harmful for tiny student networks that lack the capacity to learn the same function composition used by the teacher). We emphasize that a high MI between student and teacher representations suffices for the teacher's prediction to be approximately recovered from the student's intermediate representation (assuming the teacher uses deterministic output layers as is standard in today's NLP models). Given that high MI suffices for the student to match the teacher, we expect tighter MI bounds like MI-α can outperform looser bounds like MSE that impose additional requirements on the student's intermediate representations beyond just their information content.

3.3.1 Layer Mapping Strategy

We investigate three intermediate layer mapping strategies. 1) Skip: the student learns from every $\lfloor M/N \rfloor$ layer of the teacher, i.e., $m_{i,j} = 1$ when $j = i \times \lfloor M/N \rfloor$; 2) Last: the student learns from the last k layers of the teacher, i.e., $m_{i,j} = 1$ when $j = i + M - N$; and 3) EMD: a many-to-many learned layer mapping strategy (Li et al., 2020) based on Earth Mover's Distance. In the *Distiller* pipeline, the intermediate loss with EMD mapping can be denoted as:

$$\mathcal{L}_{\text{EMD}}(H^S_{1:N}, H^T_{1:M}) = \frac{\sum_{i=1}^{M}\sum_{j=1}^{N} w^H_{i,j} d^H_{i,j}}{\sum_{i=1}^{M}\sum_{j=1}^{N} w^H_{i,j}}, \tag{4}$$

where $D^H = [d^H_{i,j}]$ is a distance matrix representing the cost of transferring the hidden states knowledge from H^T to H^S. And $W^H = [w^H_{i,j}]$ is the mapping flow matrix which is learned by minimizing the cumulative cost required to transfer knowledge from H^T to H^S. In *Distiller*, the distance matrix is calculated via intermediate objective function: $d^H_{i,j} = l^{\text{inter}}(H^S_i, H^T_j)$.

3.4 AutoDistiller

Our experiments indicate that the best distillation algorithm varies among datasets/tasks (see in particular the top-5 configurations listed in Table 9 in Appendix). This inspires us to train a prediction model that recommends a good KD pipeline given a dataset. To represent the distillation performance across datasets which are evaluated on different metrics, we define distillation ratio as the fraction of the teacher's performance achieved by the student and use it as a general score for distillation performance. Then the prediction model can be trained to predict the distillation ratio based on features of the dataset/task as well as the features of each candidate distillation pipeline. Here we train our *AutoDistiller* performance prediction model via AutoGluon-Tabular, a simple AutoML tool for supervised learning (Erickson et al., 2020). To the best of our knowledge, our proposed method is the first attempt towards automated KD in NLP.

4 Experimental Setup

To study the importance of each component described in the previous section, we randomly sample *Distiller* configurations in the designed search space while fixing the optimizer and other unrelated hyper-parameters. We apply each sampled distillation configuration on a diverse set of NLP tasks and different teacher/student architectures. All experiments are evaluated on GLUE (Wang et al., 2019b) and SQuAD v1.1 (Rajpurkar et al., 2016) that contain classification, regression, and sentence tagging tasks. Here, we view the question answering problem in SQuAD v1.1 as finding the correct answer span from the given context, which is essentially a sentence tagging task. We adopt the same metrics for these tasks as in the original papers (Wang et al., 2019b; Rajpurkar et al., 2016).

Since Turc et al. (2019) finds initializing students with pretrained weights is better for distillation, we initialize student models with either weights obtained from task-agnostic distillation (Jiao et al., 2020) or pretrained from scratch (Turc et al., 2019). Three different pretrained models $\text{BERT}_{\text{BASE}}$ (Devlin et al., 2019), $\text{RoBERTa}_{\text{LARGE}}$ (Liu et al., 2019) and $\text{ELECTRA}_{\text{LARGE}}$ (Clark et al., 2020) are considered as teacher models in our experiments after task-specific fine-tuning. As student models, we consider options like TinyBERT_4, $\text{ELECTRA}_{\text{SMALL}}$, as well as other models detailed in Table 6 in Appendix.

Existing implementations of data augmentation in KD for NLP generally first generate an augmented dataset that is K times larger than the original one and then apply the distillation algorithm over the augmented dataset. Such implementation separates the process of DA from KD, leading to a time/storage-consuming and inflexible KD pipeline. In *Distiller*, we instead apply DA dynamically during training. In addition, we use the teacher network to compute the soft label $\hat{y}$ assigned to any augmented sample $\hat{x}$.

To analyze the importance of different components in *Distiller*, we adopted fANOVA (Hutter et al., 2014), an algorithm for quantifying the importance of individual hyper-parameters as well as their interactions in determining down-stream performance. We use fANOVA to evaluate the importance of the four components in *Distiller* as well as their pairwise combinations: data augmentation, intermediate distillation objective, layer mapping strategy, and prediction layer distillation objective.

5 Experimental Results

Under the previously described experimental setup, we conducted a random search over *Distiller* configurations on each dataset and collected more than 1300 data points in total. Each collected data point contains a particular *Distiller* configuration, the dataset/task, the teacher/student architectures, and the final performance of the student model. Analyzing the data reveals three major findings:

1. Design of the intermediate distillation module is the most important choice among all factors studied in Distiller.
2. Among different loss functions for intermediate distillation, MI-α performs the best.
3. DA provides a large boost when the dataset or the student model is small.

Additionally, we observe that the best distillation policy varies among datasets/tasks as shown in Table 9 in Appendix. Thus we train a meta-learning model, *AutoDistiller*, that can recommend a good distillation policy on any new NLP dataset based on which configurations tended to work well for similar datasets in our study.

Table 1: Comparison of evaluation results on GLUE test set. $BERT_{BASE}$ (G) and $BERT_{BASE}$ (T) indicate the fine-tuned $BERT_{BASE}$ from (Devlin et al., 2019) and the teacher model trained by ourselves, respectively. BERT-EMD_4 and MI-α are both initialized from $TinyBERT_4$, the difference is that BERT-EMD_4 is trained with "EMD" as intermediate layer mapping strategy and MSE as intermediate loss, our MI-α model is trained with "Skip" as intermediate layer mapping strategy and MI-α as intermediate loss.

Model	#Params	MNLI-m (393k)	MNLI-mm (393k)	QQP (364k)	QNLI (108k)	SST-2 (67k)	CoLA (8.5k)	MRPC (3.5k)	RTE (2.5k)	STS-B (5.7k)	AVG
$BERT_{BASE}$ (G)	110M	84.6	83.4	71.2	90.5	93.5	52.1	88.9	66.4	85.8	79.6
$BERT_{BASE}$ (T)	110M	84.5	83.6	71.7	90.9	93.4	49.3	87.0	67.3	84.7	79.2
BERT-PKD_4 (Sun et al., 2019)	52M	79.9	79.3	**70.2**	85.1	89.4	24.8	82.6	62.3	82.3	72.9
BERT-EMD_4 (Li et al., 2020)	14M	**82.1**	**80.6**	69.3	87.2	91.0	25.6	**87.6**	66.2	82.3	74.7
MI-α ($\alpha = 0.9$, ours)	14M	81.9	**80.6**	69.8	**87.4**	**91.5**	**25.9**	87.0	**67.4**	**84.0**	**75.1**

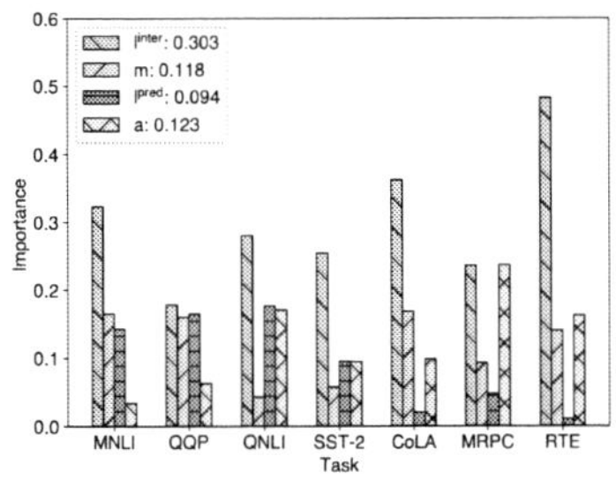

Figure 2: As assessed via fANOVA, we report the individual importance of the four Distiller components in this figure and importance of interactions between any two of the four components in Figure 6 in Appendix. Four components are: l^{inter} for intermediate distillation objective, l^{pred} for prediction layer objective, a for data augmentation and m for layer mapping strategy. Average importance for each component (across tasks) is listed in the legend.

5.1 Importance of Distiller Components

Figure 2 illustrates that the objective function for intermediate distillation l^{pred} has the highest individual importance out of all components in *Distiller*, and the combination of the intermediate distillation objective and layer mapping strategy has the highest joint importance. Thus these are the components one should most critically focus on when selecting a particular KD pipeline. One hypothetical explanation is that the teacher can provide token-level supervision to the student via intermediate distillation, which can better guide the learning process of the student. Our finding is also consistent with the previous observations (Sun et al., 2019; Li et al., 2020).

5.2 MI-α for Intermediate Distillation

We submitted our MI-α model predictions to the official GLUE leaderboard to obtain test set results and also report the average scores over all tasks (the "AVG" column) as summarized in Table 1. The results show that the student model distilled via the MI-α objective function outperforms previous student models distilled via MSE or PKD loss. To further verify the effectiveness of MI-α, we compare how different choices of l^{inter} affect the distillation performance. In detail, we first pick the top 5 best *Distiller* strategies according to the evaluation scores for every task and then count how many times each intermediate objective function appears in these strategies. Figure 3 shows that MI-α appears more frequently than all other objectives on both classification and regression tasks. And the results for SQuAD v1.1 in Table 2 indicate the MI-α also works well for sentence tagging.

Table 2: Ablation study of distillation performance on SQuAD v1.1 dev set. The first line shows the performance of the $BERT_{BASE}$ teacher. $ELECTRA_{SMALL}$, $TinyBERT_6$ and $TinyBERT_4$ are three student networks. $ELECTRA_{SMALL}$ (FT) means to fine-tune without KD. $TinyBERT_6{}^{\dagger}$ and $TinyBERT_4{}^{\dagger}$ are results obtained from Jiao et al. (2020). Models that end with "(MSE)" are trained with the MSE loss. "+ MI-α" means to distill the student with MI-α (α=0.9) as the intermediate loss function. "+ mixup" means to further apply the mixup augmentation.

Model	**SQuAD v1.1** EM	F1
$BERT_{BASE}$ (T)	80.9	88.2
$ELECTRA_{SMALL}$ (FT)	75.3	83.5
$ELECTRA_{SMALL}$ (MSE)	79.2	86.8
+ MI-α	79.0	86.8
+ mixup, MSE	80.1	87.4
+ mixup, MI-α	**80.2**	**87.6**
$TinyBERT_6{}^{\dagger}$ (Jiao et al., 2020)	79.7	87.5
$TinyBERT_6$ (MSE)	77.8	85.5
+ MI-α	80.0	87.8
+ mixup, MSE	78.6	86.2
+ mixup, MI-α	**81.1**	**88.6**
$TinyBERT_4{}^{\dagger}$ (Jiao et al., 2020)	**72.7**	82.1
$TinyBERT_4$ (MSE)	72.7	81.7
+ MI-α	71.7	81.2
+ mixup, MSE	72.4	81.4
+ mixup, MI-α	71.9	**82.5**

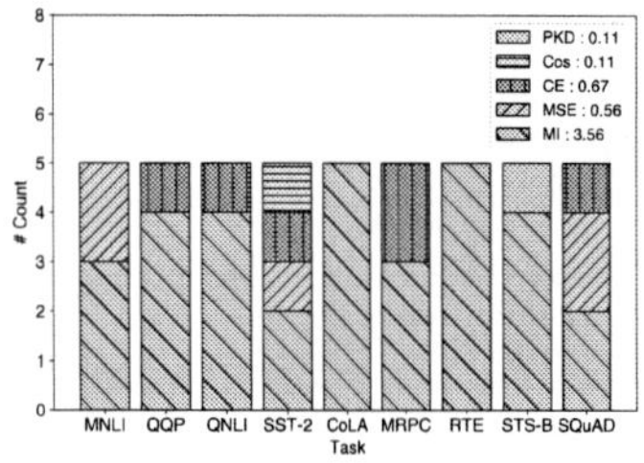

Figure 3: Intermediate objective functions used in the top-5 performing KD configurations on each dataset. The average count of each objective function is listed in the legend. Configurations are detailed in Appendix.

Table 3: Student performance with(out) augmentation (augmenter initialized as CA+RA+mixup). We report the relative improvement for rows starting with "+ aug".

Model	#Params	CoLA mcc	MRPC f1/acc	RTE acc	STS-B spearman/pearson	AVG
$BERT_{BASE}$ (T)	110M	55.0	89.6/85.0	65.0	88.4/88.6	78.6
$TinyBERT_6$	67M	51.3	**92.5/89.7**	**75.5**	89.6/89.8	**81.4**
+ aug		**+0.1**	-1.1/-1.8	-3.3	**+0.2/+0.2**	-1.0
$BERT_{MEDIUM}$	41M	44.1	**89.3/84.8**	65.3	88.3/88.6	76.7
+ aug		**+5.3**	-0.4/-0.7	**+4.4**	**+0.6/+0.5**	**+1.6**
$BERT_{SMALL}$	29M	37.4	86.8/80.6	64.6	87.7/88.0	74.2
+ aug		**+5.0**	**+0.1/+0.8**	**+0.4**	**+0.3/+0.2**	**+1.1**
$TinyBERT_4$	14M	23.6	88.9/**83.8**	67.1	88.0/88.1	73.3
+ aug		**+7.9**	**+0.3/+0.0**	**+2.2**	**+0.7/+0.7**	**+2.0**
$ELECTRA_{SMALL}$	14M	42.8	88.3/83.8	66.4	87.4/87.5	76.0
+ aug		**+16.2**	**+3.4/+3.7**	**+1.8**	**+1.0/+1.0**	**+4.5**
$BERT_{MINI}$	11M	11.2	**86.1/80.1**	62.8	87.1/**87.2**	69.1
+ aug		**+23.2**	**+0.0**/-0.1	**+3.3**	**+0.2/+0.0**	**+4.4**
$BERT_{TINY}$	4M	6.0	83.2/73.3	60.0	84.0/83.6	65.0
+ aug		**+6.6**	**+1.7/+3.7**	**+4.3**	**+0.1/+0.7**	**+2.9**

5.3 Benefits of Data Augmentation

Data augmentation in KD provides the student additional opportunities to learn from the teacher, especially for datasets of limited size. Thus, our experiments investigate the effect of DA on four data-limited tasks: CoLA, MRPC, RTE and STS-B. We also study whether students with different architectures/sizes benefit dissimilarly from DA. Table 3 demonstrates that DA generally provides a boost to student performance and is especially beneficial for small models ($BERT_{MINI}$ and $BERT_{TINY}$).

5.4 Performance of AutoDistiller

Recall that we train our *AutoDistiller* performance prediction model on the previously collected experimental results via AutoGluon-Tabular. Once trained, *AutoDistiller* can recommend distillation pipelines for any down-stream dataset/task by fixing the dataset/task features and searching for configurations that maximize the predicted distillation ratio. *AutoDistiller* operates on features that represent the dataset domain, the task type, and the task complexity, which are detailed in Appendix.

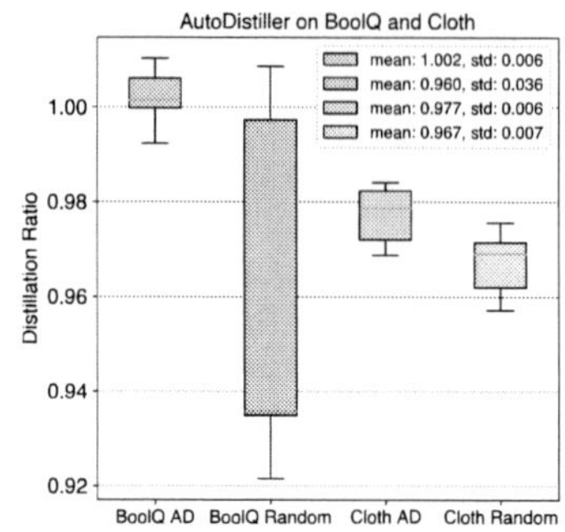

Figure 4: Distillation ratio of *AutoDistiller* (AD) top-5 KD strategies vs. 5 randomly selected strategies, for a fine-tuned $BERT_{BASE}$ teacher and $TinyBERT_4$ student. Higher ratio indicates better distillation performance. Mean and standard deviation of the four groups of ratios are listed in the legend.

We evaluate the performance of *AutoDistiller* on the 8 GLUE datasets via a leave-one-dataset-out cross-validation protocol. Figure 5 in Appendix shows that *AutoDistiller* achieves positive Spearman's correlation coefficients for most datasets.

Finally, we applied *AutoDistiller* on two unseen datasets "BoolQ" (Wang et al., 2019a) and "cloth" (Shi et al., 2021) not considered in our previous experiments. We compared the distillation ratio obtained by each of the top-N strategies suggested by *AutoDistiller* with the distillation ratio from each of N randomly selected strategies. The best strategy suggested by *AutoDistiller* achieves accuracy of 74.2 on "BoolQ" and 70.1 on "cloth", close or superior to the teacher performance (73.4 on "BoolQ" and "71.2" on cloth). Figure 4 shows that *AutoDistiller* significantly outperforms random search, indicating its promise for automated KD.

6 Conclusion

We provided a systematic study of KD algorithms in NLP to understand the importance of different components in the KD pipeline for various NLP tasks. Using data collected from our study, we fit a *AutoDistiller* to predict student performance under each KD pipeline based on dataset features, which is helpful for automatically selecting which KD pipeline to use for a new dataset. Here we unified the existing intermediate distillation objectives as maximizing the lower bounds of MI, leading to a new MI-α objective based on tighter bounds, which performs better on many datasets.

References

David M Blei, Alp Kucukelbir, and Jon D McAuliffe. 2017. Variational inference: A review for statisticians. *Journal of the American Statistical Association*, 112(518):859–877.

Tom Brown, Benjamin Mann, Nick Ryder, Melanie Subbiah, Jared D Kaplan, Prafulla Dhariwal, Arvind Neelakantan, Pranav Shyam, Girish Sastry, Amanda Askell, Sandhini Agarwal, Ariel Herbert-Voss, Gretchen Krueger, Tom Henighan, Rewon Child, Aditya Ramesh, Daniel Ziegler, Jeffrey Wu, Clemens Winter, Chris Hesse, Mark Chen, Eric Sigler, Mateusz Litwin, Scott Gray, Benjamin Chess, Jack Clark, Christopher Berner, Sam McCandlish, Alec Radford, Ilya Sutskever, and Dario Amodei. 2020. Language models are few-shot learners. In *Advances in Neural Information Processing Systems*.

Cristian Buciluă, Rich Caruana, and Alexandru Niculescu-Mizil. 2006. Model compression. In *Proceedings of the 12th ACM SIGKDD international conference on Knowledge discovery and data mining*, pages 535–541.

Daoyuan Chen, Yaliang Li, Minghui Qiu, Zhen Wang, Bofang Li, Bolin Ding, Hongbo Deng, Jun Huang, Wei Lin, and Jingren Zhou. 2020. Adabert: Task-adaptive bert compression with differentiable neural architecture search. In *IJCAI*.

Kevin Clark, Minh-Thang Luong, Quoc V Le, and Christopher D Manning. 2020. ELECTRA: Pre-training text encoders as discriminators rather than generators. In *ICLR*.

Ekin D Cubuk, Barret Zoph, Dandelion Mane, Vijay Vasudevan, and Quoc V Le. 2019. AutoAugment: Learning augmentation strategies from data. In *CVPR*, pages 113–123.

Jacob Devlin, Ming-Wei Chang, Kenton Lee, and Kristina Toutanova. 2019. BERT: Pre-training of deep bidirectional transformers for language understanding. In *NAACL*.

Monroe D Donsker and SR Srinivasa Varadhan. 1975. Asymptotic evaluation of certain markov process expectations for large time, i. *Communications on Pure and Applied Mathematics*, 28(1):1–47.

Sergey Edunov, Myle Ott, Michael Auli, and David Grangier. 2018. Understanding back-translation at scale. *arXiv preprint arXiv:1808.09381*.

Nick Erickson, Jonas Mueller, Alexander Shirkov, Hang Zhang, Pedro Larroy, Mu Li, and Alexander Smola. 2020. Autogluon-tabular: Robust and accurate automl for structured data. *arXiv preprint arXiv:2003.06505*.

Rasool Fakoor, Jonas W Mueller, Nick Erickson, Pratik Chaudhari, and Alexander J Smola. 2020. Fast, accurate, and simple models for tabular data via augmented distillation. In *Advances in Neural Information Processing Systems*, volume 33.

Hongyu Guo, Yongyi Mao, and Richong Zhang. 2019. Augmenting data with mixup for sentence classification: An empirical study. *arXiv preprint arXiv:1905.08941*.

Manish Gupta and Puneet Agrawal. 2020. Compression of deep learning models for text: A survey. *arXiv preprint arXiv:2008.05221*.

Geoffrey Hinton, Oriol Vinyals, and Jeff Dean. 2014. Distilling the knowledge in a neural network. In *NIPS 2014 Deep Learning Workshop*.

Lu Hou, Zhiqi Huang, Lifeng Shang, Xin Jiang, Xiao Chen, and Qun Liu. 2020. DynaBERT: Dynamic bert with adaptive width and depth. In *Advances in Neural Information Processing Systems*.

Frank Hutter, Holger Hoos, and Kevin Leyton-Brown. 2014. An efficient approach for assessing hyperparameter importance. In *ICML*, pages 754–762. PMLR.

Xiaoqi Jiao, Yichun Yin, Lifeng Shang, Xin Jiang, Xiao Chen, Linlin Li, Fang Wang, and Qun Liu. 2020. TinyBERT: Distilling BERT for natural language understanding. In *EMNLP*.

Jared Kaplan, Sam McCandlish, Tom Henighan, Tom B Brown, Benjamin Chess, Rewon Child, Scott Gray, Alec Radford, Jeffrey Wu, and Dario Amodei. 2020. Scaling laws for neural language models. *arXiv preprint arXiv:2001.08361*.

Taehyeon Kim, Jaehoon Oh, NakYil Kim, Sangwook Cho, and Se-Young Yun. 2021. Comparing kullback-leibler divergence and mean squared error loss in knowledge distillation. In *IJCAI*.

Lingpeng Kong, Cyprien de Masson d'Autume, Wang Ling, Lei Yu, Zihang Dai, and Dani Yogatama. 2020. A mutual information maximization perspective of language representation learning. In *ICLR*.

Jianquan Li, Xiaokang Liu, Honghong Zhao, Ruifeng Xu, Min Yang, and Yaohong Jin. 2020. BERT-EMD: Many-to-many layer mapping for bert compression with earth mover's distance. In *EMNLP*.

Kevin J Liang, Weituo Hao, Dinghan Shen, Yufan Zhou, Weizhu Chen, Changyou Chen, and Lawrence Carin. 2021. MixKD: Towards efficient distillation of large-scale language models. In *ICLR*.

Yinhan Liu, Myle Ott, Naman Goyal, Jingfei Du, Mandar Joshi, Danqi Chen, Omer Levy, Mike Lewis, Luke Zettlemoyer, and Veselin Stoyanov. 2019. RoBERTa: A robustly optimized bert pretraining approach. *arXiv preprint arXiv:1907.11692*.

Seyed Iman Mirzadeh, Mehrdad Farajtabar, Ang Li, Nir Levine, Akihiro Matsukawa, and Hassan Ghasemzadeh. 2020. Improved knowledge distillation via teacher assistant. In *AAAI*.

XuanLong Nguyen, Martin J Wainwright, and Michael I Jordan. 2010. Estimating divergence functionals and the likelihood ratio by convex risk minimization. *IEEE Transactions on Information Theory*, 56(11):5847–5861.

Aaron van den Oord, Yazhe Li, and Oriol Vinyals. 2018. Representation learning with contrastive predictive coding. *arXiv preprint arXiv:1807.03748*.

Jeffrey Pennington, Richard Socher, and Christopher D. Manning. 2014. Glove: Global vectors for word representation. In *EMNLP*, pages 1532–1543.

Ben Poole, Sherjil Ozair, Aaron Van Den Oord, Alex Alemi, and George Tucker. 2019. On variational bounds of mutual information. In *ICML*.

Colin Raffel, Noam Shazeer, Adam Roberts, Katherine Lee, Sharan Narang, Michael Matena, Yanqi Zhou, Wei Li, and Peter J Liu. 2019. Exploring the limits of transfer learning with a unified text-to-text transformer. *arXiv preprint arXiv:1910.10683*.

Pranav Rajpurkar, Jian Zhang, Konstantin Lopyrev, and Percy Liang. 2016. SQuAD: 100,000+ questions for machine comprehension of text. In *EMNLP*.

Victor Sanh, Lysandre Debut, Julien Chaumond, and Thomas Wolf. 2019. DistilBERT, a distilled version of BERT: smaller, faster, cheaper and lighter. *arXiv preprint arXiv:1910.01108*.

Xingjian Shi, Jonas Mueller, Nick Erickson, Mu Li, and Alex Smola. 2021. Multimodal automl on structured tables with text fields. In *8th ICML Workshop on Automated Machine Learning (AutoML)*.

Siqi Sun, Yu Cheng, Zhe Gan, and Jingjing Liu. 2019. Patient knowledge distillation for BERT model compression. In *EMNLP*.

Michael Tschannen, Josip Djolonga, Paul K Rubenstein, Sylvain Gelly, and Mario Lucic. 2020. On mutual information maximization for representation learning. *ICLR*.

Iulia Turc, Ming-Wei Chang, Kenton Lee, and Kristina Toutanova. 2019. Well-read students learn better: On the importance of pre-training compact models. *arXiv preprint arXiv:1908.08962*.

Ashish Vaswani, Noam Shazeer, Niki Parmar, Jakob Uszkoreit, Llion Jones, Aidan N Gomez, Łukasz Kaiser, and Illia Polosukhin. 2017. Attention is all you need. In *Advances in neural information processing systems*, pages 5998–6008.

Alex Wang, Yada Pruksachatkun, Nikita Nangia, Amanpreet Singh, Julian Michael, Felix Hill, Omer Levy, and Samuel R Bowman. 2019a. Superglue: A stickier benchmark for general-purpose language understanding systems. *arXiv preprint arXiv:1905.00537*.

Alex Wang, Amanpreet Singh, Julian Michael, Felix Hill, Omer Levy, and Samuel R Bowman. 2019b. GLUE: A multi-task benchmark and analysis platform for natural language understanding. In *ICLR*.

Jason Wei and Kai Zou. 2019. EDA: Easy data augmentation techniques for boosting performance on text classification tasks. In *EMNLP*.

Jing Yang, Brais Martinez, Adrian Bulat, and Georgios Tzimiropoulos. 2021. Knowledge distillation via softmax regression representation learning. In *ICLR*.

Hongyi Zhang, Moustapha Cisse, Yann N Dauphin, and David Lopez-Paz. 2018. Mixup: Beyond empirical risk minimization. In *ICLR*.

Appendix – Distiller: A Systematic Study of Model Distillation Methods in Natural Language Processing

A Relationship with Other Distillation Methods

Distiller is a generic meta-framework that encompasses various KD pipelines used in previous work. For example, Distiller with the following configurations corresponds to the KD pipeline used in each of the cited works: $l^{\text{pred}} = \text{CE}$, $l^{\text{inter}} = \text{MSE}$, $m_{i,j} = \text{Skip}$, $a = \text{CA}$ (Jiao et al., 2020); $l^{\text{pred}} = \text{CE}$, $l^{\text{inter}} = \text{MSE}$, $m_{i,j} = \text{EMD}$ (Li et al., 2020); $l^{\text{pred}} = \text{CE}$, $a = \text{Mixup}$ (Liang et al., 2021).

B Proof of Theorem 3.1

We denote the Mutual Information (MI) between two random variables X and Y as $I(X;Y)$. Based on the results on variational bounds of MI (Poole et al., 2019), we derived that optimizing common knowledge distillation objectives, including Mean Squared Error (MSE), L2 distance, and cosine similarity between X and Y, can be viewed as maximizing certain lower bounds of $I(X;Y)$.

Lemma B.1 (I_{TUBA}) . *Assume that $f(x,y)$ is an arbitrary neural network that takes x and y as inputs and outputs a scalar and $a(y) > 0$. The lower bound of x and y can be estimated by:*

$$I(X;Y) \geq E_{p(x,y)}[\log \frac{e^{f(x,y)}}{a(y)}] - E_{p(x)p(y)}[\frac{e^{f(x,y)}}{a(y)}] \triangleq I_{TUBA}$$

Proof.

Based on the definition of MI, we have:

$$\begin{aligned} I(X;Y) &= E_{p(x,y)}[\log \frac{p(x|y)}{p(x)}] \\ &= E_{p(x,y)}[\log \frac{p(y|x)}{p(y)}] \end{aligned} \tag{5}$$

Replacing the intractable conditional distribution $p(x|y)$ with a tractable variational distribution $q(x|y)$ yields a lower bound on MI due to the non-negativity of the KL divergence:

$$\begin{aligned} I(X;Y) &= E_{p(x,y)}[\log \frac{q(x|y)}{p(x)}] + E_{p(x,y)}[\log \frac{p(x|y)}{q(x|y)}] \\ &= E_{p(x,y)}[\log \frac{q(x|y)}{p(x)}] + E_{p(y)}[KL(p(x|y)||q(x|y))] \\ &\geq E_{p(x,y)}[\log q(x|y)] + H(X) \end{aligned} \tag{6}$$

where $H(X)$ is the entropy of X.
We choose an energy-based variational family that uses a critic $f(x,y)$ and scaled by the data density $p(x)$:

$$q(x|y) = \frac{p(x)}{Z(y)} e^{f(x,y)}, \, Z(y) = E_{p(x)}[e^{f(x,y)}] \tag{7}$$

Substituting this distribution into (6) gives a lower bound on MI:

$$I(X;Y) \geq E_{p(x,y)}[f(x,y)] - E_{p(y)}[\log Z(y)]$$

However, this objective is still intractable. To form a tractable bound, we can upper bound the log partition function by this inequality: $\log(x) \leq \frac{x}{a} + \log(a) - 1$ for all $x, a > 0$. Apply this inequality to get:

$$\begin{aligned} I(X;Y) &\geq E_{p(x,y)}[f(x,y)] - E_{p(y)}[\log Z(y)] \\ &\geq E_{p(x,y)}[f(x,y)] \\ &\quad - E_{p(y)}[\frac{E_{p(x)}[e^{f(x,y)}]}{a(y)} + \log a(y) - 1] \\ &= E_{p(x,y)}[f(x,y)] - E_{p(x,y)}[\log a(y)] \\ &\quad - E_{p(x)p(y)}[\frac{e^{f(x,y)}}{a(y)}] + 1 \\ &\geq E_{p(x,y)}[\log \frac{e^{f(x,y)}}{a(y)}] - E_{p(x)p(y)}[\frac{e^{f(x,y)}}{a(y)}] \end{aligned} \tag{8}$$

This bound holds for any $a(y) > 0$

Theorem 1. Minimizing the MSE, L2, PKD loss, and maximizing the cosine similarity between two random variables x,y can be viewed as maximizing lower bounds of $I(X;Y)$. In knowledge distillation, x and y are hidden states generated by student model and teacher model.

Proof. We prove this theorem by constructing $f(x,y)$ and $a(y)$ in Lemma B.1 for each loss function.

MSE $L_{\text{MSE}}(x,y) = ||x-y||_2^2$, let $f(x,y) = -||x-y||_2^2, a(y) = 1$, we have:

$$\begin{aligned} I(X;Y) &\geq E_{p(x,y)}[\log e^{-||x-y||_2^2}] - E_{p(x)p(y)}[e^{-||x-y||_2^2}] \\ &\geq E_{p(x,y)}[\log e^{-||x-y||_2^2}] - E_{p(x)p(y)}[e^0] \\ &= E_{p(x,y)}[\log e^{-||x-y||_2^2}] - 1 \\ &= E_{p(x,y)}[-||x-y||_2^2] - 1. \end{aligned}$$

Thus, minimizing the MSE loss between x and y can be viewed as maximizing the lower bound of $I(X;Y)$.

PKD Loss $L_{\text{PKD}}(x,y) = ||\frac{x}{||x||_2} - \frac{y}{||y||_2}||_2^2$, let $f(x,y) = -||\frac{x}{||x||_2} - \frac{y}{||y||_2}||_2^2$, we have:

$$
\begin{aligned}
I(X;Y) &\geq E_{p(x,y)}[\log e^{-||\frac{x}{||x||_2} - \frac{y}{||y||_2}||_2^2}] \\
&\quad - E_{p(x)p(y)}[e^{-||\frac{x}{||x||_2} - \frac{y}{||y||_2}||_2^2}] \\
&\geq E_{p(x,y)}[\log e^{-||\frac{x}{||x||_2} - \frac{y}{||y||_2}||_2^2}] - E_{p(x)p(y)}[e^0] \quad (9) \\
&= E_{p(x,y)}[\log e^{-||\frac{x}{||x||_2} - \frac{y}{||y||_2}||_2^2}] - 1 \\
&= E_{p(x,y)}[-||\frac{x}{||x||_2} - \frac{y}{||y||_2}||_2^2] - 1.
\end{aligned}
$$

Thus, minimizing the PKD loss between x and y can be viewed as maximizing the lower bound of $I(X;Y)$.

L2 Loss $L_{L_2}(x,y) = ||x-y||_2$, let $f(x,y) = -||x-y||_2$, a(y)=1, we have:

$$
\begin{aligned}
I(X;Y) &\geq E_{p(x,y)}[\log e^{-||x-y||_2}] - E_{p(x)p(y)}[e^{-||x-y||_2}] \\
&\geq E_{p(x,y)}[\log e^{-||x-y||_2}] - E_{p(x)p(y)}[e^0] \\
&= E_{p(x,y)}[\log e^{-||x-y||_2}] - 1 \\
&= E_{p(x,y)}[-||x-y||_2] - 1
\end{aligned}
$$

Thus, minimizing L2 loss between x and y is equivalent to maximizing the lower bound of $I(X,Y)$.

Cosine Similarity The cosine similarity between two hidden states x and y is calculated as $\frac{x \cdot y}{||x|| \times ||y||}$, let $f(x,y) = \frac{x \cdot y}{||x|| \times ||y||} - 1, a(y) = 1$

$$
\begin{aligned}
I(X,Y) &\geq E_{p(x,y)}[\log e^{\frac{x \cdot y}{||x|| \times ||y||} - 1}] - E_{p(x)p(y)}[e^{\frac{x \cdot y}{||x|| \times ||y||} - 1}] \\
&\geq E_{p(x,y)}[\log e^{\frac{x \cdot y}{||x|| \times ||y||} - 1}] - E_{p(x)p(y)}[e^0] \\
&= \frac{1}{e} E_{p(x,y)}[\log e^{\frac{x \cdot y}{||x|| \times ||y||}}] - 1 \\
&= \frac{1}{e} E_{p(x,y)}[\frac{x \cdot y}{||x|| \times ||y||}] - 1
\end{aligned}
$$

Thus, maximizing cosine similarity between x and y can be viewed as maximizing mutual information between x and y.

C Architecture of Teacher and Student Networks

In Table 1, we use two baseline models BERT-PKD$_4$ and BERT-EMD$_4$. As described in the original paper (Sun et al., 2019), we initialize BERT-PKD$_4$ with the first 4 layers of parameters from pretrained BERT$_{\text{BASE}}$. BERT-EMD$_4$ is initialized from TinyBERT$_4$ so they have the same architecture. We list the detailed configurations of the teacher and student architectures investigated in our study in Table 6.

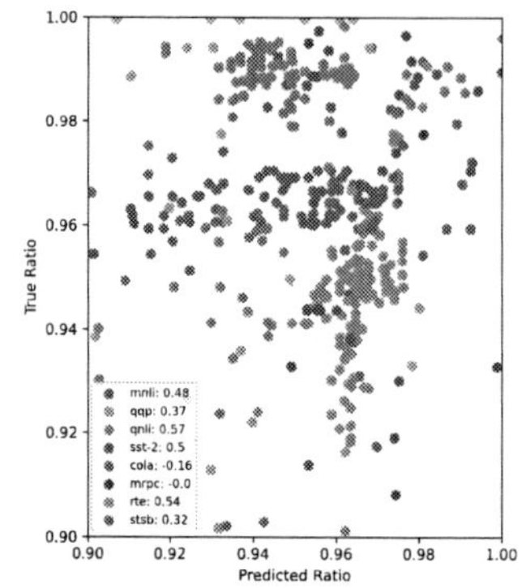

Figure 5: Evaluating held-out AutoDistiller predictions on GLUE via leave-one-out estimates. We use dataset-level cross-validation that holds out each GLUE dataset from AutoDistiller training. For each held-out dataset, the legend lists Spearman's rank correlation between the predicted vs. actual distillation ratio across different KD pipelines. The average Spearman's rank correlation value across the 8 datasets is 0.33.

D Benefits of Intermediate Distillation

Table 5 shows the experimental results of distillation with(out) intermediate distillation across different tasks/datasets. All the experiments are trained 20 epochs and the intermediate distillation constitutes of "Skip" as intermediate mapping strategy and CE as intermediate distillation object.

E Dataset Embedding

As features for the AutoDistiller model, we extract features from datasets and represent them as a fixed dimension embedding. Details are shown in Table 7.

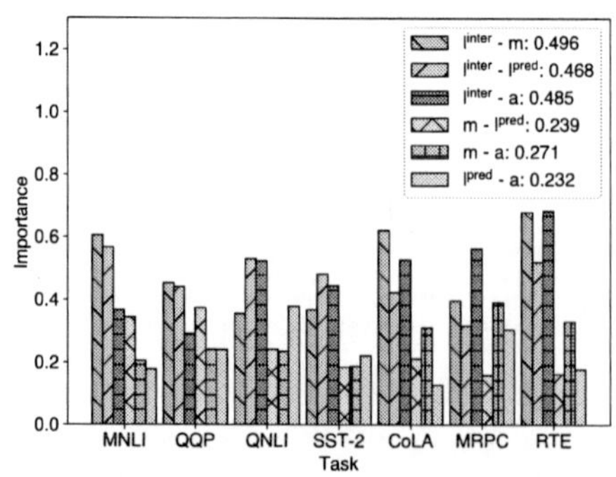

Figure 6: Importance of interactions between hyperparameters.

Table 4: Comparison of evaluation results on GLUE test set. We compare the distillation performance when using MLP and Transformer as critic functions in MI-α respectively. $\text{BERT}_{\text{BASE}}$ (T) indicates the teacher model trained by ourselves. Both of the students are initialized with TinyBERT_4 (Jiao et al., 2020) and distilled with "Skip" as intermediate layer mapping strategy and MI-α as intermediate objective functions. The difference is, TinyBERT_4 (MLP) is trained with a 4-layer MLP with hidden state of 512 as critic function while TinyBERT_4 (Transformer) uses a 2-layer Transformer with feed-forward hidden size 256. The result shows that a small Transformer architecture performs as a better critic function than an MLP in MI-α especially when the task is a token-level task (SQuAD v1.1).

Model	MNLI-m (393k)	MNLI-mm (393k)	QQP (364k)	QNLI (108k)	SST-2 (67k)	CoLA (8.5k)	MRPC (3.5k)	RTE (2.5k)	STS-B (5.7k)	SQuAD v1.1 (108k)	AVG
$\text{BERT}_{\text{BASE}}$ (T)	84.5	83.6	71.7	90.9	93.4	49.3	87.0	67.3	84.7	88.2	80.0
TinyBERT_4 (MLP)	81.7	**80.6**	69.7	**87.6**	**91.6**	24.9	**87.0**	**67.4**	81.9	70.1	74.3
TinyBERT_4 (Transformer)	**81.9**	**80.6**	**69.8**	87.4	91.5	**25.9**	**87.0**	**67.4**	**84.0**	**71.7**	**74.7**

Table 5: Comparison of evaluation results on GLUE dev set. We compare the distillation performance with(out) intermediate distillation. A $\text{BERT}_{\text{BASE}}$ model is used as the teacher and TinyBERT_4 is the student. TinyBERT_4 (KD) represents using a vanilla knowledge distillation (student only learns from the outputs of teacher) and "+intermediate distillation" represents using vanilla KD and intermediate distillation.

Model	MNLI-m (393k) acc	MNLI-mm (393k) acc	QQP (364k) f1/acc	QNLI (108k) acc	SST-2 (67k) acc	CoLA (8.5k) mcc	MRPC (3.5k) f1/acc	RTE (2.5k) acc	STS-B (5.7k) spearman/pearson	SQuAD v1.1 (108k) f1/em	AVG
$\text{BERT}_{\text{BASE}}$ (T)	84.1	84.7	88.0/91.1	91.7	93.0	55.0	89.6/85.0	65.0	88.4/88.6	88.2/80.9	83.8
TinyBERT_4 (KD)	80.1	80.3	86.4/89.7	85.8	89.1	16.1	**89.6/85.3**	**66.8**	**88.4/88.5**	77.3/66.8	77.9
+intermediate distillation	**80.7**	**81.3**	**87.0/90.2**	**86.8**	**90.0**	**21.3**	89.3/84.8	65.3	88.2/88.4	**79.4/69.4**	**78.7**

Table 6: Network architectures of the teacher and student models used in the paper.

Model	#Params	h_{units}	n_{layers}	h_{mid}	n_{heads}
	Teacher architectures				
$\text{RoBERTa}_{\text{LARGE}}$	335M	1024	24	4096	16
$\text{ELECTRA}_{\text{LARGE}}$	335M	1024	24	4096	16
$\text{BERT}_{\text{BASE}}$	110M	768	12	3072	12
	Student architectures				
TinyBERT_6	67M	768	6	3072	12
BERT-PKD_4	52M	768	4	3072	12
$\text{BERT}_{\text{MEDIUM}}$	41M	512	8	2048	8
$\text{BERT}_{\text{SMALL}}$	29M	512	4	2048	8
TinyBERT_4	14M	312	4	1200	12
$\text{ELECTRA}_{\text{SMALL}}$	14M	256	12	1024	4
$\text{BERT}_{\text{MINI}}$	11M	256	4	1024	4
$\text{BERT}_{\text{TINY}}$	4M	128	2	512	2

F How much does larger/better teacher help?

Table 8 shows the performance of different students distilled from teachers of different sizes and pretraining schemes. From the results, we found that although the teacher $\text{ELECTRA}_{\text{LARGE}}$ has the best performance on average score, most of the students of $\text{ELECTRA}_{\text{LARGE}}$ performs worse than students of $\text{RoBERTa}_{\text{LARGE}}$. $\text{ELECTRA}_{\text{SMALL}}$ is the only student that performs the best with $\text{ELECTRA}_{\text{LARGE}}$ as teacher, that may be attributed to $\text{ELECTRA}_{\text{SMALL}}$ and $\text{ELECTRA}_{\text{LARGE}}$ are pretrained on the same pretraining task, so they have a similar knowledge representation scheme. And also, for datasets (MNLI, QQP, QNLI and SST-2) which have abundant amount of data, students of $\text{BERT}_{\text{BASE}}$ perform better.

G Computing Details

All the experiments are performed on a single machine with 4 NVIDIA T4 GPUs. For hyperparameters in Equation 1, our experiments suggest that setting β_1 and β_2 to 1 produces the best overall performance so we fix their values to 1 in subsequent results. γ_1 and γ_2 are set to 0.5 when DA is used (otherwise β_2, γ_1 and γ_2 are set to 0). For controlled experiments, unless specified explicitly, we fix l^{inter} as MI-α ($\alpha = 0.9$) and the layer mapping as "Skip". Critic functions in MI-α are powered by a two-layer Transformer($h_{\text{mid}} = 256$, $n_{\text{heads}} = 8$) and the comparison of using Transformer and MLP to estimate critic functions is described in Table 4. To reduce the hyper-parameter search space, we fix the batch size as 16 and the learning rate as 5e-5 for all experiments. We used automated mix precision for training. Maximum sequence length is set to 128 for sentence-pair tasks in GLUE, 64 for single sentence tasks and 320 for SQuAD. Most of the experiments are trained for 20 epochs except 50 epochs for the challenging task CoLA and 30 epochs for SQuAD.

Table 7: We extract features from downstream datasets so that every task can be represented as a fixed-dimension embedding. The extracted embedding can be fed into *AutoDistiller* as dense features. In this table, we describe how the embedding is acquired.

Feature	Description
Context Embedding	Every document can be represented as a weighted average of the GloVe vectors, where the weights are defined by the TF-IDF scheme. Each down-stream dataset is viewed as a "document" in the TF-IDF scheme. Precisely, the embedding of a dataset s is $v_s = \frac{1}{\lvert s \rvert}\text{IDF}_w v_w$, where $\lvert s \rvert$ denotes the number of words in the dataset, and $\text{IDF}_w := \log \frac{1+N}{1+N_w}$ is the inverse document frequency of word w. N is the total number of datasets, and N_w denotes the number of datasets containing w. Intuitively, this feature represents the content of datasets.
Task Embedding	For the dataset, we collect their literal descriptions, usually one or two sentences. Then aggregate GloVe vectors of every words in these sentences and get a description embedding. This feature is used to represent what is the NLP task and how the data is formatted.
Baseline Score	We use a lite Bi-LSTM model as the baseline model and finetune it on the down-stream dataset. This feature aims to measure the difficulty of each task by measuring how well a simple architecture can perform on the specific dataset.
Teacher Score	The fine-tuned teacher score on the dataset. Comparing teacher score to aforementioned baseline score tells how much boost can a complex model has on this dataset.
Number of Examples	How many training samples in the dataset.

Table 8: Performance comparison with different teacher and student models. We abbreviate three teacher models $\text{BERT}_{\text{BASE}}$, $\text{RoBERTa}_{\text{LARGE}}$ and $\text{ELECTRA}_{\text{LARGE}}$ as B, R, E. Results are evaluated on GLUE dev set and best results are in-bold.

Model	#Params	Teacher	MNLI-m	MNLI-mm	QQP		QNLI	SST-2	CoLA	MRPC		RTE	STS-B		AVG
			acc	acc	f1	acc	acc	acc	mcc	f1	acc	acc	spearman	pearson	
$\text{BERT}_{\text{BASE}}$ (T)	110M		84.1	84.7	88.0	91.1	91.7	93.0	55.0	89.6	85.0	65.0	88.4	88.6	83.7
$\text{RoBERTa}_{\text{LARGE}}$ (T)	335M		90.2	90.1	89.6	92.1	94.7	96.3	64.6	91.3	88.0	78.7	**91.7**	**91.8**	88.3
$\text{ELECTRA}_{\text{LARGE}}$ (T)	335M		**90.5**	**90.4**	**90.3**	**92.8**	**95.1**	**96.6**	**67.4**	**91.7**	**88.5**	**84.5**	88.7	88.9	**88.8**
$\text{BERT}_{\text{BASE}}$	110M	R	**84.5**	**84.6**	88.6	91.5	**91.7**	**93.2**	59.3	91.6	88.0	66.4	89.0	89.4	84.8
		E	84.4	**84.6**	**88.8**	**91.7**	91.6	92.8	**59.5**	**91.9**	**88.7**	**69.3**	**89.1**	**89.6**	**85.2**
TinyBERT_6	67M	B	**83.9**	**84.0**	**88.1**	**91.2**	**91.3**	91.6	**50.5**	90.3	86.5	75.5	89.4	89.4	**84.3**
		R	83.5	83.5	88.0	**91.2**	90.8	**92.2**	48.0	**91.9**	**88.7**	72.6	**89.9**	**90.0**	84.2
		E	83.0	83.0	87.8	91.0	90.6	91.3	48.6	91.6	88.5	**76.2**	89.1	89.3	84.2
$\text{BERT}_{\text{MEDIUM}}$	41M	B	**82.6**	**83.0**	**87.9**	**91.0**	**90.0**	90.8	48.3	88.9	84.1	**65.0**	**88.2**	88.4	**82.4**
		R	80.9	81.4	87.6	90.8	89.0	**91.4**	50.5	88.9	84.6	64.3	**88.2**	**88.6**	82.2
		E	81.0	81.3	87.5	90.7	89.0	90.9	**51.0**	**89.5**	**85.3**	64.3	88.0	88.2	82.2
$\text{BERT}_{\text{SMALL}}$	29M	B	**81.0**	**81.0**	**87.4**	**90.6**	**87.3**	**90.5**	**43.1**	87.8	82.4	63.5	87.0	87.2	**80.7**
		R	78.7	78.6	87.0	90.4	87.0	88.6	41.2	**89.1**	**84.1**	**64.3**	**87.1**	**87.3**	80.3
		E	78.6	78.8	87.2	90.5	87.0	89.3	43.0	88.7	**84.1**	63.9	86.8	87.1	80.4
TinyBERT_4	14M	B	**81.1**	**81.6**	**87.2**	**90.4**	**87.4**	**90.6**	12.3	89.4	85.0	66.4	87.7	87.8	78.9
		R	80.0	80.7	86.5	90.0	86.0	89.4	**24.6**	90.4	86.5	67.9	**88.0**	**88.1**	**79.8**
		E	80.0	80.2	86.2	89.6	85.9	88.9	21.8	**90.9**	**86.8**	**68.6**	87.6	87.6	79.5
$\text{ELECTRA}_{\text{SMALL}}$	14M	B	**82.7**	**83.8**	87.8	90.9	**89.7**	91.3	**60.6**	91.3	87.7	60.6	87.4	87.5	83.5
		R	82.3	83.2	88.1	91.2	89.5	90.6	58.6	91.3	87.5	67.5	**87.6**	**87.8**	83.8
		E	82.0	82.7	**88.5**	**91.5**	89.3	**91.4**	**60.6**	**92.3**	**89.0**	**69.7**	86.6	86.7	**84.2**
$\text{BERT}_{\text{MINI}}$	11M	B	**78.5**	**79.7**	**86.6**	**90.0**	**84.9**	**87.8**	20.1	**87.0**	**81.6**	61.0	**86.2**	86.1	77.5
		R	76.6	77.3	86.0	**90.0**	84.6	85.9	32.2	86.6	81.1	**65.3**	**86.2**	**86.3**	**78.2**
		E	76.3	77.1	85.9	89.5	84.2	85.9	**33.8**	**87.0**	**81.6**	65.0	85.7	85.5	78.1
$\text{BERT}_{\text{TINY}}$	4M	B	**72.8**	**73.4**	**83.5**	**87.2**	**81.3**	**83.9**	0.0	84.5	75.7	58.5	81.4	**79.9**	71.8
		R	71.5	72.0	82.9	86.7	80.2	83.1	6.2	84.9	76.2	60.3	**81.9**	**79.9**	**72.1**
		E	71.2	71.8	82.9	87.0	80.0	82.8	**6.7**	**85.2**	**77.0**	**62.8**	78.4	77.3	71.9

H Distiller Search Space

Here we recap the full search space considered for each stage of the KD pipeline in Distiller:

- $l^{\text{inter}} \in$ {MSE, L2, Cos, PKD, MI-α ($\alpha = 0.1$, 0.5, or 0.9)}
- $l^{\text{pred}} \in$ {MSE, CE}
- $\{m_{i,j}\} \in$ {Skip, Last, EMD}
- Augmentation policy a is one or combinations of elementary augmentation operations in {CA, RA, BT, Mixup}.

I Top Configurations in Distiller

Here we list the top 5 configurations from the Distiller search space that performed best on each dataset in Table 9.

Table 9: Top 5 configurations to distill a $\text{BERT}_{\text{BASE}}$ teacher to a TinyBERT_4 student on every dataset. To reduce the search space, we only compare configurations that don't use data augmentation. As Hyper-parameter α is only valid for MI-α, the value of α is set to N for other intermediate loss in the table.

Task	Intermediate Loss	α	Layer Mapping Strategy	KD Loss	#Example	Score
MNLI	MI-α	0.9	EMD	MSE	393000	81.7
MNLI	MI-α	0.1	EMD	MSE	393000	81.7
MNLI	MI-α	0.5	Skip	MSE	393000	81.7
MNLI	MSE	N	EMD	MSE	393000	81.6
MNLI	MSE	N	Skip	MSE	393000	81.6
QQP	MI-α	0.9	EMD	MSE	364000	90.2
QQP	MI-α	0.1	EMD	MSE	364000	90.2
QQP	CE	N	Skip	MSE	364000	90.2
QQP	MI-α	0.1	EMD	MSE	364000	90.1
QQP	MI-α	0.1	Skip	MSE	364000	90.1
QNLI	CE	N	Last	MSE	105000	87.4
QNLI	MI-α	0.5	Skip	MSE	105000	87.4
QNLI	MI-α	0.5	Last	CE	105000	87.3
QNLI	MI-α	0.9	Skip	CE	105000	87.2
QNLI	MI-α	0.1	Skip	CE	105000	87.1
SST-2	Cos	N	Last	MSE	67000	90.6
SST-2	MSE	N	Skip	CE	67000	90.5
SST-2	MI-α	0.1	Last	CE	67000	90.3
SST-2	CE	N	Skip	MSE	67000	90.3
SST-2	MI-α	0.9	Skip	CE	67000	90.3
CoLA	MI-α	0.1	EMD	MSE	8500	22.3
CoLA	MI-α	0.5	EMD	MSE	8500	21.6
CoLA	MI-α	0.5	EMD	CE	8500	21.1
CoLA	MI-α	0.1	Last	MSE	8500	21.1
CoLA	MI-α	0.5	Skip	MSE	8500	21.0
MRPC	MI-α	0.1	EMD	CE	3700	90.3
MRPC	MI-α	0.5	EMD	CE	3700	90.2
MRPC	CE	N	Skip	CE	3700	89.9
MRPC	MI-α	0.9	EMD	CE	3700	89.9
MRPC	CE	N	Last	MSE	3700	89.7
RTE	MI-α	0.1	Skip	CE	2500	70.8
RTE	MI-α	0.9	Skip	CE	2500	70.4
RTE	MI-α	0.5	Skip	CE	2500	70.0
RTE	MI-α	0.1	Last	CE	2500	70.0
RTE	MI-α	0.5	Last	CE	2500	69.3
STS-B	MI-α	0.9	Skip	MSE	7000	88.0
STS-B	MI-α	0.5	Skip	MSE	7000	88.0
STS-B	MI-α	0.9	EMD	MSE	7000	87.9
STS-B	MI-α	0.1	Last	MSE	7000	87.9
STS-B	PKD	N	Skip	MSE	7000	87.9
SQuAD v1.1	MSE	N	Skip	MSE	130000	72.6
SQuAD v1.1	CE	N	Skip	MSE	130000	72.4
SQuAD v1.1	MSE	N	EMD	MSE	130000	72.3
SQuAD v1.1	MI-α	0.9	Skip	CE	130000	71.9
SQuAD v1.1	MI-α	0.9	Skip	CE	130000	71.7

Shrinking Bigfoot: Reducing wav2vec 2.0 footprint

Zilun Peng[1] **Akshay Budhkar**[1] **Ilana Tuil**[2] **Jason Levy**[2]
Parinaz Sobhani[1] **Raphael Cohen**[2] **Jumana Nassour**[2]
[1]Georgian.io [2]Zoominfo
`{zilun.peng, akshay, parinaz}@georgian.io`
`{ilana.tuil, jason.levy}@zoominfo.com`
`{raphael.cohen, jumana.nassour}@zoominfo.com`

Abstract

Wav2vec 2.0 is a state-of-the-art speech recognition model which maps speech audio waveforms into latent representations. The largest version of wav2vec 2.0 contains 317 million parameters. Hence, the inference latency of wav2vec 2.0 will be a bottleneck in production, leading to high costs and a significant environmental footprint. To improve wav2vec's applicability to a production setting, we explore multiple model compression methods borrowed from the domain of large language models. Using a teacher-student approach, we distilled the knowledge from the original wav2vec 2.0 model into a student model, which is 2 times faster, 4.8 times smaller than the original model. More importantly, the student model is 2 times more energy efficient than the original model in terms of CO_2 emission. This increase in performance is accomplished with only a 7% degradation in word error rate (WER). Our quantized model is 3.6 times smaller than the original model, with only a 0.1% degradation in WER. To the best of our knowledge, this is the first work that compresses wav2vec 2.0.

1 Introduction

Speech recognition technologies enhance people's lives through a wide range of applications such as virtual assistants, home automation, and real-time transcription and captioning. Neural network-based speech recognition models achieve superior performances, but successfully training them requires a lot of labeled data (Amodei et al., 2016).

Wav2vec 2.0 (Baevski et al., 2020) is a framework that combines self-supervised masking pre-training with a tuning step that achieves impressive results with little labeled data. With only 10 minutes of labeled data, wav2vec 2.0 achieves word error rates (WER) of 4.8% and 8.2 % on LibriSpeech (Panayotov et al., 2015) dev-clean and dev-other datasets, respectively. Moreover, Wav2vec 2.0 achieves state-of-the-art performances on the LibriSpeech benchmark while using a minimal amount of labeled data. Self-supervised learning enables wav2vec 2.0 to learn speech representations efficiently without much labeled data. This allows easily training an end-to-end automatic speech recognition (ASR) system for a low resource language[1] or for a specific domain. The largest version of wav2vec 2.0 has 317 million parameters, which makes real-time inference inefficient in production.

Language modeling is a central research question in natural language processing (NLP). In recent years massive LM architectures, based on novel pre-training approaches, revolutionized NLP (Devlin et al., 2019; Howard and Ruder, 2018). The BERT (Devlin et al., 2019) architecture of masked pre-training and transformers is similar to wav2vec2.0. To improve wav2vec's applicability to a production setting, we explore multiple model compression methods borrowed from the domain of massive LMs.

A significant drawback of massive LM models is high resource consumption. The negative impact of such models, beyond the costs for organizations using this technology in production, is cause for concern (Strubell et al., 2019; Bender et al., 2021). Various compression methods have been developed to overcome the problem, such as (Sanh et al., 2020). To compress wav2vec 2.0, we explore quantization and knowledge distillation methods. Our quantized model is 3.6 times smaller than the original model, with a 0.1% loss in WER, making it easy to deploy in a production environment. Our student model is at least 2 times faster on both CPU and GPU and 4.8 times smaller than the original model, with a 7% loss in WER through knowledge distillation.

Since the knowledge distilled model is smaller

[1]For example, an Arabic ASR model `https://huggingface.co/elgeish/wav2vec2-large-xlsr-53-arabic`

Proceedings of the 2nd Workshop on Simple and Efficient Natural Language Processing, pages 134–141
November 10, 2021. ©201 Association for Computational Linguistics

than the original model, it is more energy efficient. In Section 7, we estimated that the distilled model could potentially save 21 tons of CO_2 equivalents (comparing to the original model) if running inferences on 54 millions of hours of speech data.

Our work makes two key contributions: 1. This research is the first work that compresses the state-of-the-art wav2vec 2.0 speech recognition model to the best of our knowledge. 2. Our distilled student model has a faster inference speed and makes wav2vec 2.0 more cost-efficient and environmental friendly.

2 Related work

In this section, we relate research works done on model compression in ASR systems. Then we describe compression methods applied in language modeling, which we wish to explore for compressing wav2vec.

2.1 Model compression in ASR systems

Several works have been done on compressing end-to-end ASR systems to make them more applicable to production settings. The compression method varies depending on the ASR architecture used. Some of the methods result in approximately 2-3% reduction in accuracy (Mehrotra et al., 2020; Li et al., 2019; Mori et al., 2018), while others result in an improved accuracy (Winata et al., 2020; Kurata and Audhkhasi, 2018). Mehrotra *et al.* (Mehrotra et al., 2020) use reinforcement learning and low rank factorization to compress a system composed of an encoder-attention-decoder with unidirectional LSTMs, while Kurata *et al.* (Kurata and Audhkhasi, 2018) and Takashima *et al.* (Takashima et al., 2018) employ knowledge distillation to train a UniLSTM model from a BiLSTM one. Winata *et al.* (Winata et al., 2019) applied low rank factorization to compress LSTMs. Mori *et al.* (Mori et al., 2018) start with "Deep Speech 2" architecture, which consists of both convolution layers and bidirectional gated recurrent unit layers (GRU), reduce the number of parameters using Tensor-Train decomposition on the weight matrix of the GRUs (TT-GRU).

Some attempts have been made to compress transformer-based ASR systems, like the work done to share parameters across different layers by incorporating additional features related to the topic and the speaker (Li et al., 2019), leading to less than a two-point decrease in accuracy. Another work proposed using a low-rank transformer (LRT) to reduce the number of parameters and boost the speed of training and inference (Winata et al., 2020). The proposed LRT model improved accuracy without using a language model or acoustic data in addition to the improvement in size and speed.

2.2 Classic compression methods in language modeling

Knowledge distillation, quantization, and pruning are few techniques employed in research for compressing language models.

Knowledge distillation involves the use of a teacher model (or models) to improve the performance of another model (student model). When used for compression, the student model's size is significantly smaller than that of the teacher model.

Knowledge distillation in ASR is used both to improve accuracy (Futami et al., 2020; Gao et al., 2020; Mori et al., 2018), and to make the model more applicable to production by reducing its size (Kurata and Audhkhasi, 2018; Takashima et al., 2018), see subsection 2.1. Futami *et al.* (Futami et al., 2020) use knowledge distillation to generate more syntactically or semantically likely results by providing a left context seq2seq ASR system (student model) with soft labels of context to the right. The authors produce soft labels by using a pre-trained BERT model (teacher model). Gao *et al.* (Gao et al., 2020) use multiple teacher models to train a student ASR model to improve ASR accuracy jointly. Moriya *et al.* (Moriya et al., 2020) improve the accuracy by adding another term to the loss function called self-distillation (SD), which comes from incorporating the teacher model.

BERT (Devlin et al., 2019) is one of the most prominent language models in NLP. Like wav2vec, it is based on the transformer model, but it uses only encoders without decoders. DistilBERT (Sanh et al., 2020) is a distilled version of BERT, with a 40% decrease in model size, a 60% increase in speed, and a 97% preservation of language understanding capabilities. Hence, it would be interesting to apply a similar distillation technique to wav2vec. TinyBERT (Jiao et al., 2019) and MobileBERT (Sun et al., 2020) also applied knowledge distillation to compress BERT.

Quantization involves reducing the number of bits used to represent weights. Normally, networks use 32-bit floating-point weights. Because neural networks have millions of such weights, quantizing these weights can make neural networks more energy efficient (Dally, 2015). Several works have been published on quantization, reducing weights to 8-bit (Vanhoucke et al., 2011), 4-bit (Choi et al., 2018), 2-bit (Hwang and Sung, 2014), and 1-bit (Courbariaux et al., 2015) integers. Weights are static and can be quantized through scaling and shifting, but this is not true for activations. Activations vary depending on input samples and can be quantized through static or dynamic quantization. Static quantization learns scaling and shifting of activations through a batch of samples, while dynamic quantization scales and shifts activations in each forward pass. There are two popular software packages for quantization: Distiller (Zmora et al., 2019), and PyTorch (Paszke et al., 2019). Distiller simulates quantization; hence, weights are still represented using 32-bit floating-point numbers but are restricted to integer values. Since we are interested in studying the efficiency of quantizing wav2vec 2.0, we decided not to explore Distiller for quantization. In section 5, we discuss the pros and cons of using PyTorch for quantizing wav2vec 2.0.

Pruning is executed by removing small weights that are likely redundant and can be removed without much loss in accuracy (Han et al., 2015). Han *et al.* (Han et al., 2016) proposed deep compression, an efficient compression pipeline, which first prunes the neural network model and then quantizes the remaining effective weights. We conducted a preliminary study on pruning using the Distiller (Zmora et al., 2019) sensitivity pruner. We set the sensitivity for each convolution layer to 0.1. We set the sensitivity in layers 3 to 16 of the transformer to 0.3 and layers 17 to 23 to 0.4. We pruned weights smaller than the product of the sensitivity and standard deviation of weights on that layer. The pruned model has a 23% sparsity while maintaining the same WER as the original model. We, however, didn't observe any significant improvement in the inference speed.

3 Wav2vec

Wav2vec 2.0 (Baevski et al., 2020) achieved a breakthrough in ASR by adopting the masked pretraining method employed in the massive language model BERT. BERT masks a few words in each training sentence, and the model learns by attempting to fill the gaps. Instead of masking words, wav2vec 2.0 masks parts of the audio representation and lets the transformer network fill in the gaps. This self-supervised setup makes it possible to learn mainly from unlabeled data while only fine-tuning on a small labeled dataset. The wav2vec 2.0 model comprises two significant components that we consider for compression: the CNN layers and the transformer layers.

In the following sections, we explore how compressing a fine-tuned version of wav2vec 2.0[2] using knowledge distillation and quantization affects the size of the model and its inference speed.

4 Knowledge distillation for wav2vec 2.0

We based our distillation on the knowledge distillation used by Sanh *et al.* to compress BERT (Devlin et al., 2019) to DistilBERT (Sanh et al., 2020). They initialized their student models by taking alternating layers from a well-performing larger model and scheduled the learning rate by first increasing, then gradually decreasing it.

Since it is possible to reduce either the CNN layer or the transformer layers of wav2vec 2.0, we decided to reduce the transformer ones since wav2vec 2.0 has only 7 CNN layers, which does not constitute a substantial computational bottleneck compared to transformer layers, see Table 3.

4.1 Knowledge distillation loss

The classic knowledge distillation approach (Hinton et al., 2015) focuses on transferring knowledge between classification neural networks, where both the teacher and the student models output probability distributions over M labels. In our case, the output is latent representations of the input speech audio waveform. We project these representations into probability distributions over M tokens, where a token could map to a character or word boundary. Let T and S be the output probability distributions of the teacher and the student model, respectively. Inspired by (Hinton et al., 2015), we define the knowledge distillation loss to be the Kullback–Leibler (KL) divergence between T and S:

$$L_{distill}(T, S) = \frac{1}{N} \sum_{0 \le i < N} \sum_{0 \le j < M} T_{ij} \log \left(\frac{S_{ij}}{T_{ij}} \right) \quad (1)$$

[2] We used wav2vec_big_960h as our base/original model. (`https://dl.fbaipublicfiles.com/fairseq/wav2vec/wav2vec_big_960h.pt`)

The dimension of T and S is $N \times M$, where N is the length of the representation and M is the number of tokens. The KL divergence signals how far off is the student model's prediction is from its teacher, and the student model learns from the teacher by optimizing this loss.

4.2 The architecture of the student model

The only difference between our student model and the original wav2vec 2.0 model is the number of transformer layers. The largest version of wav2vec 2.0 has seven convolution layers and 24 transformer layers, while our student models have a reduced number of transformer layers. Our smallest student model has four transformer layers. We have also trained student models with 6, 8, 10, 12 transformer layers. See section 7 for a discussion on the trade-off between the number of transformer layers and the performance of the different student models.

4.3 Objective function

Our objective function for knowledge distillation training consists of the knowledge distillation loss and feature penalty (Baevski et al., 2020), $L_{distill} + L_{feature}$. $L_{distill}$, the knowledge distillation loss, is defined in equation 1, and $L_{feature}$ is the L2 norm of the final output of convolution layers and serves as a regularization term for convolution layers. The original wav2vec 2.0 uses $L_{feature}$ during training.

We have tried to use the cosine embedding loss (Sanh et al., 2020) in our objective function, but it didn't help with the student model's performances.

4.4 Training techniques

After trying different optimizers, step size scheduling, objective functions, and other techniques to help the student model learn faster, the two approaches that significantly improved the student model's performance were using DistilBERT's initialization strategy and training on more data.

5 Quantization for wav2vec 2.0

In this section, we discuss how the two quantization techniques available in Pytorch apply to our task of quantizing wav2vec 2.0.

5.1 Static quantization

Static quantization quantizes weights and requires calibration before inference to determine scaling and shifting for quantizing activations. PyTorch does not support quantization for gelu activation (Hendrycks and Gimpel, 2020) (as of March 2021), one of the activations used in the wav2vec 2.0 model. A closed pull request [3] shows they were trying to add the support but suspended it temporarily due to some test case failures. One possible workaround is to dequantize before gelu and requantize afterward, but this causes some performance degradation.

5.2 Dynamic quantization

Dynamic quantization only quantizes weights and dynamically quantizes activations in each forward pass. As of March 2021, there are no supports for dynamically quantizing the multi-head attention (MHA) mechanism, which is an essential part of a transformer layer. Related issues remain open in PyTorch [4] and fairseq [5]. As a result, tensors entering MHA must not be quantized. We observed that dynamic quantization wraps weights and biases of MHA with some methods, requiring a costly *linear_unpack* operation to access them during inference. We save weights and biases before inference so that *linear_unpack* is not performed for every sample during inference, hence increasing inference efficiency.

6 Experiments

The wav2vec 2.0 model we are trying to compress was trained with 960 hours of unlabeled data from the LibriSpeech dataset (Panayotov et al., 2015), and then fine-tuned with the labeled version of the same 960 hours. We did not attempt to compress the model before it was fine-tuned. We used a Viterbi decoder to convert the output of the student wav2vec 2.0 model into text. We conducted training on 4 Nvidia V100 GPUs and set the batch size to 1 per GPU. We trained with 16-bit floating-point arithmetic and fixed the seed at 42 in all our runs to make the results reproducible.

For knowledge distillation, we used the Adam optimizer with weight decay. We set $eps = 10^{-6}$, $betas = (0.9, 0.98)$, and the weight decay coefficient to 0.01. We scheduled the learning rate by the number of epochs. The learning rate starts from 2.5×10^{-5} and linearly increases for the first two epochs. After two epochs, we linearly decrease the learning rate in every epoch. Also, we assessed the

[3] https://github.com/pytorch/pytorch/pull/34396
[4] https://github.com/pytorch/pytorch/issues/32764
[5] https://github.com/pytorch/fairseq/issues/1901

effect of using a different number of transformer layers on the target metrics, see Table 2.

For quantization, we used PyTorch's dynamic quantization to quantize linear layers of wav2vec 2.0. Table 1 contains the results of evaluating the different compression methods on LibriSpeech dev-clean.

Our implementation is available at `https://git.io/JmpJM`.

7 Results and discussion

Table 1 shows the performance of the largest version of wav2vec 2.0 compared to the compressed models. The distilled model has a 7% loss in terms of word error rate (WER) compared with the original model. However, the distilled model is at least two times faster than the original model on both CPU and GPU, in addition to being 4.8 times smaller than the original wav2vec 2.0 model. We trained the distilled model for 32 epochs.

Table 1 shows that our distilled model is at least 2 times more efficient than the original model in terms of CO_2 emissions and energy consumption. The distilled model is expected to consume less energy since it is smaller than the original model. Our test set contains 5.4 hours of speech data, and the distilled model emits 0.0019 kg of CO_2 equivalents less than the original model. We roughly estimate the potential saving on a larger dataset: if we have 54 millions of hours of speech data, and inference using the distilled model, then it's possible to save $\sim$21 tons of CO_2 equivalents. This shows the energy efficiency of the distilled model, especially when applying it to a large dataset. We used CodeCarbon (Schmidt et al., 2021) to estimate CO_2 emissions and energy consumption. While CodeCarbon should be able to track CPU energy consumption, for our quantized model (which can only be used on a CPU), our machines were not supported by CodeCarbon (as seen in this pull request[6]), and hence we were not able to report CO_2 emissions for our quantized model. Other tools like carbontracker (Anthony et al., 2020) and experiment-impact-tracker (Henderson et al., 2020) can be used in the future to track both CPU and GPU energy consumption.

Considering the quantized model, we notice that even though the model is 3.6 times smaller than the original model, it is not significantly faster. This discrepancy can be attributed to the need for dequantize tensors entering multi-head attention; see section 5.2 for more details. PyTorch does not support GPU quantization; therefore, we report only CPU inference time for the quantized model. Its significant reduction in size, together with its ability to maintain the original WER, albeit with a slight loss, make the quantized model easily deployable in a production environment.

7.1 Knowledge distillation using different settings

There is a wide range of settings that can be tweaked when distilling a model. We explore some of them to understand their effect on the resulting model and the target metrics.

We conducted some experiments to evaluate the trade-off between the size of a model and its performance when performing knowledge distillation by varying the number of kept transformer layers in the student model. LibriSpeech train-clean-100 was used to train the student models. We trained each student model for ten epochs. We performed inferences on a single GPU. Table 2 reports the results of these experiments. The performance of the original wav2vec 2.0 is shown in the first row. We observe that as the number of transformer layers decreases, the inference time decreases, but WER increases. Thus, as expected, as the model becomes smaller, its inference time improves, but its accuracy degrades.

In section 4.2, we introduced the student wav2vec 2.0 model's architecture, where we mentioned that reducing the number of convolution layers will probably not have much effect on the inference time of the distilled model. We tested this claim by reducing the convolution layers to 4. Table 3 shows the result of this experiment compared to the original setting. GPU inference time is only 0.7 seconds faster in the four convolution layer model, whereas CPU inference time is slower. This behavior is because we replaced convolution layers with max-pooling, and PyTorch has a slower max-pooling operation on the CPU.

DistilBERT initializes layers in the student model by taking alternating layers from a larger model. It's possible to initialize layers in the student model by taking the last few layers from a larger model. Figure 1 shows the effectiveness of DistilBERT's initialization strategy, as the student wav2vec 2.0 model initialized using DistilBERT's approach significantly outperforms the

[6]https://github.com/mlco2/codecarbon/issues/156

Model	#Parameters	Model Size	CPU Inference Time	GPU Inference Time	WER	Emissions as CO_2-equivalents	Energy Consumed
Original	317 M	1262 MB	4433 s	123 s	**2.63%**	0.0032 kg	0.0087 kWh
Distilled	**65 M**	**262 MB**	**1560 s**	**51 s**	9.51%	**0.0013 kg**	**0.0036 kWh**
Quantized	317 M	354 MB	4079 s	N/A	2.75%	N/A	N/A

Table 1: Performances of the original wav2vec 2.0 model, a student model trained using knowledge distillation, and a quantized wav2vec 2.0 model.

Layers	Parameters	Model Size	Inference Time	WER
24	317 M	1262 MB	123 s	2.63%
12	166 M	665 MB	81 s	6.6%
10	141 M	564 MB	75 s	7.59%
8	115 M	464 MB	69 s	10.42%
6	91 M	363 MB	60 s	16.54%

Table 2: Performance of a student wav2vec 2.0 model with different number of transformer layers on GPU.

Layers	GPU Inference Time	CPU Inference Time
7	2.97 s	**161 s**
4	**2.26 s**	387 s

Table 3: Inference time of wav2vec 2.0 model with different number of convolution layers. Original wav2vec 2.0 model has 7 convolution layers.

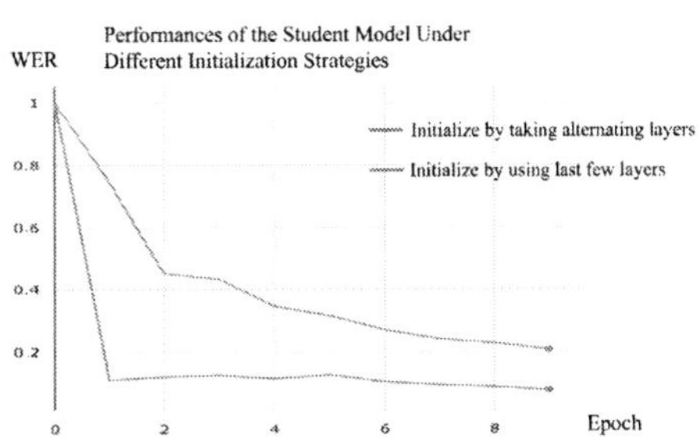

Figure 1: A student wav2vec 2.0 model initialized using different strategies, then trained with knowledge distillation.

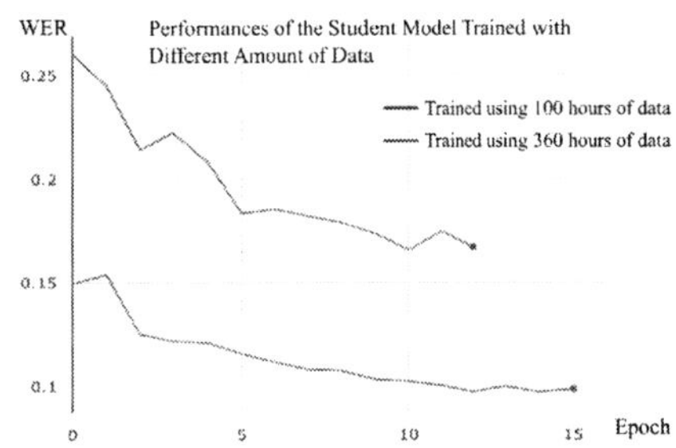

Figure 2: A student wav2vec 2.0 model trained with knowledge distillation using different amount of data.

other method from the beginning of training. We split the dev-clean dataset into two parts for this experiment, one for training and the other for validation, which we used for reporting WER.

We observed that a student model trained with more data tends to obtain a better WER. As figure 2 shows, the student model trained using 360 hours of data (train-clean-360) achieves better WER than the student model trained with less data (train-clean-100).

8 Conclusion

Jointly training teacher and student model has become a popular technique for compressing ASR systems (Swaminathan et al., 2021; Yu et al., 2020). In contrast, we employed a traditional knowledge distillation approach and it will be an interesting future work direction to investigate why such approach did not achieve great performances for the student model. Despite performance limitations, we found that knowledge distillation is the most effective compression method for wav2vec 2.0 for saving energy by lowering CPU or GPU inference time. Using knowledge distillation, we trained a student wav2vec 2.0 model, which is at least two times faster than the original model on both CPU and GPU. Moreover, the trained student model is also two times more energy efficient than the original model.

Wav2vec models present a valuable technology for democratizing ASR. We explored multiple methods for reducing memory usage and speeding up such models for deployment. More remarkably, our compressed model is environmental friendly during inference. Maintaining low carbon footprint and improving model's performance will be our future research direction.

References

Dario Amodei, Sundaram Ananthanarayanan, Rishita Anubhai, Jingliang Bai, Eric Battenberg, Carl Case, Jared Casper, Bryan Catanzaro, Jingdong Chen, Mike Chrzanowski, Adam Coates, Greg Diamos, Erich Elsen, Jesse H. Engel, Linxi Fan, Christopher Fougner, Awni Y. Hannun, Billy Jun, Tony Han, Patrick LeGresley, Xiangang Li, Libby Lin, Sharan Narang, Andrew Y. Ng, Sherjil Ozair, Ryan Prenger, Sheng Qian, Jonathan Raiman, Sanjeev Satheesh, David Seetapun, Shubho Sengupta, Chong Wang, Yi Wang, Zhiqian Wang, Bo Xiao, Yan Xie, Dani Yogatama, Jun Zhan, and Zhenyao Zhu. 2016. Deep speech 2 : End-to-end speech recognition in english and mandarin. In *Proceedings of the 33nd International Conference on Machine Learning, ICML 2016, New York City, NY, USA, June 19-24, 2016*, volume 48 of *JMLR Workshop and Conference Proceedings*, pages 173–182. JMLR.org.

Lasse F. Wolff Anthony, Benjamin Kanding, and Raghavendra Selvan. 2020. Carbontracker: Tracking and predicting the carbon footprint of training deep learning models. ICML Workshop on Challenges in Deploying and monitoring Machine Learning Systems. ArXiv:2007.03051.

Alexei Baevski, Yuhao Zhou, Abdelrahman Mohamed, and Michael Auli. 2020. wav2vec 2.0: A framework for self-supervised learning of speech representations. In *Advances in Neural Information Processing Systems 33: Annual Conference on Neural Information Processing Systems 2020, NeurIPS 2020, December 6-12, 2020, virtual.*

Emily M Bender, Timnit Gebru, Angelina McMillan-Major, and Shmargaret Shmitchell. 2021. On the dangers of stochastic parrots: Can language models be too big? In *Proceedings of the 2021 ACM Conference on Fairness, Accountability, and Transparency*, pages 610–623.

Jungwook Choi, Zhuo Wang, Swagath Venkataramani, Pierce I-Jen Chuang, Vijayalakshmi Srinivasan, and Kailash Gopalakrishnan. 2018. Pact: Parameterized clipping activation for quantized neural networks.

Matthieu Courbariaux, Yoshua Bengio, and Jean-Pierre David. 2015. Binaryconnect: Training deep neural networks with binary weights during propagations. In *Advances in Neural Information Processing Systems 28: Annual Conference on Neural Information Processing Systems 2015, December 7-12, 2015, Montreal, Quebec, Canada*, pages 3123–3131.

William Dally. 2015. High-performance hardware for machine learning. *NIPS Tutorial*, 2.

Jacob Devlin, Ming-Wei Chang, Kenton Lee, and Kristina Toutanova. 2019. BERT: Pre-training of deep bidirectional transformers for language understanding. In *Proceedings of the 2019 Conference of the North American Chapter of the Association for Computational Linguistics: Human Language Technologies, Volume 1 (Long and Short Papers)*, pages 4171–4186, Minneapolis, Minnesota. Association for Computational Linguistics.

Hayato Futami, Hirofumi Inaguma, Sei Ueno, Masato Mimura, Shinsuke Sakai, and Tatsuya Kawahara. 2020. Distilling the knowledge of bert for sequence-to-sequence asr.

Yan Gao, Titouan Parcollet, and Nicholas Lane. 2020. Distilling knowledge from ensembles of acoustic models for joint ctc-attention end-to-end speech recognition.

Song Han, Huizi Mao, and William J Dally. 2016. Deep compression: Compressing deep neural networks with pruning, trained quantization and huffman coding. *International Conference on Learning Representations (ICLR)*.

Song Han, Jeff Pool, John Tran, and William Dally. 2015. Learning both weights and connections for efficient neural network. In *Advances in Neural Information Processing Systems*, volume 28. Curran Associates, Inc.

Peter Henderson, Jieru Hu, Joshua Romoff, Emma Brunskill, Dan Jurafsky, and Joelle Pineau. 2020. Towards the systematic reporting of the energy and carbon footprints of machine learning.

Dan Hendrycks and Kevin Gimpel. 2020. Gaussian error linear units (gelus).

Geoffrey Hinton, Oriol Vinyals, and Jeff Dean. 2015. Distilling the knowledge in a neural network.

Jeremy Howard and Sebastian Ruder. 2018. Universal language model fine-tuning for text classification. In

Proceedings of the 56th Annual Meeting of the Association for Computational Linguistics (Volume 1: Long Papers), pages 328–339, Melbourne, Australia. Association for Computational Linguistics.

Kyuyeon Hwang and Wonyong Sung. 2014. Fixed-point feedforward deep neural network design using weights+ 1, 0, and- 1. In *2014 IEEE Workshop on Signal Processing Systems (SiPS)*, pages 1–6. IEEE.

Xiaoqi Jiao, Yichun Yin, Lifeng Shang, Xin Jiang, Xiao Chen, Linlin Li, Fang Wang, and Qun Liu. 2019. Tinybert: Distilling BERT for natural language understanding. *CoRR*, abs/1909.10351.

Gakuto Kurata and Kartik Audhkhasi. 2018. Improved knowledge distillation from bi-directional to uni-directional lstm ctc for end-to-end speech recognition. In *2018 IEEE Spoken Language Technology Workshop (SLT)*, pages 411–417. IEEE.

Sheng Li, Dabre Raj, Xugang Lu, Peng Shen, Tatsuya Kawahara, and Hisashi Kawai. 2019. Improving transformer-based speech recognition systems with compressed structure and speech attributes augmentation. In *INTERSPEECH*, pages 4400–4404.

Abhinav Mehrotra, Łukasz Dudziak, Jinsu Yeo, Young-yoon Lee, Ravichander Vipperla, Mohamed S Abdelfattah, Sourav Bhattacharya, Samin Ishtiaq, Alberto Gil CP Ramos, SangJeong Lee, et al. 2020. Iterative compression of end-to-end asr model using automl. *Proc. Interspeech 2020*, pages 3361–3365.

Takuma Mori, Andros Tjandra, Sakriani Sakti, and Satoshi Nakamura. 2018. Compressing end-to-end asr networks by tensor-train decomposition. In *Interspeech*, pages 806–810.

T. Moriya, H. Sato, T. Tanaka, T. Ashihara, R. Masumura, and Y. Shinohara. 2020. Distilling attention weights for ctc-based asr systems. In *ICASSP 2020 - 2020 IEEE International Conference on Acoustics, Speech and Signal Processing (ICASSP)*, pages 6894–6898.

Vassil Panayotov, Guoguo Chen, Daniel Povey, and Sanjeev Khudanpur. 2015. Librispeech: An ASR corpus based on public domain audio books. In *2015 IEEE International Conference on Acoustics, Speech and Signal Processing, ICASSP 2015, South Brisbane, Queensland, Australia, April 19-24, 2015*, pages 5206–5210. IEEE.

Adam Paszke, Sam Gross, Francisco Massa, Adam Lerer, James Bradbury, Gregory Chanan, Trevor Killeen, Zeming Lin, Natalia Gimelshein, Luca Antiga, Alban Desmaison, Andreas Köpf, Edward Yang, Zachary DeVito, Martin Raison, Alykhan Tejani, Sasank Chilamkurthy, Benoit Steiner, Lu Fang, Junjie Bai, and Soumith Chintala. 2019. Pytorch: An imperative style, high-performance deep learning library. In *Advances in Neural Information Processing Systems 32: Annual Conference on Neural Information Processing Systems 2019, NeurIPS 2019*, pages 8024–8035.

Victor Sanh, Lysandre Debut, Julien Chaumond, and Thomas Wolf. 2020. Distilbert, a distilled version of bert: smaller, faster, cheaper and lighter.

Victor Schmidt, Kamal Goyal, Aditya Joshi, Boris Feld, Liam Conell, Nikolas Laskaris, Doug Blank, Jonathan Wilson, Sorelle Friedler, and Sasha Luccioni. 2021. CodeCarbon: Estimate and Track Carbon Emissions from Machine Learning Computing.

Emma Strubell, Ananya Ganesh, and Andrew McCallum. 2019. Energy and policy considerations for deep learning in NLP. In *Proceedings of the 57th Annual Meeting of the Association for Computational Linguistics*, pages 3645–3650, Florence, Italy. Association for Computational Linguistics.

Zhiqing Sun, Hongkun Yu, Xiaodan Song, Renjie Liu, Yiming Yang, and Denny Zhou. 2020. Mobilebert: a compact task-agnostic BERT for resource-limited devices. *CoRR*, abs/2004.02984.

Rupak Vignesh Swaminathan, Brian King, Grant P. Strimel, Jasha Droppo, and Athanasios Mouchtaris. 2021. Codert: Distilling encoder representations with co-learning for transducer-based speech recognition. *CoRR*, abs/2106.07734.

Ryoichi Takashima, Sheng Li, and Hisashi Kawai. 2018. An investigation of a knowledge distillation method for CTC acoustic models. In *2018 IEEE International Conference on Acoustics, Speech and Signal Processing, ICASSP 2018, Calgary, AB, Canada, April 15-20, 2018*, pages 5809–5813. IEEE.

Vincent Vanhoucke, Andrew Senior, and Mark Z. Mao. 2011. Improving the speed of neural networks on cpus. In *Deep Learning and Unsupervised Feature Learning Workshop, NIPS 2011*.

Genta Indra Winata, Samuel Cahyawijaya, Zhaojiang Lin, Zihan Liu, and Pascale Fung. 2020. Lightweight and efficient end-to-end speech recognition using low-rank transformer. In *2020 IEEE International Conference on Acoustics, Speech and Signal Processing, ICASSP 2020, Barcelona, Spain, May 4-8, 2020*, pages 6144–6148. IEEE.

Genta Indra Winata, Andrea Madotto, Jamin Shin, Elham J. Barezi, and Pascale Fung. 2019. On the effectiveness of low-rank matrix factorization for LSTM model compression. *CoRR*, abs/1908.09982.

Jiahui Yu, Wei Han, Anmol Gulati, Chung-Cheng Chiu, Bo Li, Tara N. Sainath, Yonghui Wu, and Ruoming Pang. 2020. Universal ASR: unify and improve streaming ASR with full-context modeling. *CoRR*, abs/2010.06030.

Neta Zmora, Guy Jacob, Lev Zlotnik, Bar Elharar, and Gal Novik. 2019. Neural network distiller: A python package for dnn compression research.

On the Role of Corpus Ordering in Language Modeling

Ameeta Agrawal, Suresh Singh, Lauren Schneider, Michael Samuels
Department of Computer Science
Portland State University, USA
{ameeta, singhsp, lbraun, msamuels}@pdx.edu

Abstract

Language models pretrained on vast corpora of unstructured text using self-supervised learning framework are used in numerous natural language understanding and generation tasks. Many studies show that language acquisition in humans follows a rather structured simple-to-complex pattern and guided by this intuition, curriculum learning, which enables training of computational models in a meaningful order, such as processing easy samples before hard ones, has been shown to potentially reduce training time. The question remains whether curriculum learning can benefit pretraining of language models. In this work, we perform comprehensive experiments involving multiple curricula strategies varying the criteria for complexity and the training schedules. Empirical results of training transformer language models on English corpus and evaluating it intrinsically as well as after fine-tuning across eight tasks from the GLUE benchmark, show consistent improvement gains over conventional vanilla training. Interestingly, in our experiments, when evaluated on one epoch, the best model following a document-level hard-to-easy curriculum, outperforms the vanilla model by 1.7 points (average GLUE score) and it takes the vanilla model twice as many training steps to reach comparable performance.

1 Introduction

Pretrained language models are the foundation for achieving impressive results on many natural language processing tasks today (Peters et al., 2018; Devlin et al., 2019; Yang et al., 2019) but they are also prohibitively expensive to train, requiring enormous computing resources to be effective. The exploding demand of computations, together with the resulting massive energy cost (Strubell et al., 2019), pose serious obstacles to the development of new pretrained models, thus, leading to a number of recent research efforts aimed towards addressing this problem by proposing approaches for improving model efficiency (Sanh et al., 2019) or sample efficiency (Clark et al., 2020), to name just a few.

The primary method researchers have explored to address this problem is to develop smaller language models (Sanh et al., 2019; Jiao et al., 2020). In this paper we study a complementary approach to simplify pretraining of language models based on corpus ordering via curriculum learning (Bengio et al., 2009). The motivation is that curriculum learning has been shown to help with faster convergence (Guo et al., 2018; Hacohen and Weinshall, 2019) which, in combination with simpler language models, will give us a sustainable platform for future research into language models.

Although curriculum learning strategies have been successfully employed in many areas of machine learning, on a wide range of tasks (Wang et al., 2020; Soviany et al., 2021), little is understood about the role of corpus ordering in the context of pretraining language models with the exception of some notable early works on language modeling (Bengio et al., 2009; Graves et al., 2017). In this paper, we continue this line of investigation by asking the question whether curriculum based pretraining of *transformer language models* provides any benefits when compared with traditional vanilla training.

In order to create a curriculum from an unlabeled text corpus for such self-supervised form of learning, one needs to define a measure of complexity. We explore if metrics of text readability difficulty designed for humans can serve as beneficial metric in creating a curriculum for machine learning models. The intuition behind this approach is to mimic the manner in which humans learn. Training samples are organized by levels of difficulty and training proceeds in steps where the model is first trained on a subset of the corpus at a given difficulty level before being trained on another difficulty level, and so on.

Proceedings of the 2nd Workshop on Simple and Efficient Natural Language Processing, pages 142–154
November 10, 2021.

For our experiments, we pretrain from scratch multiple models of $\text{BERT}_{\text{BASE}}$ using the WikiText-103 corpus (Merity et al., 2016), a collection of English articles from Wikipedia. We explored standard length-based metrics of complexity as well as document-level complexity using Flesch Reading Ease readability index to organize the corpora into a curriculum. We also investigated two different methods of accessing such an ordered training set – one where the bins remain disjoint (BINNED) and another where the bins are incrementally joined together to increase the training data size (STEPPED) over n epochs. An extensive evaluation is conducted in terms of metrics related to not just pretraining but also fine-tuning on eight downstream tasks, specifically the suite of datasets from the GLUE benchmark (Wang et al., 2018).

Our results demonstrate that while sentence-level and document-level complexity metrics work comparably well, they outperform the vanilla models in all experiments. Furthermore, while easy to hard is a good strategy when complexity is computed at sentence-level, the reverse is true when complexity is measured at document-level. Finally, the most encouraging results suggest that corpus ordering takes significantly less time (measured in terms of training steps) as compared to vanilla training, while yielding comparable results as measured by the average GLUE score.

In summary, this work makes the following contributions,

- We propose a novel paradigm defined by document-level metrics of text complexity for ordering a training corpus.
- We explore two strategies for learning from such a curriculum in the context of pretraining of language models.
- We conduct extensive experiments by training several versions of transformer model from scratch and evaluating their performance in terms of metrics computed at both pretraining and fine-tuning stages.

2 Corpus Complexity

We begin by describing the unlabeled corpus of text used during training and the metrics adopted for measuring its complexity.

Corpus. In this work we choose the WikiText-103 corpus (Merity et al., 2016), which has served as a popular choice of text corpus for language modeling in prior works (Khandelwal et al., 2019; Press et al., 2021). It consists of a set of verified Good and Featured articles[1] from English Wikipedia, containing a total of around 103.2 million tokens[2]. For all experiments, the predefined splits of the corpus are used.

Complexity. Before we can order the unlabeled text instances in WikiText-103, we need to define some criteria for ranking them. Designing a ranking criteria in a self-supervised setup is a challenging problem, especially due to the dual pretraining and fine-tuning paradigm. We choose to estimate sample complexity in terms of human-centered notion of 'difficulty', specifically text readability and lexical richness. In other words, we construct a heuristically informed pre-defined curriculum, and adopt metrics that measure the difficulty of text, based on readability and complexity, at two levels of granularity - sentence and document. The corpus is then divided into bins, from which batches of training input are constructed at random.

2.1 Sentence-level complexity

The length of a sentence (or a sequence) is a straightforward, intuitive, and attractive (easy to implement) measure for indicating difficulty or complexity of a piece of text, and indeed, numerous works have used length as a criteria for ordering samples (Spitkovsky et al., 2010; Cirik et al., 2016; Kocmi and Bojar, 2017), although, to our knowledge, none in the context of pretraining of *transformer* language models. Note that sentence length as discussed here is different from sequence length (Press et al., 2021), with the former being the number of contiguous words in an entire sentence (linguistic unit), whereas the latter is the number of tokens in a subsequence that serves as an input to the model (machine unit)[3].

We first split each article into non-overlapping sentences, which are further tokenized into words[4].

[1]In this paper, the words 'articles' and 'documents' are used interchangeably.

[2]`https://blog.einstein.ai/the-wikitext-long-term-dependency-language-modeling-dataset/`

[3]To further illustrate the difference between the two notions of length, sentence vs. subsequence, consider this very simple sentence '*This is a very long sentence.*'. Here, the length of the sentence is 6, whereas subsequences of varying lengths can be created from this sentence, with their length being anywhere between 1 and 6, depending on the user specified parameter. Moreover, the subsequences can be non-overlapping or otherwise (Press et al., 2021).

[4]We use NLTK's sentence segmentation and word tokenization.

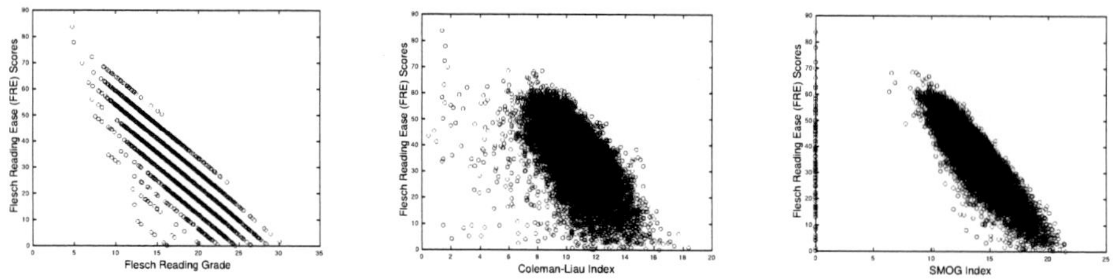

(a) FRE vs Grade (b) FRE vs Coleman-Liau (c) FRE vs SMOG index

Figure 1: Comparison of the four metrics of readability on the WikiText103 corpus.

Length	FRE	Grade	Coleman-Liau	SMOG
2-10	52.8	8.4	8.0	9.2
11-15	49.2	9.8	9.9	10.5
16-20	44.7	11.5	10.3	11.6
21-25	48.5	12.1	10.8	12.6
26-30	43.7	13.9	10.7	13.5
31-35	38.8	15.8	10.9	14.4
36-40	33.9	17.7	10.9	15.2
41-45	29.0	19.6	11.1	16.0
46-50	24.0	21.5	11.1	16.7
51-55	18.9	23.5	11.1	17.4
56-60	05.3	26.6	11.0	18.1
61+	-12.7	33.6	11.2	20.2

Table 1: Sentence length and its connections to Flesch Reading Ease (FRE), Flesch-Kincaid Grade, Coleman-Liau index and SMOG index. For FRE, higher scores reflect easier samples (in terms of readability difficulty); for all others, a smaller value reflects easier to read. In general, there appears to be a consistent monotonic mapping between length and all other metrics, except for an occasional outlier (underlined).

Then we compute the number of tokens in each sentence and create bins consisting of sentences of similar lengths – 2 to 5 words, 6 to 10 words, and so on, together, thus organizing the corpus to create a length-based curriculum.

It is important to note that by binning sentences based on length this way, it is possible that we may (completely) lose the surrounding context of the sentences. However, in looking closely at the bins, we noticed that multiple sentences of similar lengths from the *same* document ended up assigned to the same bin successively, thereby still maintaining some relevant context. Some examples are included in the Appendix A.

In order to address any issues that may arise due to a corpus shuffled so thoroughly, we also explore document-level metrics of complexity.

2.2 Document-level complexity

This time, we conduct a very different analysis of the WikiText-103 focusing on text readability for approximating text complexity. We initially studied four measures of readability[5] to classify the documents – the Flesch Reading Ease (FRE) (Kincaid et al., 1975), Flesch-Kincaid Grade Level (Kincaid et al., 1975), Coleman-Liau Index (Coleman and Liau, 1975), and Smog Index (Mc Laughlin, 1969).

Comparison of the four readability metrics. Figure 1 plots the FRE scores against the other three readability metrics for WikiText computed at the document level. We observe that the FRE score and the Grade-level scores exhibit a linear relationship implying that both these metrics rate the documents similarly. However, there is some variability because at any Grade level we have a range of FRE scores. This is consistent with the manner in which Grade levels are computed since each Grade level is based on a range of computed scores. There is a similar linear relationship between FRE and SMOG index. The relationship between FRE and Coleman-Liau is similar though there is a larger spread of values for a given FRE value. However, we generally observe a linear relationship between FRE values and the other indices, and for this reason we settle on the FRE measure for scoring documents. Further, since FRE has a larger range compared to the other indices, it gives us the fidelity, i.e., fine-grained classification, needed to bin documents.

In FRE, higher scores denote *easier* samples, in terms of their readability difficulty, whereas lower values indicate *harder* samples. Concretely, for a document, FRE is computed as,

$$\text{FRE} = 206.835 - 1.015\left(\frac{\#w}{\#s}\right) - 84.6\left(\frac{\#l}{\#w}\right)$$

where w denotes the words, s denotes sentences, and l denotes syllables.

We also ran the FRE metric on each of the sentence length bins as described earlier. As Table 1

[5]These metrics were computed via TextStat library: `https://pypi.org/project/textstat/`

Bin	% tokens
easy	32.8%
medium	32.6%
hard	34.5%

Table 2: Statistics of binning the WikiText103 corpus based on FRE scores.

shows, there is indeed a direct correlation between FRE scores and the length of sentences in the bin. As the sentence length increases, FRE scores drop (indicating greater difficulty). To validate this we ran the other three metrics as well and those results are also displayed in the table. Like FRE, the other three metrics also provide strong correlation between sentence length and difficulty.

In order to create a curriculum based on differing levels of complexity, we use a histogram of FRE scores to identify boundaries for splitting the corpus. Additional details on the distribution fit of the FRE sccores are included in Appendix B. Table 2 provides a summary of how we split the corpus into three bins of roughly same size in terms of number of tokens but varying difficulty of documents, namely, *easy*, *medium*, and *hard*. Based on this split, we can consider different curriculum learning strategies including training easy-to-hard or hard-to-easy with variations where either we train on each bin individually or cumulatively, as described in the next section.

As an additional experiment, we also computed the type token ratio score (TTR) of each document, a ratio of the number of unique words (types) to the total number of words (tokens) in a document – the closer the TTR is to 1, the greater the lexical richness, and thus, considered as 'complex' for our purposes. This is because none of the other metrics described earlier take word types into account, which have been shown to be helpful in prior works (Zhang et al., 2018). Appendix C includes some comparison between FRE and TTR scores.

3 Corpus Ordering for Pretraining

We first summarize the process of creating the curriculum and then explain the strategy for training over it. As described in the previous section, sentences or documents are sorted by their complexity score, which are then distributed into non-overlapping bins, essentially subsets of data (also known as shards (Zhang et al., 2018)), such that samples in each bin are similar in complexity.

The training consists of t sequential phases, where t denotes the different points of time during the training, where training samples are fetched only from a subset of bins. For instance, $t = 1$ may correspond to the first epoch or first n steps, $t = 2$ may correspond to the second epoch or the next n steps, and so on. In our experiments, t denotes an epoch. A subset consists of one or more bins, and for creating and iterating over these training subsets during training, we explore two different strategies - BINNED and STEPPED.

(i) **BINNED**: In this variant, the model is trained sequentially on each bin, one at a time. In other words, the model is first trained on the first bin and its state is saved. The training then continues from the saved checkpoint on the next bin, and so on. This is similar to the case where a subset consists of only one bin, and we iterate over it for one epoch.

The bins themselves can be accessed in order of either increasing difficulty (from easy to medium to hard), an approach that can be intuitively seen as mimicking the way humans learn, or in the reverse order of decreasing difficulty (from hard to medium to easy), a technique shown to benefit machine learning algorithms (Weinshall et al., 2018). In doing so, the question we ask is whether curriculum or anti-curriculum help in the context of language modeling, if at all.

It is worth mentioning that while the bins are accessed in a pre-defined order (i.e., easy to hard or reverse), the samples within the bins are still randomly selected, thus combining a deterministic schedule with the benefits of randomization that serve neural models well.

(ii) **STEPPED**: Alternatively, the bins could be accessed cumulatively where the training set progressively increases in size by addition of newer bins while retaining earlier bins (also referred to as Baby Steps curriculum (Bengio et al., 2009; Spitkovsky et al., 2010)). Basically, samples of increasing (or decreasing) complexity are added to the training set after each phase t while the samples from the previous phase still remain in the training set. For instance, at the first phase $t = 1$, only the first bin is presented; at the next phase $t = 2$, the training set comprises of both the first and second bins; at $t = 3$, samples from the first, second, and third bins are accessed, and so on until the model iterates over the entire corpus in the last phase. Essentially, the first bin's samples are seen n more times (n =

number of bins) than the last bin. So in our case of three bins, the easy samples are iterated over thrice as compared to the samples from the hard bin if following an increasing level of complexity, and vice versa for a schedule of decreasing complexity.

To sum it up, if we set a phase t to be an epoch, in the BINNED models, all the bins (and by extension, the entire corpus) are/is iterated over just once, whereas in the STEPPED models, since newer bins are progressively added in addition to existing bins in the training set, a process that not only modifies complexity but also increases data size over time, on average, this is similar to iterating over the entire corpus n^2 times.

Finally, the VANILLA model, where the corpus is not sorted or binned in any way and data from the entire corpus is accessed randomly at any phase, serves as the baseline model.

4 Experiments and Discussion

In this section, we perform a series of experiments for evaluating the effects of corpus ordering strategies in the pretraining of language models.

4.1 Evaluation Metrics

We conduct experiments for evaluating different aspects of the language model and report the results pertaining to, (i) **pretraining**: As intrinsic metrics of evaluation, we measure *loss* and *perplexity* on the validation set which provide some insight into the language modeling capabilities of the pretrained models; (ii) **fine-tuning**: The benefits of better pretraining gained in terms of validation loss or perplexity will be lost if they do not transfer over to downstream natural language processing tasks after fine-tuning, which currently remains the predominant way of using these pretrained language representations. Thus, we further fine-tune the pretrained models on a range of task datasets and report metrics of extrinsic evaluation including *F1 scores*, *Spearman Correlations* and *Accuracy*; and, (iii) **compute resources**: Finally, we perform an analysis of the training time measured in the *number of training steps* taken to reach a certain threshold of performance.

4.2 Model Combinations

We train from scratch and fine-tune the following models:

- Training can go from easy to hard (EASY) or hard to easy (HARD).
- The criteria for determining complexity of text is specified at (a) sentence-level using length (LENGTH), or (b) document-level derived from FRE scores (FRE) or TTR scores (TTR).
- For BINNED, the training set consists of any one bin during a phase, whereas for STEPPED learning, the bins are cumulatively added to the training set at each phase.
- Finally, the standard way of training where the original corpus is used as is, without any ordered curriculum, serves as our baseline denoted as the VANILLA model.

4.3 Pretraining

For training all the models from scratch, we adopt a transformer model, i.e., $\text{BERT}_{\text{BASE}}$ (Devlin et al., 2019), uncased version, with 12 transformer layers, and masked language modeling objective. The batch size is set to 8, the maximum length of the input sequence is 512, and all other settings set as default. First, we train LENGTH and BINNED models for one epoch over each bin (in other words, as the bins are disjoint, each sample in the entire corpus is seen just once). As a comparable baseline, VANILLA is also trained for one epoch.

For the STEPPED models, since the earlier bins are iterated over more times than the latter bins, it has the complexity of O(n^2). Thus we re-run the VANILLA and BINNED models for two epochs for a comparable evaluation.

4.4 Finetuning

Subsequently, we fine-tune each pretrained model for two epochs over eight distinct task datasets from the General Language Understanding Evaluation (GLUE) benchmark, a suite of diverse natural language understanding tasks, including CoLA, MNLI, MRPC, QNLI, QQP, RTE, SST-2 and STS-B, described in detail in Wang et al. (2018).

4.5 Implementation

All runs are trained on a single GPU (Nvidia GeForce RTX 2080) and all pretraining and finetuning experiments are performed using HuggingFace[6] library (Wolf et al., 2019).

[6] https://github.com/huggingface/transformers

Model		Pretraining ↓ Loss	PPL	Fine-tuning ↑ CoLa	MNLI	MRPC	QNLI	QQP	RTE	SST-2	STS-B	Avg.
VANILLA		**6.09**	**441.2**	69.0	62.0	69.6	60.8	76.9	55.2	79.4	25.1	62.2
BINNED$_{LEN}$	INC.	6.61	748.5	**69.1**	**63.8**	**72.0**	**61.3**	**80.9**	**55.6**	79.7	25.6	**63.5**
	DEC.	6.72	835.1	**69.1**	62.6	68.8	60.8	78.1	**55.6**	**80.2**	**25.8**	62.6

Table 3: Results of bins derived from sentence length (increasing/decreasing) and vanilla training, in terms of loss and perplexity (↓ is better) on the valid set at the end of training, and F1 scores for QQP and MRPC, Spearman Correlations for STS-B, and accuracy scores for the other tasks after fine-tuning (↑ is better). The last column reports the average GLUE score. Each bin (or the entire corpus in the case of VANILLA model) is iterated over for one epoch.

Model		Pretraining ↓ Loss	PPL	Fine-tuning ↑ CoLa	MNLI	MRPC	QNLI	QQP	RTE	SST-2	STS-B	Avg.
VANILLA		6.09	441.2	69.0	62.0	69.6	60.8	76.9	55.2	79.4	25.1	62.2
BINNED$_{LEN}$	INC.	6.61	748.5	**69.1**	63.8	72.0	61.3	80.9	55.6	79.7	**25.6**	63.5
BINNED$_{TTR}$	HARD	**5.96**	**388.9**	68.1	31.8	71.5	50.5	81.3	50.9	81.4	23.8	57.4
BINNED$_{FRE}$	EASY	6.06	430.8	**69.1**	61.9	70.3	**62.1**	**82.2**	55.6	**81.5**	24.5	63.4
	HARD	6.11	450.8	**69.1**	**64.6**	**72.3**	61.4	81.7	**56.0**	81.4	24.5	**63.9**

Table 4: Results of training over bins derived from document level complexity (TTR and FRE scores) in easy to hard (EASY)or hard to easy (HARD) order. Results of vanilla training and length (increasing) are included from Table 3 as baselines. Loss and perplexity (↓ is better) is measured on the valid set at the end of training, and F1 scores for QQP and MRPC, Spearman Correlations for STS-B, and accuracy scores for the other tasks are reported after fine-tuning (↑ is better). The last column reports the average GLUE score. Each bin (or the entire corpus in the case of VANILLA model) is iterated over for one epoch.

4.6 Results

The goal of this work is to examine the role of corpus ordering inspired by curriculum learning in the pretraining of transformer language models. In particular, we seek to explore the following questions:

Q1. Effect of Sentence Complexity (BINNED)

We first compare the simple sentence-level LENGTH based curriculum learning with the VANILLA way of training language models, the results of which are presented in Table 3. We observe that while the VANILLA model performs better in terms of loss and perplexity on the validation set at the end of one epoch, those improvements fail to carry over to the fine-tuning stage. Instead, both the BINNED$_{LEN}$ curriculum models perform better in terms of the average GLUE score, with the increasing LEN schedule outperforming the other two.

These results are encouraging considering that a simple approach of iterating over the corpus in bins of progressively increasing sentence length seems to be quite effective.

Q2. Effect of Document Complexity (BINNED)

Next we investigate the effect of accessing the corpus organized based on document-level notion of complexity as measured using FRE scores (and some preliminary experiments using TTR scores, which did not perform as well as FRE scores and, therefore, were not included in further experiments), as compared to VANILLA and BINNED$_{LEN\ (INC.)}$ models. The results are reported in Table 4 and once again we notice a disconnect between the intrinsic and extrinsic evaluation scores. That is, while BINNED$_{TTR}$ (HARD) does well in terms of validation loss and perplexity, it is the poorest performing model when measured in terms of average GLUE score after fine-tuning, and instead, the overall best performance is achieved by the BINNED$_{FRE}$ (HARD) model.

There appears to be little difference between the performance of LENGTH models and FRE models even though it has been noted that it may be better to use a document-level corpus rather than a shuffled sentence-level corpus (Devlin et al., 2019). We hypothesize that this may be because in length-based bins, multiple sentences of similar lengths

Model		Pretraining ↓ Loss	PPL	Fine-tuning ↑ CoLa	MNLI	MRPC	QNLI	QQP	RTE	SST-2	STS-B	Avg.
VANILLA		5.98	398.6	**68.7**	**63.5**	73.5	61.2	79.1	55.2	**81.3**	**24.9**	63.4
BINNED$_{FRE}$	EASY	5.97	394.4	68.1	63.2	**73.8**	50.5	77.0	52.7	80.6	**24.9**	61.4
	HARD	6.00	406.5	68.5	62.4	71.8	**62.5**	82.7	57.4	81.2	23.9	**63.8**
STEPPED$_{FRE}$	EASY	**5.86**	**351.7**	67.3	62.7	71.1	50.5	**83.0**	**58.4**	80.2	24.4	62.2
	HARD	5.98	398.2	68.1	63.4	71.3	61.6	82.7	53.4	79.5	24.7	63.1

Table 5: Results of training over bins derived from FRE scores in easy to hard (EASY)or hard to easy (HARD) order using BINNED or STEPPED algorithm. Loss and perplexity (↓ is better) is measured on the valid set at the end of training, and F1 scores for QQP and MRPC, Spearman Correlations for STS-B, and accuracy scores for the other tasks are reported after fine-tuning (↑ is better). The last column reports the average GLUE score. The entire corpus in the case of VANILLA model is iterated over for two epochs whereas for BINNED versions, each bin is iterated over twice.

belonging to the *same* document get binned successively, thereby continuing to maintain their context when long contiguous sequences as extracted for input. The main observation, however, is that some notion of ordering certainly seems to help as compared to no ordering such as in the case of the VANILLA model.

Crucially, this experiment also allows us to analyze the question whether metrics of text readability designed for humans could also benefit machine learning algorithms, and it appears that an anti-curriculum derived from FRE scores, i.e., from *hard to easy* ordering works better for machines. This result is especially interesting and in line with prior work (Weinshall et al., 2018) where it was noted, in the context of visual object recognition, that what makes an image difficult to a neural network classifier may not always match whatever makes it difficult to a human observer. Here, we notice a similar behavior, albeit in the context of language modeling.

Q3. Effect of STEPPED vs. BINNED

This experiment compares the effect of the two strategies of accessing the bins during training. Recall that in BINNED, the bins are disjoint and training samples are randomly selected from only one bin during a given epoch. On the other hand, in STEPPED, at each epoch, a new bin is added to the training set in addition to the previous bin, thereby, increasing the size of the training dataset progressively. For a fair comparison between the two approaches, we iterate over the VANILLA and BINNED models twice to reach the same number of steps as the STEPPED models.

Table 5 reports the results of this experiment allowing us to make the following key observations: (i) the BINNED (HARD) model yields the most competitive results, which is somewhat surprising given that one might consider such a strategy of training over non-overlapping bins to perhaps lead to catastrophic forgetting. To further analyze this phenomenon, when we compute the ratio of common word types between any two consecutive bins, we find an overlap of up to 40%, which could possibly explain why disjoint training works just as well as progressively incremental training; (ii) once again, we observe that adopting a document-level anti-curriculum learning, i.e., hard to easy sequence is beneficial especially after fine-tuning; and, (iii) the disconnect between the intrinsic and extrinsic evaluation results continues to persist.

Q4. What about Sustainability?

In Table 6 we summarize the results of the top performing model and the vanilla training runs in order to compare them in terms of the compute power consumed, i.e., the number of training steps, along with their validation loss and average GLUE score. We find that while, unsurprisingly, VANILLA model improves given more epochs, it still does not match the performance afforded by the BINNED model which is reached in almost half the number of steps[7], and this we find to be one of the most interesting findings of this study. This is particularly encouraging because it suggests that simple corpus ordering can not only improve the quality of the language model, but also its efficiency in terms of

[7]Even though the same base corpus is used for all the experiments, the slight difference in the number of steps is due to the way data is randomly sampled and chunked into input sequences during training.

Model	Loss ↓	GLUE ↑	# steps ↓
VANILLA (1 epoch)	**6.09**	62.2	28.2K
VANILLA (2 epochs)	**5.98**	63.4	56.4K
$\text{BINNED}_{\text{FRE}}$ (HARD) (1 epoch)	6.11	**63.9**	32.1K

Table 6: Compute resources in terms of training steps.

the training steps needed to reach a certain level of performance after fine-tuning.

We acknowledge that this work's conclusions are largely drawn based on experiments run on a reasonably sized transformer language model over a relatively small corpus[8] and a handful of epochs. We hope that future research can build upon these simple yet effective ideas.

5 Related Work

There is a growing awareness of the benefits of Green AI (Schwartz et al., 2020; Bender et al., 2021), with an emphasis on not just accuracy, but also efficiency, with the desirable goal, amongst many, of decreasing the environmental carbon footprint of pretrained language models, during training or inference. Tremendous progress is being made towards sustainable or 'greener' models with many efforts in improving model efficiency in order to reduce the amount of compute required (Hinton et al., 2015; Sanh et al., 2019; Jiao et al., 2020; Mao et al., 2020; Anderson and Gómez-Rodríguez, 2020; Schick and Schütze, 2021; Stock et al., 2021; Iandola et al., 2020).

Scaling laws (Kaplan et al., 2020) suggest that optimal compute-efficient training involves training very large models on a relatively modest amount of data and indeed, many studies explore the relationship between the volume of training data and consequent model performance (Banko and Brill, 2001; Sun et al., 2017; van Schijndel et al., 2019; Hu et al., 2020; Raffel et al., 2020; Brown et al., 2020; Zhang et al., 2021), generally concluding that rapid improvements in performance are observed as the amount of training data increases, at least until a certain point, after which the improvements slow down.

In this work, our focus is on studying the role of *corpus ordering* in language modeling, and although a handful of works explored this idea via length-based metrics (Bengio et al., 2009; Graves et al., 2017), they did not integrate document-level measures of complexity, nor did they study this in the context of transformer models. Furthermore, we perform an extensive evaluation reporting metrics pertaining to both pretraining and fine-tuning stages.

Prior work has typically measured the complexity of text in terms of the length of a sequence (Spitkovsky et al., 2010; Cirik et al., 2016; Kocmi and Bojar, 2017; Subramanian et al., 2017; Zhang et al., 2018; Platanios et al., 2019; Chang et al., 2021). Other metrics include features such as diversity, simplicity, and prototypicality (Tsvetkov et al., 2016), or the norm of a word embedding (Liu et al., 2020). The effects of these prior efforts have mostly been studied at the fine-tuning stage. At the pretraining stage, Babanejad et al. (2020) studied the effects of preprocessing training corpora in the context of affective tasks, while more recently, Press et al. (2021) showed that initially training a model on shorter subsequences before moving onto longer ones has benefits in terms of training time and model perplexity, although they did not study the impact on downstream tasks.

Although in regular settings curriculum learning has often led to mixed results, under limited training budgets, curriculum has shown to improve the performance (Cirik et al., 2016; Wu et al., 2020), which motivated us to explore the effects of corpus ordering in the task of transformer-based language modeling, and evaluating the metrics related to not just accuracy but also training efficiency as measured in the number of training steps.

6 Conclusions and Future Directions

In this paper, we investigate several corpus ordering and training schedules as a way of exploring the effectiveness of curriculum learning, specifically with regards to obtaining better models and potentially reducing training time and/or cost, for pretraining transformer language models (English, in this case). Between the two notions of complexity, one computed at sentence-level, and the other at document-level, we find them to perform relatively comparably. In the document-level curriculum, our findings suggest that going from hard to easy training samples may be an effective strategy. Furthermore, iterating over disjoint bins one at a time seems comparably effective to incrementally increasing the training data size. Finally, interestingly, our empirical results on eight down-

[8] 103.2 million tokens of WikiText-103 corpus as compared to some recent models leveraging upto 130 billion words (Linzen, 2020).

stream tasks from GLUE benchmark reveal that an ordered corpus yields competitive performance as compared to vanilla training in almost half the number of training steps, as measured over two epochs of training.

Many interesting avenues for future work remain such as devising more efficient corpus ordering algorithms or verifying whether these simple yet effective strategies generalize to different training corpora or model architectures, thus enabling development of sustainable language models.

Acknowledgments

We thank the anonymous reviewers for their insightful comments.

References

Mark Anderson and Carlos Gómez-Rodríguez. 2020. Distilling neural networks for greener and faster dependency parsing. In *Proceedings of the 16th International Conference on Parsing Technologies and the IWPT 2020 Shared Task on Parsing into Enhanced Universal Dependencies*, pages 2–13, Online. Association for Computational Linguistics.

Nastaran Babanejad, Ameeta Agrawal, Aijun An, and Manos Papagelis. 2020. A comprehensive analysis of preprocessing for word representation learning in affective tasks. In *Proceedings of the 58th Annual Meeting of the Association for Computational Linguistics*, pages 5799–5810.

Michele Banko and Eric Brill. 2001. Scaling to very very large corpora for natural language disambiguation. In *Proceedings of the 39th annual meeting of the Association for Computational Linguistics*, pages 26–33.

Emily M Bender, Timnit Gebru, Angelina McMillan-Major, and Shmargaret Shmitchell. 2021. On the dangers of stochastic parrots: Can language models be too big?. In *Proceedings of the 2021 ACM Conference on Fairness, Accountability, and Transparency*, pages 610–623.

Yoshua Bengio, Jérôme Louradour, Ronan Collobert, and Jason Weston. 2009. Curriculum learning. In *Proceedings of the 26th Annual International Conference on Machine Learning*, pages 41–48.

Tom B Brown, Benjamin Mann, Nick Ryder, Melanie Subbiah, Jared Kaplan, Prafulla Dhariwal, Arvind Neelakantan, Pranav Shyam, Girish Sastry, Amanda Askell, et al. 2020. Language models are few-shot learners. *arXiv preprint arXiv:2005.14165*.

Ernie Chang, Hui-Syuan Yeh, and Vera Demberg. 2021. Does the order of training samples matter? improving neural data-to-text generation with curriculum learning. In *Proceedings of the 16th Conference of the European Chapter of the Association for Computational Linguistics: Main Volume*, pages 727–733, Online. Association for Computational Linguistics.

Volkan Cirik, Eduard Hovy, and Louis-Philippe Morency. 2016. Visualizing and understanding curriculum learning for long short-term memory networks. *arXiv preprint arXiv:1611.06204*.

Kevin Clark, Minh-Thang Luong, Quoc V Le, and Christopher D Manning. 2020. Electra: Pre-training text encoders as discriminators rather than generators. *arXiv preprint arXiv:2003.10555*.

Meri Coleman and Ta Lin Liau. 1975. A computer readability formula designed for machine scoring. *Journal of Applied Psychology*, 60(2):283.

Jacob Devlin, Ming-Wei Chang, Kenton Lee, and Kristina Toutanova. 2019. BERT: Pre-training of deep bidirectional transformers for language understanding. In *Proceedings of the 2019 Conference of the North American Chapter of the Association for Computational Linguistics: Human Language Technologies, Volume 1 (Long and Short Papers)*, pages 4171–4186, Minneapolis, Minnesota. Association for Computational Linguistics.

Alex Graves, Marc G Bellemare, Jacob Menick, Remi Munos, and Koray Kavukcuoglu. 2017. Automated curriculum learning for neural networks. In *international conference on machine learning*, pages 1311–1320. PMLR.

Sheng Guo, Weilin Huang, Haozhi Zhang, Chenfan Zhuang, Dengke Dong, Matthew R Scott, and Dinglong Huang. 2018. Curriculumnet: Weakly supervised learning from large-scale web images. In *Proceedings of the European Conference on Computer Vision (ECCV)*, pages 135–150.

Guy Hacohen and Daphna Weinshall. 2019. On the power of curriculum learning in training deep networks. In *International Conference on Machine Learning*, pages 2535–2544. PMLR.

Geoffrey Hinton, Oriol Vinyals, and Jeff Dean. 2015. Distilling the knowledge in a neural network. *arXiv preprint arXiv:1503.02531*.

Jennifer Hu, Jon Gauthier, Peng Qian, Ethan Wilcox, and Roger Levy. 2020. A systematic assessment of syntactic generalization in neural language models. In *Proceedings of the 58th Annual Meeting of the Association for Computational Linguistics*, pages 1725–1744, Online. Association for Computational Linguistics.

Forrest Iandola, Albert Shaw, Ravi Krishna, and Kurt Keutzer. 2020. SqueezeBERT: What can computer vision teach NLP about efficient neural networks? In *Proceedings of SustaiNLP: Workshop on Simple and Efficient Natural Language Processing*, pages 124–135, Online. Association for Computational Linguistics.

Xiaoqi Jiao, Yichun Yin, Lifeng Shang, Xin Jiang, Xiao Chen, Linlin Li, Fang Wang, and Qun Liu. 2020. TinyBERT: Distilling BERT for natural language understanding. In *Findings of the Association for Computational Linguistics: EMNLP 2020*, pages 4163–4174, Online. Association for Computational Linguistics.

Jared Kaplan, Sam McCandlish, Tom Henighan, Tom B Brown, Benjamin Chess, Rewon Child, Scott Gray, Alec Radford, Jeffrey Wu, and Dario Amodei. 2020. Scaling laws for neural language models. *arXiv preprint arXiv:2001.08361*.

Urvashi Khandelwal, Omer Levy, Dan Jurafsky, Luke Zettlemoyer, and Mike Lewis. 2019. Generalization through memorization: Nearest neighbor language models. *arXiv preprint arXiv:1911.00172*.

J Peter Kincaid, Robert P Fishburne Jr, Richard L Rogers, and Brad S Chissom. 1975. Derivation of new readability formulas (automated readability index, fog count and flesch reading ease formula) for navy enlisted personnel. Technical report, Naval Technical Training Command Millington TN Research Branch.

Tom Kocmi and Ondřej Bojar. 2017. Curriculum learning and minibatch bucketing in neural machine translation. In *Proceedings of the International Conference Recent Advances in Natural Language Processing, RANLP 2017*, pages 379–386, Varna, Bulgaria. INCOMA Ltd.

Tal Linzen. 2020. How can we accelerate progress towards human-like linguistic generalization? In *Proceedings of the 58th Annual Meeting of the Association for Computational Linguistics*, Seattle, Washington. Association for Computational Linguistics.

Xuebo Liu, Houtim Lai, Derek F. Wong, and Lidia S. Chao. 2020. Norm-based curriculum learning for neural machine translation. In *Proceedings of the 58th Annual Meeting of the Association for Computational Linguistics*, pages 427–436, Online. Association for Computational Linguistics.

Yihuan Mao, Yujing Wang, Chufan Wu, Chen Zhang, Yang Wang, Quanlu Zhang, Yaming Yang, Yunhai Tong, and Jing Bai. 2020. LadaBERT: Lightweight adaptation of BERT through hybrid model compression. In *Proceedings of the 28th International Conference on Computational Linguistics*, pages 3225–3234, Barcelona, Spain (Online). International Committee on Computational Linguistics.

G Harry Mc Laughlin. 1969. Smog grading-a new readability formula. *Journal of reading*, 12(8):639–646.

Stephen Merity, Caiming Xiong, James Bradbury, and Richard Socher. 2016. Pointer sentinel mixture models. *arXiv preprint arXiv:1609.07843*.

Matthew E. Peters, Mark Neumann, Mohit Iyyer, Matt Gardner, Christopher Clark, Kenton Lee, and Luke Zettlemoyer. 2018. Deep contextualized word representations. In *Proceedings of the 2018 Conference of the North American Chapter of the Association for Computational Linguistics: Human Language Technologies, Volume 1 (Long Papers)*, pages 2227–2237, New Orleans, Louisiana. Association for Computational Linguistics.

Emmanouil Antonios Platanios, Otilia Stretcu, Graham Neubig, Barnabas Poczos, and Tom Mitchell. 2019. Competence-based curriculum learning for neural machine translation. In *Proceedings of the 2019 Conference of the North American Chapter of the Association for Computational Linguistics: Human Language Technologies, Volume 1 (Long and Short Papers)*, pages 1162–1172, Minneapolis, Minnesota. Association for Computational Linguistics.

Ofir Press, Noah A. Smith, and Mike Lewis. 2021. Shortformer: Better language modeling using shorter inputs. In *Proceedings of the 59th Annual Meeting of the Association for Computational Linguistics and the 11th International Joint Conference on Natural Language Processing (Volume 1: Long Papers)*, pages 5493–5505, Online. Association for Computational Linguistics.

Colin Raffel, Noam Shazeer, Adam Roberts, Katherine Lee, Sharan Narang, Michael Matena, Yanqi Zhou, Wei Li, and Peter J. Liu. 2020. Exploring the limits of transfer learning with a unified text-to-text transformer. *Journal of Machine Learning Research*, 21(140):1–67.

Victor Sanh, Lysandre Debut, Julien Chaumond, and Thomas Wolf. 2019. Distilbert, a distilled version of bert: smaller, faster, cheaper and lighter. *arXiv preprint arXiv:1910.01108*.

Timo Schick and Hinrich Schütze. 2021. It's not just size that matters: Small language models are also few-shot learners. In *Proceedings of the 2021 Conference of the North American Chapter of the Association for Computational Linguistics: Human Language Technologies*, pages 2339–2352, Online. Association for Computational Linguistics.

Roy Schwartz, Jesse Dodge, Noah A. Smith, and Oren Etzioni. 2020. Green AI. *Commununications of the ACM*, 63(12):54–63.

Petru Soviany, Radu Tudor Ionescu, Paolo Rota, and Nicu Sebe. 2021. Curriculum learning: A survey. *arXiv preprint arXiv:2101.10382*.

Valentin I Spitkovsky, Hiyan Alshawi, and Dan Jurafsky. 2010. From baby steps to leapfrog: How "less is more" in unsupervised dependency parsing. In *Human Language Technologies: The 2010 Annual Conference of the North American Chapter of the Association for Computational Linguistics*, pages 751–759.

Pierre Stock, Angela Fan, Benjamin Graham, Edouard Grave, Rémi Gribonval, Herve Jegou, and Armand

Joulin. 2021. Training with quantization noise for extreme model compression. In *International Conference on Learning Representations.*

Emma Strubell, Ananya Ganesh, and Andrew McCallum. 2019. Energy and policy considerations for deep learning in NLP. In *Proceedings of the 57th Annual Meeting of the Association for Computational Linguistics*, pages 3645–3650, Florence, Italy. Association for Computational Linguistics.

Sandeep Subramanian, Sai Rajeswar, Francis Dutil, Christopher Pal, and Aaron Courville. 2017. Adversarial generation of natural language. In *Proceedings of the 2nd Workshop on Representation Learning for NLP*, pages 241–251.

Chen Sun, Abhinav Shrivastava, Saurabh Singh, and Abhinav Gupta. 2017. Revisiting unreasonable effectiveness of data in deep learning era. In *Proceedings of the IEEE international conference on computer vision*, pages 843–852.

Yulia Tsvetkov, Manaal Faruqui, Wang Ling, Brian MacWhinney, and Chris Dyer. 2016. Learning the curriculum with Bayesian optimization for task-specific word representation learning. In *Proceedings of the 54th Annual Meeting of the Association for Computational Linguistics (Volume 1: Long Papers)*, pages 130–139, Berlin, Germany. Association for Computational Linguistics.

Marten van Schijndel, Aaron Mueller, and Tal Linzen. 2019. Quantity doesn't buy quality syntax with neural language models. In *Proceedings of the 2019 Conference on Empirical Methods in Natural Language Processing and the 9th International Joint Conference on Natural Language Processing (EMNLP-IJCNLP)*, pages 5831–5837, Hong Kong, China. Association for Computational Linguistics.

Alex Wang, Amanpreet Singh, Julian Michael, Felix Hill, Omer Levy, and Samuel Bowman. 2018. GLUE: A multi-task benchmark and analysis platform for natural language understanding. In *Proceedings of the 2018 EMNLP Workshop BlackboxNLP: Analyzing and Interpreting Neural Networks for NLP*, pages 353–355, Brussels, Belgium. Association for Computational Linguistics.

Xin Wang, Yudong Chen, and Wenwu Zhu. 2020. A comprehensive survey on curriculum learning. *arXiv preprint arXiv:2010.13166.*

Daphna Weinshall, Gad Cohen, and Dan Amir. 2018. Curriculum learning by transfer learning: Theory and experiments with deep networks. In *International Conference on Machine Learning*, pages 5238–5246. PMLR.

Thomas Wolf, Lysandre Debut, Victor Sanh, Julien Chaumond, Clement Delangue, Anthony Moi, Pierric Cistac, Tim Rault, Rémi Louf, Morgan Funtowicz, et al. 2019. Huggingface's transformers: State-of-the-art natural language processing. *arXiv preprint arXiv:1910.03771.*

Xiaoxia Wu, Ethan Dyer, and Behnam Neyshabur. 2020. When do curricula work? *arXiv preprint arXiv:2012.03107.*

Zhilin Yang, Zihang Dai, Yiming Yang, Jaime Carbonell, Ruslan Salakhutdinov, and Quoc V Le. 2019. Xlnet: Generalized autoregressive pretraining for language understanding. *arXiv preprint arXiv:1906.08237.*

Xuan Zhang, Gaurav Kumar, Huda Khayrallah, Kenton Murray, Jeremy Gwinnup, Marianna J Martindale, Paul McNamee, Kevin Duh, and Marine Carpuat. 2018. An empirical exploration of curriculum learning for neural machine translation. *arXiv preprint arXiv:1811.00739.*

Yian Zhang, Alex Warstadt, Xiaocheng Li, and Samuel R. Bowman. 2021. When do you need billions of words of pretraining data? In *Proceedings of the 59th Annual Meeting of the Association for Computational Linguistics and the 11th International Joint Conference on Natural Language Processing (Volume 1: Long Papers)*, pages 1112–1125, Online. Association for Computational Linguistics.

Appendix

A Sample Examples from Different Text Complexity Bins

Tables 7 and 8 present some sample text excerpts from *easy* and *hard* bins, as computed by document-level complexity and sentence-level complexity, respectively.

B Flesch Readability Ease

We computed the FRE value for each document in WikiText and create a histogram and fit a distribution, Figure 2. For WikiText, the *Epsilon-Skew-Normal* distribution provides the best fit with a mean FRE score of 36.23 and a standard deviation of 9.7.

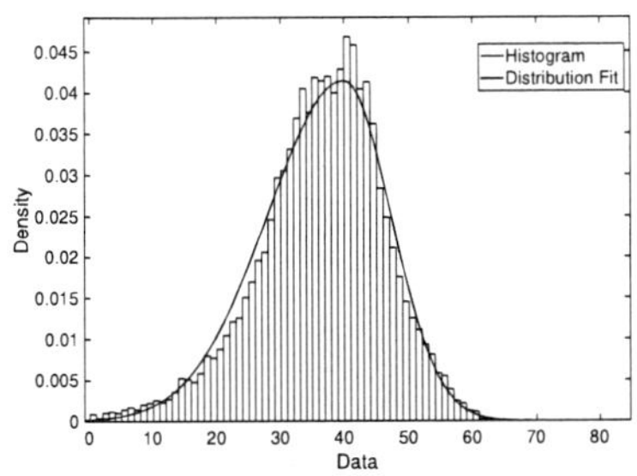

(a)

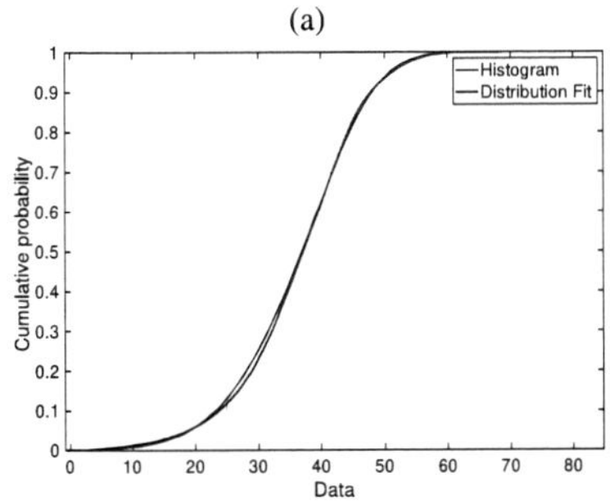

(b)

Figure 2: (a) Distribution fit and histogram, and (b) Cumulative distribution function, of the FRE scores as computed on the WikiText-103 corpus. We see that 70% of the documents have a FRE score in a narrow range between 35 and 55. We use this analysis to create the curriculum described in the text.

C Type Token Ratio

In our preliminary experiments, we also considered another document-level metric of complexity, namely, type token ration (TTR) which takes into account the unique number of word types in addition to the total number of word tokens, which may guide in creating more meaningful bins. Figure 3(a) indicates little correlation between FRE and TTR, which further motivated us to try this line of investigation, whereas Figure 3(b) shows the histogram of TTR scores which was used to identify bin boundaries. During the experiments, however, TTR's performance did not match that of FRE.

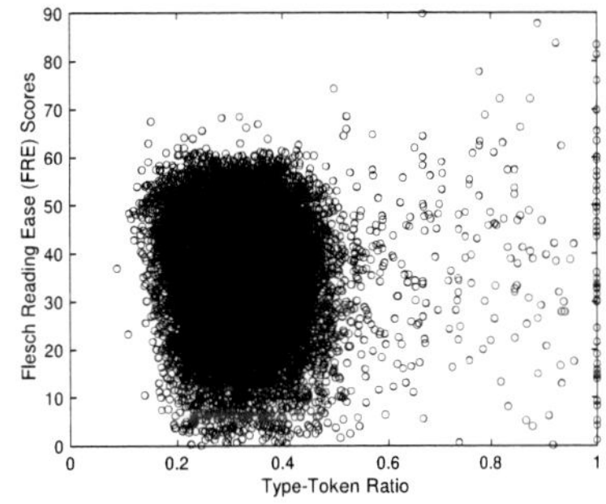

(a)

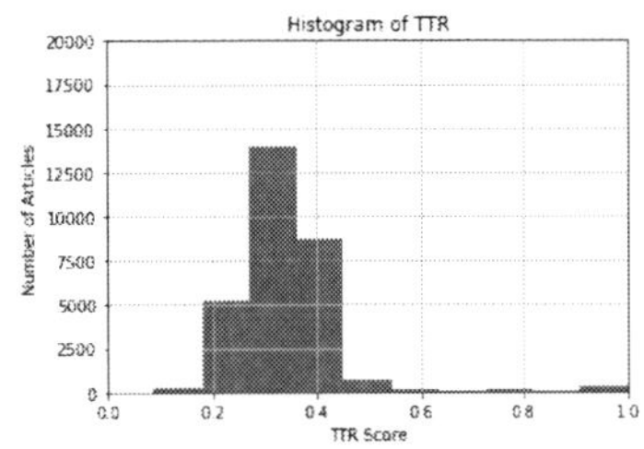

(b)

Figure 3: (a) Flesch Reading Ease vs. TTR score, and (b) Histogram of the TTR scores as computed on the WikiText-103 corpus.

Complexity	Text
EASY	A last-minute addition to the film, the simple love song was quickly written by Ashman and Menken to replace the more elaborate and ambitious "Human Again" after the latter was cut from Beauty and the Beast. O'Hara based her own vocal performance on that of American singer and actress Barbra Streisand, who Howard advised the actress to impersonate, while O'Hara herself convinced the songwriters to have Benson record the song. Critical reception towards "Something There" has been positive, with film and music critics alike praising Ashman's abilities as both a songwriter and a storyteller.
HARD	TM and Cult Mania is a non-fiction book that examines assertions made by the Transcendental Meditation movement (TM). The book is authored by Michael Persinger, Normand Carrey and Lynn Suess and published in 1980 by Christopher Publishing House. Persinger is a neurophysiologist and has worked out of Laurentian University. He trained as a psychologist and focused on the impacts of religious experience. Carrey is a medical doctor who specialized in psychiatry. He focused his studies into child psychiatry with research at Dalhousie University, and has taught physicians in a psychiatry residency program in the field of family therapy. Suess assisted Persinger in researching effects of geological phenomena on unidentified flying object sightings in Washington; the two conducted similar research in Toronto and Ottawa.

Table 7: Easy and hard text samples as measured by FRE scores at document level.

Complexity	Text
EASY	(i) Most Egyptian deities represent natural or social phenomena. (ii) But some deities represented disruption to maat. (iii) Not all aspects of existence were seen as deities. (iv) Divine behavior was believed to govern all of nature. (v) In myth, the gods behave much like humans. (vi) Some have unique character traits. (vii) Gods were linked with specific regions of the universe. (viii) Temples were their main means of contact with humanity. (ix) The gods were believed to have many names. (x) This divine assemblage had a vague and changeable hierarchy.
HARD	(i) Employing the same fusion of tactical and real-time gameplay as its predecessors, the story runs parallel to the first game and follows the "Nameless", a penal military unit serving the nation of Gallia during the Second Europan War who perform secret black operations and are pitted against the Imperial unit "Raven". (ii) Characters also have Special Abilities that grant them temporary boosts on the battlefield: Kurt can activate "Direct Command" and move around the battlefield without depleting his Action Point gauge, the character can shift into her "Valkyria Form" and become invincible, while Imca can target multiple enemy units with her heavy weapon. (iii) The three main characters are No.7 Kurt Irving, an army officer falsely accused of treason who wishes to redeem himself; Ace No.1 Imca, a female Darcsen heavy weapons specialist who seeks revenge against the Valkyria who destroyed her home; and No.13 Riela, a seemingly jinxed young woman who is unknowingly a descendant of the Valkyria. (iv) Speaking in an interview, it was stated that the development team considered Valkyria Chronicles III to be the series 'first true sequel: while Valkyria Chronicles II had required a large amount of trial and error during development due to the platform move, the third game gave them a chance to improve upon the best parts of Valkyria Chronicles II due to being on the same platform.

Table 8: Easy and hard text samples as measured by sentence length. We hypothesize that sentence shuffled corpus still yields competitive results as compared to document-level ordering is because in general, the larger context surrounding the sentences continues to be maintained as shorter sentences from the same documents remain together, and longer sentences from the same document cluster together. It is worth noting that the sentences in this table are delineated just for presentation purposes. In actual implementation, the sentences are all combined as one (very) long document for efficient processing.

Efficient Domain Adaptation of Language Models via Adaptive Tokenization

Vin Sachidananda[*]
Stanford University
vsachi@stanford.edu

Jason S. Kessler
Amazon
jasokess@amazon.com

Yi-An Lai
AWS AI HLT
yianl@amazon.com

Abstract

Contextual embedding-based language models trained on large data sets, such as BERT and RoBERTa, provide strong performance across a wide range of tasks and are ubiquitous in modern NLP. It has been observed that fine-tuning these models on tasks involving data from domains different from that on which they were pretrained can lead to suboptimal performance. Recent work has explored approaches to adapt pretrained language models to new domains by incorporating additional pretraining using domain-specific corpora and task data. We propose an alternative approach for transferring pretrained language models to new domains by adapting their tokenizers. We show that domain-specific subword sequences can be efficiently determined directly from divergences in the conditional token distributions of the base and domain-specific corpora. In datasets from four disparate domains, we find adaptive tokenization on a pretrained RoBERTa model provides >97% of the performance benefits of domain specific pretraining. Our approach produces smaller models and less training and inference time than other approaches using tokenizer augmentation. While adaptive tokenization incurs a 6% increase in model parameters in our experimentation, due to the introduction of 10k new domain-specific tokens, our approach, using 64 vCPUs, is 72x faster than further pretraining the language model on domain-specific corpora on 8 TPUs.

1 Introduction

Pretrained language models (PLMs) trained on large "base" corpora, oftentimes >100GB of uncompressed text Liu et al. (2019); Brown et al. (2020), are used in many NLP tasks. These models first learn contextual representations in an unsupervised manner by minimizing a masked language modeling objective over a base corpus. This stage of unsupervised language model training is referred to as "pretraining". Subsequently, for supervised classification tasks, the output head of this pretrained model is swapped for a lightweight classifier and trained further on a classification objective over labeled data, referred to as "fine-tuning".

Recent work has examined the transferability of PLMs Gururangan et al. (2020) and their contextual representations to domains differing from their base corpora. On text classification tasks from four different domains, it was shown that continuing to pretrain RoBERTa's contextual embeddings on additional domain (DAPT) and/or task-specific data (TAPT) resulted in performance gains over only fine-tuning a baseline RoBERTa model. These performance gains, however, were inferior to each task's start-of-the-art metrics which were largely based on training versions of RoBERTa, or other LMs, from scratch on a large sample of in-domain data.

These performance gains come at substantial financial, time, and environmental costs in the form of increased computation, with pretraining an LM from scratch being the most expensive, using additional pretraining in the middle, and only fine-turning an off-the-shelf model the most economical.

One observed advantage Gu et al. (2020) that pretraining from scratch on in-domain data has over continual pretraining is that the tokenizer's vocabulary captures domain-specific terms. This allows semantics of those terms to be directly learned in their fixed embeddings, and relieves the language model from having to encode these semantics through the contextual embeddings of these domain-specific term's subwords. Recent work Zhang et al. (2020); Poerner et al. (2020) has shown adding whole words common to the target domain but absent from a PLM's tokenizer improves performance on single tasks. In this work, we show that augmenting an PLM with statistically derived subword tokens selected for domain association with

[*] Work done during an internship at Amazon.

Proceedings of the 2nd Workshop on Simple and Efficient Natural Language Processing, pages 155–165
November 10, 2021.

simple embedding initializations and no further pretraining provide an effective means of adapting a PLM across tasks and domains. In contrast, both Zhang et al. (2020) and Poerner et al. (2020) add inefficiencies by respectively requiring further masked language model (MLM) pretraining and doubling the resources needed for inference.

In this paper, we efficiently adapt a PLM by simply augmenting its vocabulary with domain-specific token sequences. We find that this adaptation, which requires no further pretraining, rivals the accuracy of domain and task-adapted pretraining approaches proposed in Gururangan et al. (2020) but requires only a small fraction of the compute cost.

2 Related work

Gururangan et al. (2020) describes two complementary methods using a task's training data or a separate unlabeled domain-specific corpus to further pretrain an LM, denoted as Task-Adaptive Pretraining (TAPT) and Domain-Adaptive Pretraining (DAPT) respectively. This paper shows the value of employing additional in-domain data in pretraining on four domains relative to only fine-tuning a PLM. Our approach is directly comparable to DAPT, as we only use in-domain corpora for adaptation.

Zhang et al. (2020) augment RoBERTa's vocabulary with in-domain OOV whole words. The most frequently occurring whole words are added until the OOV rate drops to 5% on the task corpus. They randomly initialize weights and pretrain a model. This improves performance on TechQA and AskUbuntu. Tai et al. (2020) also augmented BERT with tokens selected by frequency (12k OOV wordpieces were used) and pretrained a modified version of BERT which allowed for only new token's embeddings to be modified while the original embeddings remained fixed. They found that using more than 12k augmented tokens didn't improve their biomed NER and relation extraction performance, and that, once augmented, performance improved with more pretraining (4-24 hours were studied.)

Poerner et al. (2020) augment BERT's vocabulary with all in-domain OOV whole words, adding 31K tokens to bert-base-cased's 29K wordpieces. They trained a word2vec model on an in-domain corpus and fit a linear transformation to project the word embeddings into the model's input embedding space. No further pretraining is done, but during finetuning, the original tokenizer and the adapted tokenizer are both used. For inference, the finetuned model is run with both the original tokenizer and the adapted tokenizer and the outputs are averaged. Their F1 score outperforms BERT on all eight biomedical NER tasks studied. The approach has the disadvantage of increasing the parameter size of bert-base-cased by 2.2x due to the embeddings of added tokens and doubles the resources needed for inference.

Hofmann et al. (2021) demonstrates how Wordpiece tokenization does not capture the semantics of derivationally complex words as well as an approach using a modified version of Wordpiece designed to produce subword segmentations consisting of linguistic prefixes, suffixes and affixes Hofmann et al. (2020). This subword tokenizer outperformed WordPiece in determining words' polarity or their source domains. Experiments were conducted on novel embedding tokens in BERT via approaches including a projection-based method and mean pooling (both similar to §3.3).

Training language models from scratch in the domain of interest has been shown to provide improved in-domain performance when compared to out-of-domain PLMs Huang et al. (2019). In addition to Gururangan et al. (2020), prior work has shown the effectiveness of continued pretraining for domain adaptation of PLMs Alsentzer et al. (2019); Chakrabarty et al. (2019); Lee et al. (2019). For the task of Aspect-Target Sentiment Classification, Rietzler et al. (2020) uses both DAPT and task-specific fine-tuning in order to adapt language models representations. Identifying domain-characteristic words is a well-studied problem, and many metrics have been proposed for this task through comparing the distributions of tokens in contrasting corpora Rayson et al. (1997); Monroe et al. (2008); Kessler (2017). Muthukrishnan et al. (2008) used the pointwise KL-divergence to distinguish informativeness of key phrase candidates in a domain corpus relative to a background.

3 Adaptive tokenization of contextual embeddings

We define adaptive tokenization (AT) as the process of augmenting a PLM's tokenizer and fixed subword embeddings with new entries taken from a novel corpus. AT consists of two goals which must be achieved for domain adaptation. First, selection of domain-specific tokens, with which to augment a pretrained tokenizer, from an in-domain corpus must be determined. Second, an appropriate initialization in the input space of the contextual embedding models needs to be determined for additions to the tokenizer vocabulary. In this section, we detail approaches for each of these linked tasks.

3.1 Tokenizer vocabulary augmentation

In this section, we detail approaches for identifying domain-specific token sequences to be added during tokenizer augmentation. Common tokenization schemes such as Byte Pair Encoding Sennrich et al. (2016) and WordPiece Schuster and Nakajima (2012); Wu et al. (2016) are greedy algorithms and, as a result, merge subwords into individual tokens if such a sequence occurs with high relative frequency. When adapting a tokenizer our goal is to identify subword sequences which occur with high relative frequency in a domain specific corpus compared to the pretraining corpus. In Table 1, we provide the corpora for each domain in which experimentation is conducted. Next, we show how to operationalize this framework to find domain-specific token sequences.

3.2 Identifying domain-specific token sequences

In this section, we detail our approach for selection of token sequences which are both difficult to represent in a base tokenizer and have large disparities in occurrence between domain-specific and base corpora. Conceptually, we would like to add new tokens to the source tokenizer which are sequences of existing tokens and, in the in-domain corpus, are extensions of existing token sequences.

(I) Computing Empirical Token Sequence Distributions We first compute counts of sequences of $[1, \lambda]$ subword tokens (s) in each corpus C, namely the source corpus for RoBERTa (S) and the in-domain corpus which is the target of our adaptation (D). The source language model's tokenizer (namely Roberta-base) is used as the source of subword tokens. The counts of each subtoken sequences are represented as C_s, where C is the corpus and ss is the subword sequence. If s does not appear in C, $C_s = 0$. We only retain sequences occurring at least $\phi = 20$ times in one corpus. The maximum subword token sequence length (λ) is 10. We limit subtoken sequences to word boundaries as detected through whitespace tokenization.

Next, we predict how "phrase-like" a sequence of tokens C_s is, using a probability $P_C(s)$. Define

$$P_C(s) = \frac{C_s}{C_t}$$

where t is first $|s|-1$ subtoken sequence of s. These probabilities should be thought of as the surprise of the sequence s in the corpus being counted and are indicative of the how phrase-like s is.

As an example, consider a hypothetical corpus consisting of documents written about classical music. Roberta-base's tokenizer splits "oboe" into the subtokens $\langle \text{ob}, \text{oe} \rangle$. In this classical music corpus, the portion of tokens following "ob" which are "oe" (composing in the word "oboe") is surely much higher than in a general base corpus where other words staring with the "ob" subtoken like "obama" (tokenized as $\langle \text{ob}, \text{ama} \rangle$) are much more frequent and "oboe" much less.

(II) Domain shift scoring of Token Sequence Distributions with Conditional KL Divergence In order to characterize these differences in probabilities, we use the pointwise KL-divergence. Letting p and q be probabilities, the pointwise KL-divergence is defined as:

$$D_{KL}(p \parallel q)) = p \log \frac{p}{q}$$

Let the sequence relevance score $R(s)$ be defined as

$$R(s) = D_{KL}(P_D(s) \parallel P_S(s)).$$

$R(s)$ indicates how much the phrase-like probability of sequence s in the in-domain corpus D ($P_D(s)$) diverges from the baseline phrase-like probability of s in the base corpus S.

(III) Selection of Token Sequences for Tokenizer Augmentation For all experiments, we add the $\eta = 10K$ sequences with the largest R, sorted irrespective of sequence length, to the domain-augmented tokenizer.

This introduces of 7.68M parameters (embedding size 768 × 10K new tokens), a 6% increase over Roberta-base's 125M.[1]

3.3 Initialization approaches for AT

In this section, we provide two approaches to impute contextual embedding input representations for tokens added in §3.1.

Subword-based initialization In this common initialization Casanueva et al. (2020); Vulić et al.

[1] github.com/pytorch/fairseq/tree/master/examples/roberta

Algorithm 1 Selection of Domain-Specific Token Sequences for Tokenizer Augmentation

Require: Base Tokenizer Tok, Base LM LM_{base}, Base and Domain Unigram Dists. U_{base}, U_{domain}, Base and Domain Seq. Dists. T_{base}= { }, T_{domain}= { } Min. Seq. Frequency F_{min}, # Aug. to make N, Max Aug. Length L, Augmentations $= []$

(I) Computing Empirical Token Sequence Distributions

for word, count $(w, count)$ in U_{base} **do** ▷ Do the same for Domain Corpus

  $Seq[t_0, t_1, ..., t_n] := Tok(w)$

  for i in [1,n] **do**

    $T_{base}[Seq[: i]] += count$

  end for

end for

T_{domain}.values() $/=$ sum(U_{domain}.values()) ▷ Normalize Sequence Distributions

T_{base}.values() $/=$ sum(U_{base}.values())

(II) Domain shift scoring of Token Seq. Dists. with Conditional KL Divergence

$Score_{DKL} = \{\}$

for Seq in $T_{base} \bigcap T_{domain}$ **do**

  $Score_{DKL}[Seq] := T_{domain}[Seq] * \log \frac{T_{domain}[Seq]}{T_{base}[Seq]}$

end for

(III) Selection of Token Sequences for Augmentation

SortDescending($Score_{DKL}$)

for Seq in $Score_{DKL}$ **do**

  if Len(Augmentations) $= N$ **then**

    break

  end if

  if Len(Seq) $< L$ **AND** $T_{domain} > F_{min}$ **AND** $T_{base} > F_{min}$ **then**

    Augmentations.append(Seq)

  end if

end for

return Augmentations

(2020); Hofmann et al. (2021), additions to the tokenizer are embedded as the mean of their Roberta-base fixed subword embeddings. In cases where all a novel word's subwords are unrelated to its specific, in-domain meaning, this initialization may cause unwanted model drift in fine-tuning for unrelated tokens with similar fixed embeddings.

Algorithm 2 Projection-Based Initialization of Augmented Tokens

Require: LM Input Embeddings C_s, Base and Domain Learned Input Embeddings X_s, X_t, and Embedding Size d.

(I) Learn Mapping $\hat{\mathcal{M}}$: $C_s \rightarrow X_s$ with SGD:

$\hat{\mathcal{M}} = \arg\min_{\mathcal{M} \in \mathbb{R}^{d \times d}} \|\mathcal{M}X_s - C_s\|_F$

(II) Get Inits. for Aug. Tokens using $\hat{\mathcal{M}}$:

$C_t = \hat{\mathcal{M}}X_t$

return C_t

Projection-based initialization To mitigate possible issues with averaging subword embeddings, we also consider projections between static token embeddings to the input space of contextual embeddings, similar to Poerner et al. (2020).

To summarize this approach, our goal is to learn a mapping between the input token embeddings in RoBERTa, C_{base}, and word2vec token embeddings learned independently on the base[2] and domain specific corpora, X_{base}, X_{domain}. The tokens in C_{base} include the original RoBERTa tokens while those in X_{base} and X_{domain} include both the original RoBERTa tokens and the augmented tokens found using adaptive tokenization detailed in §3.2. First, a mapping M, parametrized as a single layer fully connected network, from X_{base} to C_{base} is learned which minimizes distances, on the original set of tokens in RoBERTa. The goal of this mapping is to learn a function which can translate

[2]See §5.4 for how the RoBERTa source corpora is approximated to form our base corpus.

Domain	Pretrain Corpus [# Tokens]	Task	Task Type	Train (Lab.)	Dev.	Test	Classes
BioMed	1.8M papers from S2ORC [5.1B]	ChemProt	relation classification	4169	2427	3469	13
		RCT	abstract sent. roles	18040	30212	30135	5
CS	580K papers from S2ORC [2.1B]	ACL-ARC	citation intent	1688	114	139	6
		SciERC	relation classification	3219	455	974	7
News	11.9M articles [6.7B]	HyperPartisan	partisanship	515	65	65	2
Reviews	24.75M Amazon reviews [2.1B]	IMDB	review sentiment	20000	5000	25000	2

Table 1: Specifications of the various target task and pretraining datasets to replicate experiments in Gururangan et al. (2020). Due to the restrictions on accessible papers in S2ORC, we are using versions of BioMed and CS which are approximately 33% and 74% smaller than were used in Gururangan et al. (2020). Sources: S2ORC Lo et al. (2020), News Zellers et al. (2019), Amazon reviews He and McAuley (2016), CHEMPROT Kringelum et al. (2016), RCT Dernoncourt and Lee (2017), ACL-ARC Jurgens et al. (2018), SCIERC Luan et al. (2018), HYPERPARTISAN Kiesel et al. (2019), and IMDB Maas et al. (2011).

word2vec token embeddings to the input space of RoBERTa. Then, the learned mapping M is applied to X_{domain} in order to obtain initializations in the input space of RoBERTa for the augmented tokens found using the approach in §3.2. The operations involved in this approach are detailed in Algorithm 2.

4 Experimentation

In this section, we perform evaluation of our adaptation approach on six natural language processing tasks in four domains, BioMedical, Computer Science, News, and Reviews, following the evaluations in Gururangan et al. (2020). Due to resource constraints, we perform experimentation on all datasets in Gururangan et al. (2020) excluding the Helpfulness dataset from the reviews domain and the Hyperpartisan dataset in the news domain. Each of the excluded datasets contain greater than 100K training examples, resulting in greater than 12 hours of time required for finetuning on 8 Tesla V100 GPUs for a single seed.

Approaches Roberta-base, a commonly used PLM with high performance, is used as a baseline on which supervised finetuning is performed separately for each dataset. Additionally, we compare AT to the DAPT method from Gururangan et al. (2020). As we do not make use of task specific data (i.e., the training data used in fine-tuning), AT is comparable to DAPT in terms of the data utilized. We focus on using large, in-domain data sets which are commonly used in further pretraining (rather than variably sized task-data) since their size both allows for reliable extraction of characteristic subtoken sequences to use in tokenizer augmentation. Adaptive tokenization for task-specific data is future work.

Classification Architecture We use the same classification architecture as in Gururangan et al. (2020), originally proposed in Devlin et al. (2019), in which the final layer's [CLS] token representation is passed to a task-specific feed forward layer for prediction. All hyperaparameters used in experimentation are equivalent to either the "mini", "small", or "big" hyperparameter sets from Gururangan et al. (2020).

Results We find that adaptive tokenization improves performance when compared to the baseline RoBERTa model in all four of the domains on which experimentation is performed. AT provides 97% of the aggregate relative improvement attained by DAPT respectively over Roberta-base while providing an order of magnitude efficiency gain detailed in Table 3. We do not see a significant difference in the performance of AT models based on the Mean or Proj initialization schemes. Given that Mean initialization required half the time as Proj, we recommend its use over Proj.

5 Discussion

5.1 Resource Efficiency in LM Adaptation

Current approaches for training and adapting LMs have resulted in negative environmental impact and high computational resource budgets for researchers. PLMs incur significant compute time during pretraining, typically requiring numerous days of training on $\geq$ 8 GPUs or TPUs Liu et al. (2019); Devlin et al. (2019); Gururangan et al. (2020). In Table 3, we provide a runtime comparison between continued pretraining and AT. We find that AT provides a 72x speedup compared to DAPT and does not require a GPU or TPU to run. The most resource-intensive portion of this procedure involves indexing the corpora and conducting

Domain	Task	RoBERTa	DAPT	TAPT	DAPT + TAPT	AT (Mean)	AT (Proj)	State-of-the-art (in 2020)
BioMed*	ChemProt	$81.9_{1.0}$	$\underline{84.2_{0.2}}$	$82.6_{0.4}$	$\mathbf{84.4}_{0.4}$	$83.6_{0.4}$	$83.1_{0.3}$	84.6
	RCT	$87.2_{0.1}$	$\underline{87.6_{0.1}}$	$87.7_{0.1}$	$\mathbf{87.8}_{0.1}$	$87.5_{0.4}$	$\underline{87.6_{0.3}}$	92.9
CS*	ACL-ARC	$63.0_{5.8}$	$\underline{75.4_{2.5}}$	$67.4_{1.8}$	$\mathbf{75.6}_{3.8}$	$70.1_{2.0}$	$68.9_{1.6}$	71.0
	SciERC	$77.3_{1.9}$	$80.8_{1.5}$	$79.3_{1.5}$	$81.3_{1.8}$	$\underline{\mathbf{81.4}_{0.4}}$	$81.2_{1.2}$	81.8
News	HyperPartisan	$86.6_{0.9}$	$88.2_{5.9}$	$90.4_{5.2}$	$90.0_{6.6}$	$\underline{\mathbf{93.1}_{4.2}}$	$91.6_{5.5}$	94.8
Reviews	IMDB	$95.0_{0.2}$	$95.4_{0.1}$	$95.5_{0.1}$	$\mathbf{95.6}_{0.1}$	$95.4_{0.1}$	$\underline{95.5_{0.1}}$	96.2

Table 2: Results of different adaptive pretraining methods compared to the baseline RoBERTa. AT with mean subword and projective initializations are denoted as AT (Mean) and AT (Proj) respectively. Stddevs are from 5 seeds. Results for DAPT, TAPT, DAPT+TAPT, and state-of-the-arts are quoted from Gururangan et al. (2020). The highest non-state-of-the-art result is bolded, since the state-of-the-art functions as a performance ceiling, leveraging both domain-specific pretraining and an adapted tokenizer. The best of the three approaches which utilize only source and domain domain data before fine-tuning (i.e., DAPT and AT) is underlined. *Due to restrictions on accessible papers in S2ORC, The BioMed and CS pretraining corpora used were respectively 33% and 74% smaller than the versions in Gururangan et al. (2020). Note that state-of-the-art numbers are current at the time of Gururangan et al. (2020), and are from the following works: ChemProt: S2ORC-BERT Lo et al. (2020), RCT: Sequential Sentence Classification Cohan et al. (2019), ACL-ARC: SciBert Beltagy et al. (2019), SciERC: S2ORC-BERT Lo et al. (2020), HyperPartisan: Longformer Beltagy et al. (2020), IMDB: XLNet Large Yang et al. (2019).

Method	Hardware Specs.	Runtime [h:m:s]
DAPT	8x TPU V-3	94 hours
AT (Mean)	64x vCPUs	1:17:35
AT (Projection)	64x vCPUs	4:54:58

Table 3: Runtime and hardware specifications for AT compared to DAPT. The vast majority of the time is spent reading the corpus and creating token distributions. Runtimes are based on the CS 8.1B token corpus. The DAPT runtime is mentioned in Github Issue 16 in Gururangan et al. (2020) and the AT runtimes are linearly extrapolated (an overestimate) from our observed runtime on the open version of CS, a 2.1B token corpus. We needed to perform this extrapolation since the full CS corpus which was used to benchmark Gururangan et al. (2020) is unavailable in S2ORC. "64x vCPUs" indicate the equivalent of an AWS ml.m5.16xlarge EC2 instance was used to determine which subtoken sequences to use for vocabulary augmentation and compute their embeddings. The times reported for AT (Mean) and AT (Projection) where from a single run, with precomputed base corpus token counts and embeddings.

subtoken sequence counts.

In addition to time and resources, the environmental impact of pretraining BERT with a single set of hyperparameters incurs a carbon footprint of approximately 1.5K pounds of CO_2 emissions, more than the average monthly emissions of an individual Strubell et al. (2019). Continued pretraining, which has a similar resource budget to BERT, exacerbates this problem Schwartz et al. (2019). Lastly, we find that the cloud computing costs associated with continual pretraining for both a single domain and set of hyperparameters are $750 compared to around $4.77 (using a ml.m5.16xlarge EC2 instance for 1:17) for AT on cloud computing platforms when using non-preemptible instances. High costs associated with the training of NLP models has led to inequity in the research community in favor of industry labs with large research budgets Strubell et al. (2019).

5.2 Augmented Token Sequences selected in each domain

In Table 4, we provide examples of augmented vocabulary selected by our adaptive tokenization algorithm for each of the four domains used in experimentation. In each domain, the augmented tokens identified by AT correspond to domain-specific language. For instance, augmented tokens in the Reviews domain token sequences often contain contractions such as "I've" and "it's", which are frequently used in informal language. In the News domain, augmented tokens include financial terms such as "NYSE" and "Nasdaq" along with media outlets such as "Reuters" and "Getty". Many of the augmented tokens in the Computer Science domain are mathematical and computing terms such as "Theorem", "Lemma", "Segmentation", and "Gaussian". Lastly, augmented tokens in the BioMedical domain are largely concerned with biological mechanisms and medical procedures such as "phosphorylation", "assays", and "transfect".

5.3 Future directions

While we have evaluated this approach on Roberta-base, it can be used on any PLM which uses subword tokenization. It would be interesting future

BioMed	CS	News	Reviews
[inc, ub, ated] → incubated	[The, orem] → Theorem	[t, uesday] → tuesday	[it, 's] → it's
[trans, fect] → transfect	[L, em, ma] → Lemma	[ob, ama] → obama	[that, 's] → that's
[ph, osph, ory] → phosphory	[vert, ices] → vertices	[re, uters] → reuters	[sh, oes] → shoes
[mi, R] → miR	[E, q] → Eq	[iph, one] → iphone	[doesn, 't] → doesn't
[st, aining] → staining	[cl, ust, ering] → clustering	[ny, se] → nyse	[didn, 't] → didn't
[ap, opt, osis] → apoptosis	[H, ence] → Hence	[get, ty] → getty	[can, 't] → can't
[G, FP] → GFP	[Seg, mentation] → Segmentation	[inst, agram] → instagram	[I, 've] → I've
[pl, asm] → plasm	[class, ifier] → classifier	[bre, xit] → brexit	[b, ought] → bought
[ass, ays] → assays	[Ga, ussian] → Gaussian	[nas, daq] → nasdaq	[you, 'll] → you'll
[ph, osph, ory, lation] → phosphorylation	[p, olyn] → polyn	[ce, o] → ceo	[kind, le] → kindle

Table 4: Samples of token sequences with large JSD between base and domain corpora sequence distributions; all of these sequences were added during AT to the Roberta-Base tokenizer.

work to see if the performance gain will hold on larger PLMs with richer vocabularies or on smaller PLMs. One may speculate the benefit of AT is due to encoding non-compositional subword tokens in the input embedding space. And furthermore, this lifts some of the responsibility for encoding their semantics from the LM's interior weights. Since these non-compositional tokens are characteristic to the domain corpus, their representations may be important to the end task and and need to be learned or improved during fine-tuning. If this is the case, then perhaps models with fewer interior weights benefit more from AT since the connection between the non-compositional tokens would be built into the input, allowing interior weights to better learn the semantics of novel non-compositional tokens and opposed to also having to learn the component tokens' connection.

While this work tests AT on an English language PLM, it can hypothetically be applied to any PLM regardless of its source language(s). Exploring how AT can work with additional pretraining on domain data is clear future work. Tai et al. (2020) show that specialized further pretraining on domain data on using a model augmented with domain characteristic whole word tokens results in an improved performance/pretraining time curve. It would also be fruitful to explore how that curve changes when using more efficient pretraining techniques such as in Clark et al. (2020).

While we compared different novel token sequence embedding techniques, we did not study different ways of identifying subtoken sequences to add. Comparing AT to approaches such adding whole word tokens Tai et al. (2020) would confirm our hypothesis that phrase-like token sequences are useful.

Experimenting with the number of subtoken sequences added to the tokenizer (η fixed at $10K$) may also be worthwhile. While Tai et al. (2020) found $12K$ tokens additions optimal, Poerner et al. (2020) added $310K$ tokens. Seeing the trade-off between added tokens and performance would be useful, as each additional parameter increases the model size.

Our approach requires new tokens to appear ϕ times in both the source and domain corpora. While this was necessary in order to produce source-corpus word embeddings in Proj, it does not allow for domain-exclusive subtoken sequences to be added to the tokenizer. Abandoning this requirement for Mean may lead to a better set of token augmentations.

We can also experiment with other subtoken candidate selection techniques. For example, Schwartz et al. (2013) used pointwise mutual information (PMI) to determine how phrase-like candidates word sequences were. PMI is the log ratio of the probability of a phrase vs. the product of the probability of its component unigrams. While our approach considers the probability of a subtoken given a preceding sequence, it, unlike PMI, does not consider the probability of that following subtoken in isolation. This may lead to domain-specific subtokens sneaking into augmented token sequences, such as the contraction tokens added to the reviews Reviews tokenizer in Table 4.

5.4 Implementation details

The code is in preparation for release. The hyperparameter search used was ROBERTA_CLASSIFIER_MINI from Gururangan et al. (2020) from their codebase `https://github.com/allenai/dont-stop-pretraining`. Token counts for RoBERTa-base were estimated using English Wikipedia 20200501.en and an open source book corpus from `https://storage.googleapis.com/huggingface-nlp/datasets/bookcorpus/bookcorpus.tar.bz2`. Word2vec embeddings were computed with Gensim (Rehurek and Sojka, 2011), using the following parameters: `Word2Vec(..., size=768, window=5, min_count=100, epochs=2, sample=1e-5)`

6 Conclusion

In this paper, we introduced adaptive tokenization (AT) a method for efficiently adapting pretrained language models utilizing subword tokenization to new domains. AT augments a PLM's tokenization vocabulary to include domain-specific token sequences. We provide two approaches for initializing augmented tokens: mean subword and projections from static subword embeddings. AT requires no further language model pretraining on domain-specific corpora, resulting in a 38x speedup over pretraining on the corpora without specialized hardware. Across four domains, AT provides >97% of the performance improvement of further pretraining on domain-specific data over Roberta-base. This initial work suggests that adapting the subword tokenization scheme of PLMs is an effective means of transferring models to new domains. Future work entails hybrid approaches using both AT and small amounts of LM pretraining, alternative metrics for augmented token selection, improved initialization of augmented token representations, and the use of task data.

Acknowledgements

We thank Yi Zhang, William Headden, Max Harper, Chandni Singh, Anuj Ahluwalia, Sushant Sagar, Jay Patel, Sachin Hulyalkar, and the anonymous reviewers for their valuable feedback.

Ethics statement

As mentioned in §5, pretrained language models incur significant costs with respect to time, computational resources and environmental impact. Continued domain specific pretraining, which has a similar resource budget to BERT, exacerbates this problem Schwartz et al. (2019). In this work, we provide approaches for adapting pretrained language models to new domains with an approach, Adaptive Tokenization, which seeks to minimize costs associated with continued domain specific pretraining. It should be noted that we do not decrease the resource and environmental associated with pretraining, only the costs for domain adaptive pretraining which are nevertheless sizable (e.g. 32 TPU days for DAPT).

Additionally, we find that the cloud computing costs associated with continued domain specific pretraining on a single domain and set of hyperparameters are around $750 compared to around $5 for AT on a cloud computing platform. High costs associated with the training of NLP models has led to inequity in the research community in favor of industry labs with large research budgets Strubell et al. (2019), a problem we seek to ameliorate.

This work does not address the high resource cost in fine-tuning PLMs. Risks associated with this paper are that this work may encourage the use of PLMs in more settings, such as domains with small amounts of data, and introduce potentially harmful inductive biases which have been found in many commonly used PLMs.

We include statistics about the data sets used in Table 1, these data sets were introduced in Gururangan et al. (2020) and open source.

References

Emily Alsentzer, John Murphy, William Boag, Wei-Hung Weng, Di Jindi, Tristan Naumann, and Matthew McDermott. 2019. Publicly available clinical BERT embeddings. In *Proceedings of the 2nd Clinical Natural Language Processing Workshop*, pages 72–78, Minneapolis, Minnesota, USA. Association for Computational Linguistics.

Iz Beltagy, Kyle Lo, and Arman Cohan. 2019. SciBERT: A pretrained language model for scientific text. In *Proceedings of the 2019 Conference on Empirical Methods in Natural Language Processing and the 9th International Joint Conference on Natural Language Processing (EMNLP-IJCNLP)*, pages 3615–3620, Hong Kong, China. Association for Computational Linguistics.

Iz Beltagy, Matthew E. Peters, and Arman Cohan. 2020. Longformer: The long-document transformer. *arXiv:2004.05150*.

Tom B. Brown, Benjamin Mann, Nick Ryder, Melanie Subbiah, Jared Kaplan, Prafulla Dhariwal, Arvind Neelakantan, Pranav Shyam, Girish Sastry, Amanda Askell, Sandhini Agarwal, Ariel Herbert-Voss, Gretchen Krueger, Tom Henighan, Rewon Child, Aditya Ramesh, Daniel M. Ziegler, Jeffrey Wu, Clemens Winter, Christopher Hesse, Mark Chen, Eric Sigler, Mateusz Litwin, Scott Gray, Benjamin Chess, Jack Clark, Christopher Berner, Sam McCandlish, Alec Radford, Ilya Sutskever, and Dario Amodei. 2020. Language models are few-shot learners.

Iñigo Casanueva, Tadas Temčinas, Daniela Gerz, Matthew Henderson, and Ivan Vulić. 2020. Efficient intent detection with dual sentence encoders. In *Proceedings of the 2nd Workshop on Natural Language Processing for Conversational AI*, pages 38–45, Online. Association for Computational Linguistics.

Tuhin Chakrabarty, Christopher Hidey, and Kathy McKeown. 2019. IMHO fine-tuning improves claim detection. In *Proceedings of the 2019 Conference of the North American Chapter of the Association for Computational Linguistics: Human Language Technologies, Volume 1 (Long and Short Papers)*, pages 558–563, Minneapolis, Minnesota. Association for Computational Linguistics.

Kevin Clark, Minh-Thang Luong, Quoc V. Le, and Christopher D. Manning. 2020. ELECTRA: Pre-training text encoders as discriminators rather than generators. In *ICLR*.

Arman Cohan, Iz Beltagy, Daniel King, Bhavana Dalvi, and Dan Weld. 2019. Pretrained language models for sequential sentence classification. In *EMNLP*.

Franck Dernoncourt and Ji Young Lee. 2017. PubMed 200k RCT: a dataset for sequential sentence classification in medical abstracts. In *Proceedings of the Eighth International Joint Conference on Natural Language Processing (Volume 2: Short Papers)*, pages 308–313, Taipei, Taiwan. Asian Federation of Natural Language Processing.

Jacob Devlin, Ming-Wei Chang, Kenton Lee, and Kristina Toutanova. 2019. BERT: Pre-training of deep bidirectional transformers for language understanding. In *Proceedings of the 2019 Conference of the North American Chapter of the Association for Computational Linguistics: Human Language Technologies, Volume 1 (Long and Short Papers)*, pages 4171–4186, Minneapolis, Minnesota. Association for Computational Linguistics.

Yu Gu, Robert Tinn, Hao Cheng, Michael Lucas, Naoto Usuyama, Xiaodong Liu, Tristan Naumann, Jianfeng Gao, and Hoifung Poon. 2020. Domain-specific language model pretraining for biomedical natural language processing.

Suchin Gururangan, Ana Marasović, Swabha Swayamdipta, Kyle Lo, Iz Beltagy, Doug Downey, and Noah A. Smith. 2020. Don't stop pretraining: Adapt language models to domains and tasks. In *Proceedings of the 58th Annual Meeting of the Association for Computational Linguistics*, pages 8342–8360, Online. Association for Computational Linguistics.

Ruining He and Julian McAuley. 2016. Ups and downs: Modeling the visual evolution of fashion trends with one-class collaborative filtering. In *Proceedings of the 25th International Conference on World Wide Web*, WWW '16, page 507–517, Republic and Canton of Geneva, CHE. International World Wide Web Conferences Steering Committee.

Valentin Hofmann, Janet Pierrehumbert, and Hinrich Schütze. 2020. DagoBERT: Generating derivational morphology with a pretrained language model. In *Proceedings of the 2020 Conference on Empirical Methods in Natural Language Processing (EMNLP)*, pages 3848–3861, Online. Association for Computational Linguistics.

Valentin Hofmann, Janet B. Pierrehumbert, and Hinrich Schütze. 2021. Superbizarre is not superb: Improving bert's interpretations of complex words with derivational morphology.

Kexin Huang, Jaan Altosaar, and Rajesh Ranganath. 2019. Clinicalbert: Modeling clinical notes and predicting hospital readmission. *arXiv:1904.05342*.

David Jurgens, Srijan Kumar, Raine Hoover, Dan McFarland, and Dan Jurafsky. 2018. Measuring the evolution of a scientific field through citation frames. *Transactions of the Association for Computational Linguistics*, 6:391–406.

Jason Kessler. 2017. Scattertext: a browser-based tool for visualizing how corpora differ. In *Proceedings of ACL 2017, System Demonstrations*, pages 85–90, Vancouver, Canada. Association for Computational Linguistics.

Johannes Kiesel, Maria Mestre, Rishabh Shukla, Emmanuel Vincent, Payam Adineh, David Corney, Benno Stein, and Martin Potthast. 2019. SemEval-2019 task 4: Hyperpartisan news detection. In *Proceedings of the 13th International Workshop on Semantic Evaluation*, pages 829–839, Minneapolis, Minnesota, USA. Association for Computational Linguistics.

Jens Kringelum, Sonny Kim Kjaerulff, Søren Brunak, Ole Lund, Tudor I. Oprea, and Olivier Taboureau. 2016. ChemProt-3.0: a global chemical biology diseases mapping. *Database*, 2016. Bav123.

Jinhyuk Lee, Wonjin Yoon, Sungdong Kim, Donghyeon Kim, Sunkyu Kim, Chan Ho So, and Jaewoo Kang. 2019. BioBERT: a pre-trained biomedical language representation model for biomedical text mining. *Bioinformatics*, 36(4):1234–1240.

Yinhan Liu, Myle Ott, Naman Goyal, Jingfei Du, Mandar Joshi, Danqi Chen, Omer Levy, Mike Lewis, Luke Zettlemoyer, and Veselin Stoyanov. 2019. Roberta: A robustly optimized BERT pretraining approach. *CoRR*, abs/1907.11692.

Kyle Lo, Lucy Lu Wang, Mark Neumann, Rodney Kinney, and Daniel Weld. 2020. S2ORC: The semantic scholar open research corpus. In *Proceedings of the 58th Annual Meeting of the Association for Computational Linguistics*, pages 4969–4983, Online. Association for Computational Linguistics.

Yi Luan, Luheng He, Mari Ostendorf, and Hannaneh Hajishirzi. 2018. Multi-task identification of entities, relations, and coreference for scientific knowledge graph construction. In *Proceedings of the 2018 Conference on Empirical Methods in Natural Language Processing*, pages 3219–3232, Brussels, Belgium. Association for Computational Linguistics.

Andrew L. Maas, Raymond E. Daly, Peter T. Pham, Dan Huang, Andrew Y. Ng, and Christopher Potts. 2011. Learning word vectors for sentiment analysis. In *Proceedings of the 49th Annual Meeting of the Association for Computational Linguistics: Human Language Technologies*, pages 142–150, Portland, Oregon, USA. Association for Computational Linguistics.

B. L. Monroe, Michael Colaresi, and K. Quinn. 2008. Fightin' words: Lexical feature selection and evaluation for identifying the content of political conflict. *Political Analysis*, 16:372–403.

Pradeep Muthukrishnan, Joshua Gerrish, and Dragomir R. Radev. 2008. Detecting multiple facets of an event using graph-based unsupervised methods. In *Proceedings of the 22nd International Conference on Computational Linguistics (Coling 2008)*, pages 609–616, Manchester, UK. Coling 2008 Organizing Committee.

Nina Poerner, Ulli Waltinger, and Hinrich Schütze. 2020. Inexpensive domain adaptation of pretrained language models: Case studies on biomedical NER and covid-19 QA. In *Findings of the Association for Computational Linguistics: EMNLP 2020*, pages 1482–1490, Online. Association for Computational Linguistics.

Paul Rayson, G. Leech, and Mary Hodges. 1997. Social differentiation in the use of english vocabulary: some analyses of the conversational component of the british national corpus. *International Journal of Corpus Linguistics*, 2:133–152.

Radim Rehurek and Petr Sojka. 2011. Gensim–python framework for vector space modelling. *NLP Centre, Faculty of Informatics, Masaryk University, Brno, Czech Republic*, 3(2).

Alexander Rietzler, Sebastian Stabinger, Paul Opitz, and Stefan Engl. 2020. Adapt or get left behind: Domain adaptation through BERT language model finetuning for aspect-target sentiment classification. In *Proceedings of the 12th Language Resources and Evaluation Conference*, pages 4933–4941, Marseille, France. European Language Resources Association.

Mike Schuster and Kaisuke Nakajima. 2012. Japanese and korean voice search. In *International Conference on Acoustics, Speech and Signal Processing*, pages 5149–5152.

H. Andrew Schwartz, Johannes C. Eichstaedt, Margaret L. Kern, Lukasz Dziurzynski, Stephanie M. Ramones, Megha Agrawal, Achal Shah, Michal Kosinski, David Stillwell, Martin E. P. Seligman, and Lyle H. Ungar. 2013. Personality, gender, and age in the language of social media: The open-vocabulary approach. *PLOS ONE*, 8(9):1–16.

Roy Schwartz, Jesse Dodge, Noah A. Smith, and Oren Etzioni. 2019. Green AI. *CoRR*, abs/1907.10597.

Rico Sennrich, Barry Haddow, and Alexandra Birch. 2016. Neural machine translation of rare words with subword units. In *Proceedings of the 54th Annual Meeting of the Association for Computational Linguistics (Volume 1: Long Papers)*, pages 1715–1725, Berlin, Germany. Association for Computational Linguistics.

Emma Strubell, Ananya Ganesh, and Andrew McCallum. 2019. Energy and policy considerations for deep learning in NLP. In *Proceedings of the 57th Annual Meeting of the Association for Computational Linguistics*, pages 3645–3650, Florence, Italy. Association for Computational Linguistics.

Wen Tai, H. T. Kung, Xin Dong, Marcus Comiter, and Chang-Fu Kuo. 2020. exBERT: Extending pre-trained models with domain-specific vocabulary under constrained training resources. In *Findings of the Association for Computational Linguistics: EMNLP 2020*, pages 1433–1439, Online. Association for Computational Linguistics.

Ivan Vulić, E. Ponti, Robert Litschko, Goran Glavas, and Anna Korhonen. 2020. Probing pretrained language models for lexical semantics. *ArXiv*, abs/2010.05731.

Yonghui Wu, Mike Schuster, Zhifeng Chen, Quoc V. Le, Mohammad Norouzi, Wolfgang Macherey, Maxim Krikun, Yuan Cao, Qin Gao, Klaus Macherey, Jeff Klingner, Apurva Shah, Melvin Johnson, Xiaobing Liu, Lukasz Kaiser, Stephan Gouws, Yoshikiyo Kato, Taku Kudo, Hideto Kazawa, Keith Stevens, George Kurian, Nishant Patil, Wei Wang, Cliff Young, Jason Smith, Jason Riesa, Alex Rudnick, Oriol Vinyals, Greg Corrado, Macduff Hughes, and Jeffrey Dean. 2016. Google's neural machine translation system: Bridging the gap between human and machine translation. *CoRR*, abs/1609.08144.

Zhilin Yang, Zihang Dai, Yiming Yang, Jaime G. Carbonell, Ruslan Salakhutdinov, and Quoc V. Le. 2019. Xlnet: Generalized autoregressive pretraining for language understanding. *CoRR*, abs/1906.08237.

Rowan Zellers, Ari Holtzman, Hannah Rashkin, Yonatan Bisk, Ali Farhadi, Franziska Roesner, and Yejin Choi. 2019. Defending against neural fake news. *CoRR*, abs/1905.12616.

Rong Zhang, Revanth Gangi Reddy, Md Arafat Sultan, Vittorio Castelli, Anthony Ferritto, Radu Florian, Efsun Sarioglu Kayi, Salim Roukos, Avi Sil, and Todd Ward. 2020. Multi-stage pre-training for low-resource domain adaptation. In *Proceedings of the 2020 Conference on Empirical Methods in Natural Language Processing (EMNLP)*, pages 5461–5468, Online. Association for Computational Linguistics.

Unsupervised Contextualized Document Representation

Ankur Gupta
Indian Institute of Technology, Kanpur
ankugupt@iitk.ac.in

Vivek Gupta
School of Computing, University of Utah
vgupta@cs.utah.edu

Abstract

Several NLP tasks need the effective representation of text documents. Arora et al., 2017 demonstrate that simple weighted averaging of word vectors frequently outperforms neural models. SCDV (Mekala et al., 2017) further extends this from sentences to documents by employing soft and sparse clustering over pre-computed word vectors. However, both techniques ignore the polysemy and contextual character of words. In this paper, we address this issue by proposing SCDV+BERT(ctxd), a simple and effective unsupervised representation that combines contextualized BERT (Devlin et al., 2019) based word embedding for word sense disambiguation with SCDV soft clustering approach. We show that our embeddings outperform original SCDV, pre-train BERT, and several other baselines on many classification datasets. We also demonstrate our embeddings effectiveness on other tasks, such as concept matching and sentence similarity. In addition, we show that SCDV+BERT(ctxd) outperforms fine-tune BERT and different embedding approaches in scenarios with limited data and only few shots examples.

1 Introduction

The semantics of a document is highly dependent on the constituent words, and words can have different meaning in different contexts. Approaches such as Socher et al., 2013; Liu et al., 2015a; Le and Mikolov, 2014; Ling et al., 2015 go beyond words to capture the semantic meaning of sentences but are restricted to perceiving the meaning of a single sentence, thus reducing its expressive power.

A simple weighted average of the individual word embeddings doesn't account for word ordering and long-distance semantic relationships. Gupta et al., 2016; Mekala et al., 2017 proposed clustering-based technique with tf-idf weighting to form sparse composite document vector, thus extending the simple averaging approach beyond a single sentence. Recently, Gupta et al., 2020a introduced SCDV-MS, which highlights how multi-sense word embedding resolves cluster disambiguation, which improves embedding performance, further enhancing SCDV. Gupta et al., 2020b (PSIF) additionally demonstrates that a sparsity constraint in clustering can be advantageous.

Modern contextualized representations such as BERT (Devlin et al., 2019) can capture the exact meaning of a word based on the surrounding context, which can automatically disambiguate the meaning of words in a corpus-based on its interpretations. Previous approaches for document representation, as discussed above, ignore these contextualized representation benefits. Therefore, in this work, we propose a new approach (SCDV+BERT(ctxd), which leverages a combination of clustering techniques for word-sense disambiguation and combines it with the expressibility of SCDV partition averaging method for creating better document representation. We contextualized the corpus by using the word sense disambiguation power contextualized pre-train BERT embedding. Contextual embedding from pre-train BERT disambiguate the occurrence of the same word with different context (meaning). We then use the SCDV partition averaging algorithm to convert this contextualized corpus into document embeddings using contextual pre-train BERT word embeddings as static word vectors.

We show that our unsupervised embeddings SCDV+BERT(ctxd) outperform existing techniques on several classification datasets in supervised, semi-supervised, and few-shot settings. We also demonstrate performance improvement in non-classification tasks such as concept matching and sentence similarity using our representation. The datasets along with the associated scripts, can be located at `https://github.com/vgupta123/contextualize_scdv`.

Proceedings of the 2nd Workshop on Simple and Efficient Natural Language Processing, pages 166–173
November 10, 2021. ©201 Association for Computational Linguistics

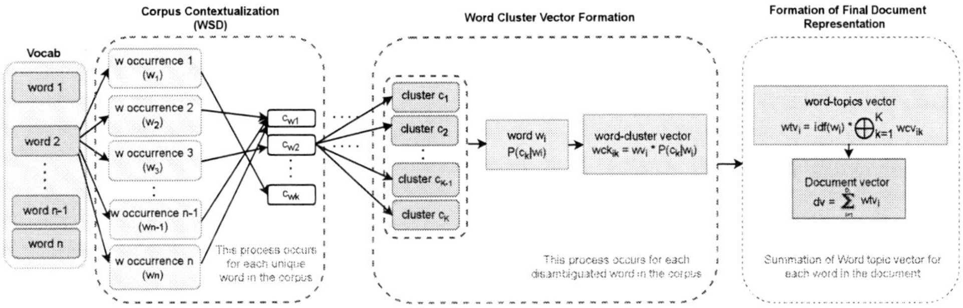

Figure 1: High level flowchart of our document representation approach a.k.a SCDV + BERT(cxtd)

2 Proposed Algorithm

Our algorithm is similar to SCDV algorithm, but uses word sense disambiguated contextualize word vectors obtained from pre-trained BERT Embedding as static word vectors. Below are details of the primary steps involved.

Corpus Contextualization (WSD): Our objective here is to disambiguate different occurrences of a word in a corpus document with its separate interpretation. For example, the word *'bank'* in *"He went to 'bank' for withdrawing money"* and *"I went to a river 'bank' during summer holiday"* has different meanings based on it's used context. Given a word w and all its occurrence in the corpus documents as w_1, w_2, ... , w_n, for each w_i , we find its contextualized embedding representation b_{w_i} using transformer based pre-trained language model such as BERT (Devlin et al., 2019).

Taking inspiration from Mekala et al., 2020, we treat the word disambiguation problem as a local clustering problem of contextualizing word vectors. For our case, we also cluster the contextualize word embedding b_{w_i}, obtained via the pre-train BERT model from the last step. We use the efficient K-means algorithm to cluster all b_{w_i} into k clusters, where k represents the total possible interpretations of word w in all the documents of the corpus.[1] We use the cosine distance between the contextualize word representation as our clustering metric. [2] The value of k i.e., cluster numbers, is decided using a similarity threshold (τ), which is a hyperparameter and a dataset property, usually set using the heuristic described in (Mekala et al., 2020).

Let $c_{w_1}, c_{w_2}, \ldots, c_{w_k}$ be the k cluster centroids obtained after the K-means clustering for the word w. We treat these k centroid representation as our polysemous word representations highlighting the k sense of the words w. After clustering for each occurrence of word w in a corpus, we perform contextualised word sense disambiguation using cosine similarity between it's BERT representation and our centroid embedding i.e. $c_{w_1}, c_{w_2}, \ldots, c_{w_k}$ to discover the closest cluster centroid j a.k.a nearest neighbour (j), the word sense for that occurrence.

Finally, we assign this nearest neighbor cluster centroids embedding c_{w_j} as the contextualized disambiguated word embedding for that word w occurrence. We repeat this procedure for all the occurrences of word w to obtain final sense disambiguated contextualized word embedding. Each of these contextualized embeddings of word w now act as our distant sense-disambiguated word vectors.

Document Representation (SCDV): Similar to the SCDV, we use Gaussian Mixture Model to cluster our final sense-disambiguated word vectors (obtain from earlier step) into K partition of the words in the corpus.[3] For each contextualized word vector w_i of word $w \in V$, we created K different word-cluster vectors of d dimensions ($\vec{wcv}_{io}$) by weighting word's embedding with sparse probability distribution for the oth cluster, i.e., P($c_o|w_i$). Then, we concatenate the K word-cluster vectors ($\vec{wcv}_{io}$) and weight them with their inverse document frequency (idf(w_i)) to form a contextualized word-topic vector ($\vec{wtv}_i$). The dimension of word-topic vector ($\vec{wtv}_i$) is $K \times d$. To obtain the final document embedding $\vec{dv}_{D_n}$, we computed the average of the contextualized word-topic vectors $\vec{wtv}_i$ from the words and it's context as appearing in that document D_n. For more details on SCDV, refer to Algorithm 1 in Mekala et al., 2017.

Figure 1 shows flowchart for our document em-

[1]K-means is computationally more efficient than other clustering approaches. Any other suitable clustering algorithm also works.

[2]L2 on normalized vectors is same as the cosine distance.

[3]Note this capital K is very different from the small k use in the word sense disambiguation. The value of K depend of number of distinct high-level concepts covered in the corpus.

Embedding	Amazon	BBCSport	Twitter	Classic	Recipe-L	20NG
SIF(Glove)	$94.1_{(0.2)}$	$97.3_{(1.2)}$	$57.8_{(2.5)}$	$92.7_{(0.9)}$	$71.1_{(0.5)}$	$72.3_{(0.11)}$
PV-DM	$88.6_{(0.4)}$	$97.9_{(1.3)}$	$67.3_{(0.3)}$	$96.5_{(0.7)}$	$71.1_{(0.4)}$	$74.0_{(0.11)}$
Doc2VecC	$91.2_{(0.5)}$	$90.5_{(1.7)}$	$71.0_{(0.4)}$	$96.6_{(0.4)}$	$76.1_{(0.4)}$	$78.2_{(0.11)}$
Word2Vec (idf-weighted)	$94.00_{(0.45)}$	$97.30_{(0.67)}$	$72.00_{(0.36)}$	$95.20_{(0.44)}$	$74.90_{(0.89)}$	$81.70_{(0.22)}$
BERT(pr)	$91.04_{(0.27)}$	$99.12_{(0.66)}$	$66.63_{(0.22)}$	$95.63_{(0.36)}$	$68.44_{(0.07)}$	$64.81_{(0.17)}$
SCDV + Word2Vec	$93.90_{(0.40)}$	$98.81_{(0.60)}$	$74.20_{(0.40)}$	$96.90_{(0.10)}$	$78.50_{(0.50)}$	$84.90_{(0.13)}$
SCDV + BERT(weight-avg)	$94.62_{(0.21)}$	$97.29_{(0.56)}$	$72.98_{(0.24)}$	$96.54_{(0.61)}$	$78.13_{(0.15)}$	$84.90_{(0.13)}$
SCDV + BERT(ctxd)	$94.16_{(0.31)}$	$99.58_{(0.41)}$	$75.98_{(0.36)}$	$97.84_{(0.40)}$	$80.71_{(0.19)}$	$86.12_{(0.11)}$
SCDV + BERT(ctxd) + Anisotropy	$\mathbf{95.88}_{(0.34)}$	$\mathbf{99.60}_{(0.59)}$	$\mathbf{77.03}_{(0.27)}$	$\mathbf{99.01}_{(0.41)}$	$80.74_{(0.15)}$	$\mathbf{86.94}_{(0.11)}$
BERT (fine-tune)	$94.60_{(0.19)}$	$\mathbf{99.67}_{(0.51)}$	$73.13_{(0.31)}$	$\mathbf{98.67}_{(0.56)}$	$\mathbf{81.13}_{(0.21)}$	$\mathbf{86.91}_{(0.28)}$

Table 1: Embedding performance with complete training i.e. full data setting. Bold represents best performance. Reported number are means performance and subscript brackets number x $_{(x)}$ represent the standard deviation over 5 random runs. Baselines are taken from Gupta et al., 2020b. We use $k = 6$ for the ainsotropic adjustment.

bedding approach (SCDV+BERT(cxtd)).

3 Experimental Results

We perform experiments with multi-class classification with data restriction settings, concept matching problem and sentence similarity task.

Datasets and Baselines: We experimented on 6 classification dataset whose statistics are shown in 4. We also validated our algorithm through the Concept Matching experiment on Concept-Project (Gong et al., 2018) dataset, where the task was to generate concepts from a given document corpus. We also perform experiments on the SemEval dataset (Y12 - Y16) involving 27 semantic textual similarity (STS) tasks from 2012 - 2016 (Agirre et al., 2012). We represent our model as SCDV + BERT(ctxd), which is SCDV using multi sense-disambiguated contextual BERT word vector for document representation. We consider the following baselines for comparison: SCDV with single sense Word2Vec (Mikolov et al., 2013), BERT(pr) (Devlin et al., 2019) i.e. pre-trained BERT vectors averaging, BERT (fine-tune)(Sun et al., 2019) i.e. fine-tune BERT model, and Word2Vec (tfidf-weighted) i.e. a tf-idf weighted Word2Vec average. We also compare SCDV + BERT(ctxd) with an ablation representation obtain without corpus contextualization a.k.a, sense-disambiguation i.e. the value of WSD clustering parameter $k = 1$ for all the words in the corpus. We referred this ablation representation as SCDV + BERT(weight-avg) in the paper. [4] Furthermore, we also adopted the work of Ethayarajh, 2019 which adjust Anisotropy (more uniformity) with our embeddings. We refer this representation as SCDV + BERT(ctxd) + Anisotropy. We followed Ethayarajh, 2019 recommendation and used BERT last layer for pre-train word embeddings.

Full Data Setting: Table 1 shows a comparison of accuracy across all the datasets. We observe that SCDV + BERT(ctxd) model outperforms the original SCDV+Word2Vec across all the datasets. To ablate the contribution of sense-disambiguation using BERT contextualization, we also compare SCDV + BERT(ctxd) result with SCDV + BERT(weight-avg). We also analyze the effect of reducing Anisotropy on SCDV + BERT(ctxd).[5]

Analysis: Contextualized BERT (SCDV + BERT(ctxd)) performs better than the average BERT (SCDV + BERT(weight-avg)), which in turn performs competitively with original SCDV + Word2Vec. This indicates that the sense-disambiguated BERT based word vectors captures multiple meaning of word (better corpus contextualization) effectively. [6]. Furthermore, reducing Anisotropy i.e. SCDV + BERT(ctxd) + Anisotropy, further boosts the performance of SCDV + BERT(ctxd). As expected, the BERT (fine-tune) performs the best on most datasets (except for Twitter and Amazon), where all versions of SCDV perform much better than pre-train BERT averaging i.e. BERT(pr). The good performance of BERT (fine-tune) is expected as fine-tuning modifies the model parameter (layer weights), producing task and domain-specific embedding, often impressed in the *[CLS]* token representation. Note that SCDV + BERT(ctxd)+ Anisotropy are unsupervised embedding but had accuracy competitive (sometimes even better) to the supervised fine-tuned BERT models i.e. BERT (fine-tune). Thus, our approach could be

[4]Model hyperparameters are provided in appendix §A.

[5]For top 1000 words, the cosine similarity reduces from 0.5468 to 0.3752 after anisotropic adjustment.

[6]Similar observation made by Gupta et al. 2020a (SCDV-MS), an extension for SCDV with multi-sense word2Vec.

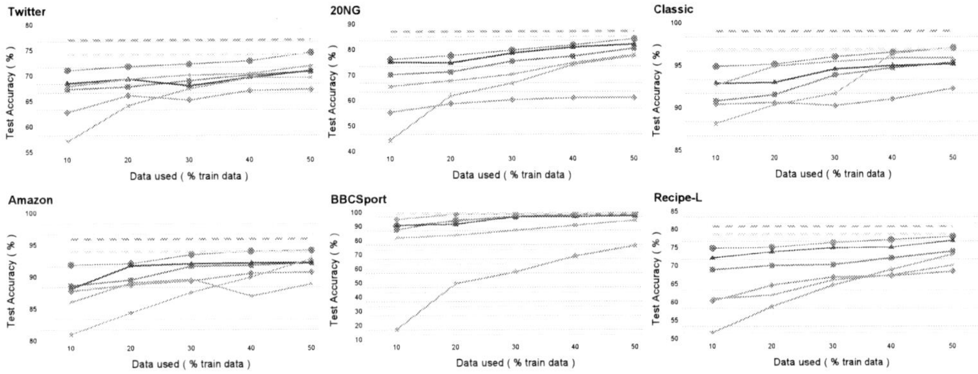

● SCDV+BERT(ctxd) + Anisotropy ■ SCDV+word2vec ▲ SCDV+BERT(weight-avg) ◆ BERT(pr) ★ BERT (finetune) × word2vec (idf-weight) — SCDV+BERT(ctxd) + Anisotropy (with 100% data) — SCDV+word2vec (with 100% data)

Figure 2: Embedding performance with limited training data i.e. semi-supervised setting. Standard deviation avg: 0.28 with range (0.03,0.81).

used as an effective alternative to fine-tuning BERT for selected classification tasks.

Limited Data Setting: BERT has produced state-of-the-art results in various NLP domains, but its use is restricted to the availability of labeled data, whereas with the help of pre-trained BERT and SCDV, our approach can also work with limited data i.e. semi-supervised setting, requiring only sufficient enough labeled data to learn the downstream classifier. To test the effectiveness of our approach in low-data conditions, we ran the same multi-class classification experiment with 10%, 20%, 30%, 40%, and 50% of the training data. See Figure 2 for the results.

Analysis: Contrast to earlier fully supervised settings, we observe that BERT (fine-tune) performed worst (except for Twitter data) due to limited training data. BERT (fine-tune) have a significant mean performance drop of greater than 33.5% across datasets with limited data training of 10% data compare to full training with 100% data. Whereas, the performance of SCDV + BERT(ctxd) (and it's Anisotropic version i.e., SCDV + BERT(ctxd) + Anisotropic) remained comparable with the full data (i.e., 100% data) setting, with the mean performance drop of just $\approx 7.2\%$ across datasets with the 10% data. [7] It also outperformed original SCDV + Word2Vec and SCDV+BERT(weighted-avg) on all datasets. [8] Under low data conditions, SCDV+BERT(weight-avg) also outperformed the original SCDV + Word2Vec due to added contextualization benefits of the pre-trained BERT word vector representation. Moreover, under significantly less data (10% or 20% data), even BERT(pr) and Word2Vec (tdf-idf weighted) performed significantly better than the BERT(fine-tune). Furthermore, we find that our method outperforms SCDV with complete training on a range of datasets while only employing limited 40% to 50% data. Overall, our unsupervised method significantly outperforms fine-tune BERT in the low data domain. We predict that fine-tuning BERT with little supervision is exceedingly difficult due to the needed learning of large-parameter space.

Few-Shot Setting: We also experimented under few-shot conditions where the available data is too low for even training a classification (and obviously for BERT fine-tuning i.e. BERT(fine-tune) too). We implemented a K-shot N-way prototypical few-shot classifier where K is the number of samples used from each class and N is the number of classes in the dataset. We set the K values from 5, 10, 15, and 20 for our setting, and N is equal to numbers of class labels (see Appendix §A). New examples are assigned the label using the nearest neighbor approach (KNN algorithm with K = 1), i.e., the label of closest averaged prototypical class point.

Analysis: We see in Figure 3 that SCDV + BERT(ctxd) and SCDV+BERT(weight-avg) outperform all other methods by a significant margin (> 11% mean across datasets). SCDV+BERT(ctxd) for most of the time marginally leads SCDV+BERT(weighted-avg), showing that contextualization also helps in the few shots settings. In contrast to earlier results adjusting anisotropy over SCDV + BERT(ctxd) only improve performance marginally.

[7] For some dataset such as BBCSport the performance drop was also < 1%.

[8] Except the BBCSport, where pre-trained BERT embeddings, i.e., BERT(pr), produced comparable results due to fewer polysemous words as evident from Appendix §A Table 1.

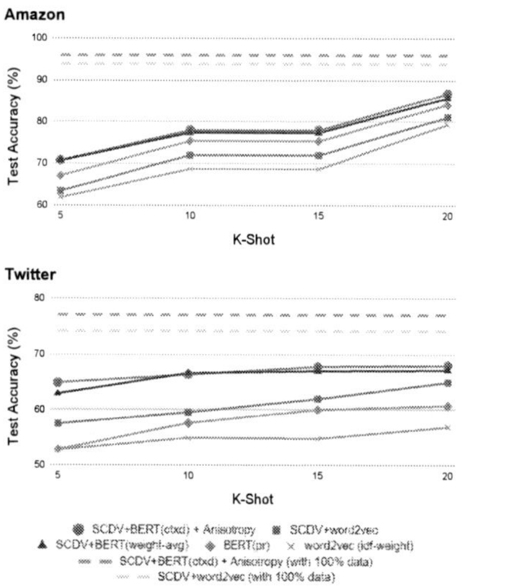

Figure 3: Results for the few-shot experiment. Reported number are mean of 5 random runs with having standard deviation average: 0.14 with range of (0.09, 0.43)

Concept Matching: The task is to link the concept with the relevant projects. Concept Matching dataset includes 537 pairs of projects and concepts involving 53 unique concepts from the Next Generation Science Standards3 (NGSS) and 230 unique projects from Science Buddies. We compare cosine similarity between our method with the TF-IDF-weighted vectors, SCDV + Word2Vec, InferSent (Conneau et al., 2017) and pre-trained BERT(pr) baselines. From table 2, we observed that our algorithm (SCDV + BERT(ctxd) + Anisotropy) outperformed pre-trained BERT and SCDV + Word2Vec by 5.2% and 4.6% on F1 and accuracy respectively on the Concept-Project (Gong et al., 2018) dataset.

Embedding	Accuracy	F1
TF-IDF	53.8	70.0
InferSent	54.0	70.1
BERT(pr)	$54.8_{(0.2)}$	$70.6_{(0.3)}$
SCDV + Word2Vec	$53.7_{(0.1)}$	$70.0_{(0.1)}$
SCDV + BERT(ctxd)	$57.1_{(0.2)}$	$73.8_{(0.2)}$
SCDV + BERT(ctxd) + Anisotropy	**58.9**$_{(0.1)}$	**74.6**$_{(0.1)}$

Table 2: Embedding performance on Concept-Marching dataset. Bold represents best performance. Baselines are taken from Zhang and Danescu-Niculescu-Mizil, 2020.

Sentence Similarity Task: The objectives of these tasks are to predict the similarity between two sentences. Performance is assessed by computing the Pearson correlation (Freedman et al., 2007) between machine-assigned semantic similarity scores and ground truth. SCDV + BERT(ctxd) + Anisotropy substantially outperform several other baselines as demonstrated in the table 3.

Embedding	Y12	Y13	Y14	Y15	Y16	Avg.
ELMO orig+all	55	51	63	69	64	60.4
ELMO orig+top	54	49	62	67	63	59
BERT(pr) Avg.	53	67	62	73	67	64.4
USE	65	**68**	64	77	73	69.4
p-mean	54	52	63	66	67	60.4
fastText	58	58	65	68	64	62.6
Skip Thoughts	41	29	40	46	52	41.6
InferSent	61	56	68	71	77	66.6
PSIF + PSL	65.7	64.0	74.8	77.3	73.7	71.1
u-SIF + PSL	65.8	65.2	75.9	77.6	72.3	71.4
SCDV + WordVec	64.1	63.9	73.0	76.9	**77.3**	71.0
SCDV + BERT(ctxd)	64.7	**64.0**	75.4	77.1	73.3	70.9
SCDV + BERT(ctxd) + Anisotropy	**66.8**	64.1	**77.3**	**78.0**	74.6	**72.2**

Table 3: Embedding performance on Semantic Textual Similarity task (STS) with several embeddings for each year with overall average (avg.). Bold represent best performance. Baselines are taken from Gupta et al., 2020b.

4 Comparison with Related Works

The closest work to our paper is SCDV by Mekala et al., 2017 that extend BoWV by Gupta et al., 2016 using an overlapping clustering technique and direct idf weighting of word vectors. Recently Gupta et al., 2020a extended SCDV to SCDV-MS via utilising the multi-sense embeddings obtained via using AdaGram (Bartunov et al., 2016) over Word-Vectors (Mikolov et al., 2013). Our idea is similar to SCDV-MS; however, it utilises pre-train BERT contextual embedding as word embedding, a.k.a a more robust sense disambiguated aware embedding (Mekala et al., 2020). Thus, our approach (SCDV + BERT(ctxd)) uses contextual word vectors as the foundational block for document representation.

5 Conclusion and Future Work

In this paper, we enhance sparse document representation (SCDV) with pre-trained BERT contextualization and propose SCDV+BERT(ctxd). We showed that one could effectively utilize the BERT contextualization for word-sense disambiguation. Our approach outperforms other unsupervised approaches in the full data regime. Our approach is also very successful for low data regime, outperforming the standard model with roughly half the training data required and few shot settings, where fine-tuning of model fails.

6 Acknowledgement

We appreciate the Utah NLP group members' valuable suggestions at various phases of the project, as well as the reviewers' helpful remarks.

References

Eneko Agirre, Daniel Cer, Mona Diab, and Aitor Gonzalez-Agirre. 2012. SemEval-2012 task 6: A pilot on semantic textual similarity. In **SEM 2012: The First Joint Conference on Lexical and Computational Semantics – Volume 1: Proceedings of the main conference and the shared task, and Volume 2: Proceedings of the Sixth International Workshop on Semantic Evaluation (SemEval 2012)*, pages 385–393, Montréal, Canada. Association for Computational Linguistics.

Sanjeev Arora, Yingyu Liang, and Tengyu Ma. 2017. A simple but tough-to-beat baseline for sentence embeddings. In *International Conference on Learning Representations, ICLR 2017*.

Sergey Bartunov, Dmitry Kondrashkin, Anton Osokin, and Dmitry Vetrov. 2016. Breaking sticks and ambiguities with adaptive skip-gram. In *Proceedings of the 19th International Conference on Artificial Intelligence and Statistics*, volume 51 of *Proceedings of Machine Learning Research*, pages 130–138, Cadiz, Spain. PMLR.

Daniel Cer, Yinfei Yang, Sheng yi Kong, Nan Hua, Nicole Limtiaco, Rhomni St. John, Noah Constant, Mario Guajardo-Cespedes, Steve Yuan, Chris Tar, Yun-Hsuan Sung, Brian Strope, and Ray Kurzweil. 2018. Universal sentence encoder.

Zhiyuan Chen and Bing Liu. 2017. *Topic Models for NLP Applications*, pages 1276–1280. Springer US, Boston, MA.

Alexis Conneau, Douwe Kiela, Holger Schwenk, Loïc Barrault, and Antoine Bordes. 2017. Supervised learning of universal sentence representations from natural language inference data. In *Proceedings of the 2017 Conference on Empirical Methods in Natural Language Processing*, pages 670–680, Copenhagen, Denmark. Association for Computational Linguistics.

Jacob Devlin, Ming-Wei Chang, Kenton Lee, and Kristina Toutanova. 2019. BERT: Pre-training of deep bidirectional transformers for language understanding. In *Proceedings of the 2019 Conference of the North American Chapter of the Association for Computational Linguistics: Human Language Technologies, Volume 1 (Long and Short Papers)*, pages 4171–4186, Minneapolis, Minnesota. Association for Computational Linguistics.

Kawin Ethayarajh. 2019. How contextual are contextualized word representations? comparing the geometry of BERT, ELMo, and GPT-2 embeddings. In *Proceedings of the 2019 Conference on Empirical Methods in Natural Language Processing and the 9th International Joint Conference on Natural Language Processing (EMNLP-IJCNLP)*, pages 55–65, Hong Kong, China. Association for Computational Linguistics.

David Freedman, Robert Pisani, and Roger Purves. 2007. Statistics (international student edition). *Pisani, R. Purves, 4th edn. WW Norton & Company, New York*.

Felix Gers, Nicol Schraudolph, and Jürgen Schmidhuber. 2002. Learning precise timing with lstm recurrent networks. *Journal of Machine Learning Research*, 3:115–143.

Hongyu Gong, Tarek Sakakini, Suma Bhat, and JinJun Xiong. 2018. Document similarity for texts of varying lengths via hidden topics. In *Proceedings of the 56th Annual Meeting of the Association for Computational Linguistics (Volume 1: Long Papers)*, pages 2341–2351, Melbourne, Australia. Association for Computational Linguistics.

Vivek Gupta, Harish Karnick, Ashendra Bansal, and Pradhuman Jhala. 2016. Product classification in E-commerce using distributional semantics. In *Proceedings of COLING 2016, the 26th International Conference on Computational Linguistics: Technical Papers*, pages 536–546, Osaka, Japan. The COLING 2016 Organizing Committee.

Vivek Gupta, Ankit Saw, Pegah Nokhiz, Harshit Gupta, and Partha Talukdar. 2020a. Improving document classification with multi-sense embeddings. In *Proceedings of the European Conference on Artificial Intelligence*.

Vivek Gupta, Ankit Saw, Pegah Nokhiz, Praneeth Netrapalli, Piyush Rai, and Partha Talukdar. 2020b. P-sif: Document embeddings using partition averaging. In *Proceedings of the AAAI Conference on Artificial Intelligence*.

Han Kyul Kim, Hyun joong Kim, and S. Cho. 2017. Bag-of-concepts: Comprehending document representation through clustering words in distributed representation. *Neurocomputing*, 266:336–352.

Stefan Kombrink, Tomas Mikolov, Martin Karafiát, and Lukas Burget. 2011. Recurrent neural network based language modeling in meeting recognition. pages 2877–2880.

Quoc Le and Tomas Mikolov. 2014. Distributed representations of sentences and documents. In *Proceedings of the 31st International Conference on International Conference on Machine Learning - Volume 32*, ICML'14, page II–1188–II–1196. JMLR.org.

Omer Levy and Yoav Goldberg. 2014. Neural word embedding as implicit matrix factorization. *Advances in neural information processing systems*, 27:2177–2185.

Wang Ling, Chris Dyer, Alan W. Black, and Isabel Trancoso. 2015. Two/too simple adaptations of Word2Vec for syntax problems. In *Proceedings of the 2015 Conference of the North American Chapter of the Association for Computational Linguistics: Human Language Technologies*, pages 1299–1304, Denver, Colorado. Association for Computational Linguistics.

Pengfei Liu, Xipeng Qiu, and Xuanjing Huang. 2015a. Learning context-sensitive word embeddings with neural tensor skip-gram model. In *Proceedings of the 24th International Conference on Artificial Intelligence*, pages 1284–1290.

Yang Liu, Zhiyuan Liu, Tat-Seng Chua, and Maosong Sun. 2015b. Topical word embeddings. In *Proceedings of the Twenty-Ninth AAAI Conference on Artificial Intelligence*, AAAI'15, page 2418–2424. AAAI Press.

Dheeraj Mekala, Vivek Gupta, Bhargavi Paranjape, and Harish Karnick. 2017. SCDV : Sparse composite document vectors using soft clustering over distributional representations. In *Proceedings of the 2017 Conference on Empirical Methods in Natural Language Processing*, pages 659–669, Copenhagen, Denmark. Association for Computational Linguistics.

Dheeraj Mekala, Xinyang Zhang, and Jingbo Shang. 2020. META: Metadata-empowered weak supervision for text classification. In *Proceedings of the 2020 Conference on Empirical Methods in Natural Language Processing (EMNLP)*, pages 8351–8361, Online. Association for Computational Linguistics.

Tomáš Mikolov, Wen-tau Yih, and Geoffrey Zweig. 2013. Linguistic regularities in continuous space word representations. In *Proceedings of the 2013 conference of the north american chapter of the association for computational linguistics: Human language technologies*, pages 746–751.

Dat Quoc Nguyen, Kairit Sirts, and Mark Johnson. 2015. Improving topic coherence with latent feature word representations in MAP estimation for topic modeling. In *Proceedings of the Australasian Language Technology Association Workshop 2015*, pages 116–121, Parramatta, Australia.

Matthew Peters, Mark Neumann, Mohit Iyyer, Matt Gardner, Christopher Clark, Kenton Lee, and Luke Zettlemoyer. 2018. Deep contextualized word representations. In *Proceedings of the 2018 Conference of the North American Chapter of the Association for Computational Linguistics: Human Language Technologies, Volume 1 (Long Papers)*, pages 2227–2237.

Pranjal Singh and Amitabha Mukerjee. 2015. Words are not equal: Graded weighting model for building composite document vectors. In *Proceedings of the 12th International Conference on Natural Language Processing*, pages 11–19, Trivandrum, India. NLP Association of India.

Richard Socher, Alex Perelygin, Jean Wu, Jason Chuang, Christopher D. Manning, Andrew Ng, and Christopher Potts. 2013. Recursive deep models for semantic compositionality over a sentiment treebank. In *Proceedings of the 2013 Conference on Empirical Methods in Natural Language Processing*, pages 1631–1642, Seattle, Washington, USA. Association for Computational Linguistics.

Chi Sun, Xipeng Qiu, Yige Xu, and Xuanjing Huang. 2019. How to fine-tune bert for text classification? In *China National Conference on Chinese Computational Linguistics*, pages 194–206. Springer.

John Wieting and Kevin Gimpel. 2017. Revisiting recurrent networks for paraphrastic sentence embeddings. In *Proceedings of the 55th Annual Meeting of the Association for Computational Linguistics (Volume 1: Long Papers)*, pages 2078–2088.

Justine Zhang and Cristian Danescu-Niculescu-Mizil. 2020. Balancing objectives in counseling conversations: Advancing forwards or looking backwards. In *Proceedings of the 58th Annual Meeting of the Association for Computational Linguistics*, pages 5276–5289, Online. Association for Computational Linguistics.

A Hyper parameter Details

We obtain the word embeddings using BERT-base-uncased pre-trained model and use k-means for contextual clustering for given word. For simplicity we used similarity threshold (τ) of 0.8 for all words in all the datasets (see datasets details in Table 4) which lead to multiple polysemous word representation for each word, the distribution for the same is shown in Table 5. For SCDV, we set the dimension of word embeddings to 200 and the number of mixture components in GMM between $30-90$ (dataset dependent) as shown in Table 6. For the GMM we ensure that all mixture components share the same *tied co-variance* matrix. Sparsifying the document vectors further as propose in SCDV leads to only marginal performance gain (statistically insignificant), so we skip that step for our experiments. We used LinearSVM for multi-class classification during fully supervised and semi-supervised settings and prototypical networks for few-shot setting. The choice of the classifier was the same in all baselines and the proposed model to maintain uniformity. We used 5-fold cross-validation on the F1 score to tune parameter C of LinearSVM. In semi-supervised setting the example are added in incremental setting for fair comparison. We also repeated the experiment 10 times (varying random set selection seed) and consider mean as our final performance.

Dataset	Train Size	Test Size	#Label
20NG	11314	7358	20
Amazon	5600	2400	4
Twitter	2180	935	3
BBCSport	516	221	5
Classic	4966	2129	4
Recipe-l	27842	11932	20

Table 4: Dataset Statistics.

Figure 4: t-SNE plots: SCDV+WordVec(left) and SCDV+BERT(ctxd) + Anisotropy(right). Clearly, better class separation for SCDV+BERT(ctxd) + Anisotropy.

Dataset	k=1	k=2	k≥3
20NG	80.29	13.58	6.23
Amazon	76.12	17.68	6.20
Twitter	80.79	15.60	3.61
BBCSport	87.29	11.56	1.15
Classic	73.63	17.01	9.36
Recipe-l	67.11	13.98	18.91

Table 5: Distribution (in %) of vocabulary as it's disambiguated into k = 1, 2 and ≥ 3 polysemous words.

Dataset (%)	10	20	30	40	50	100
20NG	45	45	60	60	60	60
Amazon	30	30	30	30	30	30
Twitter	30	45	45	45	45	45
BBCSport	60	60	75	75	75	90
Classic	30	30	30	30	30	30
Recipe-l	30	30	30	30	30	30

Table 6: Number of mixture components in GMM used in various experiments. [9]

STS Task Details: For the STS task, the gold score is a continuous valued similarity score on a scale from 0 to 5, with 0 indicating that the semantics of the sentences are completely independent and 5 signifying semantic equivalence is computed

B Word Sense Disambiguation Examples

Table 7 shows word sense disambiguation for few polysemous words from 20NewsGroup dataset along with the cosine similarity between BERT embedding with different context usage. We use threshold of 0.8 for sense cluster disambiguation. Figure 4 shows tha t-sne plots for SCDV+WordVec(left) and SCDV+BERT(ctxd) + Anisotropy(right) embeddings. Clearly, we see much better class separation for SCDV+BERT(ctxd) + Anisotropy than SCDV+WordVec. We can alse the anisotropic reduction conical effect.

Word	Sentence	Score
Subject	The math **subject1** is difficult He sent the mail without **subject2**	0.71
Apple	The stocks of **Apple1** have increased I eat an **apple2** everyday	0.67
Unit	Metre is **unit1** of Distance He is in 1st **unit2**	0.78

Table 7: Word Sense Disambiguation. Here, score represent the cosine similarity between BERT embedding of the **bold** subject word.

C Other Related Work

Levy and Goldberg, 2014 used unweighted averaging of word vectors, Singh and Mukerjee, 2015 proposed tfidf-weighted averaging of word vectors, Socher et al., 2013 proposed a recursive neural network defined over a parse tree with supervised training. Le and Mikolov, 2014 proposed PV-DM and PV-DBoW models which treat each sentence as a shared global latent vector. Other approaches use seq2seq models such as RNN (Kombrink et al., 2011) and LSTM (Gers et al., 2002) which can handle long term dependency. Wieting and Gimpel, 2017 proposed a neural network model which optimizes the word embeddings based on the cosine similarity. Recent deep contextual word embeddings such as ELMo (Peters et al., 2018), USE (Cer et al., 2018) and BERT (Devlin et al., 2019), which capture the word context, outperform all earlier approaches. There are also other topic based modeling approaches such as LDA (Chen and Liu, 2017), weight-BoC (Kim et al., 2017), TWE (Liu et al., 2015b) , NTSG (Liu et al., 2015a), w2v-LDA (Nguyen et al., 2015), etc, as explored in SCDV (Mekala et al., 2017).

Association for Computational Linguistics
209 N. Eighth Street
Stroudsburg, Pennsylvania 18360

ISBN 978-1-7138-9181-9

9 781713 891819

CURRAN ASSOCIATES INC.
proceedings.com